68°
40°
36°
32°
28°
60°
64°
narkand
Ashkhabad
Atrek R.
Bujnurd
Kuchan
Radkan
hyailaq
K H O R A S A N
Tus
Meshed
Sarakhs
Sabsewar
Nishapur
Sangbast
Turbat-i-
Sheikh Jam
Kishmar
Turbat-i-
Haideri
Taiabad
Herat
Bidokht
Ferdowsi
Tabas
Biri
AFGHANISTAN
Dasht-i-Lut
Za
SEISTAN
Kerman
Mahan
Zahedan
Bam
Taftan
PAKISTAN
MAKRAN
Bandar Abbas
Minab
Hormuz
Jask
Chahbehar
M.Verity

The Land
of the Great Sophy

The Land
of the Great Sophy

ROGER STEVENS

EYRE METHUEN

First published in 1962
First published as a paperback 1965
Copyright © 1962 by Sir Roger Stevens
Second edition, 1971
© 1971 by Sir Roger Stevens
Third edition, 1979
© 1979 by Sir Roger Stevens

Printed Offset Litho in Great Britain
by Cox & Wyman Ltd,
Fakenham, Norfolk

ISBN 0 413 45780 X (hardback)
0 413 45790 7 (paperback)

Contents

Illustrations

PLATES

Plates 3b, 4a, 12, 14a 15a–16b *are from photographs by Paul Popper Ltd.* Plates 10a, 10b, 13 *and* 14b *from photographs by Alex Starkey, and* plates 2a *and* 9b *from photographs by Kay Gordon. The remaining plates are from photographs taken by the author.*

MAPS

Maps drawn by Maureen Verity

Acknowledgments

It is first and foremost to Dr Roman Ghirshman and M. André Godard that I would express my gratitude for having fired my imagination with an interest in archaeology and Islamic architecture respectively. Readers of this book will be in no doubt as to the debt which is owing in these fields to these French scholars, and also to Arthur Upham Pope. Ali Sami, Archaeological Director of Fars, Ali Hannibal of Tehran, Lutfullah Honarfar of Isfahan, and many Persian friends have continued the process and helped to widen my horizons. My thanks are due as well to the benevolent governments which in one case authorized, and in the other facilitated, my various journeys about the country; to the many who, during those journeys, gave the traditional hospitality of Persia a new dimension for me; and not least to Ismail Hejazi, my driver, without whom I should often never have reached my destination.

I am also most grateful to Arthur Kellas, of the British Embassy, Tehran, for having suggested various improvements and for bringing the travel notes (Appendix II) up to date; and to George Hiller, formerly of the Embassy, for having contributed some passages relating to certain parts of the country which he was able to visit but I was not. Finally, I would thank my wife for having shared my enthusiasms and consistently encouraged me to persist, against occasional odds, in what has proved, as I hope it may appear, a labour of love.

Table of Royal Houses
with principal rulers

ACHAEMENIANS 640–323 B.C.
Cyrus	558–528
Cambyses	528–522
Smerdis	522–521
Darius	521–485
Xerxes I	485–465
Artaxerxes	465–425

SELEUCIDS 323–223

PARTHIANS 223 B.C.–A.D. 226

SASSANIANS A.D. 224–642
Ardeshir I	224–255
Shapur I	242–271
Shapur II	309–379
Yezdigird I	399–420
Bahram V	421–438
Khosrow I	531–579
Khosrow II Parviz	590–628

ISLAMIC INVASION
and minor dynasties 642–1037

SELJUKS 1037–1220
Toghril Beg	1055–1063
Alp Arslan	1063–1072
Malik Shah	1072–1092
Sultan Sanjar	1096–1157

MONGOLS 1220–1380
First Mongol invasion 1220–1227
Second Mongol invasion 1251–1256
Hulagu	1256–1265
Abaqa	1265–1281
Arghun	1284–1291
Ghazan Khan	1295–1304
Oljeitu	1304–1316

TIMURIDS 1380–1500
Timur	1395–1405
Shah Rukh	1408–1447

SAFAVIDS 1500–1736
Ismail	1499–1524
Shah Tahmasp	1524–1576
Shah Abbas	1587–1629
Shah Safi	1629–1642
Abbas II	1642–1666
Suleiman	1666–1694
Huseyn	1694–1726

THE INTERREGNUM

	1736–1794
Nadir Kuli (Afshar)	1736–1747
Karim Khan (Zand)	1759–1779

Mohammed	1834–1848
Nasr-uddin	1848–1896
Muzaffar-uddin	1896–1907
Mohammed Ali	1907–1909
Sultan Ahmed	1909–1925

QAJARS 1787–1925

| Aga Mohammed | 1787–1797 |
| Fath Ali Shah | 1798–1834 |

PAHLEVIS

| Reza Shah | 1925–1941 |
| Mohammed Reza | 1941– |

Preface to Second Edition

I understand that the first edition of this work has added to the enjoyment of many visitors and travellers to Persia; it has also been translated into Italian and received the compliment of an unauthorized edition in English produced in Iran. At the same time I have been very conscious of its imperfections, magnified after a lapse of nine years during which on the one hand the country has undergone extensive modernization and change, while on the other the rate of archaeological exploration and the discovery of hitherto unknown sites and monuments has fantastically accelerated. This new edition endeavours, with much new material compressed within the confines of a still slender volume, to bring the story up to date at both ends of this rather breathless time-scale.

It has been a complex task which I should certainly have been unable to complete without the assistance of many friends and helpers. I am particularly indebted to Jenny Housego, formerly of the Textile Department of the Victoria and Albert Museum and now working on Persian miniatures and textiles, whose husband is *Times* Correspondent in Tehran, for undertaking the heavy work of assembling much new material on my behalf as well as providing her own most valuable observations. Molli Cloake, wife of the Commercial Counsellor at the British Embassy in Tehran, has ably assisted her in this task, particularly with Chapters Four and Twelve and in providing new material about Qajar buildings and decorations. I have received most generous advice and assistance too from Sir Denis Wright, Her Majesty's Ambassador in Tehran until April 1971, from David Stronach, Director of the British Institute of Persian Studies in Tehran, from Professor Kleiss of the German Institute, from Paul

Glanfield of the British Council, and from Robert Hillenbrand of Trinity College, Oxford, who has recently completed a year of travel and research into early Islamic monuments in Persia with particular reference to tomb towers. I am also indebted to John Cloake, Commercial Counsellor at the Embassy, for the additional maps. To all these, and to others whose knowledge or good will I have drawn upon directly or indirectly, and mercifully or otherwise, I offer grateful thanks.

August 1971   R.B.S.

NOTE FOR THIRD EDITION

The seventies brought sudden and uneasy prosperity to Persia and wrought changes undreamt of even fifteen years ago. Modern tarmac highways now span the country almost from end to end; people have poured out from the villages into the big cities and swollen cities have erupted uncomfortably into the surrounding rural areas; the traditional Persia is being thrust aside by the march of progress. But the number of business visitors, foreign residents and tourists has risen tenfold, and a fair proportion of these still fall under Persia's spell and want to learn more about her past.

After a seven-year interval a further edition of this book has therefore become due. Though radical revision such as was effected for the second edition is not required, I have taken the opportunity to bring several passages up to date or in line with the latest archaeological discoveries, to correct certain inaccuracies and to elucidate some references not previously explained. For the complete revision of Appendix I (Notes on Travel) I am much indebted to Peter and Angela Westmacott of the British Embassy in Tehran.

Hill Farm, Thursley   R.B.S.
November 1978

Introduction

Persia, long a Mecca for adventurous travellers and a magnet for devotees of her literature and art, is now leaping into fame both as a modern country and as an alluring stopping-place on a trunk route round the world. Most of the books written about Persia in the past have been either personal accounts of travel or learned disquisitions for the expert. This is neither. It is written for the many who like myself find themselves living in or visiting Persia, or otherwise involved in Persian affairs or interests, without any previous knowledge of Asia or background of Persian history and civilization. It struck me, after some time in the country and a certain amount of desultory reading, that there was no single volume which, within a small compass, set out simply the essential elements in that background and related them clearly to the visible testimony of the country's great past which is to be seen both in Persia and in many of our own museums today. There is no pretence here of original research or first-hand study. I have drawn shamelessly on the researches of scholars who have devoted a lifetime of work to their particular branch of the subject and used their conclusions for the purpose of analysis, classification and exposition. I hope that one result may be at least that the reader's appetite will be whetted and that he will then turn to more original sources in search of further enlightenment.

This is in no sense a book about modern Persia – its institutions, its politics, its economic development. These are an important and fascinating field of study in themselves but one which, in my opinion, cannot properly be undertaken by a foreign representative who has had the good fortune to be accredited to the Persian Government. Persian literature is passed by; my ignorance of the language precludes any appreciation of that, as will no doubt be the case of many others. But apart from literature, there are many things in the past which are not irrelevant to an understanding of modern Persia. Persia grows out from her past to as great an extent as any evolving nation; her geography, her history, her religion and her art tell more perhaps about the Persian character and the nature of the country than any account of her modern economy or form of government. Besides, it is fairly easy to obtain up-to-date information about these things; the past is a little more elusive.

All this goes for the first part of the book. In the second part, I have tried to convey some idea of what Persia looks and feels like to the visitor without writing a guide book or a travelogue. I hope that this may be of some use to the traveller, but he will not I think derive much value from it unless he has first absorbed something of the first part. For this is essentially the background which it is desirable to have if one is to appreciate fully what one sees, and can hardly fail to admire, as one moves about that desolate, exciting, irresistible country. To the Westerner (like myself) without background, untutored admiration will not get one very far; to try to understand why things are as they are enhances the interest – and in my case doubles the pleasure. Indeed until I started enquiring (and found that getting answers was not always easy) my admiration was largely intermittent and wholly uncomprehending. This book may at any rate provide a short cut for others who have a similar experience. I hope that not too much will be expected of it. In the last century it might have been given the subtitle *Old Things seen in Persia explained.* It is no more than that; indeed, even that may be too broad a claim.

ROGER STEVENS

Hill Farm, Thursley
March 1961

Part I

CHAPTER ONE

The Setting

1. THE LAND AND THE PEOPLE

Practically speaking only the English talk about Persia. It is just like them to do so, for in reality 'Persia' is to 'Iran' what 'England' is to the 'United Kingdom'. It is the old name originally applied to a bit of the country, and it has shown remarkable powers of survival. Only for 'England' there is really more excuse. She is a clearly defined area; 'Britain' and 'the British' are hazy if handy terms; 'United Kingdom' does not roll easily off the tongue and as an adjective is excruciating. But what could be simpler to say than Iran, or more natural than that its people should be Iranians?

'Persia' is derived from the word Fars, the name of the southern province (in the neighbourhood of Shiraz) which was the cradle of the Persian Empire. It was the ruling dynasty of Fars which first married into, and then took by conquest, the neighbouring kingdom of Media to the north and west of Fars. Fars also gave its name to the language, which is called Farsi in Persia today and therefore is correctly described in English as Persian.

Iran is by origin the same word as Aryan, and throughout history has been intermittently applied to the peoples of Indo-European, that is, Aryan origin occupying the plateau, and to the plateau itself. Historically various tribes and people of similar racial origin – Persians, Medes, Hyrcanians and Sogdians among others – invaded the plateau from about 1000 B.C. onwards, just as various Nordic people from east and north – Saxons, Danes and Normans – invaded Britain some two thousand years later. But here the parallel becomes inexact. The indigenous inhabitants of

the plateau were absorbed or disappeared. The invading tribes settled the country, unified it and gave it its predominant character. The Persians were only one of these tribes and, like the others, they were Iranians. Having said this it must be admitted that the historical background for the name Iran is a little shaky, that the use of the name has not been well established over a long period, and that its propagation today smacks somewhat of conscious effort. Nevertheless, Iran is the official name of the country and Iranians is what the inhabitants like to be called. Therefore, defying long-standing tradition and ingrained and instinctive English habit, I propose generally though not invariably to refer to the country as 'Iran' and the people as 'Iranians'; some things (carpets for instance) will remain 'Persian'; and if the reader who is to live in the country follows the same practice, he will not, I think, have occasion to complain that he has been led astray.

Present-day Iran, though shrunken compared with the past, covers an enormous area (628,000 square miles). A journey by road from the extreme north-west to the south-east would involve over two thousand miles, from the head of the Persian Gulf to the Soviet-Afghan frontier somewhat less (1,350 miles). But, however approached or regarded, it is a great slab of a country.

Certain basic facts are worth noticing from the outset. Iran is exceptionally accessible by land and relatively inaccessible by water. Because of the Caspian Sea to the north and the Persian Gulf to the south it forms in effect a land bridge between Central Asia and India on the one hand, and the Arab world, Turkey and Europe on the other. But from the point of view of Europe and the West – and it is in that direction that Iran has nearly always tended to look – the Persian Gulf is a most perverse and inconvenient piece of water. It not only faces the wrong way; but it is on the wrong side of the Arabian peninsula. The sea mileage from anywhere in Europe to the head of the Persian Gulf is greater than to Bombay; and most ships from London to Persian ports take the best part of six weeks. This is one reason why during the heyday of maritime communication Iran remained relatively isolated. But today the aeroplane follows much the same routes as the medieval caravan, and Iran benefits once more from her central position athwart the deserts of Arabia and the barren steppes of Southern Russia.

Iran is one of the highest countries in the world. Except for narrow coastal and frontier strips, the whole country consists of a high plateau with an average height of between four and five thousand feet, intersected by mountain ranges running for the most part from north-west to south-east. Typical plateau scenery is a wide arid plain containing few or no settlements, bounded by tawny, jagged mountains whose highest peaks are snow-covered for five or six months in the year, and in whose folds lie green valleys and well-watered villages. Nor is it entirely true of them, as Thomas Herbert wrote in 1627, that they 'promise much at a distance, but when there delude the expectation';* for much of the charm of this scenery lies in the contrast between the barren austerity of its vast horizons and the lush fertility of its secluded intimacies.

To the north and south-west lie the great mountain ranges of the Elburz and Zagros rising in places to 14,000 or 15,000 feet, and in the case of Mount Demavend, east of Tehran, to over 18,000 feet. The outer edges of these ranges provide a startling contrast to the spacious interior of the country. To the south-west, facing the Mesopotamian plain and the Persian Gulf are a series of descending ridges alternating with deep valleys. The hills are sparsely wooded with oak and scrub, the valleys green and carpeted with flowers in winter and spring, but the country is rough, rugged, and in places almost impenetrable. To the north, towards the Caspian shore, the Elburz dips down into a region of sub-tropical forest and swamp, terraced tea plantation and rice paddy – a populated, luxuriant, once fever-ridden world, nearly 100 feet below sea level.

Over most of the country, the annual rainfall ranges between two and ten inches, and practically all of it falls between November and April, while for the rest of the year the skies are virtually cloudless and the sun beats down relentlessly. In the Zagros mountains and particularly towards the west, the rainfall is substantially higher (20–25 in) but the seasonal distribution is the

* *Travels in Persia, 1627-9.*

same. To the north of the Elburz, it varies from twenty to fifty-five inches and rain falls at all seasons of the year. Cloudy days are common and the air is heavy and damp. This accounts for the entirely different vegetation of the Caspian whose provinces are, agriculturally speaking, the richest in Iran. On the central plateau, save in a few mountain regions, cultivation is maintained only by irrigation, and for the most part by a particular system of irrigation, the principles of which date back over two thousand years. This sytem is induced by the lie of the land – a plain or trough surrounded by mountains. Its essential feature is the underground water-channel, or qanat. From an underground water-table in an elevated position in relation to the surrounding country, a channel is dug on an inclined plane beneath the slope of the land, emerging at the point where the water is needed, namely just above the village or the irrigated fields. From this point it is conducted in surface channels known as jubes for whatever purpose it is required – sometimes to be dammed by primitive weirs in the form of stone or wooden blocks and distributed in different directions for varying purposes on different days. The entire flow from the water-table out to and beyond the village or field is maintained by gravity; and the building of the qanat at the right tilt is no mean art. Both for the initial construction of the qanat and for its maintenance, holes are driven into the ground at fifty- to a hundred-and-fifty-yard intervals above it; these are the lines of craters, resembling bomb-holes, which every visitor to Iran observes with curiosity from the air. It is a skilful, ingenious system – primitive and wasteful no doubt and crying out for modernization – but one without which there would have been little cultivation, and hence little settled life, on the Iranian plateau since the dawn of history.

The cities – Tehran (over three million), Tabriz, Isfahan and Meshed (over 400,000), Shiraz (300,000), and many lesser towns (e.g. Kerman, Kazvin, Kashan, Qum, Yazd), are on the central plateau, and owe their growth to their position on the ancient trade routes. They are all situated on plains not far removed from high mountainous catchment areas and represent points of concentration of water supplies, whether by qanat (as for

example in the case of Tehran), or by perennial and strongly
flowing rivers (e.g. the Zaindeh Rud at Isfahan). The only two
large towns off the plateau (Resht near the Caspian and Abadan
near the Persian Gulf) are comparatively modern.

Round the edges of the plateau are areas where the rainfall is
sufficient to permit of dry farming or to provide good pasture.
Most of Azerbaijan (the north-west province) and the Zagros
mountain area fall into this category. In Azerbaijan and some
of the wider Zagros valleys there are permanent settlements
and numerous towns of between 10,000 and 30,000 inhabitants.
But over large areas of the Zagros southward from Lake Rezaieh to
where the mountains strike the Gulf, the population is predominantly nomadic, moving from their winter feeding grounds
on the Mesopotamian plain or the shores of the Gulf up through
forbidding gorges and defiles to their summer pastures on the
higher ranges. Though nomads are found elsewhere, on the
Elburz and in the mountains of Khorasan for example, in small
numbers, it is the Zagros which is nomad country *par excellence*.
Furthermore, though tribal organization continues to exist in
some settled parts of the country, notably at the head of the
Persian Gulf, it is in the nomadic areas that not unnaturally
the tribes have maintained their organization most effectively; the
Zagros mountains are thus the great tribal country of Iran. At
the northern end are the Kurds, as in adjoining areas of Iraq; to
the south of the Kurds the fierce and turbulent Lurs; east of the
Lurs, in the area between Isfahan and the oil fields, the large and
flourishing Bakhtiaris, and beyond them again, in a more confused mosaic, the once powerful Qashgais, the Khamseh, Kuh
Galu and Mamassani.

The tribes are only one example of the racial diversity which
over the centuries has been welded into the Iranian nation. With
the people as with geography, climate and agriculture, it is,
roughly speaking, the central plateau of Iran which is the norm,
and the fringes of the country which constitute the aberration.
The area from Kazvin to Kerman, and eastwards to the great salt
desert, not only gives Iran its most characteristic scenery but also
contains the people of purest Aryan stock. Closely allied to them in

racial origin, and speaking variants of the same language, are the Kurds and Lurs. Farther south however the tribes are of more mixed stock, the Qashgai containing an admixture of Turkish and Persian and the Khamseh of Turkish and Arab. The Mesopotamian province of Khuzistan (formerly Arabistan) is predominantly Arab, while the south-east corner of the country is inhabited (insofar as it is inhabited at all) by Baluchi who have close affinities with their neighbours in West Pakistan. In the northern areas the pattern is considerably more complex. North-west Iran (Azerbaijan) is largely Turkish speaking, though the dialect is very different from that spoken by Ottoman Turks, and the people have not, as might be supposed, walked across the border from Turkey but came originally all the way from Turkestan – they are in short Turkomans rather than Turks by origin. In the western parts of Azerbaijan, beyond Lake Urmia, there are considerable settlements of Nestorian Christians or 'Assyrians', while to the north are a number of Armenian communities. Both Kurds and Turks are to be found (though they certainly do not predominate) along the Caspian coast. But the most complex racial pattern is in the north-east (Khorasan). Here Turks from the Turkoman steppes jostle with Kurds transplanted from the Zagros; there is a sprinkling of Afghan Hazaras to the east, while along the edge of the desert are (surprisingly) a number of Arabs. But the process of assimilation, encouraged by a common religion and an intermittently effective central government, has now gone on for so long that these racial divergencies are not immediately or easily discernible except in Khuzistan and Azerbaijan.

2. HISTORY
i] THE ROYAL HOUSES
Though the history of Iran is long and complex, its shape is determined by the rise and fall of successive dynasties – with intervals of chaos and confusion. I intend to concentrate on the dynasties.* For one thing, they help to keep the story straight. For another, it is they, and they almost alone, who have left their

* See however Annex, note 1.

mark on the face of the land. The great monuments of Iran are the product and the symbol of the wealth and power of royal personages. Even the temples and mosques built to the glory of God were in many cases erected at the expense and on the initiative of the royal houses or great chieftains. There were no great feudal families dwelling in fortified castles, or, until recent times, in town palaces or substantial country houses set in the midst of well-tilled estates. The people, when they were not nomadic, lived in modest, flat-roofed, mud-built houses of flimsy construction; where these survive, they have been so overlaid by repair and reconstruction that it is difficult to assign a date to them. Domestic building, though not devoid of charm, has little historical association. The architectural glories of Iran are first and foremost the monuments of her kings and to a lesser extent those of Islam; the rest hardly count. Since the purpose of this book is primarily to describe and to explain what meets the eye of the traveller in Iran, I make no further apology here for passing off as history a schoolboy sketch of dynasties – from the Normans to the Windsors inclusive, so to speak.

The reader must be warned, however, that the names of the dynasties are very confusing and sometimes seem devised only to tease. Thus, the really big ones have an irritating habit of naming themselves after some remote ancestor – Achaemenes, or Sassan – about whom history gives us little information and whose very existence can be called in question. Tribal names – Parthian, Seljuk, Mongol or Afshar – jostle with family ones; the Parthians, for example, were also known as Arsacids. Small fry like the Saffarids, Muzaffarids and Samanids, are not at first easy to distinguish from their big brothers the Sassanians and the Safavids. A warning should perhaps be given here too that the Omayyads have nothing to do with Omar Khayyam, nor the Abbasids with Shah Abbas, nor the Ghaznavids with Ghazan Khan. The present Pahlevi dynasty takes its name from the script in use before the Islamic conquest.

The Achaemenians, 640–323 B.C. The earliest and greatest of the dynasties seems, at first glance, to spring into being like Athene, fully armed. The first world empire was indeed built up from small beginnings in two or three decades, and there is nothing else quite like it in the history of the world. Achaemenes, to whom the dynasty owes its name, could have had no inkling of what the future held in store for his family. He ruled a small province in the mountains south and west of Isfahan about 700 B.C. His son Teispes added Parsa, the modern Fars, to his dominions, but then proceeded to divide them up between his sons. They were only reunited some hundred years later by Cambyses I, who took an even more fateful step: he married the daughter of his much more powerful neighbour and overlord Astyages, King of Media. Their son, Cyrus II, or the Great, revolted against and conquered Media; he was generous to his grandfather, and the kingdom of the Medes and Persians was born.

It was already a large inheritance, including the whole of what is today North-West Iran, as well as the original Kingdom of Persia to the south-west. Not content with this, Cyrus added Assyria, much of Asia Minor and Bactria to his dominions, which thus stretched from the Aegean to the Oxus (the river which today divides Afghanistan and Russia). He was a generous conqueror and a tolerant ruler. He it was who enabled the Jews to return from captivity to Jerusalem, and Isaiah said of him, or rather quotes the Lord as saying of him:

'He is my shepherd, and shall perform all my pleasure: even saying to Jerusalem, Thou shalt be built; and to the temple, Thy foundation shall be laid.'*

Wherever he went, he built and conserved, protecting the ancient religions in the territories which he conquered, and constituting himself as the heir of the rulers he displaced.

Cyrus made Ecbatana, the seat of the Median Kingdom, his capital, while retaining his Persian capital at Susa and creating and embellishing his new residence at Pasargadae. Today the first lies buried beneath the modern city of Hamadan, but Pasargadae, some hundred miles north of Shiraz, remains one of the most evocative sites in the country.

* [Isaiah xliv. 28.]

Cyrus's son, Cambyses II, ruled for only eight years, but found time (inveigled, according to one story reported by Herodotus, by the machinations of an oculist) to conquer Egypt, and to contemplate assaults on both Carthage and Ethiopia. He seems to have been an unattractive personality and was probably an epileptic. He had no heir and there was a short period of confusion at the end of which (522 B.C.) Darius emerged triumphant. He was one of seven conspirators who had agreed to support for the throne the one whose horse neighed first; according to one story (Herodotus again) it was his groom who found an ingenious and somewhat obscene method of securing this result.

A good general knowledge question among those who know a little of Iranian history is 'Who was Darius' father?' The answer is worth remembering, for it explains why it was necessary to go back to Achaemenes to find a name for the dynasty. His name was Hystaspes, and he was descended from the older son of Teispes who had been awarded the Kingdom of Parsa, which Hystaspes' father subsequently lost to Cambyses I. Darius was thus in all probability a third cousin once removed of Cyrus and well qualified to uphold the imperial tradition of the family.

Because of his great organizing ability, his success in quelling opposition, and above all his invasions of Greece and Scythia (Southern Russia), Darius is possibly the most famous of all the Iranian kings. The story of his conquests belongs to the history of Greece more perhaps than to that of Iran. But it was during his reign that the Empire suffered its first defeat (at Marathon in 490) and that it began to pay the price of over-expansion. The process was carried further during the reign of his son Xerxes who suffered a series of crushing defeats (Salamis, Plataea and Mycale) at the hands of the Greeks; these finally brought to an end the Achaemenian dreams of European conquest.

In Iran, however, these two reigns correspond to the Augustan age, and represent the apotheosis of imperial power and wealth. Deserting the austere simplicities of Pasargadae, Darius founded a new residence at Persepolis, some forty miles to the south; and on that great artificial, sunbaked platform he and Xerxes built a

vast series of elaborate and splendid palaces which can have had no
counterpart in Asia or Europe at that time.

But these Achaemenian kings, like many of their successors of
later dynasties, were incurably restless, indeed almost nomadic,
in their habits. Not content with rushing about over more than
half the civilized world (Xerxes admittedly grew a little tired
before the close) in an attempt to conquer it, they also contrived
to travel almost incessantly while they were at home. They had
three capitals – at Susa, Persepolis and Ecbatana. Susa, the ancient
capital of the Elamite Kingdom,★ had been continuously inhabited
for over twenty centuries; Darius built a vast new series of
palaces on the site of which little, alas, now remains. They
wintered in Susa, passed the spring in Persepolis, and repaired to
the cooler heights of Ecbatana (6,000 ft above sea level) for the
summer. As the crow flies it is five hundred miles from Susa to
Persepolis, over eight hundred from Persepolis to Ecbatana, and
about three hundred miles from Ecbatana back to Susa. To
traverse these distances in winter cold or in the heat of summer,
with all the trappings and paraphernalia of the Imperial Court,
would be a formidable task even if the country were flat. It is of
course nothing of the kind. Between Susa and the two capitals
on the plateau lie a series of jagged ridges and rocky valleys
which, according to the constructors of a recently built oil pipeline, constitute some of the most difficult country in the world.
Between Persepolis and Ecbatana too lie rough mountains interspersed with stretches of inhospitable desert. I invite anyone
flying today from Ahwaz to Isfahan or from Abadan to Shiraz
to look out of the window and pay a silent tribute to the valour
and endurance and skill of the Achaemenian kings and the
industrious and devoted citizens of this vast Empire in which, so
far as historical records show, every man was paid for his work,
and slavery was unknown.

It was not only between the places of residence that roads were
constructed. Perhaps Darius's most remarkable feat was the Royal
Road from Susa to Sardis, on the west coast of Asia Minor – over
sixteen hundred miles of highway complete with posting stations,

★ See Annex, note 1.

which the King's messenger could, when pressed, cover in a week.

Good communications were essential to efficient administration of the vast Empire. Yet there was no attempt at over-centralization. Provincial autonomy was maintained by the appointment of satraps or viceroys. Each had with them a general and a state secretary, but these were not subordinate to the satrap; they reported direct to headquarters. Moreover, to obviate any risk that these three independent authorities might be tempted to combine in revolt, inspectors with strong military support were despatched to the provinces at irregular intervals. Thus was achieved a type of central control which did not eliminate provincial independence. The latter was much in evidence in the organization of the army. Apart from a small royal bodyguard and the ten thousand 'Immortals', the army was organized entirely, even in time of war, from provincial levies. This in turn determined the order of battle and in later times placed a severe handicap on the Persian Army as an effective fighting force.

The events and personalities of this Golden Age of Iranian history are better known to us and more vivid than those of any period until quite modern times. This is partly because of the abundance of Greek records, and above all the rich narrative skill of Herodotus. But it is also thanks to the ambition of the Achaemenian kings, especially Darius, to proclaim in stone a worthy record of their achievements. We do not know for certain whether they could read and write themselves; but they saw to it that their names and titles and deeds were blazoned in letters and in pictorial bas-reliefs, not only on the rock vaults of Naqsh-i-Rustam and nearby Persepolis, which are their tombs, but also in distant Kurdistan. It was at Bisitun, some thirty miles east of Kermanshah, on the great highway leading to Ecbatana, that Darius elected to engrave the story of his reign. His figure is portrayed in enormous size triumphing over his enemies, above whom floats the great winged figure of the god Ahuramazda (Ormuzd). Accompanying these bas-reliefs is an enormous cuneiform inscription, occupying a surface measuring 150 by 100 feet, describing Darius's parentage, the extent of his dominions, and how he triumphed over internal rebellion. The inscription is in three languages, Elamite, Babylonian and Old Persian, and the story of how it was deciphered by the British archaeologist Sir Henry Rawlinson, and the linguistic discoveries to which it led, has a special place in the annals of historical research. A tablet found at Susa describes in detail how the palace of Darius there was constructed, where its materials came from and who did the work. Even more than the recital of the countries over which Darius ruled, it is a testimony to the vast size, wealth and coherence of his great Empire.

The tale of the remaining Achaemenians can be briefly told. Defeated in Greece, Xerxes retired to his palaces and never again attempted to follow his father on a career of conquest. Neither his son Artaxerxes I, nor his grandson Darius II ever led their troops in battle. They were corrupted by luxury and ease; their courts were riddled by intrigue and decimated by murder. Nevertheless, despite periodical revolts in the more distant provinces, the Asian part of Darius's empire somehow held together. The Greeks still regarded it with awe; the Achaemenian monarchs were Basileus, the king, not just Kings of Persia. Their survival was due, not to military prowess, but to success in playing off one Greek state against another, with liberal use of gold, which remained, it seems, in plentiful supply. It was used most extensively and successfully by Artaxerxes II, whose brother Cyrus led in revolt, and to ultimate defeat, the Ten Thousand Greeks whose famous retreat from Cunaxa (near Babylon) to Trebizond has been immortalized by Xenophon. For a moment, during the reign of his brutal but efficient son Artaxerxes III, it seemed as though the Empire had been securely re-established. And so it might have been, had Greece remained weak and another Cyrus or Darius arisen on the plateau. In fact however the end was very near. The rise of Macedon, the unification of Greece and the military genius of Alexander were more responsible than any further deterioration within. Darius III Codomannus, last of the Achaemenian line, made a not unnatural mistake in underrating Alexander's ability and driving power. Despite superior numbers the Persians were beaten at Issus, in the extreme north-east corner of the Mediterranean, and Darius ran away. After reducing Tyre and annexing

Egypt, Alexander inflicted a further defeat on Darius in northern Mesopotamia near Erbil, and then occupied Susa. Thence he advanced, virtually without opposition, to Persepolis, where he found the equivalent of £28 million and other booty and remained for four months. Either during this time or later he visited Pasargadae and, horrified at the condition of Cyrus's tomb – touched, according to Plutarch, by the inscription 'Grudge me not this little earth that covereth my body' – ordered it to be conserved, and punished the Magi who had guarded it so incompetently. It was also during the period of Alexander's stay that Persepolis caught fire. It was long assumed that this was a deliberate act of incendiarism. Ghirshman gives some convincing reasons (without coming to any definite conclusion) for thinking that it was an accident. Whatever the truth,* it is a strange irony that there is still plenty to show for the past glories of Persepolis, while Susa, which Alexander preserved, is little but mouldering mounds of earth.

Alexander then proceeded to Ecbatana, only to find that Darius had retired beyond Rhages (Rayy, a few miles south of Tehran). He followed him there and through the Caspian Gates (identified as what is today the pass of Sardarra) and finally overtook the Persian forces near Hecatompylos, but Darius still eluded capture. The last of the Achaemenian kings had been taken, and then murdered, by the satrap of Bactria. Alexander was master of Iran.

The rest of Alexander's story, falling largely outside the scope of Iranian history, must be briefly told. He went on through Gurgan, Mazanderan and Afghanistan to conquer India, returning overland through Southern Iran to Pasargadae and Susa in 325 B.C., while his fleet under Niarchos sailed from Hormuz to Ahwaz. The following year he fought a campaign in Luristan, and in 323 B.C. he died in Babylon.

The Seleucids, 323–223 B.C. After prolonged chaos, Seleucus, one of Alexander's generals, emerged as the master of his Eastern Dominions, and married an Iranian wife; from them the dynasty descended. Its leading characteristic was the attempt to blend the

* See Annex, note 2.

Greek conquerors with their Iranian subjects. The process was by no means one-sided. Large numbers of Greek civilians were settled in the cities founded along the northern, western and southern edges of the country – in Bactria, at Hecatompylos, Rhages (Rayy), Kangavar and Nihavend in the Zagros. In and around these cities, Greeks and Iranians were fused by inter-marriage, bilingualism, and a mingling of Greek and oriental religious cults. But these were islands in a sea whose currents were running strongly in favour of the indigenous population. Nor has this period of Greek rule left much outward trace – a Greek temple at Kangavar and Khurha (near Arak), a column at Istakhr, some statuary in stone and bronze from Shami and Susa. Yet the end came, not primarily because the Greeks succumbed to oriental influences or were overwhelmed by sheer numbers, but from external causes – the rise of the Roman Empire in the West, and the first of the many great nomad invasions, that of the Parthians, in the East.

The Parthians, 223 B.C.–A.D. 226. The Parthians came from the steppes to the north-east; they first established themselves in Hyrcania (south-east of the Caspian) and ultimately made them-selves masters of Mesopotamia as well as Iran. In many ways they were an endearing people, and the prototype of later conquerors from the east – fearless, resourceful, skilled in the warlike arts, intensely feudal, tolerant towards religions, a little short on culture of their own, but capable of acquiring it from others. In the first century B.C. and again about A.D. 100 they held Rome at bay, and in the intervening period had the sense to keep peace with her when at the zenith of her power. Using the tactics of firing when retreating, which have made 'Parthian' a household word, they defeated Crassus at Carrhae (53 B.C.). The story goes that when Crassus's head was brought in triumph to the Parthian King Orades II at his capital he was watching a performance of the *Bacchae* of Euripides. Seventeen years later Mark Antony, at the head of the largest army which had invaded Iran from the west since Alexander, was thrown back and utterly defeated in his attempt to reach the great religious centre of Praaspa. In A.D.

116 Trajan became the first Roman emperor to reach the Persian Gulf, but he too was soon forced to withdraw by Parthian partisan activity.

It is difficult not to admire the Parthians. They took Iran as they found it, showed respect for Graeco-Iranian civilization, defeated the Romans and converted their soldiery to the cult of Mithraism, defended Iran against Scythian hordes from the north-east, and brought about a revival of the national spirit which came to a full flowering under their successors.

The Sassanians, A.D. 224-642. The Parthian dynasty fell, not to external assault from Rome or the East, but as a result of a national uprising in Fars, the cradle of Iranian civilization, the home of the Achaemenians, the province least touched by Greek colonization. Ardeshir I, the author of the rebellion, was a grandson of Sassan from whom the family derives its name. He defeated and killed the last Parthian king in battle, successfully withstood a hostile coalition of Rome, Scythia and Armenia, and established his sovereignty from the Euphrates to Afghanistan. The line which he founded, the only purely national dynasty between the Achaemenians and the Pahlevi (20th century), proved so powerful and so enduring that, as Ghirshman puts it, 'the civilized world appeared to be divided between it and Rome'.

In four centuries of Sassanian rule there were two periods of glory. In the first, which lasted into the fifth century, the outstanding kings (remarkable for their longevity) were Ardeshir I (226-55), Shapur I (255-71) the captor of Valerian, Shapur II (309-79) conqueror of Armenia and persecutor of Christians, and Bahram V, or Bahram Gur, the Wild Ass (421-38), famous in history and legend for his hunting exploits. In the second period, the great figures were Khosrow I (531-79), perhaps the most illustrious of all the Sassanian kings, and Khosrow Parviz (590-628), conqueror of Jerusalem, invader of Egypt, glorified in legend for his amours (both feminine and equestrian) but in fact brutal, cowardly and fairly incompetent.

The Sassanians were colourful, full-blooded, grandiose; perhaps they have come down to us a little larger than life because they lasted longer than any other purely Iranian dynasty. But they sought to impress, and were not unsuccessful. They maintained a court of unexampled splendour. They delighted in fantastic clothes. They surrounded themselves with an aura of majesty, maintaining a thirty-foot gap between themselves and their nearest nobles on ceremonial occasions. When a subject approached he was required to tie a handkerchief over his mouth so as not to pollute the Royal Presence.

These qualities are evident in what remains of Sassanian architecture and art. Their buildings, such as the palaces and temples at Ctesiphon (Iraq), Firuzabad and Bishapur, were massive, rectangular, their dominant feature the great arch leading into a great hall or court with four bays or iwans – the prototype of the Iranian mosque. Even more characteristic perhaps were the gigantic bas-reliefs with which they decorated the valley walls of frequented roads approaching their towns or palaces. These carvings were the equivalent of the modern hoarding – but they only advertised one product, the Sassanian monarchy. The kings were represented in combat, in victory, or in the process of investiture – they are more than life size and the king is always taller than his companions. Though the carvings frequently portray some connection with religion – e.g. the investiture of Ardeshir I by the God Ormuzd or Ahuramazda – their purpose is primarily secular – the glorification of the monarchy, clothed with all the pomp and majesty of the age.

Not that the Sassanian kings were indifferent to religion. For the most part they were the fervent upholders of the national creed of Zoroastrianism. Ardeshir I restored the privileges of the Magi, which had been curtailed under the Parthians, and most of the early kings displayed their valour in the persecution of Christians, who were regarded as having their first loyalty to Rome and hence as a menace to Iranian security. The only king who encouraged the Christians, Yezdigird I, received the sobriquet of 'the Wicked', and it was not until the Eastern Church broke away from Rome during the reign of Bahram V that persecution was relaxed. The monarchy sought to perpetuate its power by the encouragement of a state religion. After Shapur I had tried unsuccessfully to make Manichaeism serve this purpose, the regime became more and more fully committed to Zoroastrianism. The identification of the monarchy with an impersonal and oligarchic church, and of Zoroastrianism with what after the deposition of Khosrow II became a decaying secular power, partly explains the rapidity with which, in the early part of the seventh century, both were swept incontinently away.

Islam, 642–1037. The third decade of the seventh century was the major turning point in Iranian history, in which the pattern of the country's religious, cultural and psychological development was determined up to the present age. For anyone wanting an insight into modern Iran, the events of this period are extremely important, immensely exciting and still rather mysterious. They were certainly totally unexpected; in 620 when Khosrow Parviz had a twenty-year career of successful conquest behind him, no one could possibly have foreseen that within twenty-five years not merely his dynasty but the whole fabric of Iranian life would have been engulfed and overwhelmed.

After centuries of relative immobility, events moved with startling rapidity. It was not till 614 that Mohammed claimed to be a divinely inspired prophet. For eight years after that he was an exile from his native Arabia. He died in 632 within two years of entering Mecca. The Arab conquests only started after his death, with an attack on Mesopotamia through Kuwait in 633. Yezdigird III, the last of the Sassanian kings, was invited to embrace Islam. He contemptuously refused, pouring scorn on the Arabs for eating lizards and the practice of infanticide. Even so, the Arab conquerors might well have left Iran alone. Omar, the second Caliph, declared in 637, 'I desire that between Mesopotamia and the countries beyond the hills, shall be a barrier, so that the Persians shall not be able to get at us, nor we at them. The plain of Iraq suffices for our wants.' But, because of Iranian raids on Khuzistan, he was forced to change his mind, and in 642 he inflicted a crushing defeat on the Iranians at the battle of Nihavend. This brought to an end the last national Iranian dynasty for nearly a thousand years. In the ensuing few years Isfahan, Kerman,

Seistan, Azerbaijan and Khorasan were successively reduced. Only Tabaristan (Mazanderan) maintained its independence until about 760. The Arab conquest permeated far deeper into the structure of Iranian civilization than any other before or since. It provided the country with a new religion and a new script; it influenced its language and revolutionized its art. Yet it did not destroy utterly or absorb completely; what was indigenous in Iranian character and customs was driven underground and emerged in new and complex forms.

Various reasons can be adduced for the success of this invasion: it was more spiritual than material; the birth of a crusading religion in Arabia coincided with the exhaustion of a dynasty in Iran; Islam was democratic where Zoroastrianism was exclusive and feudal; four centuries of independence under autocratic rule had sapped initiative and reduced the will to resist. But none of these considerations fully explain the completeness with which Iran apparently succumbed to Islam.

I say apparently, because beneath the surface collapse the surrender was never quite complete. The Iranians were not in their hearts ever fully reconciled to fusion with Arab Islam; they accepted the tenets of the new religion but gave it an individual, nationalistic twist. They were helped in this by the dispute over the succession to Mohammed between the Caliphs and the sons of Ali, Mohammed's son-in-law, which led in turn to the cleavage between Sunnis and Shi'as. Since it was the second Caliph Omar who had ordered the invasion of the plateau, Iranian sympathies went naturally to Ali's descendants, the Imams, round whom there developed a curious mystique, partly religious, partly secular in its application. For instance, there grew up a legend that Ali's son Huseyn was married to Shahrbanu, a daughter of Yezdigird III. No historical evidence has been adduced to support this theory, but it served its purpose. The blood of the Sassanian dynasty flowed in the veins of those whom the Iranians, and other Shi'as, regarded as the true successors of the Prophet; the Shi'a version of the succession was thus legitimized, made respectable from a nationalistic standpoint. And the fact that the majority of the followers of Islam, and particularly the Arab conquerors,

thought otherwise, made the Shi'a doctrine all the more attractive
from the Iranian point of view.

The same separatist tendencies were encouraged by later developments within Islam. Thus in the eighth century, when another
dynastic rivalry between the Omayyad family, who held the
Caliphate for some seventy years, and the descendants of
Mohammed's uncle Abbas (who held it from 749 till 1258), came
to the surface, the latter claimed that the rights of Ali's house had
been surrendered and merged in the Abbasid branch of the family.
This legend secured for them Shi'a backing, and the inhabitants of
Khorasan were largely responsible for the overthrow of the
Omayyad dynasty in 750. As a result, the early Abbasids were
considerably dependent on Iranian support, and Haroun-al-
Rashid's son Mamun went so far as to name the eighth Shi'a
Imam, Ali Reza, as his heir in 817 – though the effect was rather
spoilt when Ali Reza died of a surfeit of grapes which Mamun
was suspected of having poisoned. All the same, under the
Abbasid dynasty Iran became increasingly self-assertive; time
brought its revenges.

The broad sweep of the history of this period is fascinating, but
its details are tedious in the extreme. It is enough to say here that,
from the middle of the ninth century onwards, the power of the
Abbasid Caliphate steadily declined. In Iran there sprang up a
number of small semi-independent dynasties such as the Saffarids,
or copper-smiths, founded by a highway robber and based on
Seistan, and the Samanids, mainly centred on Bokhara. Northern
Iran in the tenth and early eleventh centuries was racked by
rivalries between two Daylamite dynasties: the Ziyarids from
Mazanderan (of whom Kabus was the most illustrious) and the
Buyids centred on Samiran (see p. 122). The Ghaznavids, who
spread from Afghanistan to India and also made various incursions
into Persia in the early eleventh century, were rather more important since they maintained themselves in power locally for over
two centuries and have left substantial architectural remains in
Afghanistan.

The Seljuks, 1037–1220. Iran, like Western Europe, emerged at the

beginning of the first millennium A.D. from a period of major
disorder into one of minor discord; the promise of relative stability engendered a great age of building. And it is with the name of
this – and succeeding – dynasties that Islamic architecture in Iran is
associated – perhaps rather misleadingly, in the sense that the buildings were erected by Iranian architects for the most part, and were
largely Iranian in character; but the monarchs who were until
1500 foreigners and invaders provided the impetus and the
inspiration.

The Seljuks, like their successors, came from the north-east.
They were members of a Turkish-speaking tribe from Turkestan,
known as the Ghuzz, and were early converted to orthodox
Mohammedanism, that is to say Sunnism. Their first act of conquest was to seize Merv from the Ghaznavids, and by 1043 they
were firmly established in Khorasan. Twelve years later their
leader, Toghril Beg, entered Baghdad and was named 'Viceregent
of the successor of the Prophet and Lord of all the Moslems' by
the Caliph. His successors were Alp Arslan (1063–72), Malik
Shah (1072–92), and Sultan Sanjar (1096–1157). Alp Arslan
conquered Asia Minor and made several successful expeditions
against the Greeks; he is said to have had such long moustaches
that they had to be tied back when he was shooting. Both he and
his son Malik Shah owed much to the wise counsel and energy
of their vizier, Nizam-ul-Mulk, the patron of Omar Khayyam.
It was he who built the Great Dome Chamber in the Friday
Mosque at Isfahan in Malik Shah's honour, while his rival Taj-ul-
Mulk, Chamberlain to the Shah's mother, built the even lovelier
Small Dome Chamber at the other end of the great mosque.
During his long reign Sanjar was mostly preoccupied with quelling disturbances in Turkestan; towards the end of his life he was
held in captivity for two years, but escaped, and when he died
was buried in the splendid mausoleum at Merv, which became
the prototype of more elaborate later buildings, of which the
most famous is the Taj Mahal.

Order was never completely established in the Seljuk dominions. The family itself was rent by internal strife – there were
separate, and sometimes rival dynasties in Kerman and Iraq. They

completely failed to check the growing power of the Assassins (or hashish addicts), a Shi'a Ismailite sect who, under the leadership of Hassan Sabah, established themselves in the Daylamite fortress of Alamut in the mountains north-east of Kazvin and from there practised the art which has made their name a household word. They were responsible for the murder of Nizam-ul-Mulk and possibly also of Malik Shah. During the last fifty years Seljuk power was increasingly threatened by marauders from Central Asia, and it was by them that they were eventually displaced.

The Mongols, 1220–1380. The Mongol invasion of Western Asia was provoked by the weakness of the Seljuk Empire only at second remove. Owing to disputes over the succession among the sons of Sultan Sanjar, Ala-ud-Din-Mohammed, a princeling of Khiva, extended his power in the early years of the thirteenth century from Samarkand to Hamadan and Kerman. Shortly thereafter, a new and more formidable power arose in Central Asia in the person of the Mongol chief Temuchin who took the name of Yenghiz Khan. Having destroyed the Chinese Empire, he offered peace and trade to his western neighbour Mohammed, who accepted it readily – the Khiva princeling was not cast in an heroic mould. Unhappily, however, one of his governors put to death a trade mission despatched to Otrar by Yenghiz Khan; Mohammed, so far from offering an apology, beheaded the leader of a Mongol expedition sent to demand it; and the war of revenge which then became inevitable had dire consequences not only for the lord of Khiva himself but for all Western Asia and much of Eastern Europe.

Once again, as six hundred years before, events moved with startling rapidity. Between 1219, the year of Mohammed's defiance, and 1227 when Yenghiz Khan died, Mongol hordes had overrun and largely destroyed Bokhara, Samarkand, Merv, Nishapur, and all of Northern Iran. Yenghiz Khan himself had pursued Mohammed's son Jelal-ed-Din across the Indus, and his lieutenants had marched through Georgia and defeated Russian armies beyond the Dnieper. The loot, murder, rape and destruction which attended these conquests was without parallel in history; the loss to art and learning in Northern Iran was incalculable. Fortunately the south escaped, and this greatly assisted eventual recovery.

A second wave of Mongol invasion took place between 1251 and 1256 when Hulagu Khan, Yenghiz's grandson, set out to destroy the Assassins in their mountain fortress and to extinguish the Caliphate in Baghdad. He was successful in both – at the price of further extensive bloodshed and destruction. Like other ruthless conquerors, Hulagu was obsessed with the desire to read his destiny. His superstitious zest for astrology gave him his one creative urge; and it was he who ordered the astrologer Nasir-ed-Din to build him an elaborate observatory at Maragheh, the Azerbaijan town which he chose for his capital and where he died, unregretted, in 1265.

The later Mongols, however, as though to amend for the shortcomings of their forebears, really went in for Civilization, and even Culture. At intervals, too, they flirted with Christianity; but this was perhaps a sign less of doctrinal tolerance than of political calculation. Moreover they were wooed; the Pope sent a mission to Abaga (1265–81), and Edward I received a Mongol emissary, all in aid of an alliance against Islam. Arghun (1284–91) went so far as to plan a joint Mongol-Christian attack on the Holy Land, but the fall of Acre intervened. The Mongols also encouraged tourism; having been indefatigable travellers themselves, this was no doubt a form of public relations which came to them naturally. Marco Polo was their most famous beneficiary. His route across Iran is an indication of the important centres of that time: Tabriz (soon to become the Mongol capital), Saveh, Kashan, Yazd, Kerman, Hormuz, Sirjan, Kerman again, Tabas and Nishapur. And as they settled down the Mongols initiated another era of great building. Ghazan Khan (1295–1304) established magnificent religious and educational institutions at Tabriz, and built, on the outskirts of that city, a tomb for himself which was intended to excel that of Sultan Sanjar at Merv. Oljeitu (1304–16) completed the city of Sultaniyeh, including the great mausoleum which still stands and bears his name. Both these sovereigns pursued moreover a religious policy of subtlety and skill. Ghazan, declaring himself a Moslem, earned merit with his Moslem subjects by persecuting Jews and Christians. At the same time, aided perhaps by indifferent communications, he managed to give the impression abroad that he was not hostile to Christianity; and one Geoffrey de Langley was despatched by Edward I to his court, the first of a long, if broken, line of British emissaries. As for Oljeitu, he was a regular Vicar of Bray. He was brought up as a Christian by his mother – converted to Sunnism by his wife – nearly reverted to paganism as a result in part of terror induced by a thunderstorm – became an ardent Shi'a after a visit to the tomb of Ali at Nejef, planned to bring his body and that of Huseyn to Sultaniyeh as an encouragement to pilgrim traffic – and when that failed, went back to Sunnism again. Even more remarkable, throughout these operations he kept up with various Western European monarchs a correspondence which gave them the impression that, basically, he was an enemy of Islam.

After Oljeitu's death in 1316 the dynasty broke down through domestic squabbles and a period of chaos ensued, in which the only relatively stable element was provided by the Muzaffarid dynasty in South Persia, one of whom, Shah Shuja, is famous in history as the patron of the poet Hafez. The collapse of organized central government meant that the way lay open to the next wave of invasion from Central Asia – that of Timur Lang.

The Timurids, 1380–1500. Timur, the original of Marlowe's Tamburlaine, was descended from a member of the Berla tribe of Central Asia who was Minister to a son of Yenghiz Khan. For some reason, he has traditionally enjoyed a higher reputation in Europe than any other Asiatic conqueror. His renown, based on a series of sweeping victories, the splendour of his court and the humanity of his behaviour, echoed down the centuries and struck a responding chord in the Renaissance concept of glory and adventure. Though his fame may have exaggerated his virtues, and he may not be the author of the memoirs attributed to him, Timur was undoubtedly a remarkable man; the extent of his conquests, at the end of his long career, was greater than that of either Alexander or Yenghiz Khan. But he was kept so busy with fresh conquests that he had little time to give to the administration of the countries conquered, nor was his hold upon them altogether secure. All in all, he has left less to show for himself in Iran than his reputation would warrant – not even an orgy of destruction. His crazy son Miran Shah destroyed Sultaniyeh, the Mongol capital, it is true; but Timur is said to have been furious when he heard and punished him for it.

Nor did Timur's successors leave any great mark in Iran proper. They were for the most part absentee monarchs who preferred to reside to the north-east. Shah Rukh (1408–47) removed his capital from Samarkand to Herat, which he did much to beautify; his wife, Gawhar Shad, was responsible for building the great mosque in the heart of the shrine at Meshed; his son, Ulugh Beg, was a renowned astronomer, a poet and a patron of literature. But what they did not manage to do was to govern their southern dominions effectively. After the middle of the fifteenth century a state of chaos and confusion, perhaps more complete than ever before or since, was the order of the day. The only clear thread running through this period (which oddly enough corresponds in time to that of the Wars of the Roses in England) is the deadly rivalry which developed between two tribes of Turkoman origin, the Kara Kuyunlu or 'Black Sheep' and the Ak Kuyunlu or 'White Sheep'. The first were established in the area of Lake Van (E. Turkey); the second in the neighbourhood of Diarbekr. The White Sheep leader Uzun Hasan (d. 1478) achieved some prominence; it was his ambition to conquer the Ottoman Empire and to this end he formed an alliance with Venice. The Venetian emissaries Caterino Zeno, Josefa Barbaro, and Contarini wrote memoirs which throw valuable light on the history of this period.

The Safavids, 1500–1736. At this point, Iranian history again takes a strange turn. For out of this welter of disorder, following upon eight and a half centuries of alien rule, emerged a dynasty more nearly national than any since the Sassanians, and certainly comparable to it in splendour and renown.

The first Safavid monarch bore the name of Ismail and reigned from 1499 to 1524. His mother was the daughter of Uzun Hasan, and when the White Sheep dynasty broke down as a result of squabbles over the succession, his family connection provided him with a legalistic justification for the seizure of power. It was this indeed which helped him to get where he did; but it was his paternity that prevented him from being just another White Sheep leader and instead enabled him – despite the Turkoman strain in him – to become a national hero and the founder of a dynasty. He was descended from a long line of holy men (or sufis) from Ardebil. Not only had their reputation for sanctity been maintained through five generations, but the first of them, Sheikh Seifuddin Ishak, who is said to have been visited and highly respected by Timur, could trace his ancestry back to the seventh Imam.

And so it was that all the deep-seated, atavistic urges in the Iranian character could find an outlet in this new dynasty: the theory of divine right, descending from the Sassanians through Yezdigird to the Imams, and through the Imams to Ismail; the mysticism and scepticism of the sufis, perhaps the most characteristic literary and philosophical manifestation of the Iranian spirit in the Middle Ages; and finally the desire to be different from other Moslems, and particularly from Arabs, and to encourage separatist tendencies within Islam. It is extremely significant that it was not until Ismail's time that Shi'ism was adopted as the official religion of the country, or that the monarch took positive steps to proselytize sunnis and create a monolithic state based on Shi'ism – which to a large extent Iran still remains today.

Whether the name Safavid is derived from 'sufi',* or from safi (meaning purity of religion) it further illustrates the important part played by the religious traditions of the family in strengthening the new dynasty. In time this character was lost. When we read the description by English chroniclers of the court of the Sophy (Shah Abbas), it is as difficult to remember the origin of this title as to discern, amidst all the splendour, the austere lineaments and devout features of the sages of Ardebil.

Ismail's background of sanctity in no way restrained the success

* See Chap. II 2 (ii), p. 45.

of his military career. At the age of about twenty he cleared the north-western part of the country, and proclaimed himself Shah at Tabriz in 1499. The following year he captured Isfahan and Shiraz, and later had to fight campaigns to secure the pacification of Gilan and Khorasan. Before the end of his reign he came into conflict with the growing power of Turkey and suffered a serious defeat at Khoy in Azerbaijan, but this led to no lasting Ottoman invasion, and under Ismail the reunification and re-emergence of Iran as an independent and sovereign power became complete.

His son, Shah Tahmasp, reigned for over fifty years (1524–75) – a period notable chiefly for protracted and ding-dong struggles with the Turks, which resulted in the loss of Mesopotamia; the removal of the capital from exposed Tabriz to more secure Kazvin; and the courting of the Iranian monarchy by Western monarchs, hoping to exploit Ottoman-Iranian rivalry and Shi'a-Sunnite discord to the disadvantage of the Turks, and also desirous of promoting trade routes through Iran.

These contacts were the prelude to an increasing flow of travellers and chroniclers in the seventeenth century, attracted by reports of the splendour of the Safavid court and the exotic and Oriental aspect of a largely unknown country. For the first time since the Achaemenians, an Iranian dynasty won international fame.

The first monarch to benefit, deservedly, from this development was Shah Abbas (1586–1628), generally regarded as the most remarkable of all Iranian kings. On the basis of his military achievements alone he deserves his title of 'the Great'. Inheriting a kingdom threatened from without and endangered by collapse within, he repelled the Uzbeg invaders of Khorasan, suppressed rebellion in Fars, drove the Portuguese out of Hormuz in the Persian Gulf, recovered the western territories lost early in his reign from the Ottoman Empire, and captured Kandahar from the Great Mogul.

But his success in war, great as this was, was surpassed by his achievements in the arts of peace. He removed the seat of government from Kazvin to Isfahan, and constructed the most splendid and spacious capital in the world. He built magnificent palaces on

the Caspian coast and improved communications in his dominions
by creating a network of paved roads and caravanserais which are
still visible today as monuments to his enterprise. He engaged in
a great series of public works and irrigation projects, even con-
templating the removal of a mountain to bring the water of the
Karun into the valley which waters Isfahan – a dream which was
only successfully accomplished in the 1950s. He moved great
bodies of men with the object of pacifying and beautifying his
country – Kurds transplanted to Khorasan to defend the frontier
against the Uzbegs, Armenians brought from Georgia to provide
skilled labour at Isfahan, European and Chinese craftsmen to
practise their skills in fresco painting, pottery and faïence mosaic.
Western travellers who crossed half the world to do him honour
were kept waiting on his pleasure for months. Was he not the
equal if not the superior, in power and wealth, in taste and skill,
of any contemporary monarchs in Asia or Europe? And if his
reign was marred by brutalities, including the murder of his
eldest son, was his record any blacker than that of many a
Renaissance princeling?

Unhappily, for all Abbas the Great's outstanding qualities the
Iranian Renaissance was of brief duration. The Safavid dynasty
struggled on for some hundred years after his death, sustained
more by the glories of its past than by any merit in his successors.
Shah Safi (1628–41), Abbas II (1642–66), Suleiman (1666–94)
and Huseyn (1694–1726) represented a sad degeneration from
the saintly race from which they sprang.

The marvel is not that the Safavid dynasty collapsed when it
did, but that it took so long to do it. Unrest spread rapidly after
about 1715, fostered by the Afghans and Uzbegs in the north-east,
the Kurds in the west and the Arabs in the south. In 1722 a small
but highly trained force of Afghans appeared before Isfahan,
routed a large Iranian army at nearby Gulnabad, captured and
looted the city and massacred many of the inhabitants. The
Russians and Turks stepped in to seize what they could of the
spoils in the north and west; Huseyn was captured and abdicated,
and his son Tahmasp became Shah in exile and established himself
in Mazanderan, where members of the Qajar and Afshar tribes

rallied to his banner. It was one of the latter, Nadir Kuli, who took command of the armies, defeated the Afghans at Damghan in 1729, ejected them from Isfahan, and in 1730 largely cleared the country. But within two years the all-powerful general had forced the craven Shah to abdicate, and in 1736 Nadir himself assumed the title of Shah, making it a condition that the Safavid claim to the throne should be extinguished for ever. Such was the ignominious end of the dynasty.

The Interregnum, 1736–94. The eighteenth century is a horrible period in Iranian history – horrible to read about, horrible to disentangle, horrible to have tried to live in – I say tried because, at least if one was prominent, one probably stood a better chance then than in any other period of being tortured, blinded, castrated, massacred or simply put to death. I propose to treat this grisly epoch with the greatest possible brevity.

Nadir was a brilliant soldier but a hopeless ruler; he conducted a glorious campaign in India, in the course of which he captured the Peacock Throne, but he seems to have continued a career of conquest for lack of anything better to do. He made Meshed his capital and – apparently for the sake of conciliating the Afghans – favoured his Sunni subjects at the expense of the Shi'as. He was murdered in 1747, and for the next fifty years Iranian history is wellnigh unintelligible. There was in essence a three-sided struggle between the descendants of Nadir Shah, the Zand family and the Qajars, a Turkish tribe centred in Mazanderan. For much of the time Shah Rukh, grandson both of Nadir and Shah Huseyn, remained nominally on the throne at Meshed, but, blinded and intermittently imprisoned, he exercised no effective power. The Zands were Kurdish chieftains who derived their authority from the Bakhtiaris. Their leader, Karim Khan, is about the only prominent character during this period from whom one does not recoil in disgust. He ruled at Shiraz for twenty years (1759–79) and had effective control over much of Iran, but never assumed the title of Shah. He did much to beautify Shiraz and to honour her poets. With his death, the Qajars fought desperately for fifteen years to gain the upper hand. Their leader, Aga Mohammed, who

had been castrated long before by Nadir's descendants, assailed
the Zands in battle, with treachery, and finally by wholesale
massacre, first at Kerman and later at Bam. There Lutfali
Khan, the young Zand chief, was finally captured, leaving the
Qajars in undisputed possession of the bloodstained throne in
1794.

The Qajars, 1787–1925. Aga Mohammed had been proclaimed
Shah in 1787 at the conclusion of a successful campaign against
Russia; thereafter he established his capital in Tehran, where it
has since remained. Later he recaptured Khorasan, though only
after perpetrating the most horrible atrocities upon the person of
Shah Rukh. Most brutal and hated of all Iranian monarchs, Aga
Mohammed at least succeeded in bringing the period of anarchy
to an end; he fought successful campaigns against external enemies, and reconstituted the Shi'a faith as the state religion. He
was murdered in camp by his personal attendants in 1797. Under
his successors Fath Ali Shah (1798–1834), Mohammed (1834–48),
Nasr-uddin (1848–96), Muzaffar-uddin (1896–1907), Mohammed
Ali (1907–09) and Sultan Ahmed (1909–25), the whole context of
Iranian history changes; we emerge from the Middle Ages into
recent times, in which the interest of Iran lay not in her own
civilization or splendour or mystery, but in her possibilities as a
field for expansion among rival great powers – or rather, to be
more precise, as a field in which expansion of one great power
should be limited by a rival power; and it was precisely this
rivalry, rather than any inherent strength in the Qajar monarchy,
which enabled Iran to preserve her independence. Although,
therefore, the period as a whole is not one to which any Iranian
looks back with much pride, it must be said that the Qajars
started well. They established diplomatic relations with France,
England and (separately) India; they inflicted a military defeat on
the Turks at Erzerum; they reduced rebellious chiefs in the east
and threatened Herat; they concluded treaties – with England,
regulating their relations with Afghanistan; with Turkey,
designed to remove causes of friction (Erzerum 1823); and with
Russia, to regulate frontiers (Turkomanchai 1828). Thus were laid

the foundations for a pacification and new stability which, apart from a brief war with Britain over Herat in 1856, lasted throughout the century. Neither external invasion nor internal feuds ever seriously menaced the Qajar dynasty. The trouble with the later Qajars was not that they were foolhardy, reckless or despotic, but that they did little effectively to enable Iran to compete in the modern world. Internally, their policy was one of drift; externally they were compelled to play their hand from weakness. Iran in consequence entered the twentieth century in a comparatively stable but hopelessly creaky condition. The constitutional revolution of 1905 all but swept away the decrepit Qajar dynasty; thereafter its powers were severely clipped. It collapsed completely in the face of resolution on the part of Reza Khan in 1922, who had the throne made over to him by legal means. The founder of the new Pahlevi dynasty proved as Shah (1925-41) to be one of the most effective and formidable personalities that Iran has ever produced. At this point we pass beyond the sphere of history, into modern times, with which this book, deliberately, has no concern.

ii] PARA-HISTORY

No account of the dynasties of Iranian history would be complete without some reference to the Iranian legend, the national myth with its kings and heroes and lovers who loom larger perhaps in the mind of many Iranians, even today, than most historical figures. 'The tenacity of the saga,' says Eduard Meyer rather primly, 'stands in the sharpest contrast with the fact that the historical memory of the Persian is extremely defective.'* By contrast, the legend, drawn partly from folk heroes of prehistoric Indo-European mythology, later taken over and transformed by Zoroastrianism, lived on to become more real, in the minds of millions, than reality itself. The process was greatly furthered by Firdausi (d. 1020) who, in his vast *Shahnameh* or *Book of Kings*, skilfully joined those ancient tales with embellishments of the lives and loves of Sassanian kings, which by his time no doubt (thanks to the Arab invasion) had already passed into mythology. The *Shahnameh* became the national epic; it was learned by heart,

* *Encyclopaedia Britannica*, Eleventh Edition, Vol. 21, p. 204.

passed on from generation to generation by word of mouth, and thus made a far deeper impression than any historical record which only a handful of those who knew Firdausi by heart would in any case have been able to read.

And so, in the Iranian legend, the past is peopled not by those who built or really lived in Susa or Sarvistan, Persepolis or Pasargadae, but by characters rooted in varying degrees in myth or history. Khosrow (Kai Khosrow, not to be confused with his Sassanian namesakes), a king in Iranian folk-lore, is the Sushrava of the Indian legend, the son who goes on a journey to meet his father and loses his life at his hands. Jamshid is the Persian off-spring of the Vedic Yama, the first man who now rules in the kingdom of the departed. Gushtasp derives his name from the mythical patron of Zoroaster. Rustam, his ancestor Garshasp, his son Sohrab and his grandson Barzu, both of whom he slew in error, his son Jahagair and his daughter Gushasp, represent a later accretion, as do his enemy Isfandiar and Kaikus' son Siwayush. In the same world we find the Caucasian princess Shirin, beloved of Khosrow; a legendary Ardeshir and Bahram Gur (both based on their Sassanian prototypes); and Madjnun and Leila, lovers sep-arated like Romeo and Juliet by family feuds, with Madjnun dying, like Romeo, at Leila's tomb. We not only meet them in verse and in imagination; we see them portrayed, in formal gardens or on mountain-sides carpeted with spring flowers, riding to the chase or in the act of slaughter, in a stream of unforgettable and vivid miniatures. Even today in the Persian language Persepolis is Tahkt-i-Jamshid, the throne of Jamshid; the tombs of Darius and Xerxes are Naqsh-i-Rustam, the picture of Rustam. Nor is this just an academic curiosity. There can be no proper under-standing of what underlies modern Iran unless we recognize the significance of this triumph of legend over history, of art over reality, this preference for embellishment as against unvarnished fact, for ancient folk beliefs as against new-fangled creeds.

iii] THE NATION

Through twenty-six centuries of history, the Iranian nation has displayed astonishing powers of survival. Situated at a cross-roads on the great land mass of Europe and Asia, it has at times over-expanded beyond its strength, at other times been buffeted, punctured or largely swallowed by competing empires or prospective world conquerors. Yet, protected by mountains and deserts, and sustained by the resilient quality of its peoples and institutions, the nation has throughout preserved an unmistakable identity, which distinguishes it from its Turkish, Arab, Slav, Mongol and Indian neighbours. There is perhaps some peculiar suppleness, some inherent flexibility in the Iranian character which has enabled it to withstand shocks which would have sent more rigid people reeling or would have broken their national spirit. Nothing else can explain the persistence with which this people, of mixed race and language, living largely in a series of oases separated from each other by natural features of forbidding difficulty, often neglected, and until recently rarely provided with even the minimum security by its rulers, has held together and, even when temporarily split apart, has retained its sense of nation-hood – and its sense of humour. It is fashionable in these days to talk of national feeling in Asia or Africa as though it were some new or even artificially created thing. This is emphatically not true of Iran, which gives every evidence of being a living organism with an unbroken core, right through history from the earliest times. Race, monarchy, language and religion have each played their part in this process, though the part has in a sense been a paradoxical one. 'No other race except perhaps the English,' says Arnold Wilson, 'has such a mixture of blood in its veins';* yet the Iranian race has evolved a distinctive personality and held fast together despite diverse origins. The monarchy has passed frequently from one dynasty to another, and half the time the throne has been occupied by monarchs of foreign race; yet the strong monarchical tradition has exercised a most effective guiding force and commanded a powerful loyalty to the institution. Only about two thirds of the inhabitants of Iran speak the Persian language or its dialects even today; yet Persian, which has remained virtually unchanged through ten centuries, has exerted a strong unifying influence by reason of its expressive simplicity,

* *Persia*, 1932.

its liquid purity, and its unrivalled (and easily memorable) poetry – qualities which have also brought it international renown. The case of religion is even more paradoxical; the process by which Iran lost her ancient faith and took revenge on her captors is described in the next chapter. If these are the causes, there are also the effects. Nowhere is the indestructible character of the Iranian genius better illustrated than in the field of artistic achievement. Again and again the same great qualities emerge – a sense of fitness of form, a love of intricate design, skilful use of resplendent colour – and, rising like a phoenix from the ashes, they seem, as will be shown in Chapter Three, to shine most brilliantly in adversity, to receive fresh inspiration from the impact of invasion or immigration. We are apt to forget, through our habit of talking of Islamic art, Seljuk building, Mongol architecture or Timurid design, that we are concerned with the achievement of Iranian architects, designers and workers operating on Iranian soil; these bear witness to the continuity and persistence of Iranian skills and traditions.

CHAPTER TWO

Religion

———

Religion in Iran means more than Islam. The plateau is the home of Zoroaster; and though since the Arab conquest Iranians have been Moslems, they have been Moslems with a difference.

1. ZOROASTRIANISM

The idea of the Deity as a moral force first developed in Iran. Iranian folk religion differentiated itself at an early stage, before the dawn of history, from the Indian cults with which it had much in common, by attributing moral qualities to its deities and relating its religious practices to the business of living in the world, rather than using them as a means of escape from it.

The Iranians in fact took over (or, more correctly, shared) the Indian mythology and turned it inside out. To the Indians good spirits were Daeva, evil spirits Asura. The Iranians, under the inspiration of Zoroaster, their first prophet, elevated one Ahura (= Asura) to be the embodiment of all goodness and power, while the Daeva, the popular or vulgar deities, were consigned to the rôle of undesirable spirits or devils. Zoroaster's unique contribution to religious thought was to envisage the universe as the battleground of two opposing forces – Ahuramazda, the wise deity, and Ahriman, the spirit of evil. It was a struggle for the soul of man; and man's part in it was neither passive nor pre-determined. On the contrary he was faced with a positive choice: the moral problem was sharply posed, as in no other religion before Christianity. The struggle continued not only on earth but in the after-life, the nature of which was determined by man's behaviour on earth, and on this was kept a close check, so that nothing could be concealed; expiation, repentance and sacrifice were useless. Man's fate after death was decided by striking a precise balance between his good and bad deeds; if the former predominated he went to heaven, if the latter to hell. Only if there was an approximate equilibrium was the matter in doubt, and man allowed to pass into a kind of transitional purgatory, from which he was delivered at a final judgment.

Who was Zoroaster? When did he live and how do we know about his doctrines? What is his connection with the other manifestation of early Iranian religion that is well known in the Christian world – the Magi, or wise men?

These questions are difficult to answer with precision. We really know very little about Zoroaster. The probability is that he flourished in Eastern Iran between one thousand and eight hundred B.C. But there is no direct evidence of his existence, and for several centuries after his presumed death he does not seem to have attained the status of a prophet. There is nothing about him, for instance, in Achaemenian inscriptions, though there is a great deal about Ahuramazda – the god he is supposed to have invented. All assumptions made about him really derive from the traditional belief that he was the author of the Gathas, or hymns, incorporated in the Avesta, or holy book of Zoroastrianism, itself a much later compilation dating in all likelihood from Sassanian times.

Whatever the facts about Zoroaster as a person, a powerful moral influence, tending towards monotheism, was evidently exerted over varying local cults and beliefs early in the last millennium B.C. By Achaemenian times it had emerged clearly in the worship of Ahuramazda, the divine light to whom the heirs of Cyrus, though by no means claiming divinity themselves, believed they owed their throne. This influence probably exerted itself, too, over the Magi, a survival from an earlier cult* centred

* The Persian New Year, No Ruz (New Day), beginning on March 21, is a secular festival whose origins are hidden in remote antiquity. One of the customs is to plant indoors in boxes seeds that germinate on No Ruz day; they must, however, all be put outside by Seezdah No Ruz or the Thirteenth Day (April 2) (c.f. our own superstition about holly and mistletoe after Epiphany).

in Media, who themselves practised rites, e.g. sacrifices, which Zoroaster opposed. But in characteristic fashion the Magi were taken over by the unified, reformed religion. They were not merely kindlers of fire but became a powerful priestly caste wielding great political influence. Indeed it was partly due to their rigid conservatism that Zoroastrianism eventually foundered.

Apart from doctrine and origin, the characteristic features of Zoroastrianism were fairly simple. Sacrifices were disapproved, and the cow was made a sacred animal – a development which, it has been suggested, might be expected to accompany an evolution from a nomadic to a settled community. Fire, sometimes derived from gases discharged from underground petroleum deposits, as at Masjid-i-Suleiman in Khuzistan, was the central feature of worship. There were two kinds of building associated with religious rites – the fire temple where the eternal fire was guarded, and the open-air altars before which people worshipped. There were no other religious buildings, and, as Herodotus noticed, no temples in the Greek sense of the word. Finally, burial, burning or drowning of dead persons was forbidden – the dead human body must not be allowed to defile the sacred elements of earth, fire or water. The air, apparently, did not matter, for the dead were exposed on hillsides or in dakhmés (towers of silence) until only the bones remained – a custom which, if merely out of hygienic considerations, could only have developed in a dry, hilly, and thinly populated country. It originated with the Magi.

The extent to which Zoroastrianism tended towards or away from monotheism varied greatly during the period of some eleven hundred years for which it flourished. Under the early Achaemenians there is no reference in inscriptions to any god save Ahuramazda.* But Zoroaster appears to have left the door ajar for the satellite gods of the old folk-beliefs which he distilled; and from the time of Artaxerxes II the cult of others, especially Anahita, goddess of water fertility, and Mithras, the sun god, flourished and was officially encouraged partly, it is believed, for

* See Annex, note 3.

proselytizing purposes.. Under the Parthians deviation was even more marked. Anahita superseded Ahuramazda as the principal deity, and animal sacrifices formed an essential feature of the royal family's religious rites.

Shapur I was by no means a sound Zoroastrian; it was indeed his flirtations with Mani (who preached a sort of mixture of Zoroastrianism with Christianity) which provoked the conservative reaction of the Magi, and led to the full reinstatement, under Shapur II, of the old religion in its purest and sternest form. Because of its rigidities, its exclusive character and the dominance of its priests, it was ill-equipped to withstand the onslaught of Islam in the seventh century.

The later history of Zoroastrianism calls for brief notice. The followers of the old religion are known in Iran today as Guebres, long thought to have been a corruption of the Arabic word Kafir (hence the Kaffirs of East Africa) meaning Gentile or unbeliever. Only a few thousand are to be found,* mainly in Yazd (where there is a fire temple and a dakhmé) and Kerman. Their religious institutions are to some extent financed by their more numerous and more wealthy co-religionists in India – the Parsees of Bombay. Persecuted intermittently in the past, they are now officially tolerated (like the Jews and the Christians) by the Iranian state and have their own representatives in the Majlis.

2. ISLAM

We have already seen how the new democratic faith of Islam carried all before it. It is interesting to speculate whether, had Islam been truly monolithic, it would have taken permanent root in Iran. When in Yazd in 1888, the renowned Persian scholar Edward Browne met a Babi colonel who told him that, had it not been for the martyrdom of Huseyn at Kerbala, 'Islam would never have gained one tenth of the strength it actually possesses'. This may have been an overstatement, but there seems little doubt that the dynastic split inside Islam within fifty years of

---

* For a fascinating account of Zoroastrian village communities today see Mary Boyce, *A Persian Stronghold of Zoroastrianism*, Oxford U.P. 1977.

Mohammed's death did much to reconcile the Iranians to the new religion imposed upon them by their Arab conquerors.

The split took place between the elected Caliphs on the one hand and Mohammed's own descendants through his son-in-law Ali and his sons Hasan and Huseyn on the other. On one side were the Arab conquerors of Persia asserting the authority of the Qureysh tribe which stemmed from Mecca and to which Mohammed himself belonged; on the other were those who favoured divine right and the principle of heredity. In practical terms the first alone were victors. Ali's descendants failed to establish themselves in any material sense. Huseyn's rebellion was a brief, abortive, ill-planned affair. The Caliphate, which was the symbol of the physical power of Islam, remained firmly in the hands of the opposite party, and their supporters, the Sunnis, have always constituted the majority within Islam. The followers of Ali, the Shi'as, had to be content with spiritual leaders, or Imams, whose natures knew no sin and whose bodies cast no shadow, but who enjoyed no temporal power.

Nor did the Shi'as with their more easy-going attitude towards public worship, their doctrinal heterodoxy and their proneness to worship saints, hold together as a unit as successfully as the Sunnis. When spiritual leaders have no temporal power, as in the case of the Imams, there is less sanction against the exercise of personal preferences. Within a hundred and thirty years of Mohammed's death, hesitations by the sixth Imam, Jafar (d. 765), over nominating a successor produced a split between those who favoured the descendants of his elder son Ismail, and those who accepted the later choice of his second son Kazim. The former, known as Seveners (followers of the seventh Imam) or Ismailis (after Ismail), formed a separate sect famous in later history for its association with the Assassins, and serving today under the generous and enlightened leadership of the Aga Khan.

How many more such splits might have occurred had the Imamate experienced further disputes over the succession it is impossible to say. But when the twelfth Imam, Mohammed, disappeared in A.D. 873, the legend grew up that he had not died but was in miraculous concealment and would one day reappear in the Gawhar Shad mosque in Meshed. Since 873, therefore, there has been no succession problem. Shi'ism has acquired its twelve saints, who give their name to its largest sect (Ithna'-ashryia or twelvers). The greater Imamate lives on as a binding spiritual force which no longer needs to become involved in temporal affairs.

In the long run, it was paradoxically this divorce from temporal power which provided Shi'ism with one source of strength; it was not linked with the Caliphate or the Arab conquest or the Ottoman Empire; the power of the Imams was of a kind which survived physical invasion. Another source of strength was its adaptability to local circumstances, the tolerance which enabled it to absorb pre-existent customs and traditions, as in Iran.

i] SHI'ISM

The relationship between Shi'ism and Iran is complex and obscure. Shi'ism has never been confined to Iran; about two fifths of the population of modern Iraq are Shi'ite, and there are pockets of Shi'ism throughout North Africa. There are also some eight million Sh'ias* in India. Conversely, until the Safavid dynasty in the sixteenth century, Shi'ism was not the official religion of Iran. There is indeed reason to believe that, except in places like Qum which was fanatically Shi'ia from early times, Sunnis predominated. It would not therefore be true to suggest either that Shi'ism wholly captured Iran, before 1500, because it was the most powerful non-conformist body within Islam, or that the idiosyncrasies of Shi'ism are purely or even primarily Iranian in origin. The true picture is that Shi'ism, the minority faith, and the Iranians, the most civilized and individualistic converts to Islam, exercised a strong mutual attraction for each other over the course of eight centuries – an attraction which was finally consummated in the establishment of Shi'ism as the official religion of the state under the Safavids.

We have already seen how in the first stage specifically Iranian legends were grafted on to the Shi'ite heterodoxy. Ali's son was supposed to have married the daughter of Yezdigird III. The

* Estimated in about 1960.

Abbasids won some Iranian support against the Omayyads by claiming that the rights of the house of Ali had been merged in that branch of the family. It was conveniently discovered that it was on the Iranian New Year's Day that Mohammed conferred the Caliphate on Ali. Later the legend sprang up that the Safavids were descended from the seventh Imam.

The triumph of Shi'ism in the sixteenth century was not effected purely from within Iran. Many rustic scholars from the mountains of Syria and Shi'as from Bahrein flowed into the country where their religion was officially recognized, and added to the strength of the movement.

It is also worth noting (because it is not often stated) that, at least according to tradition, all the Imams with the exception of Imam Reza and Mohammed, the twelfth Imam, who disappeared, were buried in Arabia or Iraq: Ali at Nejef; Hasan at Medina; Musa al Kazim, number seven, at Kazimein; Huseyn at Kerbala; numbers four to six at Medina; and numbers nine to eleven at Samarra, where the Mahdi also disappeared.

The shortage of shrines in Iran was, however, made up for in other ways consistent with the Shi'a tendency to create and reverence saints.

This is an outstanding Shi'a idiosyncrasy. It derives from the cult of Huseyn and the belief in the divinity of the Imams, but extends to many martyrs and holy persons including, particularly in medieval times, many Sufis. The result is that Shi'a territory, and notably Iran, yields a remarkable crop of tombs, shrines and other places of pilgrimage.

Another idiosyncrasy of Shi'ism is what can be regarded as the revival within Islam of the Christian concept of martyrdom. Not only Mohammed but also Abu Bekr and Omar, the first two Caliphs, died in their beds; but Ali was murdered at Kufa, Huseyn slain in battle at Kerbala and most of the Imams were (according to legend) murdered by the contemporary Caliph. Which was cause and which effect – whether the violent deaths of the early Imams developed the passion motive in Shi'ism, or whether it was some hidden masochistic urge which first built up into a myth deaths which were in fact quite ordinary, is one of the fascinating problems which cannot on present evidence be answered confidently. What is at least clear is that the death of Huseyn occupies a central place in Shi'a religious practice and that the theme of violent death or martyrdom constantly recurs in the early centuries of Shi'ism. It is in honour of Huseyn's death on the tenth day of the Mohammedan month of Muharram that the whole of that month is regarded as a period of mourning by the Shi'as and that the tenth day itself, Ashura, is celebrated with processions in which men, stripped to the waist, flay themselves with thongs and perform a ritual dance in the course of which, calling on the name of Huseyn and Hasan (who was not martyred at all, but died of consumption at Medina), they often work themselves into a frenzy. In certain parts of central Iran enormous wooden structures, known as nakhl, are decorated in Muharram with black ribbons and streamers, covered with banners and carried in procession by as many as a hundred men. Another most important feature of Muharram celebrations is the passion play or taziya, in which episodes from the life of Huseyn, many imaginary, but with themes of persecution, cruelty, mourning and sentiment strongly emphasized, are acted before a public whose reactions sometimes border on the hysterical. These plays are believed to be of fairly recent origin, at least in Iran, but many contain survivals from earlier pre-Islamic rites. This is almost certainly true of one of the most widespread and characteristic features of Shi'a ritual – the hand. This is to be found everywhere – in mosques, in the most modest shrines, as well as in Ashura processions where it is used to summon onlookers to the festival. It takes the simplest forms – often a flat outline crudely cut from an old petrol tin. However ancient its origin, it is now associated exclusively with the murder of Huseyn, symbolizing the legend that his hand was cut off.

Another Shi'a feature is the doctrine of takiya (caution) or ketman (disguise), meaning the legalization of the practice of denying one's faith under threat of compulsion or injury. This is not exclusively of Shi'a origin; it is indeed sanctioned in the Koran (Sura XVI 106) and received approval from early authorities of all sects. But it flourished particularly in the conditions of persecution and surveillance in which the minority faith was compelled to operate, especially in the early years. There has been endless debate as to whether takiya should be regarded as a duty to be practised for the benefit of other co-religionists, or as an option which can be exercised to save one's own skin. However regarded, it is difficult to reconcile, if not with the worship of martyrs, at least with the spirit of martyrdom, and it tends to endow with doctrinal respectability practices of concealment or even of deceit in everyday life. It would be interesting to examine how far the principles underlying takiya or ketman have coloured the Iranian attitude towards such things as governmental authority, taxes, rules and regulations and, indeed, straightforward explanation of ordinary phenomena.

A fourth characteristic, more specifically associated with Shi'ism from the doctrinal point of view, is the practice of muta, or the temporary marriage. This permits the conclusion of contracts of marriage in a specified form with wives to a number in excess of the statutory four permitted by the Koran. This contract must provide for payment, in money or kind, and must name the period for which it is agreed the marriage shall last. This period cannot be prolonged with a further contract. Though by no means confined to travellers, muta is practised above all by pilgrims and others on journeys. At its worst it operates as a legalized form of prostitution, and flourishes most luxuriantly in the neighbourhood of the leading shrines.

Islam is often described as a singularly democratic faith. This certainly applies to the absence of any powerful episcopal hierarchy and to the manner in which mullahs (priests) are appointed. They are in fact self-constituted and (save for those attached to the many well-endowed shrines and religious colleges) exist on the goodwill and generosity of the community in which they live; any person capable of reading the Koran and interpreting its laws may function as a mullah. It is indeed rather like the practice of medicine in the United Kingdom, but before the days of National Health, without the British Medical Association and with a very simple qualifying examination. This much is, I believe, common to all Islam. The peculiar feature of Shi'ism is that mullahs who excel in their work (presumably in the opinion of the local community) or otherwise make the grade receive the elevated title of mujtahid (which means in effect one who lays down the law). Every large town in Iran has one or more mujtahid, and though in no formal relationship to each other they constitute perhaps the nearest thing to a religious hierarchy in Islam. It is certainly remarkable that they do not owe their position to any temporal authority, such as the Shah or the Government, and regard themselves as free to criticize both. What gives them prestige is that in theory they are the representatives and mouthpieces of the Hidden Imam. Perhaps it is not altogether fanciful to see in these powerful priests of Iran a continuation of the tradition of the Magi.

ii] SUFIS

Traditions from the earlier cults certainly survived in the Moslem variants of mysticism which have flourished abundantly on Iranian soil. The earliest Islamic mystics appeared in Baghdad in the ninth century and were known as Sufis, a name derived from suf (wool) and descriptive of the white woollen cloak traditionally worn. In a remarkably short time, the term was applied to all who preferred the contemplative or ascetic to the active life and Sufism became – and still is – synonymous with mysticism. The tenets varied from place to place and even from Sufi to Sufi, but common to all was the belief that the individual, by his own efforts, could attain spiritual union with God, that the 'human soul was an emanation from the essence', and that 'like a reed torn from its native brook, like wax separated from its delicious honey, the soul of man bewails its disunion with melancholy music and sheds burning tears like a lighted taper, waiting passionately for the moment of its extinction, as a disengagement from its earthly trammels, and the means of returning to its only beloved'.*
In the early centuries the Sufis flourished only as individuals; they had small and transient followings and were not organized into orders or communities. This however did not prevent them from falling foul of orthodox Islam, and above all of orthodox

* Sir William Jones, *Sixth discourse on the Persians*, 1799.

Shi'ism. This can no doubt be explained by two things: first, that Sufism flourished more particularly among the Shi'as and above all in Iran; and second, that Sufi doctrine, individual and anarchistic, cut at the root of the Shi'a hagiology with its elaborate structure dependent on the exclusive divinity of the Imams.

Despite official hostility, however, Sufism continued to flourish and, in the Middle Ages, went from strength to strength. In particular it profoundly influenced the literature and above all the poetry of Iran during the Golden Age (A.D. 1200–1500). It was in the twelfth century that mystics began to form themselves into permanent fraternities and sects, members of which are generally known in Persia as Darvishes, or as we know them, dervishes, probably meaning 'those who seek doors', that is to say, mendicants, or those who humble themselves at the door (dar). The two terms, Sufi and Darvish, sometimes appear almost interchangeable; latterly Sufis have often organized themselves in communities, and there is nearly always an element of mysticism in the beliefs and practices of the Darvish sects. There was a bewildering profusion of these in the Middle Ages, many engaging in extensive forms of fasting, hypnosis and collective frenzy which were far removed from the ascetic qualities of the early Sufis.

The development of mysticism in Iran is well illustrated in the career of Bayazid-al-Bastami, a famous Sufi of the ninth century who lived most of his life as a recluse at Bastam in north-east Persia. His grandfather is believed to have been a Zoroastrian priest or Magus; there was a strong admixture of Pantheism in his mysticism. There is no evidence that he had any body of disciples, still less that he founded a school. Yet a hundred years later a school of Sufis (Taifuris or Bastamis) was formed in his name and in later centuries he became the legendary patron of an order of Darvishes, the Naqshbandi, which spread through Turkey, into Russia and among the Kurds. And in the early fourteenth century the shrine over his tomb at Bastam was renovated and extended, and a dome placed over it by Sultan Oljeitu, whose spiritual adviser claimed descent from Bayazid himself.

3. BAHA'ISM

No account of religion in Iran would be complete without some reference to its novel manifestations since 1800, which culminated in the Baha'i movement.

The story can be briefly told. It begins with Sheikh Ahmad Ahsai, a Bahreini who emigrated to Kerbala and was brought to Iran by Fath Ali Shah, eventually settling at Yazd. Famous as a teacher he founded a school (the Sheikh sect), not of mystics but based on a philosophy which outdid the Shi'as in its attribution of divinity to the Imams. They were the ultimate cause of creation, and they alone provided access to the knowledge of God. Since the twelfth Imam disappeared, there had always been perfect men among the Shi'as who served as a channel of communication between the Hidden Imam and his followers; they were designated as doors or 'bab'.

It was this doctrine which gave the impetus to the teaching of the Shirazi, Mirza Ali Mohammed, born about 1817, who started life as a devout Shi'a, but in 1844 declared himself to be the Bab. He quickly acquired a large and influential following, in so doing drawing down against his movement the hostility of the authorities, both civil and religious. Forced to escape from Shiraz he enjoyed for a time the protection of the Governor of Isfahan, but on the latter's death was seized and imprisoned in Azerbaijan and in 1850 publicly executed in front of the org or citadel of Tabriz (see p. 145). But the movement he started did not end with his life – in 1852 a number of his followers attempted to murder Nasruddin Shah and a savage persecution followed, its most famous victim being the prominent woman convert, Quarrat-ul-Ayn, who on the way to the scaffold is said to have composed extempore the moving poem which begins (in E. G. Browne's translation):*

'The thralls of burning love constrain in the
    bonds of pain and calamity,
These broken hearted lovers of thine to yield
    their lives in their zeal for thee

* *A Persian Anthology*, 1927.

Though with sword in hand my darling stand with
    intent to slay though I sinless be,
If it pleases Him, this tyrant's whim, I am well
    content with his tyranny.'

As a result of the persecution, the Bab's leading followers left
Iran, and in exile bitter struggles over the succession developed
between two brothers, Mirza Hussain Ali and Mirza Yahya
Subh-i-Ezel, the first of whom settled at Acre, adopted the name
of Baha'ullah, and, together with his son Abdul Baha, was the
founder and architect of modern Baha'ism.

Doctrinally, the movement had travelled a long way from the
original tenets of the Sheikhi sect. The Bab superimposed on these
a new concept of seven attributes called Letters of Truth with
which God had created the world. He instituted rules of life and
conduct which involved a serious departure from Islamic pre-
cepts and, if they had been allowed to do so, would have shaken
the foundations of society – for example an independent system of
taxation. He even invented a new calendar of nineteen months
each of nineteen days – a number which was invested with a
peculiar symbolism in many Babi institutions. Baha'ullah went
further, for he set out to create a religion which would have a
universal appeal, incorporating principles such as humility, world
peace and the equality of the sexes and advocating practices such
as charitable works, world government and a universal auxiliary
language. The movement has made many converts in India,
Africa and also the United States, where Baha'ism continues to
have a considerable following. In Iran Baha'is are not very
numerous, but they are influential out of proportion to their
numbers and are generally regarded as law-abiding and broad-
minded citizens. Unlike the Jews, Christians and Zoroastrians,
however, they do not enjoy any political status, and are viewed
with grave disapprobation by the orthodox as a dangerous
deviation from Islam.

CHAPTER THREE

Art

It took the great American scholar Arthur Upham Pope six enormous volumes to describe and illustrate the marvellous varieties and exquisite harmonies of Iran's artistic heritage. It is difficult to believe that his magnificent work* (now republished in fourteen volumes) will ever be effectively superseded. It certainly induces a spirit of humility in anyone tackling the subject. Here I propose to do no more than give some pointers to the main features of Persian achievement, which may be useful to the traveller or foreign resident before he plunges headlong (if he is wise) into whatever branch of the subject takes his fancy most.

1. BUILDINGS

As one wanders about the country, it is primarily buildings (in the field of art) that catch the eye, or anyway, my sort of eye; that is why I make no apology for devoting what some may think disproportionate space to this section.

Pre-Islamic. Purely religious Achaemenian buildings are confined to fire altars and fire temples, the latter being small, square constructions in which the eternal fire, central to Zoroastrian religious observances, was housed in a room accessible only to the priests. It seems increasingly probable that the Cube of Zoroaster at Naqsh-i-Rustam, whose purpose has long been a subject of dispute among scholars (see p. 249), falls into this category, together

* *A Survey of Persian Art,* Oxford, 1938–39.

with related buildings, the Zendan-i-Suleiman at Pasargadae (p. 255), the Ayadana at Susa (destroyed) and the Mil-i-Azdaha at Nurabad in Fars (this last being of Seleucid or Parthian date, see p. 260). Religious ceremonies took place before fire altars in the open air.

Achaemenian secular buildings were much more substantial and their style varies according to the period. In Cyrus's time, for example, they were oblong in shape, of exquisite proportions, and generally executed in contrasting colours as between say wall surfaces and window emplacements. The buildings of Darius and Xerxes were bigger and, as they no doubt thought, better; the result was rather heavy and colourless, depending on elaborate carving applied to doorways, staircases and columns. The usual plan was a large hall often with columns surrounded by small rooms; a common feature of these were the recesses about the height and size of windows, probably used as cupboards, which are an invariable feature of the more modest houses of Iran today. The materials used included unbaked brick for walls, local stone for windows, stairways, doorways and some walls and columns, and heavy timber for columns and roofs.

From the Sassanians, by contrast, few secular buildings survive, the principal remains being at Firuzabad (p. 262) Bishapur (p. 257) and Takht-i-Suleiman (p. 162); we know the dynasty principally by their rock carvings (cf. p. 18). But the salient features – stone construction, the large arched doorway or iwan leading to the square domed chamber often surrounded by smaller domed chambers, the squinches which provide the transition from square to dome – these features reappear and are developed in the specifically Iranian type of mosque, the so-called madrasseh mosque built on the four-iwan plan. On Sassanian religious buildings, on the other hand, recent discoveries have thrown much light. They fall into two groups: the Chahar Taq, or four arches, a covered temple with a fire altar round which the faithful gathered, a building consisting of four pillars joined by arches and supporting a dome; and the Atashgah or fire chamber, accessible only to priests, in which the sacred fire was kept, also domed. Thirty-four Chahar Taq had been identified in 1971, nineteen of them since 1959; they are listed in *Memo from Belgium* (see footnote p. 61). Complexes which include both Atashgahs and Chahar Taqs generally within a single enclosure are to be seen at Takht-i-Suleiman, Kunar Siah south of Firuzabad (see p. 263), Tang-i Chak Chak in Luristan (p. 264), near Farrashband (p. 263) and at Nigar south of Kerman (where the two buildings are united). These temples, no doubt more directly than the Sassanian palaces, and despite their small scale (generally less than ten metres square) determined the plan of the Iranian mosque.

Mosques. From Cordoba to Delhi, from Sarajevo to the Niger, the mosque (masjid in Persian and Arabic) or house of prayer is the outstanding symbol of Islam, the focus of worship, the central point of this democratic faith. Its forms are more varied and its uses more widespread than those of the Christian cathedral or church. While primarily a place of worship, it is also an assembly hall, often a religious college, sometimes a court of justice, even, to some extent, a poor man's club. Its essential components are a wall, known as the qibla wall, facing, at least in principle (calculations were not always accurate), in the direction of Mecca; a niche or corner of particular sanctity in that wall corresponding in a sense to the Christian altar, and known as a mihrab; a preaching platform or pulpit nearby, called a mimbar; the surrounding area, generally arcaded or covered with a dome, which is the maqsura or sanctuary; and very often, though by no means invariably, a tower or minaret originally used for the call to prayer. Another requirement, especially in the case of the congregational or Friday mosque (masjid-i-jumeh), which is found in every sizeable town in Iran, is that the mihrab and preacher should be visible to a large number of people, and this called for a wide space, generally an open court, somewhere within sight of the qibla wall. In the larger mosques an adjoining prayer hall was sometimes constructed specifically for the use of women.

For the rest, mosque builders had a fairly free hand. No other feature was compulsory. The siting, however, was frequently determined by practical considerations. If, for example, the mosque was located in the populous centre of the city, it was better frequented and better able to serve the religious and other purposes for which it was designed. For the same reason it was desirable that access to it should be made easy from several directions, as befitted a popular institution. And, because of its multiple purposes, it was frequently a group or succession of buildings rather than a single isolated edifice like a Christian church or cathedral.

It is necessary for the Western traveller, if he is to avoid early disappointments, not to expect the mosque to look like a church. It is not a building set apart from everyday life, isolated in its sanctity, to be admired from a distance, or even seen from outside; many mosques indeed have no visible outside, except perhaps a monumental portal. Just as generally speaking the traditional house is not visible until you pass through a doorway into its garden or court, so the mosque is turned inward and can only be properly appreciated from within. Even the great Royal Mosque at Isfahan, which presents an uncharacteristically exuberant face to the world, only reveals its full splendour within. The majority of Iranian mosques, great or small, are so encumbered with surrounding buildings that you scarcely know you are upon them till you are in them. In cases where this is not true (Yazd, Kerman, Tabriz) it is generally because the buildings around have been demolished, not because they were never there.

The majority of learned works written about mosques as architecture take the early Arab buildings of North Africa and Spain as their point of departure. The mosque, they say, is an open court surrounded by arcades which are deeper on the Mecca side than on the other three sides; there may be a minaret or two, but there is no dome. This plan is treated as the norm, and other plans – the Dome of the Rock at Jerusalem, the Omayyad Mosque at Damascus, both with some reason, and the mosques of Iran and India, with considerably less justice – are regarded as aberrations. The *Encyclopaedia Britannica** goes so far as to make the astonishingly inaccurate statement that 'in

* Eleventh Edition, Vol. 18, p. 900.

Persia there are no mosques earlier than the thirteenth century, and the oldest example at Tabriz [sic] is evidently, as far as its plan is concerned, a copy of a Byzantine church departing entirely from the normal plans'. There could be no better evidence that, until the present century, study of the Iranian mosque has been sadly neglected in favour of its Arab prototype. Is it possible that our encyclopaedist had not *heard* of the Friday Mosque at Isfahan?

In fact, for purposes of rough classification there are three types of mosque in Iran. The first is what the pundits would call 'normal', i.e. the Arab plan. Of this type only two examples remain, the Tari Khaneh at Damghan and the Friday Mosque at Nain. But tenth-century writers, who do not even mention Nain, speak of 'scores' of mosques in Iran, such as that at Nishapur with marble columns, gold tiles and richly carved walls and roof, or that at Saveh which had an entrance portal rivalling the arch of Ctesiphon. At least a proportion of those vanished buildings will certainly have conformed to the 'Arab' type. The second type is thought by some to owe its origin to the plan of the Nestorian (Christian) church. The fact that it is found primarily in North-West Iran (Tabriz, Rezaieh, Varamin) is said to lend colour to this view; but it might equally be attributed to climate. For the peculiar feature of this 'kiosk' mosque is that it is covered, providing the congregation with protection against the elements. It has a central chamber with vaulted doorways leading out of it, the largest being that towards the qibla wall; but the chamber is domed, and there may be a second dome over the sanctuary which divides the central chamber from the mihrab.

The majority of Iranian mosques conform, in whole or in part, to a third plan, which in Iran must be regarded as the norm, even though elsewhere in the Islamic world it constitutes the exception. It consists of an open central court, sometimes large enough to be planted with trees or flowers, with a large portal or iwan, on the side facing towards Mecca, which leads into a domed sanctuary. On the other three sides of the court there are arcades and altars and in the centre of each side another, though smaller, iwan. To the left and right of the sanctuary there may be arcaded halls, and in addition balconies (often reserved for the use of women worshippers) from which a view of the mihrab can be obtained. In the grander mosques the south iwan, leading into the sanctuary, and sometimes also the north iwan, which is frequently the main entrance to the mosque, is flanked by minarets. This type of building is known as the four-iwan or madrasseh-mosque (madrasseh meaning religious college) because the smaller arches round the central court in early examples led into students' or teachers' rooms; later they were ornamental. Certainly the central court, the iwans, the dome and the squinches, by means of which the transition from a square base to a circular dome is achieved – invariable features of mosques of this type – derive directly from the Sassanian traditions of building. And it should be observed here that the central court, surrounded by arcades and flanked by two or more iwans, is a feature of many other buildings in Iran – religious colleges, shrines (imamzadehs) and wayside hotels or caravanserais. But it is the mosque which is the focal centre, the house of prayer and contemplation, the meeting place of man with man, and of man with God, the shelter for the poor and needy, the symbol of the freedom and equality of the Islamic world. If some mosques are used, according to our Western ideas, for some odd or secular purposes, that only goes to show that in Islam there is not the same gulf fixed as in the West between material and spiritual things.

Minarets. The word minaret is derived from the Arabic manar, which means a tower with a light on it, and which is also applied to a lighthouse. The earliest minarets were square, at least in their lower storeys, but few of these survive in Iran today (Nain). The round minaret originated in North-East Iran and was built of brick, tapering towards the summit. Seen from a distance, they bear a striking resemblance to factory chimneys, and the Western eye may need to make some adjustment before it can recognize them as objects of beauty. In Seljuk times they often carried fine brick decoration; a good example is the stubby little minaret at Bastam, so small that you can look down and admire its detail from the roof. Until at least the thirteenth century, minarets were almost invariably single, and placed in the north corner of the mosque. Later they tended to be constructed in pairs, flanking the iwan of the sanctuary and sometimes the north iwan of the court. The older minarets have for the most part lost their heads, which consisted of a projecting balcony of brick stalactites, surmounted by a wooden structure. Since the fourteenth century minarets have generally been covered with mosaic or coloured tiles, in the taste of the period. Thus the mosaic inlay on the minarets of the Mosque of Gawhar Shad at Meshed are of surprising delicacy and beauty; both the tiles and bulbous shapes of the Qajar minarets at Qum and Mahan, for instance, are characteristically florid. In general, Iran, compared with, say, Turkey, is markedly deficient in minarets. Only at Isfahan do they occupy a prominent place in the landscape.

Shrines. Shrines are the hall-mark of Shi'ism, with its partiality for local saints. Nearly every town in Iran has its quota, and village or wayside shrines are a recurring feature of the landscape. In general they are modest, circular, four-sided or octagonal buildings, surmounted by a cone or dome. Many have charm but no great architectural merit; the famous shrines, rambling structures which have received additions from generations of the devout, are among the most splendid, and in some cases most opulent, buildings in Iran. The lesser shrines, unlike the mosques, have a distinct regional character; the sturdy pine or inverted stalactite cones of Khuzistan, the whitewashed circular cones of the central plateau, the blue domes of the southern Elburz, the Romanesque octagons of Mazanderan, with their ostensibly Christian decorative features and their country churchyard settings.

Tombs. Secular tombs fall into two clearly marked architectural categories – the domed mausoleum and the tomb tower. Iran can justly claim to possess one example of each that is an architectural sensation.

The domed mausoleum has certain affinities with the larger shrine. It is frequently octagonal, rising through squinches and galleries into a circular dome. It is built for show, inside and out,

meant to be visited, the last resting place of a chieftain who may
have had no claim to sainthood, but expected to be duly revered
when he was dead. In a succession of these buildings, inside and
outside modern Iran but all in the same Iranian tradition, can be
seen the competitive spirit among monarchs. Each one deliberately
sets out to excel the last, and the result is a display of architectural
pyrotechnics for which there is no precise parallel in the world.
It was the tomb at Bokhara of Ismail the Samanid who died in
907 which began the competition. Sultan Sanjar, who died in
1157, went one better, at Merv. Oljeitu's older brother Ghazan
set out deliberately to put Sultan Sanjar in the shade. He built for
himself, at Ghazaniyeh near Tabriz, a duodecagon with a dome
460 feet high and 165 feet in diameter; Oljeitu's mausoleum at
Sultaniyeh must have been modest by comparison, yet today it
seems to us, with the Friday Mosque at Isfahan, the outstanding
architectural achievement of medieval Persia. Later examples of
mausolea are the more modest Khwaja Rabi (1622) outside
Meshed, the Qadamgah (1643) near Nishapur, and stemming
from the same principles, the tomb of Homayoun at Delhi and
the Taj Mahal at Agra.

Tomb towers, which are mainly confined to Northern Iran,
were conceived in a different spirit. They were gaunt, remote,
solitary resting places, not meant to be frequented by admirers
in generations to come. Some say that their circular design is
derived from the nomadic tent, or yaourt, of wattle and camel
skin which can still be seen among the Turkoman tribes today;
but not all are round. The high towers were designed to carry
the body of the departed suspended in the air from the roof, in
which a window was constructed to let in the air. Do we see here
a relic of the Zoroastrian custom of exposing the dead in dakhmés,
or towers of silence? It can only be said that they have no resemblance to religious buildings of the same period, and there is little
specifically Islamic about them. The most famous and most
remarkable is a great fluted conical tower, 150 feet in height,
which looks like a well sharpened pencil on the horizon and from
200 yards away appears to have been built yesterday. In fact it
dates from 1006 and is the tomb of Kabus, the Ziyarid leader, in

BUILDINGS 57

the town which bears his name – Gunbad-i-Kabus, near Gurgan
on the Turkoman steppe. There are other tomb towers in the
neighbouring mountains, but perhaps the finest group is in the
little town of Maragheh, some fifty miles south of Tabriz. These
are less monumental or austere in style, and are relieved by rich
decorations of, in one case, incomparable skill. I shall have more to
say about all these buildings as they are encountered on the
road.

Palaces. For a country which has enjoyed close on two thousand
five hundred years of virtually continuous monarchical rule, Iran
is singularly deficient in royal palaces, particularly of the Islamic
period. As we have seen, there are substantial remains of Achaemenian and Sassanian palaces, impressive both in size and in
detail, some of which, as at Persepolis, have been almost miraculously preserved; but when all is said they are ruins. Of Seljuk
and Mongol royal residences, however, all trace has disappeared;
of the Great Palace at Ghazaniyeh, for instance, not even the
foundations are visible. It is only from Safavid times that royal
houses have survived intact, and even then the crop is disappointing. A sixteenth-century pavilion still stands in the
grounds of the former royal palace at Kazvin, but it has been
sadly vandalized. There is a late seventeenth-century kiosk in
the lovely royal garden at Fin, above Kashan, in which a few wall
paintings of the period have been preserved. The little palace at
Behshahr (Ashraf) on the Caspian dates from the time of Shah
Abbas, but has been completely rebuilt by Reza Shah. For practical purposes, Safavid palaces are confined to Isfahan: the Ali Kapu,
overlooking the Maidan, which served at once as royal residence
and a kind of grandstand for parades and polo matches; the
Chehel Sutun behind it, covering the throne room; and the
Talar Ashraf, a later and more modest structure in the grounds.
Externally, these buildings appear ungainly; if in the end they
captivate, it is by reason more of their decoration than of their
architecture.

Later domestic building follows the same unwieldy pattern. At
Shiraz there are a number of large private houses, built in the

nineteenth century, apparently under the influence of the Crystal
Palace. The great Qajar Palace at Tehran, the Gulestan, rises like
a series of ill-disposed fretwork boxes in no identifiable architectural style, waiting it may be for some Persian Betjeman, as yet
unborn, to disclose its real beauties.

The medium-sized Iranian private town house was built for
nearly twenty centuries in accordance with a consistent tradition,
now abandoned in favour of the box, the bungalow, the patio
house or the terrace. The traditional house was shut off by a wall
from the street. An entrance passage or dihlaz led into a courtyard,
known as the hayat. This court was generally surrounded by one-
storey rooms, sometimes two, the main room having a large
window, perhaps with wooden tracery or coloured glass, facing
the court. The interior of this room would generally be more
richly decorated and elaborately furnished than the rest; it might
have a painted ceiling or a mirrored recess or fluted columns.
Behind the main court there would often be a second court constituting the anderun or women's quarters. While old houses are
fast disappearing, examples of this type, necessarily with variations
of feature, are still to be seen in towns such as Kazvin, Yazd,
Kerman and Sanandaj.

Caravanserais. Save in a few well-favoured areas, the traveller along
the high roads of Iran sees little evidence of the works of man. He
may drive for many miles without noticing a house. Villages are
about as infrequent as petrol filling stations; indeed the two are
frequently synchronous. Along the edge of the great deserts
ab-ambars or water storage tanks, tunnel-vaulted buildings
flanked by high wind towers, eerie in their isolation and, all
too often, desolation, are more frequent than either. But on the
old trade routes the standing feature of the landscape generally
encountered every twenty miles or so is the caravanserai.

Most of these are derelict today. But, even as ruins, they are
readily recognizable. They are generally built round a square –
in fact like the courtyard of a mosque on the four-iwan plan.
The main entrance often has an extra storey over the arch, providing cooler accommodation for distinguished guests, or for the

use of guards in troubled times. The four sides generally have vaulted recesses with rooms beyond and a corridor which served as a stable against the outer wall. This design, simple and traditional, provided security and privacy for the traveller, protection for the animals, control over admissions. 'Never,' exclaims Pope, 'was the Persian facility for practical planning better demonstrated.' In large towns caravanserai, bazaar and mosque were frequently contiguous. The grandest and remotest caravanserais often housed a mosque of their own within their precincts.

If a visitor enquires the age of a caravanserai, he is generally told that it dates from the time of Shah Abbas. This is a deceptive generalization. Some are much older. A number, probably the majority, are of more recent date. Many were built during the Qajar dynasty, as an examination of their graceful tile-covered portals easily reveals. They were for the most part in operation for travellers at the time of Curzon's visit in 1888* and it is only in the present century, mainly since the arrival of the motor-car, that they have fallen into decay.

One of the oldest caravanserais is that of Robat Sharaf, between Meshed and Sarakhs, a masterpiece of Seljuk architecture dating from 1114. Measuring some 125 yards long by 75 wide, provided with two courtyards, each containing four iwans, it is equipped with two mosques, traced in many parts with elaborate brick patterns and embellished with rich plaster decorations. This astounding building provides eloquent testimony to the care lavished by kings, even in difficult times and in insalubrious places, on the comfort of travellers – chief among whom were no doubt themselves. In more settled conditions the practice was further extended. Some of the finest Safavid caravanserais are to be found on the great roads (now no more than tracks) leading northwards from Isfahan – one through Qum to Kazvin, the other via Kashan across the edge of the salt desert to Firuzkuh and Behshahr on the Caspian. The latter route was travelled by Pietro della Valle in 1618 in search of the Shah Abbas at a time when the Sang Farsh, or stone carpet across the marshes, was under construction. Perhaps the caravanserais such as the great one near the

* *Persia and the Persian Question*, 1892.

base of Siah Kuh* were under construction too, but Pietro and
his wife Maani spent one night at least in the open although it was
February, and on another were offered a 'spacious cave which
travellers were accustomed to use as a caravanserai', and which
had been 'occupied the day before by a large consignment of
pigs'.† If all the caravanserais visible above ground today
had indeed been built by Shah Abbas, early seventeenth-century
travellers would have been spared many of these discomforts.

Bridges. More essential for the maintenance of communications
than caravanserais, bridges have been an outstanding feature of
Iranian building since earliest times. The great Sassanian bridges
were constructed under Roman inspiration: the dam and bridge
attributed to Valerian at Shushtar, which is over half a mile long,
Shapur's bridge at Dizful, the Pul-i-Dokhtar and the Pul-i-
Khosrow between Andimeshk and Khorramabad, all in
Khuzistan, and probably the lovely little Pul-i-Shahrestan downstream from Isfahan.

The building of bridges which were both sturdy and a pleasure
to the eye continued until recently. There is a magnificent
example, of which unfortunately the central piers have been
carried away, over the Qizil Uzun on the Tehran-Tabriz road
just south of Mianeh. This is thought to date from the fifteenth
century. The lovely Safavid bridge over the Karaj river, twenty-
five miles west of Tehran, has now been closed to road traffic – not
because it is weak, only because it is too narrow. Well-constructed
hump-backed bridges of ancient date are to be found in many
parts of the country – for instance at Amol (Mazanderan), on the
road from Hamadan to Sanandaj and in the Elburz valleys north
of Tehran. But the outstanding glories of Iranian bridge-building
are the two great works which span the Zaindeh Rud at Isfahan –
the Allah Verdi Khan (1629) and the Khaju (1660). The delight of
Iranian builders in creating beauty out of objects designed for
practical use, as well as turning brilliant improvisations con-

* Fifty-six miles south-east of Varamin. Now occupied by Wardens of The
Game and Fish Department.
† Wilfrid Blunt, *Pietro's Pilgrimage*, 1953.

ceived for aesthetic purposes to practical advantage, is nowhere better illustrated than in the gangways, the arched recesses, the double-tier vaulting and the ingenious barrages of the Khaju bridge. These two mighty structures are among the most impressive monuments in Isfahan, and are two of the most remarkable bridges in the world.

Pigeon towers. During the seventeenth century the lands irrigated by Isfahan's river the Zaindeh Rud, and adjacent areas round Kumisheh (Shahreza), became the centre of melon cultivation. At the same time it was found that melons waxed fat when fed with pigeon manure. To further this process, towers to house the pigeons and collect their excreta were built throughout the melon-growing area. And because this was Iran in the days of Shah Abbas, these towers, though of avowedly utilitarian purpose, were not conceived on purely functional lines. They were circular and stout, like small forts. The larger ones were built up to forty feet in height. They were covered with white plaster, given a frieze, and often surmounted with a cupola, both of which were polychromed. 'Their houses were neat', writes Thomas Herbert, of Mehiar, south of Isfahan, 'yet they were in no wise comparable to their dovehouses for curious outsides.' Today most of the decorations have disappeared but their interiors lined with pigeon perches still have a mesmeric quality (cf. Elizabeth Beazley, *Iran* VI) and they are moreover still in use; they give the densely cultivated and thickly populated oasis of Isfahan an unexpected air of grandeur. In some places at an approach to a village they stand close together, looking with their turrets or round knobs as though they were rooks or pawns in a mighty game of chess, waiting for some god from the machine to move them into the next square.

2. BRONZES*

South of Kurdistan lies the remote and mountainous Luristan.

* For a succinct account of Luristan bronzes, with illustrations, see *Memo from Belgium Sept.-Oct. 1968* by L. vanden Berghe (Belgian Ministry of Foreign Affairs).

It was in this region, and particularly round Harsin, that the now famous Luristan bronzes first came to light in the late twenties and early thirties of the present century. They were all discovered by peasants who, quickly realizing what they might fetch on the market, went systematically through some four to five hundred burial grounds each containing between ten and two hundred graves. Some of these yielded little more than the brachycephalic skull which Freya Stark presented to the Baghdad Museum; others contained shards, pottery and glass; but the great incentive for opening the graves was the bronzes.

Harsin was the principal mart, and the bulk of the bronzes was probably brought there and to other centres by the peasants who found them, or by traders from the villages, and sold to intermediaries who quickly made contact with dealers in the cities. The whole process was carried through with extraordinary speed. At the end of four years the bulk of the graves had been completely rifled; not one had been scientifically excavated. Because of the manner of their discovery, it has been extraordinarily difficult to classify them or to piece together reliable information as to exactly where they were found and with what other bronzes or other objects they were associated. Recent excavations carried out by a Belgian mission under the leadership of Professor vanden Berghe of Ghent University, chiefly in Pusht-i-Kuh (Western Luristan), have established that the earliest bronzes date from 2600–2500 B.C. and that the period in which the most characteristic pieces were produced in largest quantities was between 1200 and 800 B.C. Similar bronzes have also been found in the course of excavations elsewhere (notably at Marlik; see p. 122) but evidence suggests that the art of metal-working was developed in Luristan itself from the earliest times.

The subject matter of the bronzes shows the Elamites of the Zagros to have been great horsemen; Freya Stark encountered a tradition that in certain valleys they shared graves with their horses. Though there are many weapons, votive objects, and some personal ornaments, the most distinctive application of the Luristan bronze is for chariot or harness fittings, rein rings or bits. The designs, some strikingly realistic, others highly stylized,

1. MOUNT DEMAVEND seen from Pulur, with nomads in the foreground (*p. 83*)

2a. ISFAHAN: Madrasseh Mader-i-Shah (*p. 200*)

2b. DAMGHAN: Tomb Tower of Pir-i-Alamdar (1027) (*p. 101*)

include many representations of mountain game, such as mouflon, ibex and gazelle; human faces and figures are also portrayed, in forms more associated with India and South-East Asia than with Iran. Some of the more elaborate work (such as can be seen for example in the Tehran Archaeological Museum) is brilliantly conceived. 'It contrived,' says Pope, 'to be expressive in two ways simultaneously, as a concentrated formulation of the inner quality of the subject, and as an exciting abstract pattern – yet, side by side and apparently contemporary with these, the last word in refined naturalism.'

3. POTTERY

The continuing flow of Iranian artistic tradition is nowhere better illustrated than in the field of ceramic art. Here were objects made, not for the most part at the behest of church or state, but by the people for their everyday use, often without self-conscious artistry. The potter's art took many forms: cylinder seals and figurines; bowls, plates, pitchers and jars; inkwells, spittoons, candlesticks, lanterns, even foot-rests and bird-houses. They were made for current use, and to give pleasure, but often not intended to endure. It is surprising, given their fragility, how many have survived.

What has been discovered, at least as far as the earlier periods go, is probably only a fraction of what still exists. At many famous sites, Susa for instance, only a small part of the area has been excavated. New discoveries – as in Gurgan, and at Amlash near Resht, at Khorvin near Karaj, and at Nishapur – are constantly being unearthed. Any account of Iranian pottery must therefore be provisional and tentative.

No art is known to have been practised so continuously on the plateau – the earliest extant examples date back five thousand years. At sites like Sialk near Kashan, Susa, Tepe Hissar near Damghan, and Rayy near Tehran, where there was continuous habitation and one city was superimposed on another, it is possible to judge the date of the pottery from the level at which it is found, and hence to deduce the age of comparable pottery found elsewhere. Even so, much must remain largely guesswork. In later times too the history and origin of even distinctive pieces is not always clear. Until the Safavid period place names are never inscribed. The potter's name, even if given, offers no clue to the place of origin. Since ceramic objects were easily transportable and much used in commerce, we cannot assume that pottery was made where it was found. Finally we do not always have reliable information as to where a given piece was found, since scientifically controlled exploration has so far been limited to relatively few sites.

However, if much remains to be discovered, there is also much that can be confidently said. The Iranian potter shows an uncanny feeling for the material in which he is working and for shaping his work so that its qualities of glaze and colour are displayed to full advantage. In this respect Pope considers him superior to the Greek, who tended to use earthenware as though it were metal or stone. On the other hand Persian workmanship cannot compare with that of the Chinese. Yet at its best Iranian pottery is strikingly varied and daringly original. The variation is due at least in part to a continuation of factors themselves contradictory: on the one hand, a flourishing regional industry which in important centres like Rayy and Kashan developed its own techniques and in remoter areas – Kurdistan or Azerbaijan – preserved its local character; on the other hand, Iran's accessibility to different influences, each of which have left their mark. There is the Sassanian tradition in design; Islam, discouraging human or or animal representation in religious edifices, encouraged decorations in other forms; and finally there is the Chinese influence which was exerted long before Safavid times, even before the Mongol invasion. At the same time the work of the Iranian potter, so sensitive to cultural influences, showed extraordinary powers of resistance to physical assault. At the time of the Mongol invasion, two of the most important producing centres were virtually destroyed – Rayy in 1220, Kashan in 1224. Yet one of the finest Rayy polychrome bowls now in the British Museum is dated 1242; there are good if small examples of lustre mihrabs from Kashan in the Victoria and Albert Museum dating from

1226 and 1250; and work on the mihrab of the Maidan mosque
at Kashan was begun in 1225. Output showed little and quality
no falling off as a result of the Mongol invasion.

The history of Iranian ceramics is so complex and so full of
uncertainties that it would be misleading to try to give a consecu-
tive account of it. I propose rather to select certain points of
particular interest.

One of the most splendid achievements of Iranian pottery was
the development of lustre ware – an art unknown to the Chinese
potter, effected by a process of double firing. The origin of lustre
ware is an intriguing subject of controversy. The earliest examples
were found at Rayy, and it was therefore supposed that the art
was developed there. Then the pundits observed that a certain
gentleman from Nishapur named Nasser-i-Khosrow recorded
having visited Cairo in 1050 where he saw something in the
bazaar there which surprised him. From his description they
judged it to be lustre ware; ergo, they said, he had never seen it
in Nishapur; ergo it was not of Iranian origin but was probably
invented in Egypt. Pope challenges this conclusion, on the ground
that no lustre has ever been found at Nishapur; that it was an
expensive and therefore a relatively rare type of ware, so that
Nasser-i-Khosrow might well not have seen it if he did not move
in the right circles; and finally that the early Iranian pieces look
older than the early Egyptian ones and some of them bear what
look like Persian signatures.

Whatever the truth may be, lustre was one of the greatest contributions of the Islamic world to the potter's art, and lustre
painting reached its zenith at the end of the thirteenth century in
the city of Kashan. It was largely a family affair, in the hands of
the descendants of one Ali Tahir. Their skill was perhaps displayed
to the greatest advantage in a series of lustre mihrabs, one of the
finest being that made for the Imamzadeh Jafar at Qum, now in
the Tehran Museum. 'The most elaborate work ever undertaken
by Western potters,' says Pope, 'is child's play compared to one
of these splendid structures. . . . Nothing more effective could be
devised for inducing religious ecstasy . . . the high clear-keyed
tones and bewildering complexity of dancing lights, the sacred

message shining through the maze in stately letters, the whole enveloped in a shimmering flame, a light from another world; this formed a fitting portal to the Divine Presence.'

The Golden Age of Iranian pottery is generally regarded as tapering off in the fifteenth century. There was certainly a deterioration and a recession. But the seventeenth century, and particularly the reign of Shah Abbas, saw an astonishing revival. This did not take the form of any slavish imitation of the masterpieces of the past. Partly under Chinese inspiration – Abbas brought three hundred Chinese potters to Isfahan and much Chinese pottery was assembled for the Ardebil shrine – new subtleties and a greater degree of sophistication were introduced. This was seen particularly in the new and striking use of delicate colours – light slate, modulated greens, lavender, and aubergine. A new emphasis was placed on monochrome ware. Efforts were made, in the so-called Gombroon ware, to imitate porcelain. Not a great deal is known about centres of production, but the revived industry appears to have flourished not only at Isfahan but also at Kashan, Yazd, Kerman, Meshed, Shiraz, and possibly Nain and Ardebil.

This period provides one fascinating example of the difficulties of topographical classification. In Daghestan, on the north-eastern slopes of the Caucasus, far inside Russia, there is a mountain town named Kubachi. Hundreds of black painted plates with every appearance of Iranian origin have been found there. Yet, so far as history relates, Kubachi is innocent of potters; certainly it has never had a pottery industry. Its inhabitants were, however, long famous for their skill in decorated metal work. The explanation appears to be that in the seventeenth century there was a large demand for this metal work in Iran and the Iranians paid for it in plates. There is no conclusive evidence to show where this so-called 'Kubachi ware' really came from – perhaps Tabriz, as the nearest point in Iran through which the trade might have been organized.

4. CARPETS

It would indeed be hard to dispute the Iranian claim to have produced the most elaborate, the most decorative and the most superbly assured carpets in the world. This supremacy is not difficult to explain, for it is with design, with flowering yet ordered arrangement of pattern, that the native genius is displayed to greatest advantage. Carpets offer unlimited scope, combining large expanse with the possibility of infinite delicacy and a wide range of exquisite colouring.

Carpets were used as floor covering from early times. Among nomadic tribes rugs are of all valuables the most easily transportable. They can be laid out wherever a tent is pitched; others may be used to decorate bare walls. Carpets are found in Iran today in the humblest homes; they are an essential adjunct to the mosque; even in modern villas they are frequently the only decorative object in a room bare of everything save the minimum of functional furniture. It is considered improvident to travel without a carpet, which is an essential feature of a picnic, to lay the dust or cushion the roughness of the ground. Carpets are spread out on the pavement in front of shops; on festive occasions they are hung out like flags, and are used to cover the rough wooden framework of a kind of primitive triumphal arch. The carpet as an institution is woven well into the fabric of Iranian everyday life.

Out of this commonplace object, which is still manufactured in large quantities and varying qualities in factory, cottage and tent; out of simple origins – the new yarn spun by tribal women as they rode to greener pastures on their donkeys, the dyed wool woven by children to the sound of a foreman singing out the pattern – a great art was born. But the golden age in which the finest Persian carpets were woven was a brief period only, spanning the sixteenth and early seventeenth centuries, and, from this period, only some 1,500 carpets survive.

It is difficult to attribute the finest carpets of the Safavid period regionally with absolute accuracy. Often cartoons were designed in one place and the carpets woven in another. The master carpetmakers, who signed their names on their carpets, moved about; when their signature included an indication of their own place of origin, this frequently meant that they were working somewhere else. The great Ardebil carpet now in the Victoria and Albert Museum, whose splendid sunburst with its subsidiary satellites is like a vision of the firmament framed in an enormous window, was the work of one Maqsud of Kashan, but the wool from which it is made is characteristic of Tabriz. A remarkable series of medallion carpets are believed to have been made at either Kerman or Yazd, but no one knows for certain which. Another famous group of silk carpets, enriched with silver and gold, were once thought to have been made in Poland because so many of them were found there – nearly 400 in Europe and only two in Iran; now their Iranian origin has been firmly established, but experts cannot decide whether they were made in Isfahan, Joshagan or Kashan.

Certain regional characteristics, however, do stand out clearly. The finest carpets produced before the middle of the sixteenth century came from Tabriz, and modern Tabriz rugs still show similarities of wool and weaving. Kashan produced the most opulent carpets, unrivalled for sumptuous material and brilliance of colour; they owed much to the existence in the same city of a flourishing velvet-weaving industry. The large group of 'Vase' carpets, with distinctive characteristics – rather static design, the length three times the width, great variety of colour tones, frequent use of ogival or lozenge-shaped compartments, total absence of human or animal figures – almost certainly originate from Joshagan, a summer resort north of Isfahan with a long tradition of carpet-weaving. It is interesting to note that the form of later eighteenth-century Joshagans with their patterns in lozenge and other shaped compartments were copied by Bahktiari weavers from the neighbouring tribal country, and are a note-worthy feature of Bakhtiari tribal rugs today.

To the subject matter of Persian carpets there is no limit. Animals abound in the great 'hunting' carpets of the Golden Age. 'Garden' carpets portray trim flowering shrubs. Birds nest every-where and are freely used for decorative purposes in tribal carpets of every period. One small group, the so-called Portuguese carpets, show seascapes: ships, human figures in the water, and even a sea-monster. Human figures were also introduced into

some of the more elaborate nineteenth-century carpets. They
were not a success. But the dominant note is stylized floral ornament: lotus flowers and rosettes, leaf palmettes, arabesques of
blossom, swaying vines, and so-called cloudbands (imported from
China in the late fifteenth century). The finest carpets often have
as many as ten borders in which these varied ingredients are used
to splendid effect; the 'field' is generally alive with movement,
though sometimes rendered more static by repetition or the use
of central medallions or compartments. The less elaborate carpets
frequently have an 'all over' pattern in the field, such as palmettes
or the widely used 'Herati pear'. Large areas of solid colour,
frequently found in Chinese rugs, are unusual. Geometric designs
are rare save in tribal rugs and those originating on the fringes of
the plateau – Caucasia, the Turkoman country, and Afghanistan.
The distinctive feature of Bokhara rugs, the quartered octagons
in rows, commonly known as 'elephant's feet', occurs in rugs
woven in North-East Iran, especially among the Turkoman
tribes.

In the latter half of the seventeenth century the art of carpet-
making deteriorated, and in the eighteenth it shrank to the status
of a peasant industry. In the mid-nineteenth century, however,
there was a new development: the growing demand for Persian
rugs in Europe. A flourishing trade sprang up, centred on Tabriz,
and carpets were shipped via Trebizond to Istanbul in exchange
for Western wares. This turned out to be a highly profitable business, and Iran was denuded of her finest carpets by Europe, and
later America. Then the Tabrizi merchants, who had built their
livelihood round this trade in old carpets, decided in the 1880's
to invest their profits in a carpet-making industry, exploiting the
taste for Persian carpets which had been created by the trade.
Work of good as well as inferior quality was produced under this
system; but there has been a gradual yet steady deterioration.
Within the last fifty years a carpet industry designed to produce
carpets in large numbers to suit the alleged taste of the European
and United States markets respectively has sprung up, notably at
Arak (Sultanabad) and at Kerman. Unhappily very stereotyped
designs and in some cases chemical or poor vegetable dyes are

freely used; the workmanship is inferior, the quality coarse; the results are often horrible.

Against this, however, it must be said that carpets of superlative quality and good colours, though using rather stereotyped conventional patterns, are still produced today; Nain, Meshed, Tabriz and Tehran spring to mind as centres of this quality industry which supplies principally the Iranian market.

It would also be a mistake to suppose that there is nothing to be seen in the shops and bazaars of Iran today except tasteless modern rugs. The finest Persian carpets have long since disappeared. But interesting and attractive carpets and rugs produced within the last hundred years or so are fairly readily available, among them characteristically Qajar designs from Tehran and Tabriz; passable Kashans and Hamadans; Turkomans, Afghans, Baluchis and so-called Bokharas galore; pleasing Bakhtiari and Afshar tribal rugs; rosette designs from Varamin; gilims (tribal cotton weave) in great profusion and variety, many with good peasant designs; and finally humble serviceable zeloo, much in demand for mosques. There is still plenty of life in the industry.

5. ARCHITECTURAL ORNAMENT

The decoration which Iranian artists lavished on their buildings deserves a section to itself, for it vies with the Persian carpet as a vehicle for expressing their genius for controlled exuberance in design and colour. There is perhaps less scope for delicate refinement here, but the variety of media used, and the special skills applied to each, are truly astounding.

It was in Islamic times that the talent for architectural ornament came into its own – helped perhaps by the discouragement of any representation of the human form in religious buildings which forced the artist to concentrate his skill on abstract design.

In the Seljuk period two utterly different, almost conflicting, arts were brought to perfection: stucco encrustation and decorated brickwork. The first, derived from pre-Islamic times, becomes a riot of opulent blooms, singing designs, intricate patterns often overlaid or interspersed with beautifully executed Kufic lettering. Much of the skill of these stucco reliefs was lavished on mihrabs – the Friday Mosque at Nain, the Madrasseh Haydariyeh at Kazvin, the Friday Mosques at Abarquh, Varamin and Ardistan, and the glorious Oljeitu mihrab at Isfahan provide examples from different periods. But the art was not confined to mihrabs: witness the decorated columns of the very early Nain Mosque, or the astounding display of stucco in the Gunbad-i-Alavian at Hamadan, described by Pope as '. . . the most complete example of stucco encrustation that has survived'. One thing lacking today in this plasterwork is colour – not that one yearns for it when the design is already so rich. But even this was not always so and some trace of colour is still visible on a few mihrabs.

Seljuk brickwork was more sober, as befits the medium, but of infinite subtlety and cunning. To appreciate the astounding variety of effects one needs to compare the brick vaulting to the left of the entrance to the Friday Mosque in Isfahan, the raised brick design on the exterior of the Pir-i-Alamdar at Damghan, the superb monochrome ornamentation on the Gunbad-i-Surkh and the effect of the use of blue tiles in the Gunbad-i-Kabud, both at Maragheh. Each is so different yet each takes away the breath by its combination of simplicity and elaboration. It is lamentable that so little Seljuk brickwork should survive, for it would seem to rank among the very finest achievements of Iranian decoration.

We have already seen how the artists of Kashan applied lustre techniques to the production of mihrabs, with sensational results. But this was essentially a transient art, partly because these delicate tiles do not easily endure, but also because they were so expensive to produce. What killed lustre, in the fourteenth century, was the use of tile mosaic. This art was to hold the field for three hundred years and to contribute glory to the name of Persia throughout the civilized world.

Anyone who has watched tile mosaic being made, as one can easily do today on the roof of the Gawhar Shad Mosque at Meshed, will marvel at the skill of the worker as well as the genius of the designer. It is no easy feat to chip coloured tiles with a clumsy-looking instrument so that they fit upside down into a multi-coloured design of considerable complexity, particularly if they have to be laid on a semi-circular mould, for example for a minaret; but in the fourteenth century skilled craftsmen were there in plenty. Mosaics were cheaper than lustre and more durable. They were more satisfactory than painted tiles because they could be extended over an indefinite area, and worked into designs on any scale. They were moreover peculiarly suited to covering the massive interior spaces which Islamic architecture provides. As for the exteriors, the patterns could be made as large or as small as needed, so that in the case of the outside of a dome like Sheikh Lutfullah at Isfahan it could be on a scale which would enable it to be easily appreciated from the other side of the Maidan. Mosaic faïence appears to have been used first in Persia at the Shrine of Oljeitu at Sultaniyeh, but limited to dark and light blue, black and white. Green, eggplant and golden yellow seem to have been introduced about 1340 at Isfahan, and appear before the end of the century at Kerman. Early designs were often geometric, sometimes inlaid (Friday Mosque, Kerman). In the fifteenth century more flowing floral patterns comparable to carpet design were developed (Blue Mosque, Tabriz; Haroun al Vilayat and Darb-i-Imam, Isfahan). Under the Safavids there were further developments in technique, some in the direction of austerity; for example, unglazed brick as background to the pattern is used to marvellous effect in the dome of the Sheikh Lutfullah Mosque at Isfahan.

The vogue of tile mosaic did not altogether exclude the use of other media. Painting on plaster, for instance, had been practised in early Islamic times (Duvazdeh Imam and Vakt-u-Saat at Yazd), and in the early fourteenth century attained marvellous perfection in the gallery of the Mausoleum of Oljeitu at Sultaniyeh and the Imamzadehs of Qum. In the Safavid period there was a revival of painting on plaster – this time in flowing designs, ceilings covered with birds and flowers, a development of tile mosaic and carpet designs with a delicacy which paint facilitated. Some early examples of this work are being uncovered in the royal pavilion at Kazvin; the style reaches perfection in the Isfahan palaces,

Chehel Sutun, Ali Kapu, Hasht Behesht and, the best preserved of all, Talar Ashraf.

When Shah Abbas decided on the construction of the Royal Mosque at Isfahan, he set a time limit for completion, and with this in view he selected painted tiles (haft rangi) rather than tile mosaic. The medium was not altogether suitable for covering these vast surfaces; lovely though the colours and the total effect may be, the impression in detail is monotonous. But the royal command set a fashion in favour of haft rangi which rapidly ousted tile mosaic as the principal decorative medium during the seventeenth century, lasting well into the nineteenth. And, as Pope points out, because it was a new art, techniques probably improved as the century wore on. Good examples of later work are found in the Julfa (Isfahan) churches and at the Madrasseh Mader-i-Shah where there are subtle colours and novel geometrical designs. Qajar tilework, easily distinguishable by its realistic flower designs and recurrent use of pink, tends to be underrated in current fashion in comparison with earlier works but has great pictorial merits. Good examples are to be seen in the shrine of Shah Zadeh Huseyn at Kazvin, the Hammams and Imamzadeh of Ibrahim Khan at Kerman and the garden of the Gulestan Palace at Tehran.

Stone carving, by contrast, has been little practised in Islamic times, and the use of stone has been largely confined to dadoes, with columns carved on corners, as used in mosques. The Blue Mosque at Tabriz contained splendid slabs of carved alabaster which was quarried on the shores of Lake Rezaieh near Maragheh, an alabaster so transparent and luminous that it was often used in the place of windows, as for example in the winter prayer-hall of the Friday Mosque at Isfahan. The Friday Mosque has fine stone dadoes cut from pale jade green and roseate Yazd marble. Stone dadoes of a different character recur in the Qajar period, a branch of nineteenth-century art which would repay systematic and sympathetic study. The stone is grey, probably limestone, the face is carved with highly accomplished floral and animal designs repeated round the sides of open courtyards (Madrasseh Ibrahim Khan, Kerman; Huseyneyeh, Kazvin;

Shiraz). Secular, realistic and sophisticated, these charming reliefs form a fitting footnote to this dazzlingly brilliant branch of Persian art.

6. PICTORIAL AND MINOR ARTS

Pictorial art is mainly represented by the miniature (which contrary to popular belief does not mean 'on a small scale' but 'made from red lead') and takes the form of illustrations of famous poems like the Shahnameh of Firdausi, the Bustan of Saadi, the Ghazals of Jami, or the Khamse of Nizami: the world of Jamshid, Sohrab and Rustam, Leila and Majnun, Khosrow and Shirin, and the jackals Khalila and Dimna. Even when the works illustrated relate to historical events the illustrations reflect the costumes and customs of the period in which they were painted rather than that which they purport to represent.

The art of book illustration received great impetus from Chinese sources after the Mongol invasion and reached its highest pitch of perfection between 1400 and 1600. The Safavid miniatures show a considerable deterioration in design and refinement, and many of the best miniaturists were taken to India in the sixteenth century to work at the orders of the Great Moghuls, with marked results on their style. Thus it happens that Persian miniature painting is known to the world as much through Indian adaptations of it as in its original forms, and the results are not altogether flattering. Behzad, the greatest name in miniature painting – to a surprising extent an anonymous art – served as master of the court at Herat to the last Timurid monarch and to the first Safavid, Ismail; he introduced a human and personal note into what had till that time been a refined but conventional art. The great animated hunting scenes, against a background of desert covered with spring flowers (no perspective is attempted, so the flowers make a delightful tracery stretching *upwards* to the horizon) later give way to more static scenes in garden settings, turbaned figures bowing round a water tank, the lute player seated at the foot of a marquetry throne. Water, fences, walls, pavilions abound, but every building represented has the air of being erected specially for the occasion, like a stage setting; in this respect the Indian miniatures which sometimes show solid towers and ramparts, like those of some Italian city, in the background, are readily distinguishable. But the early Persians have a lyric quality, a combination of colour, subject and composition, which must faithfully reflect the poetry which it is intended to illustrate, a compensation perhaps for the non-Persian scholar who cannot understand the original, but at the same time a pointed reminder of what he is missing. If the painter can thus write poetry with his brush, what cannot the poet do with his pen? Perhaps no manifestation of Iranian genius gives a greater insight into the poetical and romantic side of the Iranian nature, except, of course, what is debarred for the illiterate, the poetry itself.

I will conclude this chapter with some brief notes on minor arts in more recent times. Painting on wood, for instance. Safavid examples are fine but few; a little pair of doors from the Chehel Sutun at Isfahan, with delicious figures in the panels and floral borders on a gold background, can be seen in the Islamic room at the Victoria and Albert. But this extension of the art of the miniaturist was revived in the early nineteenth century with charming results. Mirrors, stools, bookends, frames poured out in profusion, notably from Kazvin, and mostly in the form of facile but attractive flower patterns. Many collector's pieces can be found on the market today. Painting on ivory has also been practised for several centuries and extensively imitated; this again is a derivation from the miniaturist's art. In the first half of the nineteenth century there was a great vogue for papier mâché pen boxes (qalamdāns), some with floral designs, some with pictorial scenes; the first are generally delightful; the second show debased European influences and are curious rather than beautiful. Finally, marquetry is widely practised, and at its best is technically most accomplished.

Part II

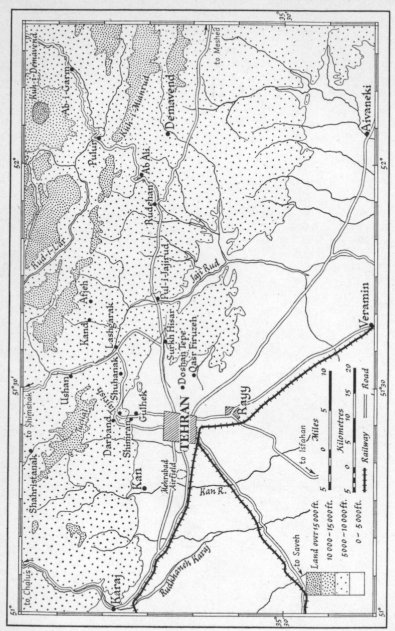

Tehran and district

Land over 15,000 ft.
10,000–15,000 ft.
5,000–10,000 ft.
0–5,000 ft.

Railway
Road

Miles
0   5   10

Kilometres
0   5   10   15   20

to Chalus
Karaj
Rudkhaneh Karaj
to Saveh
to Isfahan
Kan R.
Kan
Mehrabad Airfield
TEHRAN
Shimran
Gulhek
Shahristanak
to Shimshak
Ushan
Tuchal
Darband
Kulish
Shuhanak
Lashgarak
Kand
Afjeh
Rud-i-Lar
Kuh-i-Demavend
Ab-i-Garm
Pulur
Kuh-i-Miamrud
Rudehan
Ab Ali
Demavend
to Meshed
Pul-i-Jajirud
Jaji Rud
Surkh Hisar
Doshan Tepe
Qasr Firuzeh
Rayy
Veramin
Aivaneki

52°
51°30'
51°
35°30'
52°
51°30'
51°
35°30'

CHAPTER FOUR

South of the Elburz

Most visitors to Iran arrive nowadays by air. If they come from
the West, they fly in from Beirut or Istanbul, looking down for
some hours on a lunar landscape apparently devoid of life, criss-
crossed in places by qanat holes, and rimmed by mountains
snow-capped in late summer. At length the aircraft dips down
over a great brown chessboard, straight, tree-lined avenues
stretching from the base of the mountains far out into the plain,
at night a vast array of twinkling lights, and finally comes to
rest at Mehrabad airport before a white palace whose marbled
lobbies and pastel-shaded halls bring one very gently down to
earth.

A wide tree-lined boulevard flanked with modern factories
leads into the heart of the city, passing at the first intersection
what claims to be the largest Maidan (square) in the world,
dominated by the vast Shahyad monument, a development of
the Sassanian arch designed by a young Iranian architect and
erected in celebration of Cyrus's 2500th anniversary. A feature
of this gateway/tower is the manner of its construction: concrete poured in between the frame and the external marble
facing.

It is fashionable for visitors to decry Tehran and first impressions are bound to be mixed, to say the least. Undistinguished
buildings, wide but hideously congested avenues, brassy animation largely unrelieved by local charm or style, are not perhaps
what a superficial knowledge of Persia may have led the sightseer
to expect. It is today only to the older parts of the city that what
I wrote in 1961 applies:

The purling stream makes a delicious sound as it bears away a little of the city's refuse; the shops look so tiny but carry the most surprising treasures; behind that dingy wall there is cool shade, green grass, gay flowerbeds, perhaps a pillared mansion with deep verandahs and plastered ornament; across that squalid circle with its little blackened doorways, and dogs scavenging for refuse in vacant lots, and sticky sweet stalls, and men being shaved on the pavement, and broken down droskhys and timberyards and acrid smells – across all that lies the Golden Road to Samarkand.

Perhaps soon this will be entirely out of date; but I leave it with the reader in an attempt to convey something of the atmosphere and local colour of pre-war Tehran as it still prevailed about 1960.

For all its transformation and however little it may at first sight endear itself to the visitor, Tehran remains a place which has much to recommend it to the resident.

This is partly due to a good climate and a magnificent situation. 'The objections to the present site,' says Curzon rather baldly, 'are advanced on sanitary grounds.' He referred to the dependence of the entire city on qanats for its water supply. Until recently the objection was valid; but it has now been overcome with the construction of a modern purification plant for water brought from the Karaj river. For the rest, Tehran is perhaps happier in its surroundings than any other city in Persia. The barren tableland is redeemed by the mountains which protect it and the fertile irrigated land beyond it. In the city limits there is scarcely a physical feature, but a few miles on each side of it swirling torrents fringed with tamarisk issue from the mountains, and rich green valleys open up, old gnarled mountain villages shaded with walnut and willow, the line of cultivation marked with irrigation ditches edged with poplar giving a startling straightness to a tumbling tortuous landscape, and above them dun or green or chocolate coloured slopes studded in spring with iris and tulip, prickly milkwort, poppy and asphodel. Some of the remoter streams abound in mountain trout; ibex and mouflon roam the more distant ranges. Snow lies deep on the higher northern slopes for a full four months in winter; from Christmas to Easter skiing is in full swing. The abundant water which flows down in qanats from Tuchal, the 13,000-foot mountain behind Tehran, is brought to the surface in innumerable tanks and watercourses; social life in summer centres round the swimming pool. In the hot months evening parties can be planned in the open air, perhaps in a gaily decorated tribal tent; the tables will be lighted with candles which need only a circular glass to protect them against the light breeze, and for dancing carpets will be spread on the lawn. It should be added, with due regard to truth, that the vegetation is exclusively of the temperate zone, that the winter climate is harsh, the summer is parched and dry under a relentless sun, and the predominant colour, of earth and buildings, is a pale dun.

In the hundred and eighty odd years in which Tehran has been the capital, the city has sprawled outwards mainly towards the north and west. The older parts to the south, round the bazaar, have little to offer that is picturesque or striking. To the north of these, but within the old city walls destroyed by Reza Shah and replaced, on the north, by the avenue (Khiaban) which bears his name, are the main public buildings, the principal shopping streets and a number of foreign Embassy residences. Narrow lanes or kuchehs running between high walls often yield unexpected charms – an elaborate Qajar gateway or façade, a well-designed modern flat, or the glimpse of some scented garden. It is these quarters of the city, built on the old Iranian enclosed plan, which have most character.

Some six miles north of Tehran proper, at the foot of the mountains, are the palaces of the Shah and the Royal Family, both old and modern villas, and many luxuriant gardens. At the highest point of the settlement, nearly 2,000 feet above Tehran, and at the entrance to a mighty gorge, stands a magnificently situated hotel, the Darband (meaning closed door or end of the valley). Just before the hotel, on the right, a road leads up to Golab Darreh, where there is a tiny picturesque market square, with magnificent views, and the Imamzadeh Qassem in which the remains of Imam Hassan's martyred second son lie buried in an exquisitely carved wooden coffin dating, like the original building, from the time of Shah Tahmasp. The Tajrish-Shimran area is becoming increasingly popular for all-the-year-round residence, principally on account of its cool summer nights. In Tehran itself it is often better to sleep out of doors; and this indeed is an ancient custom. Thomas Herbert describes how he looked out from a high building one morning and saw the flat roof-tops covered with sleepers. 'I could perceive ... that most of the masters of families slept nightly with their seraglio upon the tops of their houses, which were spread with carpets; some ... had three, some six, women about them wrapped in cambolines or fine linen.' He adds that had he been observed he might have had an arrow in his brain. I would not suggest that an early morning glance over the roof-tops of modern Tehran would entail the same risks – or promise the same rewards. But wake up if you can* at five o'clock on a summer morning to the sound of the bells of a camel-train – 'the distant boom of a heavy bell' as Curzon describes it; 'mournfully, and with perfect regularity of iteration, it sounds, gradually swelling nearer and louder, and perhaps mingling with the tones of smaller bells, signalling the rearguard of the same caravan'; watch the sun rise behind Demavend and its rays steal round the blue slopes of Tuchal; breathe the ineffably light morning air as the last star is extinguished; and even in Tehran, you will have sensed something of the magic that has cast its spell on successive generations of travellers, and held their spirits captive even when like Edward Browne they only spent 'a year among the Persians' in their youth.

Even now, when modern villas stretch up to the base of Tuchal, it is still possible to find rural peace within easy reach of the town centre. A short track uphill from the airport brings you to the streams and orchards of Kan. East of Shimran, past long blank walls facing north built to collect snow from which ice is made in spring (yakhchals, or ice valleys), the village of Shuhanak, its gardens hanging on the hillsides, lies tucked away

---

* No longer possible, I am told; not to wake up, but to hear these lovely sounds on the northern fringe of Tehran.

in a high valley. Just beyond it, the road climbs up to a pass where lesser kestrels nest by the roadside, and where the whole glory of the Elburz range, pierced just below by the chasm of the Jaji Rud, bursts suddenly into view. The feeder valleys of the rich green plain below, reached by crossing the stream at Lash-garak and leading up to Kand and Afjeh, with their high arched bridges and tumbling fields and flat-roofed villages nestling in poplar and walnut, provide some of the most entrancing scenery in Iran. Farther afield, the road to Ab Ali winds up to the 8,000-foot pass (an hour and a half from Tehran) where it is generally possible to ski for four months in winter. Beyond this again, the road plunges down into the Lar valley at Pulur, and then climbs up through a natural rock garden. The summit, at nearly 9,000 feet, is one of the most delectable spots in the world. On one side, green meadows studded with tulips in spring and red and white poppies in high summer carry the eye upwards to the snow-capped and often clouded peak of Demavend. On the other, the ground falls away steeply to the rushing torrent of the Haraz some two thousand feet below; and behind it rises the breathtaking range of the Kuh-i-Mianrud, the Peaks between the Rivers, a 13,000-foot knife-edge nearly twenty miles in length. Here in this cool clear air it is difficult to believe that through that irridescent gap to the north-east, where clouds often hang, there is rich cultivation and crowded villages and the thick steamy heat of the Caspian shore.

The road continues through Ab-i-Garm, a hot spring where Reza Shah started to build a large hotel, but it was never finished and most of what there was of it was destroyed in an earthquake which inflicted great damage on this region in July, 1957. This is the best starting-point for the ascent of Demavend, the 18,500 foot mountain which dominates Tehran and towers above the Lar valley. Since it lies near one of the great trade routes across Iran, can be seen in good weather for over 100 miles, and has a shape as seductive as that of Fujiyama, it is surprising that it has not had a more distinguished career in myth, legend or religious rite. One reason may be that from the south it cannot be seen in its full glory except from a very long way off, when it rises behind the intervening ranges, or from very close up, with the intervening ranges out of the way. It also has another and more intimate defect which was well described by Thomas Herbert who visited it (or more probably Ab-i-Garm) in 1628. He calls it 'a defatigating hill', and 'a pleasant object to the eye, but so offensive to the smell that it requires a nosegay of garlic in the ascending'.

The sulphurous fumes which rise from the crater once the sun warms it, and the rarity of the air above about 15,000 feet, are today the two chief problems facing the spare-time mountaineer. There is no rock climbing and it is generally described by those who have done it as an easy walk. The best plan is to camp at about 13,500 feet, leave camp at 1 a.m. in moonlight, reach the top not later than 7 a.m., and return to Tehran in the afternoon.

Such are some of the sights which beckon the traveller out of Tehran. They are so splendid that what the city itself has to offer inevitably pales by comparison. How often have I waited in vain for that wet Sunday in early spring which would provide the excuse for a little urban sightseeing! Yet the monuments of Tehran after their fashion are not to be despised.

Tehran, it must be remembered, is a modern city. In the Middle Ages it was a savage place where people lived in holes like jerboas. Shah Abbas loathed the site, built no palaces there and avoided it like the plague. Karim Khan Zand built a hunting lodge on the outskirts, but it remained an obscure, ill-favoured provincial town until the coming of the Qajars. Agha Mohammed picked Tehran as his capital because of its proximity to Mazanderan, his native province. He proceeded to build a fortified palace surrounded by a high wall on the site of Karim Khan's pavilion. The palace was finished by Fath Ali Shah, his successor.

This, the palace of Gulestan, or Rose Garden, is the oldest substantial building in the city. Both as a whole and in many of its parts it is an eloquent testimony to the deplorable taste of the period. Yet many details are worth careful observation. The palace is set in a lovely garden, and the tilework of the surrounding walls, with its gay flowers and fresh colours, stands as proof that the art of delicate design had not been completely lost. The mirrored halls and stalactites of the interior are an acquired taste;

in the great reception rooms there are exquisite carpets, a ceremonial bed made in Isfahan for one of Fath Ali Shah's weddings,
and the so-called Peacock Throne – *not* that is to say the original
throne taken by Nadir Shah from India in 1739, or the copy he
made of it (parts of both of which may have been incorporated
in the so-called Nadir Throne now to be seen in the vaults of the
Bank Melli) but a platform throne similar in shape made for
Fath Ali Shah on the occasion of his wedding to a lady conveniently (or confusingly) called Peacock (Tavous Khanum). In
the open talar of the palace itself, filled with stucco and mirror
work and Qajar paintings, is the white marble throne built for
Fath Ali Shah in 1806. And to the right of the main entrance to
the garden stands the White Palace (Kakh-i-Abyaz) housing the
Ethnological Museum. This contains many examples of village
handicrafts, now fast disappearing, a superb collection of wax
works and many fine period costumes, the work of the late Ali
Hannibal, an Iranian citizen descended from Pushkin, who was
also responsible for initiating the restoration of the Royal Pavilion
at Kazvin and for the museum at Abadan.

The Gulestan is used today principally for Imperial receptions
('salaams') on the Shah's birthday and at the New Year, and for
State banquets. Three other palaces should be mentioned. The
Kakh-i-Marmar or Marble Palace, was built by Reza Shah in the
1930s for his town residence. It is a square building in pale green
Yazd marble, surmounted by a tiled dome derived from the
Sheikh Lutfullah Mosque at Isfahan – and it is no unworthy
imitation. The interior includes a room encased entirely in
mirrors (the effect on a sunny day or when fully illuminated at
night is blinding), another covered from head to foot, walls,
ceiling and furniture, with marquetry, and a highly ornate staircase with wall-paintings of Persepolis and the Trans-Iranian
Railway. This is now the Pahlevi Dynasty Museum.

The Summer Palace at Saadabad stands in a magnificent park
above Tajrish, just below the Darband Hotel. Fifty-five years
ago this tract was a barren hillside where donkeys roamed and
goats gnawed a few scraggy hard-bitten bushes. Today fountains
play over emerald green grass, there are dazzling beds of salvia,

and tall chenars (oriental planes) offer ample shade. Private houses of members of the Royal Family are in the grounds.

Of greater architectural interest is the summer palace of the Qajars known as Saheb Qaranieh (Lord of the Centuries) at Niavaran some three miles east of Tajrish. This was built by Nasr-uddin Shah and, as compared with Gulestan, shows considerable advance in design and the influence of European, notably Russian, taste. It is a relatively low building somewhat rococo in style; its white colonnaded porticoes give it a Colonial air, yet have the quality of stage scenery. It resembles many private residences of great charm and distinction built in and around Tehran in the middle or third quarter of the nineteenth century, many of which are now, alas, threatened with demolition. The garden of the palace at Niavaran is sheer delight. In the extensive grounds are a number of smaller pavilions where Nasr-uddin Shah kept his harem. These, with the palace itself, are used today for the reception of distinguished visitors. The Stokes Mission, which came out at the time of the Abadan crisis to try to arrive at a solution to the oil problem, was much amused to find itself in the women's quarters or anderun. The delegation, however, despite the charm of their surroundings, failed to reach agreement.

The house of Moshir-ed-Dowleh, a nobleman at Nasr-uddin's court, for many years housed the Majlis or Parliament. It is a massive stone building of 1885 with ornate iron gates leading into a big garden, a little Second Empire in manner but still characteristically Persian in spirit. A new house is in the process of construction in the northern part of the adjoining garden. To the south-west, on the Khiaban Ecbatana, is the Palace of Zil-i-Soltan, Nasr-uddin Shah's eldest son – a complex of three houses ornately covered with white stucco on grey-blue ground, with pillared galleries and ground-level dadoes decorated with full-length portraits – some in tile and some in stone – of soldiers and court officials. It now houses the Ministry of Education.

Close by the Majlis to the south stands Tehran's biggest mosque named after Sepah Salar, brother of Moshir-ed-Dowleh and Nasr-uddin Shah's War Minister. The minarets are covered with pink roses and the smaller ones flanking the entrance have

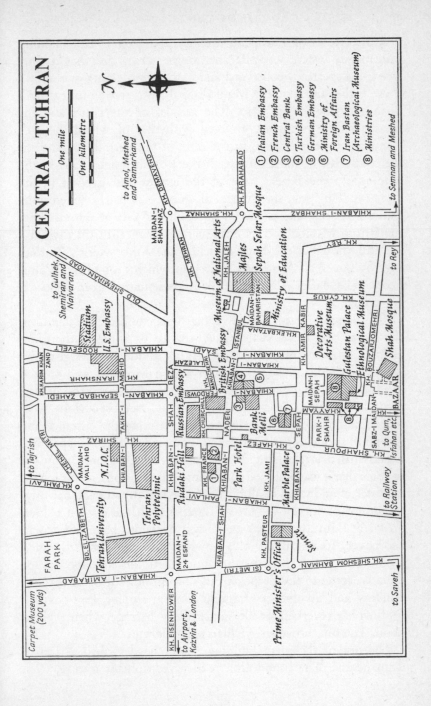

CENTRAL TEHRAN

One mile
One kilometre

① Italian Embassy
② French Embassy
③ Central Bank
④ Turkish Embassy
⑤ German Embassy
⑥ Ministry of Foreign Affairs
⑦ Iran Bastan (Archaeological Museum)
⑧ Ministries

N

to Amol, Meshed and Samarkand

to Gulhek, Shemiran and Naivaran

to Tajrish

Carpet Museum (200 yds)

FARAH PARK

Tehran University

Tehran Polytechnic

N.I.O.C.

Stadium

U.S. Embassy

Russian Embassy

Rudaki Hall

Park Hotel

Marble Palace

Prime Minister's Office

Senate

British Embassy

Museum of National Arts

Bank Melli

Majles

Sepah Selar Mosque

Ministry of Education

Gulestan Palace

Decorative Arts Museum

Ethnological Museum

Shah Mosque

BAZAAR

to Airport, Kazvin & London

to Railway Station

to Qum, Isfahan etc.

to Saveh

to Rey

to Semnan and Meshed

OLD SHEMIRAN ROAD

KH. DEMAVEND

MAIDAN-I SHAHNAZ

KH. MEHRAN

KH. FARAHABAD

KH. SHAHNAZ

KHIABAN-I SHAHBAZ

KH. JALEH

KH. REY

KH. CYRUS

KH. EKBATANA

KH. AMIR KABIR

KH. BOUZARJOMEHRI

KH. SHAHPOUR

KH. SHESHOM BAHMAN

KH. PASTEUR

KH. JAMI

KH. HAFEZ

KH. FRANCE

KHIABAN-I PAHLAVI

KHIABAN-I SHAH

MAIDAN-I 24 ESFAND

KH. EISENHOWER

KHIABAN-I AMIRABAD

BD. ELIZABETH II

KHERBE MERI

KH. PAHLAVI

MAIDAN-I VALI AHD

SEPAHBAD ZAHEDI

KH. KARIM KHAN ZAND

IRANSHAHR

KH. TAKHT-I JAMSHID

KH. SHIRAZ

KHIABAN-I ROOSEVELT

KHIABAN-I SAADI

KHIABAN-I ISTANBUL

MAIDAN-I BAHARISTAN

KHIABAN-I FERDOWSI

KHIABAN-I NADERI

KH. CHURCHILL

KH. SHAH REZA

LALEZAR

KHIABAN-I ISMAIL

KHIABAN-I SEPAH

MAIDAN-I SEPAH

PARK-I SHAHR

SABZ-I MAIDAN

KH. METRI (SI)

KH. SAADI

MAIDAN-I SHAH

postcard views of European architectural scenes. The building presents an austere brick façade to the street, but has a fine, tree-filled, peaceful courtyard and extensive tilework within.

An earlier mosque, the Masjid-i-Shah, was started by Fath Ali Shah and finished in 1840. The arcades of the court and the façades of the iwans are covered with tiles of which the predominant tone is yellow, in the taste of the period. It stands to the south-east of the Gulistan on the Bouzarjomehri, and at the entrance to the Bazaar, one of the largest and liveliest in the country. This was the centre of gravity of early nineteenth-century Tehran, and it was in the southern part of this area that the British Mission had its headquarters from 1812 till 1870 at a site still known as the Bagh-i-Elchi – the Ambassador's Garden. Nearby is a small Armenian church in which a son of Sir Walter Scott and Charles Alison, British Representative from 1860–72, are buried.

The present British Embassy on Khiaban Firdausi stands in the centre of a fifteen-acre garden shaded by some of the finest chenars (oriental planes) in Iran. The Residence, designed by Mr J. W. Wild of the South Kensington Museum, and erected in 1869/70 under the supervision of an Indo-European engineer of the Indo-European Telegraph Department, is a most curious structure. The main block of one storey containing the entrance and reception rooms is crowned by an open-sided object shaped like the howdah of an elephant, frankly Indian in inspiration. One might suppose that it was designed for ceremonial occasions, on which the Minister would stand in all his finery on this ornamental balcony, to address or survey the crowds gathered in the garden below. So far as I am aware, however, such occasions have not arisen. Moreover, to get under the howdah and still look dignified would be difficult (perhaps the same is true on an elephant) for the only route to this preposterous summit lies out of a bedroom window and involves a scramble along a sloping lead-covered roof which reverberates like an artillery barrage when walked upon. The top, however, yields a splendid view.

The rest of the main building might be described as Indian Romanesque. The round arch is the predominant feature, even in the little brick balustrades on balcony and roof, which look as though they had been built with children's bricks, and are now falling out of place. This effect is enhanced by the dingy colour of the brick, even more lifeless than the Tehran average; but in spring it forms a good contrasting background to the riotous colour of the judas trees and the enormous wistaria which conceals in its purple foam all the architectural ineptitudes of the south front. A series of portholes high up on the south side are generally presumed by the visitor on first acquaintance to light attic bedrooms; in fact they light nothing; they look down into the reception rooms and are filled with coloured glass representing the rose, the thistle – and the shamrock.

Close to the east end of the main block is a campanile which houses an ancient clock. Substantial houses built for Legation secretaries and staff create the effect, as one visitor observed, of an English public school without the boys. The mature beauty of the garden derives largely from an excellent water supply, brought by qanat from beyond Tajrish. The reputation of this water is such that, until recently, when filtered and piped water from the Karaj river was laid on by the city, the British Embassy supplied water to the neighbourhood; today even the water-cart and donkey of the Bank Melli – one of our partners in the qanat enterprise – are no more seen.

The building of the National Bank stands two blocks away down Firdausi Avenue. It presents an imposing classical front to the street, that is to say, Persian classical based on Persepolis. Behind it, well concealed from view, is an old palace and a large well-kept garden. The Bank, apart from its excellent professional reputation, is famous for two things: its jewels and its gymnasts. The jewels, the property of the Crown, are now finely displayed in a modern vault open every afternoon save Friday. They include jewelled crowns and swords of the early Qajar period. The gymnasts recall an earlier tradition. They are the most famous survival of the gymnastic clubs, or Zurkhaneh, which flourished in secret in early Islamic times, operating as cells of resistance to the Arab conquerors. In a gymnasium which, in pursuance of the tradition of secrecy, is half underground,

swarthy athletes clad in tightfitting shorts like tiger skins wield
enormous clubs, wrestle, spin round dizzily, or heave chains to
the sound of a drum and the intoning of passages from Firdausi's
epic, the *Shahnameh*.

No visitor can afford to miss the Archaeological Museum.*
Housed in a modern building in the Khiaban Qavam-al-Saltaneh
near the Ministry of Foreign Affairs, and organized with the aid
of the French archaeological mission, it contains within a small
compass perhaps the finest collection in the world of Persian art
treasures of all periods, and is a model of orderly arrangement.
Among the pre-Islamic objects, some on the ground floor, some
in the Treasure Room on the first floor are pottery from Tepe
Sialk near Kashan (fourth century B.C.), Susa, Rayy, Khorvin and
Tepe Hissar; Luristan bronzes; columns, bas-reliefs and statuary
from Persepolis; Sassanian jewellery and silverware. Nine groups
of objects are of particular interest. One is the Kalar Dasht treasure, including a gold dagger and the famous gold cup, on the
sides of which are worked the figures of lions in hammered relief,
with applied heads in the round, to serve as handles. No date can
be firmly assigned to this astounding piece, but it is probably of
the tenth or eleventh century B.C. It was found, with other objects,
in a tomb near Kalar Dasht in the course of excavating a site for
one of the Shah's palaces in the 1930s. As gold belonging to the
Crown it was handed in to the National Bank of Iran, the Bank
Melli, and is said to have been subsequently purchased from
them by the Tehran Archaeological Museum at the value of its
weight in gold. Another is the golden plaque found in a stone
box at Persepolis in the 1930s which contains an inscription in old
Persian, Babylonian and Elamite. It is said to have been the
discovery of this foundation stone which fired Reza Shah's
interest in Iran's Imperial past and the great tradition which he
had inherited. A third is the Shami statuary: a large male bronze
figure complete with what look like a clubman's moustache and
fisherman's leggings (in fact riding-trousers), a bronze statuette,
a bronze head and a marble head, all dating from the Parthian
period, probably the second century B.C. Greek influence, par-
* For opening hours of this and other Tehran museums see Appendix I.

ticularly in the marble head, is clearly visible. They were found
some thirty years ago by peasants on the site of an even more
ancient temple near the upper reaches of the Karun. A fourth
is the mosaic pavement from the iwan of the Sassanian palace at
Bishapur. These mosaics consist of portrait heads and full-length
figures and show strong traces of Graeco-Roman influence. They
were discovered by Dr Ghirshman in 1938. The other five are: a
silver beaker from Marv Dasht with the raised figure of a woman
and an Elamite inscription of the third century B.C.; the Zuwiye
treasure described on p. 174; a fabulous collection of gold beakers
from Marlik (see p. 122) found by Dr Negahban in 1961–62; the
Golden Bowl of Hassanlu uncovered by Dr Dyson; and Achaemenian gold including rhytons, swords and jewellery, and
Xerxes's beautiful bowl found by David Stronach at Pasargadae.
All these last together with the Kalar Dasht treasure and the
Luristan bronzes are in the Treasure Room (1st floor).

The Islamic section of the Archaeological Museum is on the
first floor. Here again the collection is highly representative. It
includes lovely examples of pottery, plaster mihrabs from Rayy
and Ashtarjan, lustre mihrabs from the Imamzadeh Jafar at Qum
and the Imamzadeh Habib ibn Musa at Kashan, a carved wooden
mimbar from Fars, alabaster windows from a mosque at Abarquh,
Safavid carpets and brocades and part of the collection of Chinese
pottery belonging to Shah Abbas I – to name only a few high-
lights. There can be no better introduction to the wealth and
variety of Persian Islamic art.

Other museums worth visiting are:

(i) The Museum of National Arts, Khiaban Kamal-ol-Molk,
opposite the Majlis, in a small Qajar house which was
originally the Howz-Khaneh of the Negarestan Palace, Fath
Ali Shah's picture gallery and summer-house. It has a vaulted
ceiling covered with baroque stucco work in white on a
startling deep blue-mauve ground supported by graceful
columns with spiral reeding and stalactite capitals which are
gilded and painted with tiny flowers. This is the show place
for the work of the craftsmen of the (adjacent) Ministry of
Culture. A shop nearby sells handwoven silk brocades copied

from old patterns, Khatam work (inlaid wood with ivory and brass) in picture frames and boxes, and modern pottery.

(ii) The Museum of Decorative Arts, Khiaban Amir Kabir, between the Gulestan and the Majlis also in a Qajar house of much charm. The collection of folk art, primarily Islamic, includes brocades, embroidery, carpets, armour, jewellery, miniatures, Khatam work, Qajar papier mâché, metal work and qalamkar (cotton stamped by hand with wooden blocks).

(iii) The Carpet Museum, Khiaban Arya Mehr and Amirabad, north of the University (under construction in 1971).

(iv) The Wild Life Museum, Khiaban Shah Abbas, on the ground floor of the Game and Fish Department, contains a small collection of stuffed animals native to Iran.

(v) The Borghese Gallery, Khiaban Villa, shows the work of living Iranian artists.

This said, it must also be noted with regret that much in and around Tehran has gone beyond recall: the Arg, or citadel, and walls surrounding the Gulestan; Nasr-uddin Shah's pavilion at Doshan Tepe (Hill of the Hare); his hunting pavilion in the hills, the Qasr-i-Firuzeh or Turquoise Palace; many fine Qajar mansions; and perhaps above all the walls and gateways built by Nasr-uddin Shah in 1871 to surround the enlarged town. They were removed by Reza Shah, and when we look at photographs of their narrow portals and then at the traffic flowing round Firdausi's statue or out to the airport, we can understand the necessity. Yet it is impossible not to regret that their coloured façades and twirling minarets are no more. The most curious extant building of the late Qajar period is the palace of Farahabad, to the east of the city and adjoining the Royal Hunting Reserve. It was built by Muzaffar-uddin Shah and has been described as the architectural counterpart of a Mississippi steamboat. It is circular in shape and said to have been modelled on the Trocadero in Paris.

Needless to say there is no lack of modern buildings in Tehran, many striking and original if not architecturally outstanding. Among these may be mentioned the new opera house (the Rudaki Hall (Khiaban Hafez)); the Senate building near the Marble

Palace; the Bank of Tehran opposite the Park Hotel; a new
circular theatre on Khiaban Pahlevi; the new Armenian Cathedral
(Khiaban Villa and Chelmetri) and the Lycée Razi on Pahlevi;
also the new Carpet Museum mentioned above.

Rayy, the Rhages of the ancients, lies seven miles south-east of
Tehran at the base of a sun-baked precipice. Today it is little
more than a village, but still retains a few traces of its former
greatness. Visited by Alexander, fortified by the Parthians, the
birthplace of Haroun al Rashid, a flourishing city of the Seljuk
Empire and perhaps the finest source for early Islamic pottery,
Rayy was utterly destroyed by the Mongols in 1220 and its
population dispersed to Varamin, Saveh and elsewhere. The
Seljuk walls of the old city are clearly visible between the modern
town and the mountainside, and on the hill to the north of the
Varamin road there stands an octagonal Seljuk tomb tower with
the base of a duodecanal Buyid tower nearby, a Zoroastrian
tower of silence (dakhmeh) and the tomb of Bibi Shahrbanu,
daughter of Yezdigird III and wife of the Imam Huseyn, dating
from the tenth century with Qajar tilework. But the principal
ancient monument of Rayy within the walls of the town is the
Seljuk tomb tower which is often referred to, inaccurately, as
the tower of Toghril Beg. To the passer-by it might appear to
be a large Victorian water-tower. This effect is enhanced by its
having lost whatever dome or cone (probably the latter) it once
possessed; its flat top looks severely functional. But a closer
study of its architectural features is rewarding; the triple-vaulted
cornice which crowns the deep pleats of its cylindrical surface is
deceptively simple and brilliantly effective; the monumental
doorway at the south side has an impressive simplicity. It is built
entirely of brick and dates from 1139.

Also within the confines of the walled city is the famous spring
known as Chashmeh Ali. This is much frequented for the purpose
of washing carpets. Often the contents of a whole house are to
be seen submerged in the clear, shallow water, or stretched out
drying on the rocks above, a gay patchwork of reds, purples and
blues. No doubt it was the popularity of this spot which caused
Fath Ali Shah to follow the old Sassanian custom of having rock

carvings representing him enthroned and hunting chiselled on the rock face nearby. The central portion depicts him seated on the Marble Throne and surrounded by ten of his sons; by the steps to the Throne stand two diminutive soldiers. Four more sons (all identified by names carved in the rock) stand in the left-hand panel, while on the right Fath Ali Shah appears again standing with a falcon on his wrist under an umbrella held by a figure standing behind him. Not far from here is the mound or tepe where some of the finest prehistoric Rayy pottery was discovered, and the remains of the walls of a Parthian palace can be seen.

At the centre of modern Rayy stands the shrine of Abdul Azim, a sanctuary and place of pilgrimage covering the remains of three Shi'a martyrs or notables: Abdul Azim, a martyred grandson of the second Imam Hassan, under the bulbous and brilliant golden dome; Hamzeh, a brother of the eighth Imam Reza, under the tiled turquoise dome; and Taher, son of the fourth Imam Zem-ol-Abedin under the third dome. The façade is Safavid but the greater part of this great pile was reconstructed in the nineteenth century. It was on leaving this shrine after Friday prayers that Nasr-uddin Shah was assassinated in 1896. Non-Moslems are not permitted to enter this holy place.

In the spacious grounds of the shrine but accessible to visitors is a high building of white marble and Yazd alabaster. This is the tomb of Reza Shah, brought back to rest here after his death in South Africa in 1945. His body lies in an open vault surrounded by a circular balcony, after the same fashion as Napoleon at Les Invalides; part of the ceremony of receiving distinguished visitors or newly accredited ambassadors consists of laying a wreath on his tomb. Adjoining the tomb itself is a small museum of Imperial relics.

At Mesgarabad, about 12 km from Rayy at the junction of the Aminabad-Khorassan road, a track leads off into the mountains to the Zendan-i-Haroun, a square, tenth-century building alleged to have been Haroun al Rashid's prison. The road to Varamin, twenty miles south-east, passes the Sassanian building (purpose unknown) of Tepe Mil. Varamin itself, which attained

3a. BASTAM: The northern group of buildings from the East; a Seljuk minaret on the left (*p.102*)

3b. CARAVANSERAI NEAR ISFAHAN. 'They are invariably built round a square like the courtyard of a mosque' (*p. 58*)

4a. (*above*) MESHED: Second Court of the Shrine, showing the Golden Dome of Imam Reza's tomb (*p. 107*) 4b. (*below*) KAZVIN: Gateway of the Shrine of Shah Zadeh Huseyn, 'with five gay minarets at slightly drunken angles' (*p. 143*)

some importance in the thirteenth and fourteenth centuries, stands near the centre of a large fertile plain watered by the Jaji Rud which issues from the mountains nearby, and is cut up into numerous irrigation channels before losing itself in the desert beyond. Benefiting by the presence of water and the proximity of Tehran, there are a number of interesting agricultural and social experiments in this area, and near the railway station Reza Shah constructed a sugar beet factory. Modernization is now starting to affect the village of Varamin itself, dominated by a Mongol tomb tower (1289) with its honeycomb cornice of glazed terracotta and its conical roof, the broken crown of which is a favourite nesting place for storks. The chief glory of the place, the Friday Mosque, stands a little apart from the village, on the edge of a greenish plain dotted with small domed imamzadehs, including the fourteenth-century Imamzadeh Yahya, one of those spots – there are perhaps a dozen others in Iran – in which the past has been so much more eventful than the present that time is extinguished, and the shades of those who lived and worshipped there fill the place with a miasma of sanctity which is almost tangible – or so it seemed to me in the fitful sunlight of a February afternoon.

The Friday Mosque at Varamin was built in 1322; it is one of the earliest extant examples of the enclosed type in its full vigour, a triumphant vindication of the Iranian capacity for revival after Mongol depredations. Its proportions are exceptionally harmonious. The use of decorated brick and of tilework and the vaulting of the dome are among the most splendid examples of their time. The mihrab is so 'intensely rich', as Pope says, 'that it defies pictorial presentation'. This mosque is unquestionably the most interesting building immediately south of the Elburz between Sultaniyeh and Damghan. Nevertheless, as an introduction to early Islamic architecture for the newly arrived visitor (which, because of its situation near Tehran it is rather apt to be), it is not to be recommended unreservedly. It has long been in a ruinous state though now well repaired. One needs to know a good deal about what a mosque ought to look like in order to appreciate what this one must have been. Moreover, decorated brick and sculptured plaster owe more to the subtlety of their design than to their colour, and cannot at first make the same impact as, say, faïence mosaic. Varamin, therefore, is not perhaps the best place to acquire the taste for early Iranian mosques; but once that taste is acquired, one returns to this lovely building with greater understanding and ever-growing respect.

Tehran's largest neighbour, Qum, lies at 3,000 feet in a hot sandy hollow between the mountains of Kashan and the Great Salt Desert, some ninety miles to the south. It belongs in climate, scenery and architecture to the desert rather than to the Elburz region; here we see the first wind towers and ab-ambars (water storage buildings), and a few miles further on the first palm trees. It can, however, be conveniently visited in a day from Tehran.

Qum's history centres round Islam. Opinions vary on its antiquity. What is certain is that from the early years of the Arab conquest it was noted for the fanaticism of its inhabitants and for the preponderance of Shi'as among them. If there is one place in Iran which can be called the cradle and centre of Shi'ism, Qum is that place. No doubt it was on this account that when Fatima, the daughter of the seventh Imam and the sister of Imam Reza, fell ill in 816 at Saveh it was to Qum that she was brought. There she died and was buried; and her tomb, as was natural, became a revered place of pilgrimage. So it remains today, and Qum, after Meshed, is the foremost Shi'a shrine in Iran.

In later history Qum experienced many vicissitudes. It was wrecked by the Mongols and again by Timur, but enjoyed a revival under the Safavids who, it will be recalled, made Shi'ism the official faith of Iran. Shah Abbas rebuilt Fatima's shrine, and his three successors were buried there. The Joshagan carpets which adorn the shrine of Shah Abbas II are noteworthy. Fath Ali Shah further enlarged the shrine, and what we see today, including the magnificent golden dome, dates from his reign.

The approach to Qum, whether from the south, west or north, gives warning of its religious importance. 'That it was a large town,' says Thomas Herbert, 'is discernible both by the rubbish appearing in several places, the foundation of temples, and other public structures.' Today we can be more precise and less un-complimentary. On the Isfahan road we observe the striking outline of two modern theological colleges or madrasseh. In all directions, the horizon is dotted with the blue cones or domes of shrines. No other place in Iran has so rich a collection; an exceptionally large number of domed sanctuaries on square or octagonal (in one case twelve-sided) bases with tent domes, tile covered, were erected here in the fourteenth century. There are in fact over a dozen dating from that period, most of them in fair condition; six are near or to the south of the old Kashan gate (south-east of the town), two between there and the Isfahan road (south), and two beyond the station (west). Several interiors contain excellent polychrome relief work, the best extant anywhere except for the gallery at Sultaniyeh; the most noteworthy are Ibrahim (1321), Ali ibn Jafar (1339), Ali ibn Abil Ma' li (1360), and Khwaja Imad Uddin (1389), all near the old Kashan gate.

Fatima's shrine is no place for infidels. We have to be content with the view of the golden dome and minarets rising behind the baked brick buildings which face the dried-up stream-bed of the Qum river, which gives the city such character as it has – or a glimpse through a doorway into the great court of the shrine from a street near the market-place. The streets of Qum are full of animation, and the shops do a flourishing trade in religious objects and in coloured earthenware animals, which (together with the surrounding oil derricks) are one of the modern features of the Iranian Canterbury.

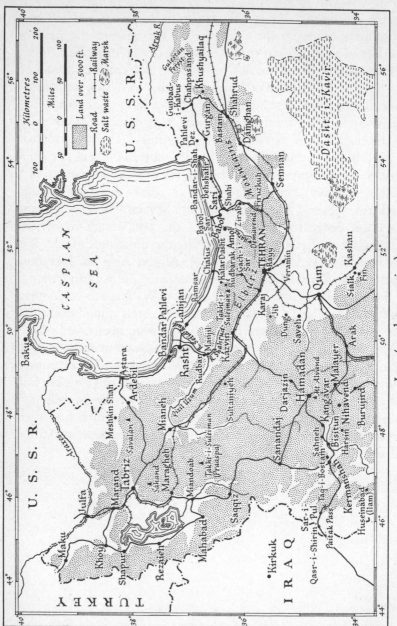

Iran (northern section)

CHAPTER FIVE

To Khorasan

> 'Away! for we are ready to a man
> Our camels sniff the evening and are glad.'

Thus opens the final scene of Flecker's *Hassan*; and the words
seem apt enough here. Unless the weather is exceptionally hot
it is not usual, or necessary, to follow the custom of leaving in
the evening and travelling by night; nor yet the more normal
Iranian practice of setting out in the afternoon of the first day
and travelling only a short stage – so that the servants can go
back and fetch what has been inadvertently left behind. But,
apart from the timing, Flecker's lines fit our case; we are glad,
like the camels; the morning air, too, is good to sniff; moreover
our route lies over the Golden Road to Samarkand.

Let this, however, give rise to no misunderstanding. Meshed is
nearly 600 miles from Tehran. The nearest route* lies mainly
along the edge of howling desert. The road is badly corrugated.
The scenery is monotonous in the extreme. It is in short the
longest and dreariest road between any two major towns in Iran.
The Golden Road to Samarkand is an ordeal, and it is as well to
know this in advance.

Nowadays, the faint-hearted can of course fly to Meshed. It is
also possible to take the train to the fine modern railway station.
For those who prefer such insulated forms of travel there is no
point in reading the next few pages. But I would hope that those
who do read them would, after reflection, take the road. I do not
think they would regret it.

* The longer route, via the Caspian and Bujnurd, is now (1978) a good tarmac
road.

There are two routes to Semnan (150 miles from Tehran): one along the edge of the desert, the other through the foothills of the Elburz. The first passes good caravanserais (notably at Khalilabad) and abandoned citadels at Padek and Aradan. The second is more beautiful. The scenery to Firuzkuh, and indeed for some way beyond it, is enchanting. The road runs near the base of the great range flanking Demavend, which at its western end is known as the Kuh-i-Mianrud; there is one stretch where it passes over the fingers of this range, which is unadulterated switchback. Demavend village, well away from its eponymous mountain on the southern slopes of the Kuh-i-Mianrud and just north of the road, possesses four tomb towers, one of which, the Tomb of Sheikh Shibli, a Sunni mystic born in Baghdad who was Wali of Demavend up to 901, is eleventh century and has fine brick work. In May, when the villages near Demavend are like emerald lakes, and the telegraph lines blue with bee-eaters and rollers (where, one wonders, did they perch before the invention of the telegraph?), the slopes are a purple cloud of spiky cushions of milkwort. After a pass, however, the road descends towards the Kavir and the scene of desolation begins. The south-east wind blows the sand off the desert towards the mountains. I have seen sand scattered in great waves over a wide area of mountain, stifling the last struggling remnants of vegetation. Not far from all this, on the edge of the desert, is Semnan, an ancient town (now a felt-making centre) which possesses a tomb tower, a Seljuk minaret, a thirteenth-century mosque, another built by Fath Ali Shah, mainly, and a Hamman with an amusing entrance and a Qajar gateway.

Fifty miles to the east across a monotonous plain and we see to the south a vast, windswept expanse of hard-baked mud with a series of great mounds. This is Shahr-i-Qumis which can probably be identified with the site of the Greek city of Hecatompylos (see pp. 15 and 16). Recent excavations here by the British Institute have found two funerary towers containing both human and horse skulls, coins suggesting a date of 70 B.C. and the base of an unusual circular building of uncertain date.

Twenty miles on is Damghan, a shrivelled place with a great history. This region has been inhabited from very early times;

pottery of 2–3000 B.C. has been discovered in the Tepe Hissar
nearby. At the time of the Arab conquest Damghan became the
site of one of the first mosques in Iran. In addition to being sacked
by Yenghiz Khan and Timur, Damghan was also laid low by the
Afghans in 1723, but Nadir Shah made some effort to reconstruct
it.

For all its unpretentious air, Damghan possesses two monuments of outstanding interest. One, at the southern edge of the
town, is the Tari Khaneh, or mosque of forty columns, the oldest
surviving Islamic building in Iran, and the one in which traces of
the Arab plan are most plainly visible. The place is a ruin, but we
can see the square court surrounded by arcades, largely standing,
which are deepest on the qibla side. The massive columns of the
arcades give a good indication of the age of the building (c. 775);
those at right angles to the walls once bore mud brick tunnel vaults.
The mosque once had a square minaret; the detached minaret beside
it, which can be climbed, is part of the Seljuk restoration.

The other monument is the Pir-i-Alamdar, a particularly lovely
tomb tower dating from 1027, the oldest extant building of this
type south of the Elburz. The use of kufic inscription in brick for
the purpose of decoration is particularly striking. Rising above a
mass of narrow streets and walled gardens, its happy proportions
give an impression of cheerful solidity; this is enhanced by the
liveliness of the kufic and by the squat dome which is thought to
have been originally covered with a cone.

Damghan also possesses another Seljuk tomb tower, the Chehel
Dukhtaran, or Forty Daughters (a common Persian appellation,
forty being regarded as a lucky number). This stands near the
western entrance to the town; it was built in 1056 and still retains
its cone. In the same enclosure is the Khanqah of Shah Rukh, a
Seljuk building with a Timurid inscription. There is also one
other Seljuk minaret in the town. Seventeen miles west is
Cheshmeh Ali a fine pool with a Qajar pavilion. The road
passes Gerd Kuh an Assassin's castle on the way.

Another dreary forty miles, relieved only by the Seljuk Tower
of Mehmandoost on the right of the road, brings us to Shahrud,
roughly the half-way point between Tehran and Meshed. It is a

modern town of prosperous appearance, remarkable mainly for
the size and number of its poplar trees. A side road leads left from
here and after about eight miles passes, on the left, a large fortified
village, well concealed in orchards. This is Bastam, an ancient
town, with two curious and impressive groups of medieval
religious buildings, about a quarter of a mile apart. They are
interrelated, and their history and topography are more involved
than those of any other buildings in Persia.

Though Bastam was the capital of the whole region south of
the Elburz in Seljuk times, its main claim to fame was, even then,
that it was the birth and burial place of a particularly renowned
Sufi, commonly known as Bayazid-al-Bastami, who died in 874.
It is to honour his memory that so many buildings have pro-
liferated in his native town. They in their turn illustrate one trend
in Islamic architecture, the tendency to concentrate many buildings serving different purposes in one place, to add to them and
even to change their association, so that their original purpose
may be obscured. Such groups stand in the same relation to our
single-purpose building as a symphony to a fugue. The pity is that
at Bastam it is so difficult to disentangle the various themes and
movements.

The larger and more prominent group stands to the north of
the other, and I shall refer to it as the northern group. Seen from
the east its profile consists of a minaret, an iwan (the main
entrance), a conical tower covered with blue tiles, another iwan
and another conical tower. The tall arch of the entrance portal is
covered with intersecting geometrical patterns in high relief
faïence; the moulded flowers in plaitwork, more than any architectural monument of the period, resemble contemporary illuminated manuscripts. A long tunnel-vaulted corridor, simple and
superbly white, leads into a large courtyard generously endowed
with trees. Straight in front of the entrance, between it and the
high iwan which it faces, there is a low, simple tomb; this I
understand to be the grave of the saint himself. Behind it, in a
little room let into the wall opposite, there is some elaborate
plaster-work and a grille; this, to judge from various accounts, is
the tomb or shrine of someone else. The big iwan ahead leads

only into the street behind; the conical tower to the right, on its rectangular base, cannot, so far as I could discover, be entered. Somewhere in this direction there is a madrasseh, but look the other way, for the northern exit from the courtyard is through a modern gateway of unexampled horror.

The iwan on the left, i.e. to the south, with its faïence mosaic in deep relief, leads to better things. On the right is a sanctuary which cannot be entered, but its wooden doors are, according to Pope, the finest that have survived from the fourteenth century. Beyond this we pass through a lobby into a mosque, with winter mosque adjoining. The former has a wooden roof, supported by wooden columns (like Persepolis or the Chehel Situn), and windows with wooden tracery. On the qibla wall is a good plaster mihrab, formerly painted blue.

The peculiar character of this group of buildings is to some extent explained by its history. The oldest, Seljuk, part is the mosque and adjoining minaret (which can only be seen from without). Under Oljeitu the whole place was renovated and enlarged. The mosque had to be re-roofed. A Damghan artist named Mohammed was responsible for this work and probably for the mihrab, which is signed M. The two iwans date from 1313 and were part of this restoration. The madrasseh was built by Shah Rukh. Towards the end of the nineteenth century the dome of the mosque collapsed, so the building was given a wooden roof, which had to rest on wooden columns. Hence its odd look today.

The southern group of buildings at Bastam is less conspicuous, less assorted, but no less interesting. They lie down a series of byways past the minaret, on the edge of open space from which the town has receded. They consist of the Friday Mosque, which is devoid of interest, an unusual cloister and a splendid tomb tower. This is best seen from the dilapidated area beyond it. It was begun in 1300 by the same Mohammed of Damghan who rebuilt the shrine of Bayazid and is one of the great circular fluted towers in the tradition of Gunbad-i-Kabus and Rayy. As with the Pir-i-Alamdar at Damghan, its conical roof has dis-appeared, leaving it with a smaller circular dome. The interior of the adjacent mosque is reached through an inconspicuous door jutting out into the street. To the right of the mosque is the fine cloister. Its qibla wall is divided into three bays separated by short partitions, each pierced by a door crowned by a broken-headed arch. The walls are covered with a handsome stucco design. But the glory of the cloister is the mihrab, also stucco, with inscription panels and intertwining arabesques. This belongs to the same period as the mihrab in the mosque of the shrine, and may well be by the same artist.

The tract of road for a hundred miles east of Shahrud was once known as the 'Stages of Terror' and small circular towers still visible were erected as a protection against Turkoman raids. Apart from Sabzevar whose gaunt Seljuk minaret has an illegible inscription and an unusual cut brick design, the only place of interest in the three hundred miles between Shahrud and Meshed is Nishapur. This, the home of Omar Khayyám, has had an even more chequered history than most ancient Iranian cities. Founded in Sassanian times and named after Shapur, it became the capital of Khorasan after the Arab conquest, and rose to great importance during the tenth century. Like Rayy and Gurgan it is one of the main sources of the pottery of this period. Toghril Beg, the first of the Seljuks, made it his capital in 1037. Omar Khayyám, who is known in Iran as a respectable astronomer and philosopher but not highly rated as a poet, died there in 1123. Nishapur was damaged by an earthquake in 1145 and by the invasion of the Ghuzz Turkomans in 1153, yet rebuilt by the time Yaqut visited it in 1216. But its revival was short lived, and it was the first city in what is now Iran to feel the full force of the Mongol invasion in 1221. Farid uddin Attar, a mystic poet more honoured in his own country than Omar, was killed here at that time. Despite a further Mongol invasion in 1269, and another earthquake in 1281, Clavijo found it a substantial city at the beginning of the fourteenth century. But it was soon overtaken and surpassed by Meshed, and after its further destruction at the hands of the Afghans in 1722, Nadir Shah made Meshed his capital and Nishapur ceased to have even symbolic importance. Curzon was probably right when he said that it 'had certainly been destroyed and rebuilt more than any other city in the world'.

Nishapur is a place of tombs. Omar lies buried in the garden of the shrine of Muhammed Mahruq, built about 1570; this is a dome on a high drum with light blue tiles, in a charming setting, and with a dazzling white interior. Not far away is the tomb of Farid uddin Attar. Some of the finest turquoise is mined in the mountains near Nishapur.

Farther along the road towards Meshed is the Qadamgah, a shrine built for pilgrims by Shah Suleiman in 1643 to cover two black stones on which the Imam Reza is said to have left his imprint. An octagonal building covered with a blue dome, it is in its small way in the tradition which begins with the tomb of Ismail the Samanid, who died in 907, at Bokhara.

At last we come to Meshed, the fourth city of Iran. Lying in a broad green plain bounded by mountain ranges on the south-west and north-east, it is approached by long straight avenues of poplars, a well-planned city with many of the attributes of a capital. Meshed has a northern air. Though nearly a thousand feet lower than Tehran, the climate is harsh and changeable, and the predominant tone of the place is pale – its setting is a gentle blue sky, soft greens, and buildings of toneless brick; nevertheless Meshed seems to have less mud or dust than elsewhere in Iran.

Meshed owes its site and size not to its commercial importance or its position on great trade routes, but to accidents of religion. Had Imam Reza not died here in 817 in the little village of Sanabad, there would be no city on this site. The very name means the place of martyrdom. The first shrine on the site was built by Haroun al Rashid's son, and the history of the town is largely the history of the shrine. It may be summarized briefly. A new shrine was built by Mahmud of Ghazna in 1009. The town was sacked by the Mongols in 1221, but the shrine was restored by Oljeitu in about 1300. The city grew as a result of the destruction of Tus by the Mongols in 1390; it was favoured by Shah Rukh whose wife Gawhar Shad built the great mosque which bears her name in 1414. It became increasingly a place of pilgrimage under the Safavids, and the shrine was further enlarged by

Shah Abbas. Meshed was the capital of Iran under Nadir Shah from 1736 to 1747; further additions were made to the shrine by Fath Ali Shah. By now Meshed had become an important point on the trade route between Turkestan and the West, but it was adversely affected by the Russian advance into Central Asia and the building of the trans-Caspian railway. Today, as capital and commercial centre of the relatively fertile province of Khorasan – the largest in the country – and as the terminus of the eastern railway, Meshed is a thriving place; but its main source of income and prosperity is still the pilgrims, and it is visited by up to one million Shi'as annually, accommodated for the most part in large caravanserais. And the shrine is the most important institution in Meshed; moreover, it is the largest owner of land in Iran, not excluding the Royal Estates and government lands. The process of acquiring property started nearly a thousand years ago when a certain rich man presented his land to the shrine in order to salve his pricking conscience – for what crime history does not relate. Outside Meshed there is a large estate which was taken over only fifty years ago from a merchant named Malik who owed money to the shrine. The shrine as an economic entity dominates Meshed and is without rival in Khorasan; furthermore it owns property or villages in Azerbaijan, Kerman, near Karaj and even in Afghanistan.

For the non-Moslem visitor, Meshed is a tantalizing place. With one glorious exception, it is totally lacking in buildings of historical or architectural interest. The little mausoleum of Khwaja Rabi, to the north of the city, built by Shah Abbas to the orthodox mausoleum design, an octagon surmounted by a blue dome, is overrun by picknickers and pilgrims. For the rest, everything is concentrated in and immediately round the shrine, and, with certain very limited exceptions, is barred to the unbeliever. Reza Shah bent a great circle of avenues round the central complex of buildings, which enables them to be seen from without, but any attempt to enter any part of the great circle, except the short alleyways of the old bazaar, without proper authorization is emphatically not recommended. With proper credentials, however, it is possible to enter the Museum, which lies at the end of a garden carved out of the circle on its south-east side, to visit the tile factory on the roof of the Mosque of Gawhar Shad, and to look down from there, or even from one of the minarets, into its great court. What follows, therefore, is based on only a little personal observation, and much more on reading and hearsay.

The proliferation of buildings within the great circle, which is some 400 yards in diameter, is staggering. It must be one of the greatest, if not the greatest, concentration of religious buildings in the world, Mecca not excluded. The shrine proper, with its two great Old and New Courts, the Sahn-i-Kohneh and the Sahn-i-No, and its innumerable sanctuaries, covers a vast area to the north, and on both sides of the central avenue. The Gawhar Shad Mosque is only surpassed by the Royal and Friday Mosques at Isfahan in size. In addition there is another mosque, the New Mosque, and no less than five madrassehs. The garden in front of the museum occupies nearly two acres. The edges of the circle are indented with numerous alleyways and streets; and there are great gates at the east and west end of the circle, leading respectively to the Khiaban-i-Pain (Lower Avenue) and Khiaban-i-Bala (Upper Avenue), the two main thoroughfares of Meshed.

As its history would indicate, the shrine complex is a jumble of periods and styles. The oldest part of the building consists of a dado, frieze and three mihrabs dating from the thirteenth century. There is evidence of Oljeitu's restoration in the base of the dome. To the early Timurid period belong not only the Mosque of Gawhar Shad but also two rooms in the shrine, the Dar-al-Huffiz and the Dar-as-Siyada (both subjected to Qajar restoration). The Madrasseh Do-Dar, the most interesting of the subsidiary buildings, lying to the west of the Sahn-i-Kohneh, with its four-iwan plan and characteristically Timurid dome, dates from the middle of the fifteenth century. The south-west side of the Sahn-i-Kohneh, with its gold iwan known as the Tala-i-Naderi, was constructed at the end of the same century. The minaret on the opposite side of the same court is sixteenth century (Shah Tahmasp). Shah Abbas was responsible for the redecoration of the great golden dome in 1606, and for the completion of the Sahn-i-Kohneh, including the construction of the sanctuary of Allah

Verdi Khan, named after one of his generals who is also associated with one of Isfahan's great bridges. This sanctuary alone, Pope tells us, will bear comparison with the Sheikh Lutfullah Mosque at Isfahan; with its seventy-foot dome, thirty-six feet in diameter, it is more energetic in form, an effect enhanced by the bewildering mass of stalactites in the interior. The floor is plain turquoise, the dado of a yellowish marble. The quality of the faïence mosaic may fall short of that in the Lutfullah and the general effect be less serene and spacious, but if anything it surpasses its contemporary in opulence.

Nor is this the only comparison with Isfahan. The northern iwan of the Sahn-i-Kohneh, beside Shah Tahmasp's minaret, dates from the time of Shah Suleiman (1680), as does the madrasseh behind it. This iwan, according to Pope, 'rivals if it does not surpass the portal of the Royal Mosque (at Isfahan)'. Finally the second golden iwan in the Sahn-i-No was added by Fath Ali Shah.

It is difficult, without having been inside, to convey an impression of this variegated patchwork of holy places. But what one can glimpse through the portals and from the Museum garden or the roof of the Gawhar Shad – the golden dome and minarets, the bejewelled courtyard of the mosque, the superb tracery of the faïence mosaic in high relief on its minarets – makes one quite ready to believe Pope when he says, 'no other group of buildings in the world gives such an effect of opulence'. The Gawhar Shad Mosque in particular is, or would be, a paradise for the student of faïence mosaic at its heyday, in the fifteenth century. Robert Byron notes* that architectural ornament is applied here in no less than nine different forms. The mosque, like the shrine, is in a splendid state of preservation. A minaret damaged in an earthquake in 1948 has been repaired, the modern tile mosaics issuing from the little factory on the roof where the arts of glazing and chipping are still jealously preserved in skilled hands. New decoration, too, is constantly being added to the iwan and arcades on the outside of the mosque, facing the garden of the Museum.

The Shrine Museum, the only place within the holy precinct

* Chapter contributed to *A Survey of Persian Art* (Pope).

in which the non-Moslem visitor may easily set foot, is well worth a visit. It contains a small, well-arranged collection of pottery, textiles, silver, carpets and other treasures presented to or acquired by the Shrine. Particularly remarkable are a stone basin, eight feet in diameter dating from 1201; an iron window with gold lettering in the name of Shah Rukh (1414); a sculptured wooden door of 1547; and a particularly fine Safavid carpet, twenty feet by eight feet with a striking yellow border and floral vine meander.

A magnet which draws pilgrims from far and near, Meshed is also the border town of Turkmenistan, the gateway of Central Asia, the capital of what is racially the most variegated province in Iran, and a neighbour to the desert. The heart of this secular Meshed is the Khiaban-i-Pain, the long avenue which runs east from the Shrine. It is not a beautiful street; the buildings, with the exception of a few set back in alleys, are modern and tawdry; it has nothing of the glamour and mystery of the covered bazaars of Isfahan, Yazd, Tabriz and elsewhere.* But it is pulsating with activity and full of colour and contrast. For once the women, with their uniformly blue chadors, provide less variety than the men. White-turbaned Baluchis with swarthy features jostle with high-cheekboned Turkomans, wearing not the fur caps of the steppe but dashing yellow turbans. The green bandana, too, the hallmark of the sayyid, is much in evidence, covering, maybe, a bearded face, whose owner strides arrogantly through the crowds with an impatient sweep of the shoulder. Donkeys or camels jog wearily out of side streets, and merchants fill the air with cries of their wares. This is not the place for hidden treasures or the finer fruits of the Persian artistic genius; but the Khiaban-i-Pain provides a dazzling display of local homely objects of a kind which, divorced from their home surroundings, look exotic: textiles, hats, beads and ropes. The first, some perhaps imported from Russia, offer a bewildering variety of colour and design; they are the frame or background of every second shop. Hats range from the regular shab kola or night cap, an embroidered cloth affair used as a base for the turban, to every shape and shade of

* Written in 1961.

the turban itself. He who resists them is strong-minded indeed. The beads are for religious use and of all shapes and colours, with amber predominating. The rope shops are beautifully arranged and have a paradoxically nautical air. Rope is available in many forms, including those admirable rope slippers known as givehs, the normal footwear of the Iranian peasant, equally suitable for sandy plain or rocky mountains provided the weather is dry. The Meshed giveh is of exceptional design and particularly well made. Finally, one will almost inevitably surrender before the poustine, a short coat cut from mountain sheep, the unclipped hair forming the inside and the smooth skin, dyed yellow and embroidered, on the outside of the jacket. These are beautifully warm and exceptionally cheap; when transported to a damper climate, they can be guaranteed to evoke the authentic scent of the steppe; whether this is an advantage or not is a matter of taste.

From the Khiaban-i-Pain, it is an easy transition to the open country, a phrase more appropriate to much of Khorasan than to most of the rest of Iran, which is open enough, but not an Englishman's idea of country. The central valley of Khorasan in which Meshed stands and which runs from near Bujnurd in the north-west to the Soviet border in the south-east, is glorious open country, with gentle rounded mountains and great pastures filled with sheep. The predominant tone is whitish-grey – the soil, the sheep, the turbans of the shepherds, the snow on the distant peaks. Khorasan as a whole embraces a wide range of scenery, from the oases and windswept deserts of the south-east to the grim fast-nesses of the Kalat-i-Naderi on the Soviet border north of Meshed and the fields and valleys around and beyond Bujnurd. As befits a frontier zone exposed to the first onrush of the Asiatic invader, but at the same time one of the cradles of Iranian civiliza-tion, the province is rich in historic remains, with ruined caravan-serais, crumbling mosques and madrassehs and lonely Seljuk and Mongol tomb towers. Only a few examples can be mentioned here.

If we cover Khorasan anti-clockwise, starting at seven o'clock, so to speak, we begin with Tabas,* a large oasis at 2,000 feet above sea level in a wide flat hole between the Dasht-i-Kavir and the

* Largely destroyed, alas, in the 1978 earthquake.

Dasht-i-Lut, the remotest town of its size, about 8,000 inhabitants, in all Iran. In early times Tabas had considerable importance owing to its position on the trade route; it was later taken in hand by the Zand dynasty and considerably embellished in the eighteenth century. Although time has long stood still there, Tabas has an air of grandeur about it, such as you would not expect to find in a mud village three hundred miles from anywhere. This is due, not to the costumes of the inhabitants, which are surprisingly featureless, but in some measure to its monuments: the remains of an ancient citadel which straddles the road impressively as you enter from Yazd; a large Friday Mosque and two Seljuk minarets of baked brick studded with blue tiles; an eighteenth-century madrasseh; outside the walls, the tomb of Sultan Huseyn, brother of the Iman Reza, a twelfth-century building reconstructed like much else in Tabas under Karim Khan Zand, with attractive wall paintings of the period; and 20 km to the west, the Mazar-i-Sipahsalar Tabas, an open mausoleum largely constructed of mud brick with a minimum of internal decoration, perhaps fifteenth century. But the planning and setting of the town perhaps contributes even more to its grandeur. A long avenue flanked by old houses with wind towers and domes, with large gardens behind, leads up from the market-place between two purling streams to the Municipal Park. This was constructed in the eighteenth century, and has a pool and a water-chute, neat hedges and formal borders, cool shade from palms and cypresses, and a hilarious ornamental doorway with painted military figures in relief, of more than life-size, a startlingly realistic example of local art.

Tabas as a whole, with its date groves and orange trees, its tropical shrubs and heavy heat, is an exotic growth in Central Persia. Few foreigners, or indeed Persians for that matter, have visited it, but among those that have I have heard it described as a Paradise on earth, a perfect place for retirement, and an ideal winter resort. Through the kindness of my host, I found it the perfect resting place between two arduous journeys.

The first day's drive from Tabas in the direction of Meshed takes one past walled, wind-towered villages of weird beauty, the once charming town of Firdaus (that is to say, Paradise itself,

formerly known as Tun or Hell) which was largely destroyed in
the 1968 earthquake, though the very fine early thirteenth-
century Friday Mosque with elegant brickwork and red plaster
decoration has survived; and beyond that a great deal of desert,
which at one point howled so hard we had to stop the car. At
Gunabad there is another pre-Mongol mosque while Bidokht a
little further is notable for a Sufi monastery with a guest-house
(where we stayed) and orange groves; the ladies of the place wear
pale grey chadors which accord well with the general dusty grey-
ness of this bleak region.

Apart from Tabas, the most interesting place in Khorasan
after Meshed is Turbat-i-Shaikh Jam, on the road to Herat not
far from the Afghan frontier (see *Iran* IX). Its principal glory is
the Shrine of Ahmad ibn Abu'l Hasan, Shaikh Jam, a Sufi theologian and preacher (d. 1141). The building bears an inscription
of 1440 and to the left of the great portal a splendid stucco mihrab
of the fifteenth century has recently been discovered. The shrine
was restored by Shah Abbas who, tradition avers, set out to
destroy it in the belief that Shaikh Jam was a Sunni; but most of
the building was saved and the restoration effected when a docu-
ment was produced claiming that, in fact, he was a Shi'a. Behind
the shrine is an enchanting little Friday Mosque and on the south-
east side the remains of a Sunni oratory with some fourteenth-
century stucco and brickwork (most of the mihrab is in the
Tehran Archaeological Museum).

Pope suggests that the Shrine of Shaikh Jam may have been
built by the same architect as the Khwaja Abd Allah Huseyn at
Gazur Gah, Herat, and the mausoleum to Zayd-al-Din at Taiabad
on the Persian side of the frontier. The latter dates from the reign
of Shah Rukh and has splendid tilework of this (or a slightly
later) period.

From Taiabad a road leads west and then north to Haideri,
passing Kerat with a Seljuk minaret and Sang-i-Pain with two
Seljuk mosques, the Masjid-i-Gunbad with a splendid mihrab
and the Friday Mosque with fine brickwork. Khargird (off to
the left) has the earliest identified madrasseh on the four-iwan
plan (1092) named the Nizamiyeh after Nizam ul Mulk, and a

later madrasseh with magnificent Timurid tilework from the same hand as that of the Gawhar Shad at Meshed. Reshkhar (farther on, also to the left) boasts a domed building with a Timurid inscription and remarkable painted plaster work usually associated with an earlier (or later) period.

There is another ancient road eastwards from Meshed leading to Sarakhs where the Soviet frontier turns south. It passes various minor monuments, including the interesting open-domed building at Mazar-i-Sangvar and two stumps (the Do Barar) which could have been the base of a ceremonial arch on the road between the two great caravanserais the Robat Mahi (1020–21) with an unusual early squinch and the Robat Sharaf (see p. 59). Sarakhs itself has a domed mausoleum of 1356 with brick and stucco decoration. It is here that one (or rather the road) crosses the frontier to Samarkand. It is also the site of a large natural gas field in which a petro-chemical and fertilizer plant has been constructed.

Tus, the city of the plain which flourished before the Imam Reza died or Meshed was born, lies some fifteen miles to the north. There is little to show for it today except the so-called Harounieh, or mausoleum of Haroun-al-Rashid, a square domed building, which is in fact believed to be the tomb of the mystic poet el Ghazali who died in 1111. Nearby is the tomb of Firdausi, who was born at Tus in the early tenth century, and whose great patriotic epic, the *Shahnameh* or *Book of Kings*, has a unique appeal and can still be recited by many who are otherwise illiterate.

Beyond the tomb, though scarcely accessible from it, runs a track into the mountains towards the Kalat-i-Naderi, the great natural fortress formed by a wall of mountains fifty miles long, where Nadir Shah concealed his Indian loot and to which Curzon failed to gain admission in 1889. It is a plateau about eighteen miles long and six to ten miles wide completely enclosed by precipitous cliffs. In the village of Gugumaz (Kalat), three miles down-stream, is a curious building with exquisite floral reliefs, very Indian in style, which is thought to have been Nadir's tomb or treasure house though it may in fact date from the nineteenth century. To reach Kalat-i-Naderi both Land-Rover and prior permission are essential. Perhaps because it was his first glimpse of Persia, Curzon penned these uncompromising lines about the mountains of Khorasan:

'Nothing can exceed the bleak sterility of their outward forms. Unredeemed by any verdure but a stunted and scanty growth of juniper, watered by a few springs, and with little or no soil upon the slopes, the grey limestone tells with frank and forbidding effrontery its remote geological tale.'

Also in this area between Meshed and the northern frontier, near the town of Darreh-Gaz is the newly discovered Mongol mausoleum of Auliya Shadmin at Nowkhandan, with kite-shaped squinches and delicate inscriptions.

There are other tombs in Khorasan worth a passing mention. At Sangbast, on the road to Herat, not far from Meshed, is the presumed tomb of Arslan Jadib, a squat brick structure with an octagonal base and a flat dome having fine brickwork on the interior. More finished are three later tomb towers, all round, of outstanding interest. That at Radkan East (about 1280, restored in 1968) between Meshed and Kuchan, has round columns with lozenge decorations in the brick, the spaces between the heads of the columns being ingeniously finished off with a trefoil or fleur-de-lys moulding which would look at home in North Oxford. Another at Kishmar, a prosperous village west of Turbat-i-Haideri, was clearly built under the inspiration of Radkan. It has alternating round and square pointed columns, the same trefoil effect and with a lozenge decoration executed in relief. The third at Ahangan, twelve miles north of Meshed, has eight columns which correspond to its octagonal interior, and a furrowed or pleated brick dome. The whole surface is studded with sea-blue and turquoise tiles in the form of flowers, stars or crosses. These buildings, especially the first two, betray a riot of imagination and an opulence of taste which may surprise those unfamiliar with Mongol architecture. Mention must also be made of an isolated twelfth-century minaret some fifty feet high at Firuzabad near Kishmar.

The westernmost town, where we leave Khorasan, is Bujnurd,

lying in a rich basin above the valley of the Atrek, which later forms the Iran-Soviet boundary. The country around is green and varied and what the French call *accidenté*; indeed I would say that there was no prettier tract in Iran. The greenness derives from the fact that clouds from the Caspian blown by the west wind up the Atrek valley deposit rain here in moderate quantities at most seasons of the year. Bujnurd is thus a happy half-way house between high desert and sub-tropical forest, and agriculture can be practised without irrigation. The inhabitants of the region are mostly Kurdish or Turkoman, with the Kurds predominating. Certain Kurdish tribes, among them the vigorous Shadloo, were brought here by Shah Abbas to defend the frontier against the Turkoman; and here they have remained, and flourished, and made an even pleasanter and greener land than in their own native Kurdistan. The Turkomans, easily distinguishable by their features and their fur hats, are responsible for the elephant-foot carpets which are a feature of the bazaar. At a private shrine up the valley, an idyllic spot belonging to the Shadloo tribe, there is a large spring and a pool filled with enormous barbel. The traveller leaves Bujnurd, and Khorasan, with regret.

CHAPTER SIX

The Caspian Rain-Belt

The Iranian plateau and the Caspian hinterland have almost no features in common. All that we associate with the plateau – the harsh light, the parched air, the vast expanse of desert and mountains occasionally fringed with green, the sparse but tidy vegetation, the crowded domed mud villages of the plain, the flat-roofed stone settlements clinging to the mountains which seem to have come out of Central Asia, the irrigation channels and clear streams, the mighty if scattered relics of an ancient civilization, the blue-domed shrines, the peasant cap or kola, the camel and the donkey – all these disappear. We enter instead a closed world, shut in on itself, and cut off from all save the sea by a great green wall of mountains. The air is heavy, the light fitful, the vegetation almost everywhere relentlessly lush. The houses are mostly of wood roofed with thatch or shingles and often on stilts, the villages scattered and half concealed in trees, the earth sodden. Human habitation here seems ageless, yet somehow not very old, like a labourer in his forties seared with toil and sweat. Even the mosques are like barns with little peaked towers for minarets. The peasants are bowed and wrinkled with generations of malaria and damp heat, but often gaily dressed; they carry large umbrellas even on the finest days and are often seen with long poles slung horizontally across their backs bearing baskets filled with melons, like Chinese coolies. Splendid Turko-man horses graze in the pastures, and ungainly water buffaloes wallow in the swamps. By turns India, Indonesia, Northern Italy or the Riviera, the Caspian rain-belt has nothing to show that we normally associate with Iran.

'The Caspian Sea,' wrote Herbert, . 'is deservedly ranked amongst the wonders of the world. . . . Many great and noble rivers enter . . . thus swelling her concave womb. . . . Considering how these mighty rivers are incessantly vomiting their full gorged watery stomachs into it, in reason it may be granted it would overflow its banks did it not empty as well as receive.' What Herbert did not know was of the loss by evaporation. Clouds thus formed over the great inland sea, which to the west, north and east is bounded by desert, are blown south and east towards the mountains and give rainfall throughout the year varying from fifty-five inches in the west to twenty in Gurgan. The rain is heaviest on the coast itself, and on the northern slopes which are densely forested; the higher mountains are drier, and in the interior there are southern slopes and basins protected from the north where the all-pervading forest stops, and there is instead a dry pastureland which bears some resemblance to the deserts of the plateau. These freaks of nature give extraordinary variety to the scenery, and provide an object lesson on the effects of climate upon landscape.

The esteem in which this exotic region is held varies considerably according to the point of view. For the inhabitant of the plateau, scorched by summer sun or chilled by winter frosts, blinded by light or parched by dust, or perhaps a little jaded by altitude, or social life, the Caspian offers ease, relaxation, generous greenery, and limitless grey sands facing a tepid salty sea. For the Safavids it was a favourite place of repose from the ardours of Isfahan. Reza Shah put it high in his priorities for development, building a new railway and a new road, repairing existing roads, and constructing two ports, textile factories, and a surprising number of civic centres in the coastal towns. In addition he built three hotels, two of them larger than anything else known in Iran at the time; his dream was to make this coast the Riviera of the Middle East. These hotels and other resorts are greatly frequented by Tehran society at all seasons, and the forest-clad hills, mountain streams, and great inland marshes at each end of the coast are the sportsman's paradise. For the visitor from rainier climes, however, the Caspian does not offer the same beneficient contrasts. The authentic tang of the plateau is missing, the coast is drab, the forests oppressive, the atmosphere foetid and soggy.

But to obtain a complete picture of Iran a visit to the Caspian region is imperative. Between a fifth and a quarter of the population live in these provinces. With their rice paddies, their tea plantations, their caviar factories and their forests, they play a vital role in the economy of the country. The Caspian provinces were the last to be overwhelmed by the Arab conquest. They had a flourishing and largely independent existence in the ninth and tenth centuries. They were harried by the Mongol invaders, both Yenghiz and Timur, and in more recent times, especially in Mazanderan, by Turkomans and earthquakes. Shah Abbas settled here thirty thousand Christian families threatened by Turkish invasions, constructed a 'stone carpet' (sang farsh) across the mountains into Mazanderan, and built two great palaces at Farahabad and Ashraf (the modern Behshahr). Relatively inaccessible to the rest of Iran, the Caspian provinces have always been exposed to the north, more especially the north-east. Consequently the Russians have from time to time nourished territorial ambitions here; there was a Bolshevik republic in Gilan after the First World War, a Soviet naval station in Astarabad Bay, and Russian-owned and operated caviar factors at Pahlevi and Babolsar until 1952. At the same time, the talent and ability of the Gilani and Mazanderani have made an important contribution to Iranian development, and the number of prominent Iranians today who originate from these provinces is noteworthy. The provinces have much in common with Scotland: a last stronghold of original inhabitants against invaders from the south; historically a remote, rather undeveloped region protected by mountains; favoured by kings for pleasure purposes and patronized by holiday-makers today; the land from which royal families and leading men of affairs stem.

A journey through the highlands in the eighteenth century was child's play compared with that between the Caspian and the plateau at almost any time before the present day. The forests were infested by lions and tigers and the lowlands by snakes and malarial mosquitoes. The weather was treacherous in the extreme and the route unbelievably perilous. In the seventeenth century, no doubt, travellers to the Caspian, like Pietro della Valle, only went in search of the monarch or in the wake of some ambassador himself in search of the monarch, as in Thomas Herbert's case. But up to and even after the First World War, the normal route from Western Europe to Tehran lay across Russia, by sea from Baku to Enzeli (now Bandar Pahlevi) and thence by road up the Sefid Rud valley to Kazvin. This, as we shall see later, is by far the easiest of the routes through the Elburz, but it was difficult enough. Harold Nicolson describes in his biography of his father* how Arthur Nicolson, his wife and family made the journey in 1887. It took six days, and when riding along a narrow path beside a precipice, strapped on to the side of her horse, the children's governess (immortalized as Miss Plimsoll in *Some People*) took one look over the edge and exclaimed: 'Take me back to Littlehampton', whereupon her stern employer leapt from his saddle and strapped her on more firmly than before.

For practical purposes the Caspian coast is no longer an international thoroughfare; the traveller arrives, as is aesthetically correct, on the plateau, and has a choice of eight road routes, and one railway, by which he can pay his visit to Persia's playground by the sad grey sea. I have travelled over these routes almost without a qualm, certainly without a backward thought for Littlehampton; they could not be more varied, and each is exciting in a different way.

The eight routes are: from Ardebil to Astara on the Soviet frontier, from Mianeh, via Heroabad, to Hashtpar; from Kazvin through Manjil to Resht; from Tehran (Karaj) to Chalus; from Tehran by the Haraz valley to Amol; from Firuzkuh beside the railway to Shahi; from Shahrud to Shahpasand (Gurgan); and from Bujnurd to Gunbad-i-Kabus. Each merits description in some detail.

The Ardebil-Astara road is perhaps the most startling. For fifteen miles east of Ardebil (see p. 154) there is no hint of change. The road rises slowly across a dusty plateau rimmed by bare hills. It enters a little valley whose grassy slopes are studded with

* *Sir Arthur Nicolson, Bart., First Lord Carnock*, 1930.

hawthorn bushes, the best imitation I know of the South Downs. One expects at the top – and the track gives a curve as it rises to the summit – to see the English Channel sparkling a few hundred feet below. Instead, one looks down five thousand feet into a great green chasm. Rich grassy slopes fall steeply away in a vast amphitheatre; a whole series of wild valleys, all tributaries of the main cleft, open up to the left and later to the right; row on row of densely wooded mountains fill the horizon; the road dips down precipitously in great sweeps and circles, pirouetting dizzily into the abyss. Even the most politically innocent traveller must observe the contrast between the two sides of the main valley; to the right, broad stretches of wheat and pasture, tilled lands at the most improbable angles rescued from the forest, substantial grey shingled villages nestling in their bowers of walnut and hazel. This is Iran. To the left, across the valley, is Russia; unbroken forest without sign of cultivation or life until, descending and approaching, one sees look-out towers, a little white settlement of frontier guards, and the double barbed wire barrier cutting like a swathe through the trees. At the bottom of the valley, where the air is steamy and the thicket closes in, the road runs beside the stream which forms the boundary, and the iron curtain is scarcely a stone's throw away. When we enter the fertile coastal plain, only a few miles wide here, the line of look-out towers disappears to the left behind the trees, and we almost forget that this is a frontier town. Astara, with its relaxed air, its well-built symmetrical red-roofed buildings spaced out round a sort of green, can lay some claim, on a sunny day, to looking the gayest and sprightliest little town in Persia. It is now the terminus of a gas line to the U.S.S.R.

The second route starts on a bad road from Mianeh, ascending long fertile valleys to Heroabad, capital of the Khalkhal district where there is a simple hotel. From here the road climbs to the summer pastures where Gilani nomads encamp during the hot months in a downland landscape from which the traveller looks down to forested slopes and the Caspian Sea shimmering (in the right weather) several thousand feet below. The road then descends through dense woodland to the sawmill at Khalifabad (permission required) though an alternative route is under construction to Hashtpar ten miles farther north. This whole region of the Talesh Hills is otherwise largely inaccessible; it is also ravishingly beautiful.

The Kazvin-Rasht road, *pace* Miss Plimsoll, is altogether more staid. It crosses no great range of mountains, but slips over the edge of a gaunt plateau behind Kazvin into a dry, rocky valley which leads into the Sefid Rud. This is the greatest river of northern Iran. On part of its course, where it passes through Turki-speaking country, it is known by its Turkish name, the Qizil Uzun. At Manjil it is joined by another mighty stream, the Shahrud, whose upper courses, the Alamut and Taleghan rivers, rise respectively in the Takht-i-Suleiman massif and the Elburz north of Tehran. This complex of valleys running north-west and south-east through the heart of the Elburz is protected from the north by high mountain ranges, and so, like the plateau, the valleys are dry; but they differ from the plateau in their altitude, for their lower reaches, Manjil, for instance, are less than 2000 feet above sea level. The country round Manjil is in consequence hotter, drier and dustier than any other place in northern Iran. In another respect, too, the climate is disobliging. After Manjil the Sefid Rud runs north, first through a small gorge and then into a broader valley. This serves as a vent-hole between the dry air of the interior and the humid atmosphere of the coast. There are, they say, few days in the year when the wind does not blow at Manjil at between thirty and forty miles an hour, at least in the afternoon.

But this uncomfortable bottleneck is a place of both economic and historical significance. Manjil is the site of the enormous Empress Farah dam, harnessing the waters of both Shah Rud and Sefid Rud (opened 1962). At first sight it might appear odd that a large dam should be built in dry country to supply more water to the rain-belt. But on the Caspian rain supply is fickle when most needed during the rice-growing season in June and July. The dam in addition to providing electric generating capacity will help to remedy this deficiency.

Historical significance resides in a site some fifteen miles

upstream from Manjil which, despite the reservoir, is still accessible, though the last kilometre must be undertaken on foot or by
Land-Rover, and when the dam is up some wading may be
required. This is Samiran, the Buyid capital of Dailam, a tenth-
century kingdom in north-west Iran accurately described by the
Arab geographer Yakut. There can still be seen here two well-
preserved tomb towers, the remains of a presumed Assassin's
castle and of a mosque, city walls, and the more modern shrine
known as the Imamzadeh Qasim.

After passing the dam the road descends a narrow gorge to
the straggling village of Rudbar, fourteen miles to the north-east
of which the Iranian Archaeological Service under the leadership
of Dr Negahban, discovered in 1961 the Royal Tombs of Marlik,
dating from about 1000 B.C. and found to contain an unusual
quantity of valuable objects in gold and silver and bronze, the
finest perhaps a 17 cm gold bowl decorated in high relief with a
double row of unicorns (illustrated in *Iran* II and to be seen in
the Tehran Museum).

The road to Rasht continues winding round a curious windswept basin, the only place in Iran where the olive flourishes.
Across the valley there are upland meadows, and stretches of
forest on the northward-facing slopes. Farther on, the river
widens out into a great bed about half a mile wide, which forms
a vast lake in spring. Only after this does the road enter woodland. First the steep banks are covered with scrub, and later with
forest. There are splendid views over the river, fringed here by
rice-paddies. As often as not, one turns round a headland to find
mist or driving rain. The last twenty miles into Resht run across
a flat fertile plain dotted with thatched houses on stilts and clut-
tered with untidy hedgerows. The river scenery on this route,
its most impressive feature, is seen to best advantage going
north.

The Karaj-Chalus road, the route best known to weekend
visitors from Tehran, is the most dramatic of the eight crossings.
It was completed by Reza Shah in the 1930s in furtherance of
his design to develop the Caspian as a holiday resort; it is well
designed and beautifully engineered. It passes close to some of

the finest mountain scenery in Iran, and crossing the Elburz at over 9,000 feet is substantially higher than any other motor road to the Caspian. The first section of the road climbs over a shoulder to bypass the Karaj dam, then winds for a long way up the dry valley enclosed between gigantic rock formations of sinister aspect. Occasionally the valley opens a little, giving a narrow thread of pure emerald, only to close in again in claustrophobic seclusion. Gone are the great vistas of the plateau; one has the sense instead of moving into the bowels of the earth. But there are some lovely side valleys leading out of this purgatory; in one, the Do-ab, on the east, the river is well stocked with trout, and a track winds past rocks and orchards to the village of Shahristanak, a favourite summer residence of Nasr-uddin Shah, which he would approach with all his retinue of servants, mules and camels by a broad track, still visible, leading over the summit of Tuchal. Soon after this the scenery suddenly changes; we enter a red land, in which the soil is scarlet and the plentiful vegetation a brilliant emerald. Large villages hang on the slopes amid well-watered fields, poplars marking irrigation ditches rise high above the valley, snow peaks appear, and black streaks on the hillsides give evidence of coal. At the village of Gach-i-Sar, lying at over 7,000 feet, there is an outcrop of chalk; the elegant little building in a grove of poplars by the roadside is Reza Shah's hotel. Just after this the road turns sharply to the left and starts to climb. A new ski-resort at 9,000 feet, Dizin, is 16 kilometres from here. There are grand views down the valley and away to the northern slopes of Tuchal. In spring these broad-backed hills are faintly green, but the snow still lies in the shady hollows; lorries fill up here with grey paste to stock the icehouses of Tehran. Avalanches are frequent, though the road is protected in several places by snow barricades. After some four miles we reach the tunnel, open only to one-way traffic and often involving a tedious wait. It is three miles long, unlighted, rough, and in summer very, very wet. It is a shock to come out of the blinding sunlight into this dark hole, and receive a cataract of water on the bonnet which washes away all the dust accumulated during that long toil up the Karaj valley. After this watery introduction, many people expect to find the Caspian scenery they have heard about in full vigour on the other side. But in fact, as a clear day will reveal, the Caspian end of the tunnel is different only in colour and tone from the southern side. There is more green grass, the rocks are less naked; but we are at 9,000 feet, well above the tree line. Only as the road descends does the vegetation appear. There is a hillside ablaze with purple and yellow iris;* then the bushes begin. In one delectable spot, where the road curves by the first village, I once in June found forty varieties of wild flowers within a hundred yards. The road swings round the tousled buttresses of a gigantic valley; wooded hills open upon every side, and little mountain villages blackened by their only industry, that of charcoal burning, stand out far below in their islands of green fields. After burrowing through a rock, the road descends in a series of sharp curves two thousand feet to the bottom of the valley floor and runs for ten miles or so through a terrifying gorge with overhanging rocks, rushing streams, and torrential waterfalls. It emerges at last, soon after passing a little dank pavilion built by Reza Shah, now a chaikhaneh, to rise above the valley into open fields and reach at length the more substantial settlement of Murzanabad. From here a road leads left for Kalar Dasht. This road, a morass in wet weather, winds up over mountain fields and pastures, giving entrancing glimpses both of distant ranges and also, nearer at hand, of large prosperous-looking villages set among walnut and chestnut trees, fronted with rich cornfields. The farmers have a curious habit in these parts, no doubt induced by the prevailing humidity, of putting their hayricks in trees, and until the harvest the landscape on both sides of the road is dotted with strange deformed trees, looking as though they have had their hearts cut out, waiting for the crops. From a low col we look down into the triangular plain of Kalar Dasht, formed by the waters of the Sardab, and once a lake. To the east and west wooded hills converge towards a funnel, the Sardab valley, at the head of which on clear days Takht-i-Suleiman and Alam Kuh, the highest peaks in the Elburz after Demavend, shine in all

---

* *I. dermavencica* and *I. flavescens,* to judge from an article by Patrick Synge in the *Journal of the Royal Horticultural Society*, June, 1961.

their glory. The plain itself is well tilled; near its centre stands a large tepe, the site of the medieval town destroyed by the Mongols and still unexcavated. Where the valley narrows Reza Shah's summer palace stands on a promontory; near this spot was found the gold cup of Kalar Dasht, now in the Tehran Museum; and in this palace the present Shah and his Queen were staying in August 1953, when they received the news that Musaddeq had abolished the monarchy – a short-lived gesture. Above the palace, straddling the mouth of the valley, is Rudbarak, which can fairly claim to be the prettiest village in Iran. A track runs from here over the Harchal pass to the Taleghan valley, whence peasants and donkeys tramp regularly in summer with their cargoes of salt, returning loaded with timber and other Caspian products. Its situation at the mouth of a wooden ravine, with a wide trout stream bisecting it, is superb; and the village itself has a character all its own. 'Here,' says Freya Stark, 'one really comes into a tradition of an old prosperity and finds buildings designed for ornament as well as comfort, as good as many a country cottage in the Alps. There are balconies and out-jutting eaves; ceilings fashioned in little wooden squares reminiscent of Italy and the Renaissance; open fireplaces, niches worked in stucco, and rough ornaments in relief, cocks, flower baskets and geometric figures, which evidently belonged to a day when Kalar was a flourishing city.'* The people, Khavajavends from Kurdistan, settled here by the early Qajars, are equally picturesque, the women in particular with their white headscarves, loose red blouses and short pink or white petticoats hanging out over their dark blue trousers. On feast days both sexes don their traditional ceremonial costumes, embroidered and hung with jewellery and silver ornament; the streets of the village and the fields round it glow with colour. Rudbarak, moreover, is still sufficiently off the beaten track for visitors to be a curiosity; the villagers 'press round friendly but overwhelming', as Freya Stark observed, asking for cures for their ailments, and a lavish supply of aspirin is recommended.

Murzanabad is only some nineteen miles from Chalus. The

* *The Valleys of the Assassins,* 1934.

road descends a wide valley, and then enters a gorge flanked by
strange grey hills covered with boulders and gnarled pines, like
a magnified version of some rocky island in the Baltic. The valley
narrows, the road gets wetter, the trees thicker. The forest,
ingrown and impenetrable, presses in on every side, varied only
by an occasional firewarden's hut; this is Caspian coastal scenery
in earnest. The hills recede, and we come suddenly and with no
warning to Chalus. The first impression is almost glossy: a smooth
tarmac road, a pink-washed plaster wall running round what is
clearly a Royal pleasaunce, banana trees and the scent of orange
blossom, and an ornamental circle in front of an hotel portico in
the best Russian Colonial (Pahlevi) style.

The road from Tehran to Amol via Pulur and the Haraz valley
(the first part of a new route to Meshed) is now the shortest
route between Tehran and the Caspian. It has the unique merit
of passing close to Mount Demavend (see pp. 83, 84) and then
plunges down into the Haraz valley whose villages contain many
old houses with wooden tracery windows as at Yazd of local
manufacture and considerable ingenuity. The mountains are still
bare as the road beside the Haraz passes through the first of
fifteen rock-cut tunnels. From Ab-i-Ask scrub appears on the
mountainside heralding the approach of the Caspian forests and
gradually the road levels out into rich pastures as it approaches
Amol (see p. 135).

The main highway from Tehran to Mazanderan follows the
Meshed route to Firuzkuh and then, together with the Caspian
railway built by Reza Shah, winds down the Mirud valley to
Shahi. It is an old, ill-constructed curling road, best travelled from
north to south, in an open car, for its principal attractions are the
views of the Elburz massif looking south up the valley, and the
antics of the railway as it crosses and recrosses the road and
tunnels into the hillside to reappear facing in the other direction
two or three hundred feet above. There is one place where the
railway performs a treble feat of this kind on one tract of hillside.
There are some sixty tunnels within fourteen miles, which must
represent one of the most remarkable engineering feats in the
world. Unfortunately, however, the railway has also left its

5. GUNBAD-I-KABUS (1006): 'a great earth-coloured pencil cleaves the horizon. (*p. 130*)

6a. PAHLEVI DEZH: A yaourt or movable round felt tent of the Turkoman tribe (*p. 129*)

6b. PAHLEVI DEZH on market day (*p. 131*)

cloven hoof in this lovely valley. The village of Pul-i-Sefid or White Bridge, for instance, belies its name, for it is black with smoke; and some of Iran's principal coal mines are nearby. So is a Seljuk tomb tower in red brick, the Darvish Mohammed probably of the eleventh century; and in the wild country a day's march to the east of Zirab there are two tomb towers at Resget (1009) and Lajim (1022) both of brick with tall conical domes, and with Radkan West (see p. 132) the last monuments to carry Pahlevi inscriptions, a reminder that Mazanderan was the last stronghold of resistance to Islam.

The Shahrud-Shahpasand road is of recent construction, and is not yet properly charted. After passing Bastam it continues for some way across a dusty plain, rising gradually to a 7,000-foot pass. There is some splendid game country to the east of this road, where herds of ibex and mouflon can often be seen at close quarters. From the pass, with its wide views over rolling country, the road descends in sweeps across grassy moorland past a romantically situated chaikhaneh named Khushyailaq, and then, still in dry country, enters a valley which curls round to the west. The transition to rain-belt vegetation is slow, and, when it comes, is unimpressive. Only when we emerge on to the level of the plains does the old magic reassert itself. A green, grassy headland guards the entrance to the valley; and round the corner is the Gurgan steppe, with its unsuspected beauties.

The last of the eight routes, Bujnurd to Gunbad-i-Kabus, also emerges on to the Gurgan plain. This is quite unlike any of the other Elburz crossings. It runs not from north to south but from east to west. It passes through no spectacular mountain scenery and involves no long ascents or descents. Some might maintain that it hardly qualifies as an Elburz crossing at all. It is, however, a road of great variety and unexpectedness. Astara and Chalus are good melodrama; this is a theatrical masterpiece.

Bujnurd itself, as we have already seen (p. 115), is an idyllic spot. We climb its rim of green hills to the west and follow a switchback course through rolling pastoral country with white villages nestling in the valleys. As the view unfolds, there is no doubt as to the subject matter of the drama: it is water. This is a truly Iranian theme. Away to the north, towards the frontiers of Russia, fold on fold of rounded reddish and whitish hills can be seen, lifeless and seared with erosion. But in the foreground the broad valley is thick with corn; the verges sparkle with wild anchusa and meadow-sweet; and to the south, facing the wet winds, are rich meadows rising above large prosperous villages, patches of woodland, oxen ploughing, and fortified farms; an almost Mediterranean scene. The valley narrows, the hills rise, the dry land disappears, and we are encircled with green benevolence. But the road is now running up towards treeless hills; and we suddenly emerge into an open desolate plain, as drab and grey as anything on the plateau, dry, sunbaked and empty. A range of low hills to the right shuts out the rain-belt, but to the observant eye an occasional tree on the summit gives an indication of what is on the other side. After some ten miles of barren flatness the road drops gently down into a fold in the hills; then comes a second surprise. Flowers, whole fields of them, suddenly appear, then bushes; there is a bramble by the roadside twittering with rose-coloured starlings (this in mid-May). The descent is hardly perceptible, yet within a matter of minutes we are in woodland; the hills rise up on either side into overgrown and hanging rocks, the trees close in, and soon the road is flanked with tremendous virgin forest. This is the famous Gulestan forest, a royal domain where the timber, instead of being felled for house-building or charcoal, has been most carefully conserved. It stretches for miles upwards and outwards on both sides of the road, glades of giant oaks alternating with maple and sycamore. There is no choking surfeit of undergrowth here as in the lesser and ravaged forests; these great trees have won their struggle for survival and only the fittest stand. If there are other forests in Gurgan as noble as this, there are none half as accessible. This is the crowning glory of the Persian woodland. It is green and fresh, but neither suffocating nor soppy. The subtropical lushness encountered further west is not found here. It is a freak of nature, a verdant valley open towards the sea, but far enough removed from it not to be enveloped in its vapours, preserved in its perfection not only by royal command but also by the healthy proximity of the dry plateau on one side and the Turkoman steppe relapsing into desert on the other.

The road runs through the true forest only for a few miles; it then emerges into a broad green valley of gentle curves and kindly aspect, which in turn gives way after a few miles to the plain. The first sight of this is breathtaking: on one side a surging range of forest-clad hills with snow-capped peaks beyond, and on the other a sea of green fading into pallor, on a vast, completely flat, horizon. Robert Byron says of it: 'I never saw that colour before. In other greens, of emerald, jade or malachite, the harsh deep green of the Bengal jungle, the sad cool green of Ireland, the salad green of Mediterranean vineyards, the heavy full-blown green of English summer beeches, some element of blue or yellow predominates over the others. This was the pure essence of green, indissoluble, the colour of life itself.'* This is the recently reclaimed Gurgan steppe, the best wheat-growing area in Iran, and a region of great potential wealth; it is potential rather than actual, as the villages with their wattle huts and nomadic-looking inhabitants clearly proclaim. For this is frontier country. Long subject to raids from across the border, inimical to settled habitation, it was until recently peopled only by the nomadic Turkoman tribes who grazed their herds right up to the edge of the hills. Even today they have not lost their wandering habits, and some prefer to live in movable round felt tents (yaourts) held up by wicker or wood, vertical for about six feet and then curving inwards and attached to a hoop in the centre. Except for this circular opening, which serves as a ventilator, the frame is covered with thick felt or camel-skin, while carpets or felt are placed against the inner wall. There is a lack of skilled farm workers, and many Baluchis have been imported to fill the gap. It is a land of strange contrast, this immensely fertile plain with its scenic backdrop, great mounds or tepes in places so close as to give the look of a golf course for prehistoric giants, mere wisps of villages, and the long-faced dark Baluchis with their white turbans, jostling with slant-eyed Turkomans, the men fur-capped even in the hottest weather, the women aflame in purple, red and orange.

* *The Road to Oxiana*, 1950.

As the road runs across the steppe it edges almost imperceptibly into drier country; the trees disappear; and in their place, straight ahead, a great earth-coloured pencil cleaves the horizon. This is the famous Dome of Kabus – Gunbad-i-Kabus – built in 1006 to receive the body of Shams el Ma'ali Kabus, who died in 1012, the Ziyarid ruler. During Kabus's reign the city of Jurjan (not to be confused with the modern Gurgan some fifty miles to the east) became a fine city and a centre of cultural activity, despite its exposed position and the dynastic rivalries which threatened the security of its rulers. Kabus's body is said to have been suspended in a glass coffin high up in the 160-foot tower, and there is a good deal of evidence which lends colour to this theory. For example, in 1899, the Russians, believing that he might have been buried there, sank a 35-foot shaft in the middle of the monument. They found only brick foundations, still continuing at that fantastic depth. Again, the only window in the whole building is in the conical roof, and faces due east, just as the door of the tent traditionally faced the rising sun. This window could have little purpose unless Kabus's body was suspended at the same level. Today there is no means, within or without, of ascending the tower, and nothing remains to testify to its use as a tomb save an antique and penetrating odour of decay.

As for the architecture of the tower itself, it is impossible to improve on Robert Byron.

'A tapering cylinder of *café au lait* brick springs from a round plinth to a pointed grey-green roof, which swallows it up like a candle extinguisher. The diameter at the plinth is fifty feet; the total height about a hundred and fifty. Up the cylinder, between plinth and roof, run ten triangular buttresses which cut across two narrow garters of Kufic text, one at the top underneath the cornice, one at the bottom over the slender back entrance.'

And thinking over it, two years later, in Peking, Byron reasserted his opinion that it ranked with the great buildings of the world.

There is much to support this view. The simplicity of its design is sensational. It is daringly original. Its sturdy construction has

withstood the test of time and the ravages of men – not to mention the birds which nest in its roof. On the other hand its
appearance is strictly utilitarian, and some may find it lacking in
refinement or charm. Moreover, its surroundings are not what
they were in Byron's day (1934). The encircling wall has been
pulled down; the artificial mound on which the tower stands is
dusty and bare; the town below might well be a drab modern
settlement in the prairies of the Middle West. A visitor nourished
on the more glowing accounts of this extraordinary tomb may
therefore experience some disappointment. Yet the fact remains
there is no other tomb tower in Persia of such massive proportions, and it is one of the unique monuments of the world.

The town now bearing the name of Gurgan lies at the base of
the mountains some twenty miles east of the south-eastern corner
of the Caspian Sea. Formerly known as Astarabad, it was a place
of considerable importance in the Middle Ages but has been
destroyed so frequently, first by Mongol invasions and later as
recently as 1928 by a particularly violent earthquake, that little
of historical interest remains except the Imamzadeh Nur, Seljuk
work with a Seljuk or Mongol mihrab, and the minaret of the
Friday Mosque, possibly Seljuk, surmounted by a modern wooden
canopy. Gurgan is a well-laid-out place of somewhat European
aspect, which Reza Shah rebuilt in an attractive style, with well-
equipped bazaars. But, if this is Europe, it is only ten miles to the
heart of Central Asia. Pahlevi Dezh to the north is the emporium
of the steppe; here at seven o'clock on Thursday morning, market
day, the Yamut Turkomans, whose grazing areas straddle the
Irano-Soviet frontier, gather in their broad fur caps and bright
colours to bargain for horses, carpets, textiles and foodstuffs. The
streets are so crowded with stalls and buyers that one can scarcely
move along them; carpets are slung over the railing round the
statue marking the centre of the town; there is a big open space
behind where splendid Turkoman horses are tethered or shown
off; Mongolian features predominate everywhere. Pahlevi Dezh
on market day provides the greatest concentration of local colour
in Iran. It is, indeed, the frontier. Just beyond, on the steppe,
stands the celebrated Wall of Alexander, a brick wall running

some hundred miles from the Caspian eastwards to the mountains of Khorasan. The name is legendary; the wall is thought to have been built in fact by the Sassanians as a first line of defence against invaders from Central Asia. It has been much despoiled but still stands, a mighty witness to efforts to afford Iran protection against barbarian conquerors.

West of Gurgan but across the first range of mountains to the south is the Nika valley and difficult of access is one of the finest of the early tomb towers, a hundred feet high, dated 1016, with a Pahlevi inscription – Radkan West. And between there and the sea south of Bandar Gaz are the recently excavated remains of Tamis or Tammisha, described by Arab geographers as the first of the cities of Tabaristan after Jurjan but which disappears from history in 1220. Traces have been found of a wall probably Sassanian which once ran 20 km to the sea; of a palace which may date from the first century A.D.; of an early Islamic citadel; and of roof tiles similar to those used in Caspian towns today. The village nearest to the site is still known as Sarkalata Kharab-shahr, or the ruined city.

Another fifty miles to the west, and Central Asia is left far behind. The steppe has been replaced by the sea. The vegetation has grown more lush. At Behshahr we are in Italy, the land-scape is of Tuscany or Verona. The illusion is almost complete. The little whitewashed Imamzadeh Abdullah stands back from the road amidst its grove of cypresses. An avenue of cypresses crowns the hill that overlooks Behshahr, a town of spacious houses with low-slung brown-tiled roofs, deep eaves and white-washed vine-covered walls. It is no wonder that Shah Abbas with his sense of pageantry and colour chose this part of Mazanderan as his country retreat. At Behshahr, formerly Ashraf, he built a pavilion beside a pool, enclosed by wooded hills; at Farahabad, further to the west, he constructed a palace and a town reputedly as large as Rome or Constantinople. It was at Ashraf that Pietro della Valle finally caught up with Shah Abbas, and was permitted to kiss his hand in the course of a long and exhausting ceremony which lasted deep into the night. We can feel for Pietro that, after over a year's waiting at Shah Abbas's court, he was required

to drink wine, which he abhorred, squat on his heels for hours
on end, and finally when the hour was late, answer searching
questions from the monarch about Rome, the Pope, Christian
sects, the policy of the King of Spain, and methods of conducting
warfare. Yet he conveys to us faithfully the typically Persian
charm of the scene – the splendid gathering on rich carpets in
the open air, night falling, the chandeliers being lighted, and soft
music playing in the background. The proceedings, too, though
dignified and inconsequential were not formal or solemn; Abbas
arrived in a turban deliberately put on back to front, and kept up
continuous banter and laughter in which he expected others to
join. Nine years later, in 1628, when Shah Abbas received the
English Ambassador, Sir Dodmore Cotton, in the same spot, the
atmosphere seems to have been more constrained. Herbert, at
least, was less impressed by the Shah's hilarity than by the terror
which he inspired in his subjects, 'who like so many inanimate
statues were placed crosslegged, joining their bums to the
ground, their backs to the wall and their eyes to a constant
object; to speak to one another, sneeze, cough or spit in the
Potshaw's (Padishah's) presence being, ever since the time of
Astyages, held no good breeding'.

Of Shah Abbas's palace at Ashraf nothing is left today except
the garden, and Farahabad has been totally destroyed. But at
Behshahr at least enough remains to enable us to conjure up the
beauties of the setting, and moreover Shah Safi's palace Safiabad,
built on an adjoining hill twenty years later, can still in some
sense be seen. The site is superb. The hill, its slopes dotted with
cypresses, juts out in a commanding position over the plain; a
formal garden surrounded by a stone balustrade occupies the
ridge. But the palace itself was found in a ruined condition by
Reza Shah and virtually rebuilt in a style quite out of keeping
with its florid surroundings. In this building no one could ever
wear his turban back to front. It is now a radar station.

The water near Behshahr is not the open sea but Astarabad
Bay; soon after, the coastline proper of the Caspian begins. Italy
now recedes; the cypresses grow rarer, the orange groves disappear, and we enter a country of wide fields, English hedgerows

prosperous walled farms, thatched villages and spreading elms
and chestnuts. This is the broad plain of Mazanderan, where there
is a thirty-mile gap between the mountains and the sea. It is one
of the three regions into which the Caspian coast may be roughly
divided, the others being the narrow coastal strip from Mahmudabad to Rud-i-Sar, and the Gilan plain, in effect the delta of the
Sefid Rud. The Mazanderan plain also contains many objects of
interest. Babolsar, for instance, appears at first sight a typical
resort town with hotels, a number of villas, an estuary and a
caviar factory; but turn off the beaten track into the old village,
and you will find winding country lanes, thatched cottages
standing in well-tilled gardens, village greens, a wooden village
hall, and the tomb tower of Ibrahim Abu Jawad with its flying
angels in plaster relief. This apparently Christian piece of symbolism is characteristic of the Mazanderan tomb towers. Dating from
the fifteenth century, built in an area which ever since its late
conversion has been fanatically Moslem, these little buildings have
for the European traveller a more familiar look about them than
perhaps anything else in Iran. Their octagonal plan, the use of
round arches for cornice and other decoration, their conical roofs,
the equilateral cross used as a decorative motif, the churchyard
setting, even the colour of the bricks and tiles, resemble features of
Romanesque architecture so closely that we may well rub our
eyes and ask ourselves how they can possibly be of Islamic inspiration. Yet Islamic they are, and indeed many of them are now used
as village shrines and have red tiled entrance halls used for prayer
and meeting purposes attached to them. The most impressive of
all, despite its dilapidation, is perhaps the Imamzadeh Abbas in
the centre of a village just north of the main road about a mile
east of Sari. There are several others in Sari itself, six in Amol,
two in Babol, and one also in a village on the road from Babol to
Shahi. The tomb towers of Mazanderan still await systematic
analysis.

The Mazanderan plain contains four fairly large towns of
about 40,000 inhabitants: Sari, the capital of the province, Shahi,
Babol, and Amol. Sari is a rambling, rather featureless place,
Shahi a largely modern textile town. Babol has some fine streets

lined with patrician houses with deep eaves and mellowed brown tiles, and outside the town is a Royal Palace built about 1900 in a lovely mature garden filled with the scent of orange blossom. But the most picturesque of these towns is Amol, the capital of Tabaristan in the ninth century, and an important pottery centre in Seljuk times. Herbert, who visited it in 1627, called it 'once this country's metropolis' and speaks of the Friday Mosque in which four hundred and forty-four Princes and Prophets are entombed. He also took a tour by the river, noted a little hump-backed stone bridge, and then observed 'seven or eight more beautiful than bashful damsels who sprang out of the water as I supposed to admire my habit'. He took them for ladies of easy virtue but later learnt that at midday the men go to sleep and then women 'have the benefit of the river'. Though much reduced in importance, Amol can boast a Safavid Mosque, the Mir Bozorg, a rambling shrine with a few painted tiles; the Masjid-i-Imam Askeri, with wooden galleries, a truncated mina-ret with conical roof, and a nice courtyard of orange trees; and some pleasant houses with overhanging eaves and outside paint-ings of birds and trees. There is also a fifteenth-century funeral tower one mile out on the road to Mahmudabad.

The narrow coastal strip which begins at Mahmudabad con-tinues for nearly two hundred miles, ranging in width from five to ten miles. Most of the way the road runs close to the sea, crossing little rivers near their mouths, where there are generally a few thatched cottages for fishermen. On the seaward side the road is bounded by dunes covered with scrub or groves of pome-granate, whose red flowers in early summer impart the only touch of bright colour to a grey-green landscape. Inland there are rice paddy fields and clearings marking villages, and, clouds permitting, impressive views of mountains. The chief variety is provided by the small towns – Mahmudabad, Nau Shahr, Chalus, Sabsewar and Ramsar – which were embellished by Reza Shah, often with an imposing circular civic centre, its plaster façade painted in white and blue, with the fragility of a stage set. Occasional villas stand amongst cypresses behind low white-washed balustrades. The show place of the Pahlevi Riviera is

Ramsar, where there is a large flamboyant hotel covered with statues on a knoll standing back from the sea, with steep woodland paths behind, subtropical gardens, and an avenue a mile long flanked with orange groves leading down to the casino and the beach.

The Gilan plain beyond Rud-i-Sar has a very different aspect from that of Mazanderan. Round Lahijan and Langerud there are extensive tea and cotton plantations, not only on the plain but running up the hillsides which fringe the road at this point. One mile east of Lahijan and just south of the main road stands the interesting fourteenth-century Tomb of Shaikhanvar. Its blue and white stepped and pointed pagoda dome sits on a wide sloping square roof of red tiles.

The Sefid Rud delta is a country of small holdings, large sandy rivers and swamps. The villages are poor and tightly packed. This is the most thickly populated agricultural region of Iran, and yet one has the impression that, in contrast to the lands farther east, man has not really got the better of nature; nature, malignant nature, is steadily catching up on him. The countryside round Resht, itself more like an overgrown village than a town, is stifling, not merely on account of its climate but by reason of the excess of vegetation and population. Only when we emerge on to the green duncs near Pahlevi, which are open and windswept, do we breathe fresh air again. This is in fact a peninsula, separated from the foetid mainland by a great inland lake or swamp, the Murdab (Dead Water) whose creeks and inlets provide some of the finest duck-shooting in the world; it is a paradise too for migratory birds and for the ornithologist. Bandar Pahlevi, formerly Enzeli, is built on both sides of the estuary through which the Murdab debouches into the Caspian; it has the best natural harbour on the coast. Here steamers ply to Baku, and the town has a distinctly Russian look, particularly within the compound of the caviar factory or shilat, which until 1953 was in Russian ownership. Abadan itself is a less exotic growth than this enclave of Czarist Russia, with its little broken-down Victorian villas with lace curtains and wooden balconies surrounded by shabby wooden palings and gardens full of rambler roses, a setting straight out of Tchekov. Even the furniture in the houses is still Russian; and we were given vodka for breakfast! (1956)

Beyond Pahlevi the coastal plain narrows once more and for much of the way the mountains, covered with particularly dense forest, come to within a mile of the sea. This is the wettest corner of Iran, with an irregular rainfall which averages about fifty-five inches a year. Torrents rush steeply from these moist hills into the sea, and the most serious problem on this fertile coast is the maintenance of communication. The Russians built an impressive asphalt road from Astara to Pahlevi during the Second World War. But by 1956 no less than ten bridges of war-time construction had been swept away in floods; motor traffic had to cross stream-beds which in places were as much as a hundred yards wide, and these in wet weather became a mass of swirling water and hidden rocks. Now, however, all the bridges over the major streams have been rebuilt. The landscape is wild and grand; in the Talish hills to the west live some of the most primitive tribesmen of Iran. The coastal folk are friendly enough, as I had occasion to discover when marooned among them for two days during a flood; they live largely on rice, and I found that when offered the flat yeastless bread of the plateau they did not know what it was. This is the measure of the isolation here; forests and floods are an even more effective barrier than the deserts to which we now return.

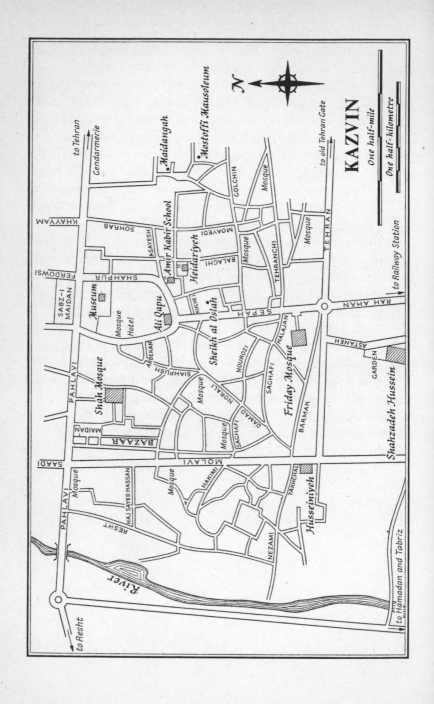

KAZVIN

One half-mile

One half-kilometre

N

to Tehran

Gendarmerie

•Maidangah

•Mostoffi Mausoleum

to old Tehran Gate

KHAYYAM

SOHRAB

ASAYESH

SHAHPUR

Amir Kabir School

Heidariyeh

GOLCHIN

Mosque

MOAYEDI

BALCHI

Mosque

TEHRANCHI

Mosque

TEHRAN

to Railway Station

FERDOWSI

SABZ-I MAIDAN

Museum

Ali Qapu

Mosque Hotel

KUCHEL

Sheikh al Oslah

SEPAH

RAH AHAN

ARDEKAN

SIAHPUSH

Mosque

NOUROZI

NORALI

HALAJAN

SAGHAFI

Friday Mosque

ASTANEH

GARDEN

PAHLAVI

Shah Mosque

MAIDAN

BAZAAR

Mosque

SAGHAFI

DAMAD

BARMAK

Shahzadeh Hussein

SAADI

Mosque

HAJ SAYED HASSAN

MOLAVI

HAKIMI

Mosque

YAKHCHAL

Husseiniyeh

PAHLAVI

RESHT

NEZAMI

to Hamadan and Tabriz

River

to Resht

CHAPTER SEVEN

To Azerbaijan

The road to Samarkand sounds more romantic, but the road to Trebizond is easier on the eye. Passing over Tehran through Kazvin and Sultaniyeh to Tabriz, it provides a history of Iran from 1260 to 1560, told in reverse. And the scenery improves as we proceed. The deserts are left behind when we enter Azerbaijan, the Atropatene of the ancients, named after Atropates, a former general appointed by Alexander as satrap of Northern Media in 328 B.C. The Persian language too is left behind, for the Azerbaijanis, though taught Persian in their schools, still speak a Turki dialect in their homes.

For the first ninety miles a fast road skirts the Elburz foothills. At Km. 73 on the right at Yang-i-Imam is the tomb-sanctuary of Hady and Naghy, two brothers of Imam Riza, with conical turquoise dome and blue painted interior. The adjacent nineteenth-century caravanserai is in army occupation. At Km. 115 there is another tomb sanctuary with several vaulted rooms on two floors, in poor repair, described as the tomb of Agha Mirza Hassan Shaikh-ul-Islam Ghaziri. At Km. 126 on the left stands a low, very small, square mud-brick shrine, like an ab-ambar, with a squat bun-shaped dome of yellow and blue tiles. Opposite this is the easternmost of the three routes to the remote, romantic, and fantastically beautiful Valley of the Assassins (see p. 23) formed by the Taleghan river (see p. 125) which continues as the Shahrud (cf. p. 121) and its tributary the Alamut.

The principal Assassin castles still to be seen out of some sixty once built and later destroyed by the Mongols, are Alamut, Maymum-Diz and Lammassar. The first is approached by a mountain track from Km. 126 motorable by Land-Rover in dry weather as far as Shuter Khan. The second, Maymum-Diz, stands above another valley running north from the Alamut Rud; it can be reached on foot from Shahrak (a few miles west of Shuter Khan) or from Maolem-Kelaiyay which is accessible by car direct from Kazvin. To reach Lammassar it is necessary to take a third track from the centre of Kazvin to Zirishk, then down to the Shahrud, proceeding thence, preferably with guide, to the village of Shahrestan Bala. It is vividly described by Freya Stark in *The Valleys of the Assassins*.

Kazvin is the first place of importance on the main road. It stands on a fertile plain well back from the Elburz, about ninety miles west-north-west of Tehran. It owes its existence largely to its position as a communications centre. Roads to Tabriz, Hamadan and Tehran radiate from here; to the south-east runs the old cara-van route across the desert to Saveh and Isfahan; the easiest road to the Caspian drops down into a deep valley to the north-west.

Largely for this reason Kazvin has a stormy history. In early Islamic times it served as a base against the unruly Daylamites who occupied the mountain valleys to the north-east. It was raided by and formed a base for attacks upon the Assassin sect in their mountain fastness of Alamut. It was pillaged by the Mongols and seized by the Afghans. Occupied by Russian forces in both world wars, Kazvin also served as headquarters for the operations of General Dunsterville's forces against the Bolsheviks in 1919-20. But this battered town knew two periods of relative prosperity: in the sixteenth century, when Shah Tahmasp made it his capital; and in the early nineteenth century when it was favoured and embellished by the Qajars.

Today Kazvin is a shrunken town with an unmistakably old-fashioned air. I know of no better place in which to get the feel of nineteenth-century Persia – long-standing neglect, dignified decay side by side with seedy respectability, life running on among the ruins and grinding gradually to a stop, the sort of hopelessness which pervaded provincial life after a century of indifference. Much of the older, southern part of the city is dilapidated. Even the newer northern section, through which the

highroad passes, is innocent of any modernization at the hands of
Reza Shah, though an industrial estate is now growing up 10 km
to the east. Instead of the usual wide avenues, flanked by one-
storeyed shops blocking out the tortuous maze of byways that
lie behind, which give a brisk and prosperous, if standardized, air
of improvement to most Iranian cities today, the main thorough-
fare of Kazvin is lined with top-heavy two-storeyed houses
fronted with wooden balconies and covered with crazily angled
tin roofs. Brassware, sugared sweets and musty antiques, including
a surprising number of crude Christian pictures, jostle each other
in the shops. In the spring Kazvin is a green town, not only
because of its encircling halo of vineyards but also because grass
and wild flowers grow in unexpected places, in the streets, in the
Friday Mosque, and on every mud roof. Quietly and wearily the
severely veiled women and sombrely dressed men of Kazvin
move about their business, gathering in little knots at street
corners, sunning themselves or intoning gently in the vast court
of the Friday Mosque, or weaving their way sadly among the
tightly packed graves of the vast cemetery beyond the shrine of
Shah Zadeh Huseyn. Outside the walls on the eastern side of the
town there is another cemetery, little frequented but of special
and melancholy interest to British visitors. There lie buried some
seventy men of the Dunster force, whose deaths in the joyful
months between September 1918 and 1920 are coldly recorded
on neat finely engraved grey slabs of stone.

Though no *ville monumentale*, Kazvin can still boast of several
interesting buildings preserved from its historic past, but they have
to be sought out, for many are concealed behind modern façades.
At the heart of the city lie the gardens of the old royal palace
which was built in the fifteenth century on what were then the
northern outskirts. The great gateway of Ali Kapu, architecturally
indistinguishable from the iwan of a Safavid Mosque, stands at
the southern end of the garden facing a wide avenue, the Khiaban-
i-Sepah, also constructed by the early Safavid kings. Inside the
gate a double row of ancient oriental plane trees, heavily pollarded,
leads to the site of the former royal palace, now covered by
undistinguished buildings which serve as police headquarters. More

interesting than these is the square top-heavy building which
stands facing a little square, the Sabz-i-Maidan or vegetable
market. In appearance like a broken-down hotel in the Middle
West, this curious structure has an interesting history. It was
originally a one-storey building which served as a pavilion to
the royal palace. About 1840 an upper storey with balcony, and a
ground floor balcony were added. The ground floor consists of a
series of charming vaulted rooms leading into a central chamber,
also vaulted. The devastations of successive generations of white-
washers are gradually being removed to reveal tantalizing patterns
of flower and wall paintings, the earliest of their kind in the
country, the prototype of the more ambitious and better preserved frescoes of the Ali Kapu, Chehel Sutun and Talar Ashraf
at Isfahan. The pavilion is being turned into a museum, and
already houses a fine collection of the painted wooden panels –
doors, ceiling slats, cupboards, mirrors – for which Kazvin was
renowned in the period of its revival, the early nineteenth century.

Kazvin also possesses a large Friday Mosque lying off the
Khiaban-i-Sepah about four hundred yards south of the Ali
Kapu. It is remarkable for its vast size, the florid splendour of its
plaster inscriptions, and the impressive dignity of its situation.
Many Friday Mosques lie adjacent to, if not in the heart of the
bazaar, and are entered through narrow doorways out of tortuous
alleys. You are on them before you know it, and they create no
sense of expectation. Not so the Friday Mosque of Kazvin. A
splendid ornamented gateway constructed in the time of Shah
Ismail leads into a long wide passage like the approach to some
great cathedral. At the end of this passage, instead of the expected
open gateway leading into the great court of the mosque, there
is a large grille of blue tiles, through which can be obtained
glimpses of the iwan's minarets and dome within. On each side
of the grille a narrower passage leads to the court itself. The
charm of this derives more perhaps from its grassy floor, its giant
plane trees, and its cloistered tranquillity than from any single
architectural feature. The tilework is inferior, a mixture of un-
inspired Safavid and overblown Qajar; the minarets are a little
vulgar, the arcades in bad repair. But the Seljuk sanctuary behind

the south iwan, has a certain massive splendour, and the inscriptions with a floral background which run in two tiers round the building are remarkably intricate and beautifully executed. Between the inscriptions the wall is decorated with fine brick ends and unusual great ornamental loops of outset brick inscription that describe sweeping curves. The exterior of this dome (A.D. 1113) over the sanctuary has an unusual spiral of diagonal stripes on a turquoise ground.

The other Seljuk monument in Kazvin is the Madrasseh Haidariyeh, which stands in the courtyard of the Dabirestan Rahnema in Kuche Bulaqi in the eastern quarter of the town. The setting, unlike that of the Friday Mosque, could scarcely be more unpromising. The dome chamber is totally concealed from view by a row of modern red brick buildings. The court is a dusty playground. All that remains from the Seljuk period is the ungainly looking building at the southern end of the courtyard. But what is left of this is beautiful and well worth preserving. There is some lovely brick vaulting; a splendid plaster mihrab of great size, the background formerly painted blue; and near the corners of the rectangle are elaborate niches with gracefully curved arches, like some Elizabethan tomb.

Farther east still, at the end of a maze of alleys, in a large depression some ten feet below present ground level, stands the tomb of Hamidullah Mustawfi, the fourteenth-century historian and geographer. It is a square brick building which changes through rather a startlingly violent transition into a cylinder surmounted by a conical blue dome. The interior, with vaulting picked out in various colours, has been admirably restored and conserved by the Archaeological Department.

In addition there are several interesting or curious buildings in Kazvin dating from the Qajar epoch. There is the shrine of Shah Zadeh Huseyn, son of the eighth Imam, Reza. According to local legend Huseyn gave water to a blind man whose sight was thereupon restored; but this attracted such a crowd that the roof on which the miracle occurred fell in and the boy was killed. His monument stands on the southern outskirts of the city, at the end of a long and leafy avenue not far from the Friday Mosque.

It is the only building in Kazvin which by reason both of its scale
and of its colour can be described as opulent. A charming if
rather decadent gateway, with a curved silhouette and five gay
minarets at slightly drunken angles, leads into a vast court immediately inside which stands an octagonal ablution pavilion. The
shrine beyond is covered with green and pink tiles in typically
Qajar floral designs, built over a tomb dating from the Safavid
period. On the side of the shrine which faces the gateway there
is a large recess, the walls and vaulted roof of which are covered
with mirrors; the effect, in an otherwise graceful building, is
shattering. The whole of the courtyard, and a vast area to the
south of it, is filled with tombs, many of them delicately carved
slabs of marble.

Another early Qajar building, the Huseyneyeh, stands on a
long avenue of caravanserais at No. 709 in the Khiaban-i-Malavi
in the western quarter of the town. This is a house of prayer,
built 150 years ago by the Amini family who still live in the
adjoining courtyards. It is opened to the inhabitants of Kazvin
for communal prayer during the lunar months of Moharram,
Safar or Ramadan. During Ramadan the poor of the city are
supplied with food and drink after nightfall. The charming courtyard in which a Russian bomb fell in 1941 has a dado of delicate
stone carvings of birds and flowers well repaired by workmen
from Yazd. To the right is the Prayer House whose façade
comprises a magnificent window of wooden Qajar tracery filled
with much coloured glass. Below the house is a delightful cool
room or Zirzamin with fountain and columned arches. The
interior consisting of three adjoining rectangular halls has been
beautifully restored; the stained glass, mirror stucco work and
brightly painted ceiling are dazzling in effect and there are enchanting decorative details. The ceilings consist of small geometric
plaques of wood painted with tiny flowers on a bright vermilion
ground and set in narrow mirror frames. Behind these rooms is a
highly picturesque vaulted kitchen in which food for the poor
is cooked on open wood fires. On the opposite side of the same
street is a splendid bath house or hammam* consisting of two

* Closed in 1977.

rooms, one hot and one cool, both octagonal, vaulted, columned and covered with marble from head to foot. The hammam is at once a public utility, a social institution, and a hygienic antidote to the dry, spare air of the Iranian plateau. A dim light comes through alabaster slats. At the approach of strangers, wizened figures wrapped in purple towels start out of the recesses in which hot water flows from half hidden tanks.

Though of relatively recent date, the plan and equipment of this hammam stem from an older tradition, vividly described by John Fryer in 1676,* at Isfahan. 'On these Marble Floors,' he writes, '[the bathers] at last extend themselves, when they think they have tarried long enough, that the Barbers whose business it is should wind and turn every limb and joint of the body before, behind and on every side ... then with a coarse Haircloth and Hot Water they scrape off all the Filth and Sweat; and last of all by a Depilatory they take clean away all manner of Hairs growing either in secret parts, or any Emunctuary to cause either nasty smells or troublesome chafing. ... When they are dressed they emplaster their feet and hands with a red Paste, which wonderfully helps sweaty and moisty palms, as also stinking feet.'

Other interesting Qajar relics include the Royal Mosque, at the entrance to the bazaar built in the reign of Fath Ali Shah and the Khaneh Ektendar-es-Sultan, a private house on the Khiaban-i-Sepah near the Ali Qapu. This is approached through a vaulted brick gateway which probably dates from an earlier period. The original tracery windows have been preserved, and in one small but highly ornate room there are fine painted wooden doors. Perhaps these paintings, from the first half of the nineteenth century, with birds and roses, vines and tulips woven into intricate patterns and resplendent with sombre colours, are Kazvin's most significant contribution to Iranian art.

After Kazvin the Tabriz road curves southward across a plain in which monuments compensate for lack of scenery. At Takistan where the Hamadan road forks there is a square Seljuk mausoleum known as 'Pir' with a decorated brick façade in good condition.

* *A New Account of East India and Persia.*

Some ten miles farther on before Qurveh there are two Mongol
towers both visible on the right of the road – the Imam Zadek
Abdullah at Farsadjan and the Kemal-üd-Din at Haydariyeh. At
Qurveh itself there is a Friday Mosque dated 1022, a square
building with dome in good repair. At Abhar off the main road
to the left ten miles farther on there is another tower also Mongol.
But these are but curtain raisers to Sultaniyeh. There is little to
mark the end of your journey there except a large dome, like an
egg in an egg-cup, on the south-west horizon. Nor, having seen
this, can you be sure of getting there. A track meanders across
fields, swampy in spring; it ends by crossing a small river impassable to motor traffic when in spate. But no traveller who cares a
rap for Islamic monuments can afford to pass by, and there is
even a sporting chance that a traveller who had not until that
moment cared might leave Sultaniyeh feeling that the visit had
after all been worth while.

It is difficult to describe the mausoleum of Sultan Oljeitu at
Sultaniyeh except in superlatives. Though plundered, shaken by
earthquakes, partially ruined (in 1976 still under repair), its
massive construction is so admirable that it remains one of the
great architectural wonders of the world. No photograph can
convey an adequate idea of its magnificence, still less of the genius
which inspired its decorations. It is an octagon, eighty feet across
inside, with walls twenty-three feet thick at the base; it carries its
egg-shaped dome some one hundred and seventy feet above the
ground. To it is attached on the south side a mortuary chapel
about sixty feet long and forty-five wide overall. The mausoleum
is constructed entirely of brick, including the dome which long
defied architectural analysis. It was thought to consist of two
concentric vaults, whereas it is in fact a single vault whose thickness diminishes towards the summit. 'Here is a dome,' says
Godard, 'which simply stands by virtue of a perfectly conceived
and constructed profile. The cross section of its construction is as
great a delight to an architect as the vision of the splendid blue
dome is to the traveller on the Tabriz-Kazvin road.'* From each
of the eight corners of the building rise minarets formerly covered

* Contribution to Pope's *Survey of Persian Art*, Vol. II.

like the dome with turquoise tiles, but now sadly dilapidated. Below these is an arcaded gallery, facing outwards, on all eight sides; its vaulted ceilings and walls are exquisitely decorated in polychrome plaster with great wealth and variety of design – Pope calls them 'a series of masterpieces of architectural ornament capable of holding its own with anything ever achieved in Persia'. Fortunately, the stair leading to this gallery in the northwest corner of the building has been repaired, so that it is now possible to admire this fourteenth-century work at close range. The interior of the main building was originally covered largely in faïence mosaic, but this was subsequently overlaid with stucco painted with rich polychrome designs, sometimes in relief. This stucco coating has not worn well, and today it is possible to see traces of both surface finishes and to compare them. The date and purpose of the stucco overlay long constituted something of a mystery; most writers believed it to be of Safavid origin, but recent researches have proved that it is contemporary with the building, for reasons explicable only by reference to its curious history.

Oljeitu's mausoleum towers above a dilapidated village, but with the little mausoleum of Chelibi Oghlu it is all that remains of what was once a flourishing city, founded about 1290 by the Mongol ruler Arghun Khan, and extended by his sons Ghazan and Oljeitu. It was an artificial capital, owing its existence not to the commercial possibilities of its situation but to the whims of the dynasty, its agreeable summer climate, and the abundance of game in the surrounding mountains. In consequence its span of glory was brief; it was sacked and largely destroyed by Miran Shah, the son of Timur, before the end of the fourteenth century; but even before then the centre of activity had moved back to Tabriz; the shifting of the capital to Isfahan under the Safavid dynasty completed the ruin of Sultaniyeh.

The history of the building, as now pieced together by the leading authorities, suggests that even in Oljeitu's time the need was realized to inflate the prosperity of the place by adventitious aid. The original plan was for the building to serve as Oljeitu's own mausoleum. Like his predecessor Ghazan Khan he probably started building his tomb as soon as he came to the throne in 1304. In 1309, however, after construction was well advanced, he became converted to Shi'ism. He then, it seems, conceived the idea of bringing to Sultaniyeh from their resting-places in Iraq the remains of Ali, son-in-law of Mohammed, and Huseyn, Ali's son, both objects of Shi'a devotion. The name of Ali can still be read in the brick patterns and stucco ornament of the interior. The notion was not wholly religious in purpose. The shrines of saints serve as a magnet for pilgrims, and pilgrims would have helped to maintain Sultaniyeh's tenuously based economy. It is believed that Oljeitu decided to add the mortuary chapel, for the purpose of receiving the bodies of the saints. The great dome chamber would then have been used as a public place of worship adjoining the tombs in accordance with local, and still prevailing, traditions. But though the chapel was built, the plan was never executed. It is possible that the same commercial considerations set up a resistance on the part of the citizens of Nejef and Kerbala to the removal of their precious relics. However this may be, Oljeitu returned to Sunnism before he died, and his great building reverted to its original purpose, to house his remains. This change of plan, however, carried its own embarrassments. In a religious society it was scarcely possible even for a powerful monarch to surround his eventual corpse with all the splendour and panoply intended for the most revered of saints. Therefore it was arranged, in all probability in 1313, three years before Oljeitu's death, that the brilliantly decorated interior of the dome chamber should be plastered over and covered with paintings still splendid but less magnificent than the original mosaic. Today, tattered and gaping, but incomparably majestic, Oljeitu's tomb, the most astounding building in Persia, still stands.

The scale and sweep of the mausoleum can hardly fail to evoke a layman's admiration; for the architect it must be almost unbearably exciting. My own visit to the place was closely followed by that of a small party of British architectural students; and I must record with mingled regret and amusement that I was responsible for deflecting their attention in some small degree from the tomb. I was returning from a tour of Azerbaijan, accompanied by a member of my staff who carried a collection of photographs, in poster form, commemorating a visit which the Shah paid to London in 1955 and showing His Imperial Majesty and his Queen with Queen Elizabeth, the Duke of Edinburgh, and Sir Winston and Lady Churchill. It was found that local officials liked to have these photographs for display purposes. On arriving at Sultaniyeh, however, we still had a few copies left. As soon as we parked our car we were surrounded by a dense crowd of curious local youths. We saw ourselves encumbered with a large following, volunteering gratuitous advice in fervent Turkish, while we wanted to examine the mausoleum quietly and alone. My companion then hit upon an ingenious notion; he handed out to the assembled company the last of our posters. There was a short struggle, in the course of which one or two of these tokens of Anglo-Iranian friendship got torn, but they created just the necessary diversion, and we were able to see the tomb in peace.

Two days later I received a visit from the party of architects. We discovered that we had been in Sultaniyeh on the same day; we extolled its beauties; and then I told them this story. Obviously some problem that had been bothering them was suddenly resolved. 'That explains it,' they said. 'Almost before we set foot in the village small boys came running at us, offering to sell pictures of the Queen. They were very disappointed to find that we'd come for another purpose!'

Sultaniyeh is approximately half way from Tehran to Tabriz. The only object of historical interest in the second two hundred miles is the ruined bridge over the Sefid Rud, known in this Turki-speaking region as the Qizil Uzun. The central piers were carried away in a flood, though I have also heard it said that they were blown up by Russians. Even in this ruined condition it is a lovely thing; Pope considers it the finest bridge extant in Persia and thinks it dates from the late fifteenth century.

After Mianeh the road becomes undulating (too much so for speed or comfort) and the scenery is increasingly attractive. Villages are more frequent, and as we approach Mount Sahand (12,200 ft) there is cultivation as far as the eye can reach, a restful contrast after the harshness of the desert.

You need to drive all round Sahand to appreciate its vast extent. With its bastions and ramparts, the mountain occupies an area some fifty miles in diameter, blocking out direct communication between Tabriz and Maragheh; and each glimpse of it on the road between these two towns yields some fresh fascination. But the most superb view of Sahand is that from the Tabriz-Tehran road south of the Shibli pass, some forty miles from Tabriz. From here it is flanked in perfect symmetry by two great rounded hills; the foreground is treeless, but well cultivated, riven by streams, dotted with villages, a chequerboard of green young wheat, yellow cornfield and rich ploughland; and at the centre of the scene, the sky flecked with a few cumulus clouds, is the lovely smooth, rolling shape of the central massif.

After climbing the pass, the road descends in a series of curves towards a rich valley filled with orchards enclosed in light grey mud walls. Tabriz lies in the fold of the hills on the horizon.

The capital of Azerbaijan, the third largest town in Iran, enjoys an agreeable situation lacking nothing in variety. The valleys to the south are watered by the streams flowing down from Mount Sahand. The surrounding country is fertile and smiling. The blue waters of Lake Rezaieh are only just over the horizon. Mountains are visible in nearly every direction. To the east, close at hand, there is a striking, eroded range of what Robert Byron calls 'plush coloured mountains approached by lemon coloured foothills'. It can thus be seen that the setting of Tabriz has originality as well as charm.

Once inside the city, however, a considerable effort of imagination is required to realize that this is the site of some of the largest building schemes and most daring architectural adventures ever undertaken. It is essential to pore over the history of Tabriz if the place as it looks today is to have any meaning at all. What Shah Abbas did to Isfahan, even what Louis XIV did at Versailles, pales in comparison with what the Il Khanid dynasty attempted here when Tabriz or Taurus was the Mongol capital at the turn of the thirteenth century. In the suburb of Shenb, south of the city, Arghun Khan founded a city which was continued by his successor and known as Ghazaniyeh. The buildings included a

dervish monastery, two theological colleges, a residence for
Sayyeds, a hospital, a library, an academy of philosophy, a palace,
a garden kiosk known as the Gardilyeh, and a great twelve-sided
tomb covered with a dome one hundred and fifty feet high and
nearly fifty yards in diameter according to some accounts. On the
tomb alone fourteen thousand workmen were employed and
Ghazan Khan took a personal interest in the design. The city was
thronged with Chinese astronomers, physicians and theologians,
and with Venetian and Genoese merchants. Rashid uddin Fadl
Allah, Ghazan's vizier, constructed his own university quarter,
the Rashidiyeh, to the east of the city; it was intended to rival in
splendour Ghazaniyeh itself. According to the vizier's letters, it
contained 24 caravanserais, 1,500 shops, and 30,000 charming [sic]
houses. It housed 200 reciters of the Koran, 400 scholars and theologians, and 1,000 students. One quarter was known as the Street
of the Scholars. There was a large dome which may well have
been an observatory. A few years later, about 1310, Oljeitu's
vizier Ali Shah Tabrizi, Rashid's rival, ordered the construction,
in the heart of the city, of a mosque whose great iwan was to
exceed in size that of the Taq-i-Kisra at Ctesiphon, the biggest
standing Sassanian arch. This iwan was a hundred feet in span, the
springing of the vault began at eighty feet and the depth of the
sanctuary was two hundred and fifteen feet. It was the largest
brick vault ever built with the exception of Gerona Cathedral, and
it surpassed the Taq-i-Kisra by sixteen feet. The vast ornamented
courtyard in front of it, measuring in all probability two hundred
and fifty by two hundred yards, was approached over a bridge
spanned by stone arches, and through a main portal. According to
Ibn Battuta the courtyard was paved with marble and the walls
covered with tiles. Other accounts state that the portal arches
were decorated with gold, and the vault round the courtyard
sustained with marble columns resembling fine crystal some ten
to fifteen feet in height. A stream ran through the court and in its
centre was a lake about two hundred and fifty feet square and six
feet deep, in the middle of which was a platform with a lion
spouting water into the pool on each of its sides. The sanctuary
iwan was flanked by a pair of minarets whose height is estimated

at one hundred and sixteen feet. The interior of the sanctuary was lighted by lamps on bronze chains inlaid with gold and silver. Each latticed window had twenty large round pieces of gold- and silver-decorated glass. The mihrab was probably of metallic lustre faïence. To the left of the sanctuary there is thought to have been a monastery, to the right a madrasseh. This, known as the Mosque of Ali Shah, was 'certainly one of the greatest buildings ever erected in Iran' (Pope). And when Clavijo came to Tabriz in 1402 he saw a great palace, perhaps at Ghazaniyeh, which he said had 20,000 rooms and was more impressive than the Ali Shah.

All this activity took place within about thirty years. But the beautification did not end with the end of the Mongol dynasty. Tabriz was again the capital from 1430 until about 1550. During this period the White Sheep leader Uzun Hasan built a great maidan to the south of the city, the whole area being enclosed with poplars. It was a brick-paved court like a cloister with marble seats all round. A seventy-five foot portal on the garden side led to the palace of Hasht Behesht (Eight Paradises), which according to one seventeenth-century traveller resembled Fontainebleau. And in 1465 Jahan Shah completed the construction of a great mosque, known as the Blue Mosque, which contained the largest and, with the Darb-i-Imam at Isfahan the finest, display of mosaic tilework in Iran.

Of all this galaxy of buildings little, alas, remains. Ghazan's dome had already collapsed in 1305, though a seventeenth-century traveller wrote of 'a tower lifting its head to the skies'. Rashid's university town was ravaged and looted before the end of the fourteenth century; foundations and the remains of masonry are now alone visible. A section of the great vault of the Ali Shah Mosque collapsed after a few years, probably carrying with it the minarets and damaging the side walls; it was never properly repaired. Uzun Hasan's maidan and garden have disappeared without trace. The Blue Mosque has been battered and beaten almost beyond recognition in a series of earthquakes. But for all this, modern Tabriz is not a ghost town. It seems to have turned its back on its past. It is nondescript more than anything else: rather featureless, rather ugly, moderately frequented, lacking in

either character or charm. There is a large and impressive covered
bazaar, but the whole of Tabriz's pre-nineteenth-century past is
concentrated in two monuments, both disappointing: the Arg, or
Citadel, which includes the remains of Ali Shah's Mosque, and
the pathetic remnants of the Blue Mosque.

The Arg, seen from a distance, is an imposing mass of 120
feet of sheer brick wall. But inside it there is nothing except
two arches and an indication of the position of the mihrab;
Ali Shah's court has been covered with ignoble buildings,
the sanctuary walls have been rebuilt and propped up, and the
approach to the ruin is across a dusty yard which passes for a kind
of urban esplanade, the most noticeable feature of which is a
public lavatory. It is hard to believe that any part of this place
was ever a mosque.

The Blue Mosque is hardly better. Its surroundings are unimpressive. To reach the sanctuary we have to go across a dusty
waste in front of a modern school. The other chief extant feature,
the north portal, is not in use and can only be seen by going outside and round the block. It is therefore difficult to get the feel of
the place or its dimensions. But the faïence mosaic both of the
north portal and of the main sanctuary, now an open court, is
dazzlingly lovely; the brown fluted marble dado, about six feet
high, with Kufic inscription, at the south entrance to the sanctuary
gives another indication of its past glories. Efforts are being made
to restore the building, and the aisles on each side of the sanctuary
have been rebuilt in brick. It is, however, doubtful whether it
would be wise to cover them with mosaic; unless this were to fall
below the level of what remains from the fifteenth century the
cost would be astronomical. If the dome over the main sanctuary
could be rebuilt it would help to give the feel of the closed or
kiosk type of mosque (as opposed to the four-iwan plan) of
which this is the finest example. But I understand that this would
be impracticable. The earthquake which smashed the dome also
shook the vaults by which it was supported, so that a new dome
could not be erected with its weight on them in their present
condition. If on the other hand they were to be demolished and
rebuilt, some of the finest tiles would perish in the process.

So, unless future techniques cause these views to be revised, the Blue Mosque of Tabriz will continue to stand more or less as it is now, in its mutilated splendour, the saddest ruin in a country where ruins are not in short supply. According to Wilbur's calculations,* out of every ten buildings in stone or fired brick constructed more than three hundred years ago, only one is still standing.

Ardebil, capital of Azerbaijan under the Omayyads, home of the Safavid dynasty, lies one hundred and fifty miles east of Tabriz. A drab, dilapidated town, it has at least one monument in a splendid state of preservation – the shrine of Sheikh Safi ad-Din Ishak, the first of the line of holy men from which the Safavids derived their name, who lived and died (in 1334) at Ardebil. The shrine, a rambling building which has received many additions, stands in the north-west quarter of the town. Once through the deep gateway we enter a large courtyard filled with trees and flowers, with walls of pale red brick. At the far end of the court we pass through a whitewashed stalacite doorway into a lobby decorated with yellow tiles of the late seventeenth century. This leads into a smaller court, which has a tiled iwan on the right and on the left a large wooden lattice of construction similar to that of the lattice windows of many old houses in Yazd, but on a much vaster scale. Straight ahead is the shrine itself, a façade with a cornice of dazzling blue tiles, with two small blue domes at the south-west end and a larger dome in the background. The entrance to the shrine is in the far left-hand corner of this court. The interior is dark, rich and ornate. There are three aisles, with balconies; the walls are entirely covered with Safavid paintings, and there is an ugly painted ceiling. The tomb of Ismail, the first Safavid king, lies in a separate chamber at the south-west end of the building; nearby are those of two of his sons. All the bodies lie in elaborately carved ivory chests. The tomb of the saint constitutes what in a Christian building would be the altar. Behind the shrine is a large octagonal hall entirely encrusted with wooden trelliswork with recesses for bottles of all shapes and sizes, like that in the upper rooms of the Ali Qapu in Isfahan. It is painted

* *Architecture of Islamic Iran*, 1955.

and in excellent condition. Today this room serves as a museum; formerly it was a dining or drinking room.

The shrine itself dates from the fifteenth century; the inner court, domes, and drinking hall are Safavid. The building has been much restored. For two hundred years the shrine lacked a roof; the original roof had rotted. Nasr-uddin Shah ordered a new roof with a low vault covering a painted ceiling which was conceived to be in imitation of the original ceiling and to match the wall paintings. But this low vaulted roof pressed out the lateral walls, so that by 1931 the building was in a parlous state and indeed in danger of collapse. Under the aegis of the Archaeological Department the vaulted Qajar roof was then removed and replaced by a flat tin roof with small cupolas which, thanks to the high cornice, are invisible from below. The building has a particular interest to English travellers because it was the home of the famous Ardebil carpet now in the Victoria and Albert Museum.

Just north of Ardebil is the village of Kelkhoran with the mausoleum of Sheikh Jebrail, Sheikh Safi-ad-Din's father – a square domed building with good Safavid plaster and tilework and elaborate pendentive vaulting, but in poor condition and not easy to find.

From Ardebil there are two routes back to Tabriz, one to the south, the other to the north of Mount Savalan. The first runs up a wide valley to join the main Tehran road at Bastanabad. The other follows the course of the Qara Su to Meshkin Shahr, formerly Khiov, where there is a Mongol tomb tower with cylindrical red brick exterior, portal and blind windows with mihrab-like frames, and showing the use of faïence mosaic in more developed form than at Sultaniyeh. At Ahar farther east there is the tomb and Mosque of Sheikh Shahab-ed-Din the tomb chamber of which has an interesting ceiling of strap-work plaster. This route lies through the country of the Turki-speaking Shahsavan, the largest nomadic tribe of Northern Iran, who winter in the Moghan steppe, away to the north near the Soviet border, and move to Savalan and the Talish hills for summer pasture.

Savalan (15,000 ft) like Demavend is an ancient volcano, and
its slopes are steep but grassy. But its top has been blown off. If
for this reason it lacks Demavend's perfection of form, it has other
qualities in compensation. It is not merely a cone but a range, and
a range of great and varied beauty. Its magnificent rock faces far
exceed anything Demavend has to offer, and are indeed an incite-
ment to the hardy mountaineer. For the majority who, like
myself, just pass by, the most splendid thing about it is what
might be called its stance. The surroundings are perfectly contrived to enable it to appear in the most favourable possible light
from all angles. To the north it slopes steadily down to the
Moghan steppe. To the south is the wide valley along which the
road runs from Tabriz to Ardebil and the sea, a road which at
one point rises briefly to cross a shoulder of the great mountain,
providing an intimacy with its surface which the most distant
views for all their grandeur cannot provide. To my mind Savalan
is the most haunting of all the mountains of Iran. It is not surprising that, according to legend, Zoroaster compiled the *Avesta* on
its summit; nor yet that Sheikh Safi ad-Din meditated at its base.

Most of the rest of Azerbaijan centres round and drains into
Lake Urmia, now called Rezaieh, after Reza Shah. This is a salt
lake some ninety miles long and thirty-five miles broad encircled
by mountain ranges. The water will not support any marine or
vegetable life; the coastline is coated with salt; but the brilliant
blue waters framed in a setting of brown or greenish mountains
under the clean transparent sky of Azerbaijan give a landscape of
melting loveliness.

There are several islands in the lake and the largest of them,
Shahi, a peninsula save in times of high water, contains the remains
of a Mongol fortress. Tradition has it that Hulagu Khan built on
the shores of a great lake in Azerbaijan a tower in which to conceal and conserve his treasure; that his body was brought to his
treasure house for burial; that during the reign of Abaqa the
treasury collapsed into the lake, but was subsequently recovered;
and that both Abaqa and his brother were buried in the same
place. While the location of this building has never been con-

clusively established, it seems probable that it was on the eastern shore of Shahi, near the village of Serai, where the remains of a fortress and a number of rock cuttings for purposes of water catchment are clearly visible.

A tour of Lake Rezaieh by car should not be lightly undertaken. The distance by road, 425 miles, is greater than that from Tehran to Tabriz.

If we proceed anti-clockwise the first place of any size, lying in a fertile valley open to the north, is Marand, where the road and Russian-built railway for Julfa, the frontier town, turn north. The ruined Friday Mosque with a fine Mongol stucco mihrab has one unusual feature: it is completely enclosed and has neither court nor portal.

Fifty miles farther on is the walled town of Khoy, surrounded by tobacco fields and fruit gardens. Here are several caravan-serais, a fine bazaar and a Seljuk gateway with lions carved in stone, and, two miles out of the town, a gruesome minaret with skulls embedded in its brickwork.

Another road goes north to the Turkish frontier through Maku. In the regions round Maku a German archaeological expedition has recently discovered a number of Urartian citadels at Zengar (north of Maku), Shotlu Kale Siah and Kale Oglu (to the east) and at Dutshaqi and Bastam (to the south). The last, with a whole series of fortified walls on a steep mountainside, dates from the seventh century B.C. A stone cuneiform inscription (now in the Tehran Museum) says that Rusa II built there a temple for the main God and a town.

Maku itself has several houses with elaborate outside decorations and about 5 km on the way to Bazargan is a country house of about 1900 belonging to the Khans of Maku. The setting is delightful and the painted plaster work in relief, the ceiling, the mirrored upstairs rooms and the period furniture are fascinating.

In this remote corner of Iran there are also a number of Armenian churches of which the most remarkable is known as Kara Kilisa (Black Church) on account of the black stone used for the building of the eleventh-century sanctuary with its striped twelve-sided drum and tent dome. The main body of the church built of white stone is seventeenth century, restored and added to in the nineteenth. Round this walled sanctuary hundreds of Armenian pilgrims pitch their tents in honour of its patron saint Thaddeus whose name day falls in July or August according to the Armenian calendar. There is another equally impressive, fourteenth-century convent church dedicated to St Stephen, with ornament on the cupola showing Islamic influence. This lies in a gorge some 20 km north-west of Julfa facing the Soviet frontier and is at present only accessible on foot from Shehi Abbassi (4½ hours).

Going south from Khoy we approach the lake once more at Shapur, three miles south of which stands the large mound of Haftavan Tepe where Manchester University has sponsored excavations since 1968. Results so far suggest that there was a place of importance here in the third to second millennium B.C.; that a large town existed in the ninth to tenth century B.C.; that the place continued though perhaps less flourishingly under Urartian rule and that there was continued occupation in Achaemenian and Sassanian times. There is a whole crop of Urartian citadels south and east of Shapur – Pir Kamus, Kale Waziri Kazimbashi and Karniarouk. And in a range of hills south of Haftavan and about quarter of a mile from the road is the only extant Sassanian rock carving in Azerbaijan showing the Armenian Varial paying homage to Ardeshir and Shapur.

At Shapur, formerly Salmas, there once stood a cylindrical Mongol tower not unlike that at Khiov, but it was totally destroyed in a recent earthquake, probably in 1929. A few miles farther along this road there is a Sassanian rock carving.

The town of Urmia, now known as Rezaieh, like the lake, stands in the middle of an enormous, densely cultivated oasis, the largest piece of continuous greenery on the plateau. The lake, invisible here, is at a respectful distance on one side; the mighty mountains which form Iran's frontier with Turkey, and later with Iraq, fill the western horizon. Fruit, vines and tobacco grow in great profusion here; the Mayor of Rezaieh assured me that he could distinguish by look and taste seventy different varieties of the grape. The town has a prosperous air, and though

7a. SULTANIYEH: Mausoleum of Oljeitu (1310). 'Its egg-shaped dome is some one hundred and seventy feet above the ground' (*p. 146*)

7b. MARAGHEH: Gunbad-i-Surkh (1147). 'The finest brickwork in Persia' (*p. 160*)

8a. (*above*) ISFAHAN: Exterior of the small Dome Chamber (1088) of the Friday Mosque (*p. 188*) 8b. (*below*) ISFAHAN: Dome of the Royal Mosque (1616) seen from the courtyard of the Madrasseh (*p. 195*)

in fact much smaller, it seems as much of a metropolis as Tabriz. The population includes an important Christian minority, Armenian, Nestorian and Chaldean; there are several churches of these communities as well as a number of Christian missions. Rezaieh is also by tradition the birthplace of Zoroaster. The Friday Mosque adjoining the bazaar is a square dome chamber flanked by vaulted prayer halls. It is an unusual building which some think may once have been a fire temple; the large windows which pierce the zone of transition make it lighter than any Seljuk dome. The stucco mihrab bears the date 1277, interesting because it is about the earliest post-Mongol work that has survived; it appears to have been plastered over an earlier mihrab. The Sardar Mosque in the main street has an ingratiating tiled façade (Qajar) and squat metal clocktowers; and in the Khiaban Ebn-i-Sina opposite a secondary school stands a Seljuk tomb tower, the Seh Gunbad, whose finely decorated façade moved Godard to observe that in architecture it is possible to be both absurd and charming.

The southern end of the lake has several archaeological sites. At Gok Tepe, near Rezaieh, a British archaeological expedition under Burton Brown excavated in six weeks eight layers, each of which yielded pottery of widely differing types, but which served to show, at different times, Hittite, Iranian and Caucasian art.

At and around Hasanlu, not far from the southern tip of the lake (turn left at the junction 10 km after Heidarabad), the University of Pennsylvania Museum has been conducting a series of excavations since the late 1950s. They have found, within a fortified area about a mile in circumference, superimposed ceramic remains to a depth of eighty-nine feet in which nine phases are clearly recognizable, the earliest being about 6000 B.C. Their finds include a remarkable gold cup, an impressive crop of Mannaean pottery and funerary ornaments and at Hajji Firuz Tepe one mile to the south a unique figurine the Hajji Firuz Venus of the sixth millennium B.C. The excavations lead to the conclusion that about 1000 B.C. the great citadel of Hasanlu was constructed with walls ten-foot thick, probably as a defence against the Assyrians, that it was destroyed about 800 B.C. by the

Urartians and reoccupied after an interval. Other citadels of the
same period were probably spaced out along the valley which
also contains the Late Bronze Age mound of Dinkha Tepe with
a stone tomb for at least nine persons, and the tumulus field of
Se Girdan (seventh century B.C., see *Iran* IX p. 227). The plain of
Mahabad contains a number of mounds of the same period.
25 km north of Mahabad, about 1 km off the road to Miandoab
and clearly visible on the left is the rock tomb of Fakrakah, with
a columned entrance, thought to be of late Achaemenean date.
A little farther on is Maragheh, which though of comparatively
recent origin, for little is known of it in pre-Islamic times, can
fairly claim to be the most interesting town in Azerbaijan.

The small town lies in a valley filled with peach and apricot
groves and rimmed by white hills. The plain to the south and
west is dotted with large and flourishing villages full of individuality; the outskirts of Bukan, for example, are covered with curious
stepped towers for raising water, and the women wear large check
chadors. Maragheh is situated on one bank of a respectable river.
A number of buildings in pink brick give it an unusually solid
look. In the last few years it has come to boast of a large grey and
very modern railway station, on the line from Tehran to Tabriz.

Maragheh's chief claim to renown is that it was the first Mongol
capital under Hulagu. Here he built his famous domed observatory in 1259, on a site to the west of the town; but it was already
in ruins in 1340 and little remains to show for it today. Altogether
Maragheh possessed five tomb towers, but it is a little irony of
history that the three which date from the pre-Mongol period
are still in good preservation, whereas of their two Mongol
counterparts one has disappeared while the other is distinctly
dilapidated.

There is a good deal of misinformation in print (to which I
myself have in ignorance contributed) about the details and
location of these towers, which the following list is designed to
correct.

Gunbad-i-Surkh (Red Dome), 1148, in a garden east of the
    town;

Circular tower (unnamed), 1168, and Gunbad-i-Kabud (Blue
Dome), 1197, adjoining a school near the town centre;
Gunbad-i-Ghaffariyeh (damaged), c. 1330, beside the river
north of the bridge.

The Red Dome was erected to the memory of one who called
himself the Master of Azerbaijan, but of whom history records
nothing. It is a deceptively modest building which deserves close
attention on account of its exquisite proportions, the skilful brick
decoration, the sparing employment of blue tiles, and the delicate
use of cobalt stone at the base and head of the flanking brick
columns on each façade. The tower is square, with two shallow
arches on three sides and a central doorway on the fourth. The
decorated brickwork is subtle and original, and the round columns
on each corner are, in Schroeder's view, the finest brickwork in
Persia. The zone of transition is only three feet in height and is
lighted by windows. The vaulting in the crypt, also in brick, is a
fascinating study in geometrical design. The building was formerly covered with an octagonal pyramid, of which only the
brick base remains.

Elaborate decorations in ornamental brick and blue tiles are the
outstanding feature of the Gunbad-i-Kabud, an octagonal building with a richly jewelled exterior of which the lower part has
the appearance of being covered with a single piece of lace.
The shallow arch of the Red Tower is here repeated with different
effect, being filled with three rows of brick stalactites. The legend
that it housed the mother of Hulagu may have been encouraged
by its resemblance to the tomb of another woman, Mumina
Khatun, at Nahkchivan in Soviet Azerbaijan, whose 'gentle,
almost genteel elegance . . . gives it the appearance of a towering
vial of perfumes'.* In fact, Hulagu's mother was a Christian, the
inscriptions are Islamic, and it has been proved conclusively that
the tower was built before the Mongol invasion. The adjoining
circular tower is of no special interest.

Like the Red Tower, the Gunbad-i-Ghaffariyeh is square, and
like the Blue Tower, is decorated with faïence. The use of

* Schroeder in contribution to Pope's *Survey of Persian Art*, Vol. II.

colour is more varied than in the latter monument, though the exterior is less overloaded with decoration. Where the Red Tower has plain arcades, Ghaffariyeh is relieved by windows with a decorative plaque above them. Unfortunately it is in a partly ruined condition, so that for example it is not possible to say whether it was covered with a dome, and if so of what shape.

Maragheh has two mosques possibly Safavid each with five rows of eight wooden columns, with wooden stalactite capitals, all painted, and with wooden slatted ceilings Kazvin style.

A day's journey from Maragheh to the south-east in a remote area is the site of the great city known today under the all too ubiquitous name of Takht-i-Suleiman. The site is 42 km or about 2¼ hours by track from Takab, which is about half way between Miandoab and Bijar (Kurdistan) on a reasonable gravel road. On the site, once thought to have been the Parthian capital of Praaspa (cf. p. 16), recent German excavations under Dr Naumann have discovered stamped clay impressions which prove it to have been the Adhur Gushnasp, or Fire of the Male Horse, the special fire of Kings and Knights. Levels going back to Achaemenian and Parthian times have been found, but its hey-day was as a Sassanian sanctuary of the fifth to sixth centuries A.D. An extensive wall with defence towers, rebuilt by the Mongols, encircles the site. There were two entrances, one to the north which was the processional entrance of the Sassanians, and another to the south-east, still surmounted by a Sassanian arch which also provides the outlet to the lake. Within the great enclosure are the foundations of the Sassanian Palace rebuilt by Abaqa Khan with an iwan still standing; the remains of a small mosque; a fire altar and a lake measuring seventy-five yards across, its sides built up by natural deposits. Mustawfi, visiting Saturiq (as it was then called) at the beginning of the fourteenth century, describes it as a town with a great palace on a mound in the middle which had been restored by Abaqa Khan. Today the place is a desolate mass of ruins impressive for what it was and enhanced by the scenic grandeur of its setting, which includes, 3 km to the north-west, the dramatic profile of the hollow mountain which was the Mannaean sanctuary of Zendan-i-Suleiman, destroyed about the seventh century B.C.

Some 20 km south of Takab are the sacred caves of Kerefta where there is an inscription in Greek, and a crude relief of Seleucid or Parthian date. We are on the fringe of Kurdistan – and the next chapter.

CHAPTER EIGHT

Media

There is no generic name for the mountain country bounded on
the north by Azerbaijan, on the west by Iraq, on the east by the
central depression, and on the south by Khuzistan and the Bakhtiari mountains. It covers the backbone of the Zagros range, but
that is too extensive a definition. To the north of the Baghdad-
Tehran road Kurds predominate, and the region is often known
as Iranian Kurdistan; to the south, and roughly as far as the
trans-Iranian railway, it is Lur country and unofficially described
as Luristan; but the settled areas cannot properly bear tribal names
and the two largest towns of the region, Kermanshah and
Hamadan, are not strictly speaking in either Kurdistan or Luristan.
(Kermanshah is the administrative capital of a province which
bears its own name.) This is, however, the heartland of the
Median kingdom just as the country round Shiraz, Fars, is the
heartland of the Persian kingdom. It was symbolic of the union
of the Medes and Persians under Cyrus that his descendants
spent their springs at Persepolis, the city of Fars, and their summers at Ecbatana (Hamadan), the former capital of Media.

Media is a region which itself belongs to the remote past; its
dominant tone is pre-Islamic, and to a considerable extent
prehistoric. It is a land of great smooth time-worn hills and high
wide valleys. Along the ancient highways there are early rock
carvings and dark ageless tombs. The valleys are thick, not indeed
with corn, but with flat-topped mounds whose graves contain
bronzes, as in Luristan, or treasure, as at Saqqiz. The spirit of the
Magians still survives here in many a ruined Sassanian fire temple
or palace. This is an old, worn, battered country, trampled by

invading hordes and modern armies, now ramshackle and remote, tribal and scarcely tamed, with a flavour quite different from the more settled parts of Iran, and an aura of antiquity that is almost tangible. We are far indeed from Seljuk mosques, Mongol restorations or Safavid town-planning; all these upstart régimes seem to belong to a different world. In this ancient kingdom, which contains an oil refinery but no railway, everything above ground seems modern: a medieval tower, a Jewish shrine, the most elaborate of all Sassanian rock-carvings, a Parthian lion, a Seleucid column, even Achaemenian inscriptions. All these serve merely as successive bells ringing back down the centuries to an alien, much older, world whose presence we can feel but whose features, lost as they are in tombs and tells,* we can hardly discern – a Lullubi horseman, gaily caparisoned, riding across the plain; a Scythian tribe burying its hoard as it flies before the Medes; a group of Magian priests, wielding immense and semi-occult powers, bending sternly over their everlasting fire in some obscure but holy rite. In the seared faces of the Kurdish tribesmen, under their black and white turbans, or from the eyes of the Lur women which flash out from their coal-black chadors, even from beneath the flat black cloth caps of the village folk, one senses the vestiges of an ancient tradition and strange folk ways which are older than Islam and belong to a forgotten world. 'I have seen eternal fires,' says Arnold Wilson,† 'burning in the hills of Luristan. I have seen women making their bows and saying their prayers to the high places ... sacred when Baal was all-powerful. I have seen rocks ... red with the blood of recent sacrifice.'

This upland region is bisected by one great road, the main route, indeed the only relatively easy one, from Mesopotamia to the plateau; it runs from Baghdad to Tehran through Kermanshah and Hamadan, the gateway to Asia, as Herzfeld calls it. At the point where the road leaves the dusty plain and turns its back on the last large palm grove, Iran begins. The customs post, however crowded with passengers and pilgrims, has an air of faded

* Ancient mounds. (Ar.)
† *Persia*, 1932.

imperial grandeur which sets exactly the right tone for an entry into this spacious kingdom. After Qasr-i-Shirin, with a ruined fire temple called Chehar Qapu and the remains of a palace built by Khosrow II for his wife Shirin, the grandeur of Iran unfolds. 'Lit from behind by the fallen sun', says Robert Byron, 'and from in front by the rising moon, a vast panorama of rounded foothills rolled away from the Sassanian ruins, twinkling here and there with the amber lights of villages; till out of the far distance rose a mighty range of peaks, the real ramparts at last.' A little farther on at Sar-i-Pul, where the hills close in, two faded bas-reliefs reputed to date from 2300 B.C., with Akkadian inscriptions, bear witness to the antiquity of this highway. These are followed at Dukkan-i-Daud by the tomb of an Achaemenian king with a Seleucid rock relief under its doorway; and half way up the 5,000-foot Paitak pass a Sassanian ruin, the Taq-i-Girreh, variously described as toll house or hunting lodge. Fifteen difficult miles to the north, on a high plateau flanked by precipitous ranges, are the remains of a vast Sassanian fortified palace, recently described by E. J. Keall (*Iran* V, 1967). It may be the site of the Madharustan mentioned by Arab geographers; traces of decorative and figurative stucco have been found in the walled enclosure of Gach Gunbad five hundred metres west of the fortified palace of Ja-i-Dar, both overlooked by the great fortress, on an eroded pinnacle, of Qal'eh-i-Yezdigird named after the unhappy monarch (see p. 18) whose last stronghold tradition claims it to have been.

The other approach, from the east, is less dramatic. There are two routes from Tehran to Hamadan, both across the western fringes of the central desert. One goes by Kazvin, following the Tabriz road as far as Takistan (see p. 145); from Ab-i-Garm some thirty miles farther on, a track leads westwards for twenty miles to the twin tomb towers of Kharraqan, near the village of Hisar-i-Armeni. These are early Seljuk octagonal towers (1067/8 and 1093) with the earliest double domes known in Iran, rounded buttresses and astonishingly advanced brick decoration both the work of the same architect. The older tower has vivid internal wall paintings. They were discovered as recently as 1965 by David Stronach, Director of the British Institute of Persian

Studies in Tehran, and T. Culyer Young of the Royal Ontario Museum, when making a survey of Median and Achaemenian routes in Western Persia. There is no clue to the identity of the occupant; the inscriptions are illegible as Persian or Arabic. The road then crosses the Aminabad pass and beyond it a little way to the east on a route to Saveh lies Darjazin where there are two even handsomer tomb towers of the Mongol period, Hud which is octagonal and Azhat with flanged façades, both containing fine brick decoration.

The other road leaves the Isfahan road at Saveh from which there is a track to Kazvin which can still be travelled by jeep or Land-Rover in dry weather, passing the great ruined caravanserais of Dung and Jib, the first at the outlet of a fertile valley, the second cupped in an arid amphitheatre, both splendid in their desolation. Saveh itself is reputed to be the place from which the Three Wise Men set out with gold, frankincense and myrrh for Jerusalem. Marco Polo passed this way at a time when Saveh flourished as a pottery centre maintained by workers who had transferred themselves from ravaged Rayy and damaged Kashan. The Friday Mosque has a Seljuk minaret and an early Safavid polychrome relief stucco mihrab with delicate spiral vines painted in blue and white, such as we see in early miniatures, apparently the work of an illuminator or carpet designer. Pope knows of nothing else like it in Iran. This mosque was restored by the Mongols and added to by Shah Ismail, no doubt because of the importance of Saveh on the route from Kazvin to the south. The other mosque, the Maidan mosque, has what Godard believes to be the oldest minaret extant in Iran (A.D. 1061).

Hamadan has the most illustrious past, the highest elevation, and the finest situation of any living city in Iran. Founded, so the story goes, by the legendary King Jamshid, Ecbatana was the Median capital long before Achaemenes was heard of. According to Herodotus (alas, more entertaining than accurate!) it was constructed by Deioces, allegedly a Median chief of the eighth century B.C., who proceeded to establish a reputation for fair dealing, thus making himself invaluable as a dispenser of justice. After a time, however, the cunning fellow announced that he

had had enough; but his retirement was followed by such anarchy
that a general meeting had to be called at which, says Herodotus,
his friends presumably did most of the talking. The result was
that Deioces was made king by acclamation. He then built the
city, and surrounded it by seven concentric walls, each higher
than the last; the two inner rings were plated with silver and gold,
and the five outer ones painted white, black, crimson, blue and
orange. All communication with the king was by messenger, and
it was an offence for anyone to laugh or spit in his presence. The
object of this was to guard him against the jealousy and resent-
ment of his contemporaries, who might otherwise have plotted
against him. Whatever we choose to believe of this story, Deioces
built a capital which was to last for close on fourteen centuries,
or until the Arab conquest. Ecbatana was the summer capital of
the Achaemenians, then of the Parthians and of the Sassanians.
Under the Sassanians a Jewish colony was established there,
possibly by the Jewish wife of Yezdigird I. Even after the Arab
conquest the city, then known as Hamadan, had its moments
of glory. The famous philosopher-physician Ibn Sina (or Avicenna), though a native of Bokhara, finally settled here after
wandering via Khiva, Merv, Nishapur, Jurjan, Rayy and Kazvin
in pursuit of patronage and employment; and it was in Hamadan
that he died in A.D. 1037. Later, after being one of the Seljuk
capitals, Hamadan was ravaged by the Mongols and decimated
by Timur. From these invasions the city never fully recovered;
it received, moreover, an additional dose of destruction in the
eighteenth century when it was for over sixty years in the
possession of the Turkish conquerors of Mesopotamia. Modern
Hamadan with its six great avenues, built by Reza Shah, radiating
through a rabbit warren of tenements and tumuli, its flourishing
carpet factory, its blue pottery industry and its large green belt,
has more vitality than style, and could lay no claim to rank
among the great monumental cities of Persia. It is only when we
contemplate its ancient mounds, and reflect on what lies beneath
them, that its unique character can be appreciated. There can be
few cities which have so much history, or such riches as Xerxes's
Treasury and Alexander's loot from Persepolis, waiting to be

uncovered beneath their streets. And it is precisely because Hamadan, unlike Susa or Siyalk, Nimrud or Nineveh, is still a going concern that excavation is so difficult, and indeed may never be undertaken on any major scale.

So we have to be content with what is visible above the surface; and what other city in Iran can boast of a piece of Parthian sculpture, a Jewish shrine, a late Seljuk or early Mongol tomb encrusted entirely, inside and out, in decorated plaster, or a modern concrete version of Gunbad-i-Kabus?

The Parthian sculpture is a stone lion, the Sang-i-Shir, which stands on a hillock in a modern garden outside the built-up area of the city, to the south-east. It is thought to have crowned one of the gates of the old city. Today the lion is much frequented by the young ladies of the place, because of a superstition that it will help them to get a lover if they kiss its nose and deposit a little stone in one of the many depressions with which the old beast is dimpled.

The Jewish shrine is known as the tomb of Esther and Mordecai. According to tradition, Esther visited Susa to appeal to Xerxes on behalf of the Jewish people; he married her, and later she brought her uncle Mordecai to the Persian court. In one of the three tiny rooms which constitute the present shrine – of venerable appearance and uncertain age – there are, in addition to a Hebrew bible, two crudely sculptured ebony tombs, one of which perhaps conceals the remains of the Jewish wife of Yezdigird I.

The Seljuk (or Mongol) tomb, the Gunbad-i-Alavian, is the only outstanding monument in Hamadan. According to one theory it was originally a dervish monastery (khanaqah) and later became the tomb of the Alavian family, who achieved distinction in the local religious world, though not themselves sufis. The Alavians virtually ruled Hamadan for two hundred years, and the present building may well have never been anything but a family memorial. It is certainly not a 'funeral tower', as it is sometimes described. The building does not indeed conform to any known type, whether of shrine or tomb tower. Its plan is square, but hexagonal flanged buttresses at each corner give it a fortress-like appearance. Though without polychrome plaster or glazed tile, it achieves a degree of baroque floridity which is unique for its period. The soft, almost lush outline is, as Pope observes, in pleasing contrast to the aridity of the plateau. The interior is equally ornate. Each wall is divided into three deep panels marked by a niche with a pointed arch inside a rectangular frame enclosed by slender colonnettes themselves heavily covered with geometrical and honeycomb patterns. The panels are filled with a double or triple system of floral patterns in high relief. The finest work of all is reserved for the mihrab. The whole effect of the interior is breathtaking. The roof, and parts of the exterior, have been much repaired. The north-east turret in particular was damaged during the Second World War and was, I understand, well restored under the care of an imaginative British officer.

Hamadan's modern tomb is the mausoleum of Avicenna, built in 1952. It covers the tomb of the philosopher himself and of Sheikh Abu Said Dokhduh, a mystic poet with whom he lodged at Hamadan. There are good modern inscriptions in Persian and Arabic and a small museum. The flat roof from which the conical concrete tower rises provides an excellent view over the upper parts of the city, and towards Mount Alvand (11,644 ft). On the northern slopes of this majestic mountain, at Ganj-i-Nameh seven miles from Hamadan, there are two rock inscriptions in old Persian, neo-Elamite and neo-Babylonian which date from the reigns respectively of Darius and Xerxes. On the south side of Alvand is the village of Tuisarkan, which boasts an octagonal Mongol tomb tower with a remarkable round flanged roof thought to be unique; while at Songkor in the same area there is a plain domed octagonal tower also of this period.

The road to Kermanshah winds up over the Assadabad pass, snow-covered for much of the winter, and at Kangavar, midway between the two cities, are impressive remains of a Seleucid temple dedicated to Artemis or Anahita, one of the few major sites of this period, now being uncovered under the direction of Mr Kambaksh Fard of the Archaeological Service of Iran. The wide rolling valley beyond is well stocked with prehistoric mounds, to the base of which modern villages often cling. Near

Sahneh at Farhad-u-Shirin there is the rock tomb of an Achaemenian king, probably later than the tombs of Naqsh-i-Rustam.
Kermanshah owes its name, the Town of the King of Kerman, to
the fact that it was founded in A.D. 390 by Bahram IV, who had
been governor of Kerman before he ascended the Sassanian throne.
It is the capital of a province and the site of an oil refinery; it is
magnificently situated at the base of a spectacular mountain, and
possesses only one really noticeable building, the tomb and takieh
of Moaven-el-Molk, a Qajar complex standing in the middle of
the town near a stream best reached from the Khiaban Shahnaz
which runs east of and parallel to the main street. The interior is a
riot of tilework, especially noteworthy being pictures of Moaven-
el-Molk preaching (in the entrance court), of animals and mystical
emblems (in the takieh court) and in the dome chamber a fine
series of portraits of Kings throughout the ages and a representation of scenes from the life of the Prophet in nineteenth-century
garb, with decapitated enemies piled in horizontal rows like
sardines.

   Near Kermanshah are the famous rock carvings of Bisitun and
Taq-i-Bustan. Those at Bisitun, thirty miles to the east on the
Hamadan road, celebrate Darius's triumph over the magus
Gaumatas, who attempted to seize the throne after the death of
Cambyses by passing himself off as Cambyses's brother, and whose
own funeral niche is believed by Herzfeld to be at Sakavand,
south of Kermanshah. The cuneiform inscription, in old Persian,
neo-Elamite and neo-Babylonian, according to the prevailing
fashion, occupies an area of vertical rock some one hundred and
fifty feet long and one hundred feet high, and is of great importance in the history of archaeology. Sir Henry Rawlinson, who in
1839 was engaged in training the Shah's troops, succeeded in
climbing the rock five hundred feet above the plain, let himself
down by ropes, copied the inscription, and eventually deciphered
the neo-Babylonian, thus laying the foundation for a lifetime of
Assyrian and Babylonian studies which are the basis of much of
our present knowledge of early Mesopotamian history. His
method of transcribing the inscriptions naturally involved a
margin of error, as well as physical risk, and he was followed in

1948 by Dr George Cameron of the Oriental Institute of the
University of Chicago, who made a facsimile impression in latex
from the steps of a painter's ladder.

The sculptures themselves were the subject of much un-
scientific speculation until Rawlinson established their true
identity by deciphering the inscriptions. Thus Ker Porter
thought that they were Shalmenezer and the ten captive tribes
of Israel; Gardanne believed them to be Christ and the twelve
disciples; Keppel said that they were a party of prisoners led by
Esther supplicating Ahasuerus.

At the base of the rock is a raised area which recent German
investigations suggest may be the ruins of an unfinished building
of the early seventh century B.C. with a Parthian settlement, a large
Sassanian terrace and a Mongol settlement superimposed on it.*

Taq-i-Bustan, a few miles west of Kermanshah, celebrates the
revival of rock-sculpture. These carvings are of special interest.
With one exception (Shapur in Azerbaijan) they are the only
Sassanian rock carvings outside Fars. Unlike nearly all other
Sassanian sculptures they do not date from a short period of
seventy years in the third century. In subject and treatment,
moreover, the two principal reliefs at Taq-i-Bustan are utterly
different from anything else in Iran.

In the lee of a great mountain is a little garden watered from a
nearby spring. To the right of two grottoes stands a bas-relief
representing the investiture of Ardeshir II (A.D. 379–83), who is
flanked by Ormuzd and Mithras. In the small grotto, an oblong
room with simple barrel-shaped roof, are carvings of Shapur II
and III, dating from the reign of the latter (383–88). But it is the
large grotto which is of outstanding interest. Its sculptures are of
much more recent date (610–26). The carved façade, with its
Nikes floating above cornucopia and bearing a garland of
ribbons, its pilasters decorated with trees of life bursting into
intricate bouquets of flowers, has no Sassanian parallel.

On the end wall within the grotto there are two scenes, one
above the other; the upper shows the investiture of Khosrow II
and the lower portrays the same monarch on his favourite horse,

* See Annex, note 4.

Shabdiz. It is not these, however, but the side walls which command attention. For here are the famous hunting panels, with their intricate design and vivid portrayal of animals. To the left there is a boar-hunt in a swamp; to the right, a stag-hunt in a forest. A wealth of little scenes and incidents charms the eye: the elephants struggling in the swamp or carrying away the spoils; stags and riders in combat; whole ranks of boars realistically portrayed; strings of camels leading off dead stags; boatloads of women clapping their hands; a poor girl holding a parasol over a king. The parts perhaps are better than the whole. The composition may leave something to be desired, but the details are a delight. Herzfeld* contrasts the realism with which the animals are drawn with the lifeless human figures – 'poor dead kings compared with beautiful and living animals'. He alleges, without explanation, that the best parts cannot be the work of Persian artists. Only Indians could make such elephants. The principle of the design he says is Greek. The subject, of hunts among fences, is of oriental origin. The treatment is that of the painter, the miniaturist rather than the sculptor. 'Only with the Kings are we back in the true Iranian world.' Are these conclusions really necessary? Is it unreasonable for the layman to see in these sculptures, extraordinary as to both date and style, a kind of link between the delicately chiselled but static processions of Persepolis and the scenes of movement dear alike to the heart of the hunting-carpet weaver and the miniaturist?

To the north of the Hamadan-Kermanshah road, stretching away to the southern edge of Lake Rezaieh, lies Kurdistan. It is a remote region of grassy rolling hills on the east and secluded valleys, far from any beaten track, dipping down towards the Mesopotamian plain, away from the main currents of Iranian life, proud, gaunt, independent and aloof. Though the Kurds, thanks to a relatively generous rainfall, are largely settled in villages and small towns, they are still intensely tribal; they wear a distinctive dress, seen to great advantage at the village of Bukan near Miandoab in the north, and have many affinities with their fellow Kurds across the border in Iraq. They are also

* *Iran in the Ancient East*, 1941.

predominantly Sunni. The total Kurdish population of Iran, including those settled in the region of Bujnurd, is close on two million.

Sanandaj, formerly Sehna, is a rough, rambling country town with several fine Qajar houses. The orange tint of its ramshackle buildings provides a colourful background to the brightly clad country folk who throng its streets. The approach to it from Hamadan, on a bad road which dives in great curves from a broad-backed mountain into what seems like a bottomless valley, is perhaps more impressive than that to any other town in the country. A better road connects with Kermanshah.

The only other place of any size, Saqqiz, far to the north, is primarily associated with the treasure accidentally found by a shepherd near the village of Zuwiye after a landslide in 1947, and systematically collected by M. Godard since 1949. This is of great archaeological interest, because clearly Assyrian and Scythian objects are found side by side with Mannaean work which bears a close resemblance to the bronzes of Luristan. Several of the Zuwiye finds, and notably a magnificent gold pectoral, illustrate clearly the interplay of Assyrian and Scythian motifs, and are the clearest indication yet available that there was contact and cross-fertilization in this area between the arts of the Mesopotamian plain and those of the steppe, probably in the seventh century B.C. The finest single object is a silver dish in which the decoration consists mainly of concentric circles of crouching hares, lynxes, and heads of wild animals; Ghirshman believes it to be the oldest example of Scythian art in existence. Even the name, Saqqiz, is thought to derive from the Scythians or Sakka, and there is a strong likelihood that this was their capital when they settled south of Urmia after conquering the Mannaeans, to be ejected themselves, some centuries later, by the Medes.

Luristan, to the south of the road, is less settled and even more inaccessible than Kurdistan. It lies entirely to the west of the main Zagros watershed within a line drawn roughly from Kermanshah to Burujird (where there is a fine Seljuk mosque with Kufic inscription) and from there to Dorud, then down the Ab-i-Diz, the river valley which the trans-Iranian railway follows, to near

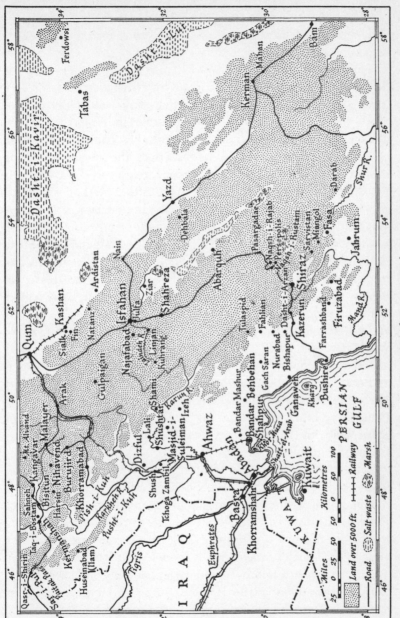

Iran (southern section)

Dizful, then north-west along the base of the mountains to near Qasr-i-Shirin. The region consists almost exclusively of a succession of whale-backed ridges running slightly south of east divided by deep valleys. Separated from the interior of Iran by the main Zagros range, from Iraq by sharp tiers of cliff and malarial valleys, and virtually closed to any sort of north-east-south-west communications by the nature of the country, Luristan is or has been a natural fortress admirably equipped to resist penetration whether from Mongols, Turks, the representatives of the central Government in Tehran – or foreign travellers. Curzon, who (unlike myself) writes with great authority, but who (like myself) seems not to have travelled into the interior of Luristan, says that the only British, or for that matter European, travellers he knows of who have done so are: Captain Grant and Lieutenant Fotheringham, who were sent by Sir John Malcolm on a reconnaissance in 1810 and were murdered at Khorramabad; Sir Henry (then Major) Rawlinson, who marched through the region with a detachment of Persian troops in 1836; and Henry Layard and a Baron de Bode, a Secretary in the Russian Legation, a few years later. Since then there have been a number of archaeological expeditions (notably the excavations of Professor vanden Berghe at Bani Surmah and elsewhere); a few visitors such as Harold Nicolson, Vita Sackville-West and Gladwyn Jebb who had a twelve-day holiday there in 1923, and the imperturbable Freya Stark who visited 'that part of the country where one is less frequently murdered' in 1931.

In the past the obstacles to visiting Luristan have not been due solely to the nature of the country. They also derive in part from the reputation of the inhabitants. Though the Lurs speak a dialect allied to Kurdish, and are closely related to the Bakhtiari farther south, they have somehow established a separate, and not altogether enviable, identity. 'A people without a history or literature or even a tradition presents a phenomenon in the face of which science stands abashed,' is Curzon's sweeping comment. In fact their recent history is fairly clear. From the middle of the twelfth until the early seventeenth century they were ruled continuously by the dynasty known as the Atabegs who held

sway over a larger area of the Zagros than what we now call
Luristan. The region over which they ruled, based on Khorramabad (a charming town with a fine Seljuk minaret and dominated
by its castle the Qal'eh Falak-ol-aflak), was described by Marco
Polo as one of the eight kingdoms of Persia. Extinguished neither
by Hulagu nor Timur, though not for lack of trying, they were
finally suppressed by Shah Abbas, who seized and put to death
the last of the dynasty and abolished the title of Atabeg. Since
then, not unnaturally, Lurs have been 'agin the Government'. A
mule track leading into the heart of Luristan from the north
passes between two mountains named Chia Dozdan (the hill of
thieves) and Pir-i-Dozd (the old thief). 'There is no one like us
for stealing in the world,' Freya Stark's guide told her proudly;
and she describes their 'expressive way of sucking their forefinger
and holding it up to illustrate the complete destitution in which
one is left' after receiving their traditional attentions. Nevertheless, she made two extended journeys in Luristan unscathed, and
found them hospitable and entertaining, though she adds 'to be
in disgrace with the law was one way of being really popular
among the tribesmen'. She has less to say of the women, but
Arnold Wilson pays them masculine tribute. 'Their powers of
endurance,' he says, 'are a perpetual source of wonder to me. . . .
They and they alone milk the sheep and the goats, weave carpets
and tent cloth, saddle-bags and much else. . . . Without a wife a
man is as helpless and useless as half a pair of anything else – and
knows it.'*

The country is divided by the Saimarreh or Karkheh river into
two parts: Pish-i-Kuh, before the mountain (Kabir Kuh) to the
north and east, and Pusht-i-Kuh, beyond the mountain, to the
south and west. In the former there were settled villages even in
Curzon's time; and now there is the Tehran-Ahwaz motor road.
It was in the northern part of this region, in the valleys accessible
to Harsin, that the bulk of the Luristan bronzes were found.
Arnold Wilson travelled extensively here in 1911. He noticed
that the area was divided theologically by the Kashgan river.
To the west of it, men swore by Baba Buzurg, to the east by

* *South-West Persia*, 1941.

Shahzadeh Ahmed; both had shrines on lofty heights. West of the
Kashgan too there were sacred groves. 'At intervals of a day's
journey or so, one sees upon a hillside devoid even of bushes a
fifty-acre patch of gnarled oaks with a few young self-sown trees
among them, the ground strewn with dead wood in a district
where wood is extremely scarce and no fuel obtainable save for
dung or grass.'

It is in this area that there have been two important archaeological finds in recent years: at Nush-i-Jan, 20 km west of
Malayer and at Baba Jan, 160 km away to the south-west. A
dig at Baba Jan sponsored by the Institute of Archaeology of
London University (1966–69) uncovered a fort, with a painted and
tiled room in close association with it, as well as a number of
fortified manor houses – all probably of the eighth century B.C.*
At Nush-i-Jan the British Institute of Persian Studies has discovered one of the principal religious sites of eighth- to seventh-
century Media. The tall remains of a lozenge-shaped fire temple
include a triangular inner sanctuary with a stepped fire altar
similar to those used in Achaemenian times. The antechamber
gave access to a spiral ramp leading to the roof – possibly to
carry the sacred fire to a position in which it would have been
visible for miles around. The recessed blind windows with projecting dentils and recessed crosses seem related to the external
decorations of Pasargadae and Naqsh-i-Rustam (q.v.). To the
west of the temple was a reception hall with four rows of three
columns and elaborate buttresses and niches. When the Median
settlement was abandoned it was blocked with mud-bricks and
plaster in a ceremonial manner.

Pusht-i-Kuh is almost exclusively nomad country; the inhabitants, says Curzon, were known as Feilis, which itself means
thieves. Though more inaccessible, Pusht-i-Kuh is lower, hotter
and poorer agriculturally; there is indeed little cultivation save
fruit trees and occasional rice paddies; and in bad years the tribes
make flour of acorns, or roast them like chestnuts, with painful
results. Freya Stark observed that there was hardly a house in the

* A detailed report on this fascinating site is contained in *Iran XIV*, pp. 19–40
and *XV*, pp. 103–40.

whole area until the Government of Reza Shah took the last Wali prisoner in 1932, dissolved his tent capital Husainabad and built in its place the new administrative centre known as Ilam, which now has over 20,000 inhabitants. Three palaces of the Walis are still standing and there is an ancient tomb which is attributed by local tradition to the father of Haroun-al-Raschid.

Three important prehistoric cemeteries have recently been excavated near Ilam by Professor vanden Berghe: at Bani Surmah, Kalleh Nisar, War Kabud (respectively 50 and 25 km north-west) and Kalwali (12 km south-east). At Bani Surmah and Kalleh Nisar large funeral vaults with copper and bronze objects dating from the early Bronze Age (2600–2500 B.C.) have been discovered. War Kabud belongs by contrast to the final phase of the 'Luristan Bronze civilization' (seventh century B.C.), and the discovery there of a large number of bronze and pottery objects has helped to date earlier discoveries rifled from other Luristan mounds in the early 1930s (see p. 62). Kalwali belonging to the second half of the seventh century B.C. appears by contrast as the poor man's cemetery. In the valleys of Kani-Chinan, north-west of Bani Surmah, too, valuable finds have been unearthed including a bronze funerary idol of 700 B.C. the first object of this character to be scientifically excavated.

It is not only with bronzes that Luristan feasts the eye. The scenery ranges from the knife-edges which curve in a vast amphitheatre along the edge of the plain in the south, to the snow-covered massifs and wide fertile valleys in the north and east. Freya Stark describes the Saidmarreh (later Karkheh) river as 'flowing through desolate hills that lie in rust-covered ridges like the upturned hulls of ships'; it was autumn at the time of her visit. In spring these lower ranges enjoy a brief honeymoon of glory; the black tents of the nomads stand out against a background of green hills carpeted with violets and purple anemones. To look out of the train window in February after an overnight journey from Tehran is suddenly to experience the breath of the south; these smooth green slopes have no parallel in the Elburz except in June at nine thousand feet. On the higher ranges spring lingers longer, and the hillsides, unlike those on the plateau, are dotted with juniper, dwarf oak and thorn, which offer shade and fodder of a sort.

Over Luristan, as over the lands to the north, the shadow of the past hangs heavily. It is not only in the regions of Harsin or Ilam that there are more mounds than villages. One of the best sources of early painted pottery, Tepe Giyan, is a few miles south-west of Nihavend. At Godin Tepe on the Hamadan side of Kangavar (p. 170) a joint Iranian-Canadian expedition has unearthed a large fortified manor with extensive magazines probably dating from the seventh or early sixth century, but with evidence of occupation going back to at least 4500 B.C. Graves, usually not more than two or three feet below ground and often placed on the sides of low foothills near a spring, are to be found in every valley; the difficulty is, not to discover their whereabouts, but to organize their scientific excavation. Wilson remarks on a number of cave dwellings near Chimashk with traces of stairs and drains; remains of Sassanian paved roads; mounds in the plains joined by ancient tracks, and shrines at intervals on these tracks; and three old bridges, the Pul-i-Kashgan, the Pul-i-Kurr-o-Dokhtar, and the Pul-i-Kalhur which he says has 'gothic' rather than 'Norman' arches. Ruined towns and villages, again of uncertain date, suggest that the population was once more numerous than it is today, and settled rather than nomadic. Even the advance of progress has entailed some destruction; at Alishtar, south of Nihavend, Freya Stark was told that a minaret which must have been like that at Saveh had been destroyed a few years earlier by Government troops in anticipation of a Lurish uprising. Thus in this troubled, unquiet country the past is constantly being effaced, history driven under-ground; but the present and the future, in the form of roads or houses, hygiene or police or security, are largely rejected too, so in the long run it is the shades that prevail.

CHAPTER NINE

Isfahan

It will soon be possible to fly from London or Paris to Isfahan in one day. Before many years Isfahan will no doubt be a five-hour stop on a world tour of Monumental Cities: Granada, Bruges, Florence, Rome, Athens, Istanbul, Delhi, Bangkok – none of these need feel ashamed to be in its company. When this happens, a great many people will know Isfahan, superficially, from the outside. But they will only have scratched its surface; and they will not have seen it, so to speak, from the inside. This will be a pity, for the peculiar distinction of Isfahan derives in part from its setting, which must be almost unique among the great historic cities of the world. To appreciate Isfahan in the round, it is better to come there by road. The journey is troublesome but infinitely rewarding.

I do not propose to describe the road. All approaches to Isfahan have one feature in common: they are long, monotonous and, by Persian standards, featureless. We of the West are used to finding places where there are reasons for them – a port, a river junction, at the heart of a rich region, in the centre of an industry or athwart a railway. We do not expect to find flourishing places separated by two hundred miles of desert from other places; it offends our practical sense. It might be thought that most towns in Iran provide an exception to this sort of principle. In some degree, yes; but not in the same degree as Isfahan. One needs to be some time in the country to appreciate this. But the quality of the desert anywhere within seventy miles of Isfahan is more intense and all-pervading than round any of the other great cities, except for those on the rim of the great Kavir; and there there are generally high mountain ranges to break the monotony. There are no high mountains near Isfahan; only tawny humps like stage backdrops. The wider setting is one of utter desolation. A few huddled villages sustained by some distant qanat; a broken caravanserai or ab-ambar; for the rest, life hardly seems to exist. What incredulity must have assailed the seventeenth-century traveller as he lumbered by slow camel train across these bleak and barren uplands, churning up the fine white dust on his way to what he had been told was the most splendid city, and the most sophisticated and luxurious court in the world? Would it not prove another mirage? And then quite suddenly the miracle occurred. Coming from the south, he swung down from a barren ridge and there it was, only the towers of the mosques and the palace gates visible over the high chenars. Soon, like John Fryer, he was crossing 'a most Magnificent Bridge with Arches over our Heads and on both sides Rails and Galleries to view the River'. If he came from the north he plunged suddenly, almost without warning, into a green, well-tilled land as intensively culti-vated as the valley of the Po, where melons and corn grew in profusion, and pigeon towers flanked the road like sentinels.*

For Isfahan does not, like Yazd for instance, grow straight out of the desert. It is at the heart of a straggling oasis formed by the Zaindeh Rud, the only great river of the plateau; a fickle stream, but on its smaller scale what the Nile is to Cairo. This, in contrast to the surrounding desert, is what gives the place its exceptional quality. One has the impression of a flourishing community which has evolved its own superlative expression in art and architecture, pressed round by its ring of green, watered as it were by an unseen hand, living its own self-contained and self-sufficient life, shut off by mountains and deserts from the rest of the world, haughty, a little arrogant perhaps, but pulsating with vitality. Air travel, pipelines, asphalt roads, will soon bring all this to an end. But is it surprising that the traveller of the past repeated, and sometimes accepted, the proud boast of its citizens: 'Isfahan nisf-i-jahan' – Isfahan is half the world?

Few cities have a lovelier name. It is tempting to seek an origin

* See Annex, note 5.

as romantic as its sound. Alas, the truth, according to the best available information, is quite untinged with poetry. It derives from Aspadana (Aspahan or Sepahan) and means the place of the army, a reference to the fact that the region was used for army concentrations or manoeuvres in Sassanian times. The English seventeenth-century visitors who, writing Spahaun, made it sound slightly martial (the words spahi and sepoy have the same derivation), and also faintly absurd, were not wide of the mark. It is the national inclination of the Persian language to poetry which has invested with magic the modern name of the city associated with the most glorious achievements of Persian art.

The mistake is sometimes made of relating these glories almost exclusively to Shah Abbas and his successors. The seventeenth century was, it is true, the golden age of Isfahan, but it was a place of great importance long before it became the Safavid capital, and a number of its finest monuments date from some earlier period.

The city originated well to the north and east of its present centre. We know that a few centuries after the Arab conquest there were in fact two built-up areas: one, called Djay or, later, Shahrestan, lay well to the east of the present city limits; the other, further to the west, was Yahoudieh, or the Jewish quarter, inhabited by Jews brought here by tradition by Nebuchadnezzar, in fact more probably by Yezdigird I. The latter area soon grew large at the expense of the former, and the Seljuk capital was centred in the region now occupied by the Friday Mosque, with the Jewish quarter still more or less in the same place – where indeed it is today, round the Sareban minaret – but to the east of what was by this time the main city. A great square or maidan extended from the Friday Mosque to the Mosque of Ali, and the royal palace of the Seljuks stood to the east of this square. There was no doubt about the prosperity of Isfahan in the eleventh century; after cataloguing its activity one Persian visitor remarked with surprise, and the observation is significant, that he did not see a single building in ruins. Unlike all cities further north, Isfahan was not devastated by either the Mongols or Timur; on the other hand, the great period of fourteenth-century reconstruction largely passed it by. When Shah Abbas decided at the end of the sixteenth century to make Isfahan his capital, he started building on what was virtually an open site. The clutter of houses which had now grown up round the Friday Mosque and the bazaar were left as they stood; the new city began where the old one left off, again to the south and west, on the site of the present Maidan-i-Shah. The Maidan was planted at a spot where the life of Isfahan as it stood would flow through it; it was to be the meeting place of monarch and citizens; 'not far from the north end', says Herbert 'are cooks' shops, where men used to feed the helpful belly, after the busy eye and painful feet have sufficiently laboured'. Into this great square, measuring 1,674 feet by 540, seven times the size of the Piazza San Marco at Venice, the bazaar debouched on the north, while to the west lay the palace quarter and to the south and east respectively the Royal and Sheikh Lutfullah Mosques. The Maidan was at once a market place, a cathedral square, a polo ground and a place of assembly. Fryer gives an interesting catalogue of the spectacles which Shah Suleiman watched in the Maidan from Ali Kapu: contests between lions and bulls; rams set to run at one another; nobles tilting; coursers trying to shoot backwards with bow and arrow at a golden bowl fixed on a high pole; wrestling; gladiators. What he does not mention, strangely enough, is polo, though the original goal posts are still to be seen at each end of the Maidan.

The other great feature of Shah Abbas's city plan was the Chehar Bagh (four gardens). Its siting seems at first sight to be a little perverse. It might have been expected to run from the Maidan to, say, the river, whose possibilities in the scheme of things then and even to this day appear to have been somewhat neglected. In fact, Pope tells us, a covered street ran in Safavid times from the south-east corner of the Maidan to the Khaju Bridge. This has now disappeared and been built over, so that one element in the harmony of the original plan has been removed. The purpose of the Chehar Bagh was different. It was to provide a thoroughfare, of unexampled width and splendour, through the heart of the new city, of which it would be the axis. Its course was deliberately chosen where there were few if any houses; it ran

across country or through gardens, indeed its name is said to
derive from the fact that it had to cut through four vineyards to
reach the river. The western side of the palace quarter backed on
to this avenue; it continued for three miles across the Zaindeh
Rud up to the royal gardens and pleasaunce of Hazar Jarib, over
the portals of which, according to Fryer, were 'curiously painted
men and women in European dress'. Thus, to an extent which
cannot be readily appreciated today, the palace grounds provided
the link between the Maidan and the Chehar Bagh. The avenue
was lined with ministers' palaces on each side, separated by open
arcades so that the gardens were plainly visible. It was planted
with eight rows of planes and poplars, with rose hedges and
jasmine bushes between them. The water channels which ran the
whole length of the avenue down to the river were faced with
onyx. Everywhere there were gardens 'which for grandeur and
fragour', declares Herbert, 'are such as no city in Asia outvie . . .
withal so sweet and verdant that you may call it another Paradise'.

There was another extension of the city for which Abbas was
responsible, of a different kind. This was not town-planning so
much as economic development. He wanted to promote trade
and industry in the new capital and to this end he decided upon a
mass movement of Armenians from the town of Julfa on the
Araxes river in Azerbaijan. His methods were high-handed: to
overcome their natural reluctance to leave home, he cut off the
water of their irrigation canals. On the other hand he offered
them special privileges, including the right to practise Christianity
and build their own churches. This being so, it was clearly
desirable in the interests of law and order that they should be
segregated. The quarter selected lay to the west of the Chehar
Bagh on the south bank of the Zaindeh Rud; it was called New
Julfa or, later, simply Julfa. Towards the end of the century we
are told it counted 60,000 inhabitants, all Christians. Though
subsequently subject to persecution, it remains a flourishing
predominantly Christian community, and the largest solid
agglomeration of Armenians in Iran.

The Armenians made a valuable contribution to the development and prosperity of the city. They were hard working, law

abiding, good traders, skilled as masons and architects. Their industry appears to have provoked a certain amount of jealousy, for Fryer tells us that at the end of the century they were forbidden to enter the city with their servants 'bearing after them their Kolyans, or Glass Vessels out of which they smoke tobacco', but were allowed to appear only as merchants. But Abbas's creation of a separate community at Julfa was doubtless a wise precaution.

Such then was seventeenth-century Isfahan: a cosmopolitan metropolis with its jangling communal problems; Moslems (both Sufis and Sayyeds), Armenians, Zoroastrians, and Banians (Indians) jostling in its streets; merchants of the British and Dutch East India companies, Swiss watchmakers, Chinese potters, discalced Carmelites settled there with royal encouragement. A city whose splendid modern buildings had been designed as a background for pageantry; Chardin says there were 162 mosques, 48 colleges, 1,802 caravanserais and 273 hammams at the time of his visit. A prosperous commercial centre whose bazaars made our markets look like 'snaps of buildings'. Gardens which were 'a compendium of sense-ravishing delights' as Herbert described Hazar Jarib. Fryer summed it up: 'The magnificently arched Buzzars which form the noble square to the Palace; the several public inns which are so many seraglios; the stately rows of sycamores which the world cannot parallel; the glorious summer houses and pleasant gardens, the stupendous bridges, sumptuous temples, the religious convents ... are so many lasting pyramids and monuments of [Abbas's] fame'; and 'people were wont to say "Shah Abbas", as we should say, "well done"'. The two cities of Spahaun and Julfa occupied more ground, he thought, than London and Southwark with their suburbs; but the area was so filled with gardens that he was prepared to believe they were not so populous.

The golden age ended early in the eighteenth century. The last major building of the Safavid era, the Madrasseh Mader-i-Shah, was completed between 1706 and 1714. In 1722 the city was besieged by the Afghans; its citizens were first reduced by famine and pestilence and later extensively massacred. Nadir Shah transferred his capital to Meshed; neglected and defenceless Isfahan was an easy prey to marauding tribes, the Bakhtiaris and the Lurs.

Considering its later history the marvellous thing about Isfahan is how much of it has survived. The city today is not in a ruinous condition; it would not be even true to say that it is but a shadow of its former self. Most of its religious and royal buildings have in fact remained more or less intact. The heaviest casualties have been among private houses and gardens, victims of depopulation and neglect. The Chehar Bagh, an animated but tawdry thorough-fare, has lost its gardens, its arches, its flowers, many of its trees and its water. The Hazar Jarib and Farahabad, its late Safavid counterpart, have disappeared. The pavilion of Hasht Behesht 'saluted by two channels in which are ships and boats to represent a naval scene of war', with its silver tank, its gold iwan, its 'posts stuck with looking glasses'* and its garden full of nightingales which Chardin thought made for the delights of love, has lost its idyllic setting. A number of the earlier mosques and madrassehs are in ruins, while some have disappeared altogether. There are few houses of any antiquity to be seen, and even the old streets and alleyways of the northern quarters are rapidly disappearing before the bulldozers which drive new avenues on every side. Nevertheless there is plenty in Isfahan to satisfy the greediest sightseer; in fact, there are well over one hundred scheduled monuments, among them some of the most outstanding Islamic buildings in the world, readily accessible and in excellent preserva-tion. No attempt will be made to describe more than about a quarter of them here. Their location will be indicated according to their position in relation to the junction of the Khiaban-i-Hafez (running east from the Maidan) and the Khiaban-i-Hatef (running north and south near the Friday Mosque). The best order in which to describe them is, perhaps, a chronological one.

This has at least one advantage: apart from the lovely brick and stucco gateway to the Daylamite Mosque of Jotjir (tenth century) near the entrance to the Mosque of Hakim (north-west) we can start with the Friday Mosque (north-west). Here is really

* Fryer, op. cit.

where any student of Persian Islamic architecture should begin. It seems almost unfair that Isfahan, which was more richly endowed by the Safavids than any other city in Iran, should also, quite independently of its later flowering, possess the most spacious and most sensational of Friday Mosques.

A narrow entrance leads down a vaulted passage into a great court. To the left rises a huge dome over the main sanctuary; this is the famous south dome chamber, flanked by arcades in great depth with brick vaulting of astonishing variety and ingenuity. Across the court, behind the western iwan, is an enclosed or winter prayer-hall, entirely lighted with alabaster windows, itself the size of a large church. To the right of the western iwan is another hall containing a plaster mihrab of wonderful intricacy and grace. The vaulted arcades, ten rows of them, behind the northern iwan are deeper than those on the south, and rival them in complexity; behind rises another dome chamber, smaller but more exquisite, the crowning glory of the mosque. To the right again, behind the eastern iwan, is a madrasseh, but this, and this alone, is partly in ruins.

This quick round indicates the general plan, the vast size, and the extraordinary riches of the building. If it has a kind of unity this is almost accidental. Its early history is obscure and its later additions most complex. A mosque probably stood on this site from the early part of the eighth century; it was rebuilt under the Abbasids in about A.D. 842. But of that which is visible today, the story begins about 1080. Then it was that Nizam-ul-Mulk, the powerful vizier of the Seljuk monarch Malik Shah, undertook the construction of the south dome chamber in honour of his master. This was to be the sanctuary, the focal point of the enlarged mosque; earlier Abbasid buildings were still probably grouped round it. Fortunately for posterity, however, Malik Shah had a mother (it is extraordinary how often women enter the story of Moslem building); that mother had a counsellor of her own, Taj-ul-Mulk; and Taj was the sworn rival of the great Nizam. He determined to make his presence felt in his own way, and the result was the northern or small dome chamber, built in 1088, probably by the same architect. In all likelihood this

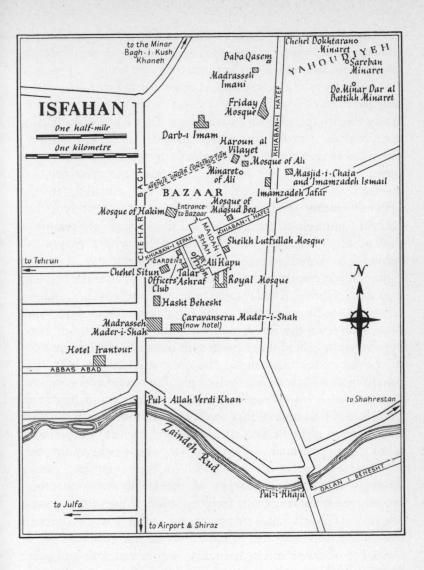

ISFAHAN

One half-mile

One kilometre

to the Minar
Bagh-i-Kush
Khaneh

Baba Qasem

Madrasseh
Imani

Chehel Dokhtarano
Minaret

YAHOUDIYEH

Sareban
Minaret

Do.Minar Dar al
Battikh Minaret

Friday
Mosque

Darb-i Imam

AVENUE UNDER CONSTRUCTION

CHEHAR BACH

Haroun al
Vilayet

Mosque of Ali

Minaret
of Ali

BAZAAR

KHIABAN-I HATEF

Masjid-i-Chaia
and Imamzadeh Ismail

Imamzadeh Jafar

Mosque of Hakim

Entrance
to Bazaar

Mosque of
Maqsud Beg

KHIABAN-I HAFEZ

MAIDAN-I SHAH

Sheikh Lutfullah Mosque

KHIABAN-I SEPAH

GARDENS

OFFICES

Ali Kapu

to Tehran

Chehel Situn

Talar
Ashraf

Officers'
Club

Royal Mosque

Hasht Behesht

Caravanserai Mader-i-Shah
(now hotel)

N

Madrasseh
Mader-i-Shah

Hotel Irantour

ABBAS ABAD

Pul-i Allah Verdi Khan

to Shahrestan

Zaindeh Rud

to Julfa

Pul-i Khaju

DALAN I BEHESHT

to Airport & Shiraz

chamber, the Gunbad-i-Khaki, was originally a separate building, and was joined on to the mosque only when the neighbouring vaults were constructed in the fourteenth century.

A further event of great importance occurred in 1121. In that year the Friday Mosque of Isfahan was ravaged by fire. Miraculously the fire spared both Nizam's and Taj's dome chambers; it consumed most of the rest. Opinions differ as to whether anything earlier than the dome chambers survived. The south iwan probably dates from the reconstruction after the great fire, but received various accretions, including the minarets, in the fifteenth century. The west iwan as we see it is entirely of late Safavid construction; the geometrical tilework closely resembles that of the Madrasseh Mader-i-Shah. The winter prayer-hall behind it is Timurid (1448). The superb plaster mihrab to the right of it was constructed in 1310, and is named after the reigning monarch, Oljeitu Khodabanda; the hall on which it stands, however, was probably built in the following century. The south iwan dates from the Seljuk reconstruction after the fire of 1121, but the vaults behind it are fourteenth century, while the oratory to the left of the small dome chamber was built in 1681. The eastern iwan is likewise Seljuk in origin, but has Safavid additions. The madrasseh is fourteenth century, with an iwan dating from 1726. It will thus be seen that the Friday Mosque brings together almost every phase of Persian Islamic architecture; no period is wholly unrepresented. Wandering in the brick vaults and admiring the perennial fascination of their patterns; gazing upwards at the soaring arches of the small dome chamber; crossing the sunlit court into the deep shade of the southern iwan where worshippers kneel in prayer, we are in a world different from almost anything else in Iran, a world not of colour but of form, not of design but of harmony, whose vast scale and sober lines evoke not religious ecstasy but simple faith, as in an early Romanesque church or a Gothic cathedral shorn of modern trappings.

The three supreme achievements are the two dome chambers and the Oljeitu mihrab. Others better equipped than I have conveyed their unique qualities. Of the great dome chamber

9a. ISFAHAN: Pul-i-Khaju (1660). 'In the Sassanian tradition, not only a bridge but a weir' (*p. 198*)

9b. ISFAHAN: Shahrestan Bridge. The piers are Sassanian, the pointed arches probably Seljuk (*p. 201*)

Byron writes: 'Twelve massive tiers engage in a Promethean struggle with the weight of the dome. The struggle in fact obscures the victory; to perceive the latter demands a previous interest in medieval engineering or the character of the Seljuks.' And of the small dome chamber: 'The very material is a signal of economy; hard small bricks of mousey grey which swallow up the ornament of kufic texts and stucco inlay in their Puritan singleness of purpose. In skeleton the chamber is a system of arches, one broad in the middle of each wall, two narrow beside each corner, four miniature in each squinch, eight in the squinch zone, and sixteen above the squinches to receive the dome. . . . I doubt if there is another building in Persia or in the whole of Islam which offers so tense, so immediate an apparition of pure form.' 'The subordinate arches appear mere incidents in the upward movement, like stars shed by a rocket,' writes Schroeder.*

Of the Oljeitu mihrab Pope himself says: 'The most subtle and perfectly proportioned of all fourteenth century mihrabs, with its exquisite overpanel of lotuses.'

All other remains of the Seljuk period in Isfahan are fragmentary. The oldest is probably that occupied by the Masjid-i-Sha'ia (north-east), with a small Seljuk minaret. In the Jewish quarter, the ancient Yahoudiyeh, there are two other Seljuk minarets of greater interest. Sareban (north-east) also known as the minaret of the camel drivers, is a slender brick tower some 150 feet in height, with kufic inscriptions in brick and blue tiles, and two rings of stalactites. This is one of the best preserved, as well as the most beautifully decorated minarets that have survived in Iran. Nearby, smaller and older, is the Chehel Dokhtaran (north-east), the forty daughters, which bears the date of 1108. The minaret of Ali (north-west) adjoining the Safavid mosque of the same name near the northern exit of the bazaar probably dates from the late twelfth century. Its top has come off but 158 feet of it are still standing.

It is often said that Isfahan was neglected during the Mongol renaissance around 1300. But one Mongol building is frequented

* In Pope's *Survey of Persian Art.*

by hundreds of visitors a year who pay little attention to its history or its architecture. It is one of the most popular, and most worthless, of the local sights. I refer to the much advertised Shaking Minarets, which are to be found some three miles west of Isfahan, at the base of a steep hill crowned by a Sassanian fire altar. The minarets are to all intents and purposes quite modern and have no architectural or decorative merit; their attraction is that they wave about a little when leant on. But the iwan below them was built about 1315; its construction resembles that of the galleries of Sultaniyeh. It covers the tomb of one Sheikh 'Amu 'Abdallah ibn Muhammad.

The Imamzadeh Jafar (north-west) is a small octagonal shrine built between 1330 and 1350, with a brick exterior and spandrels filled with faïence mosaic. To the same decade belong the two minarets built over the street, but divided by a modern portal known as the Do Minar Dar al Battikh, or Ziafeh (north-east). Another pair, the Do Minar Dardasht (north-west), adjoin a little square tomb chamber containing the body of a lady called Bakht-i-Aqa, and are probably contemporary (1330–40).

There is one later minaret on the northern outskirts, the Minar Bagh-i-Kush Khaneh (the Falcon Garden) dating from about 1400. It is named after a Safavid building which stood nearby, but belonged in fact to the mosque of Baba Sokhteh, part of which is shown still standing in Flandin's sketch, c. 1840. The mausoleum of Baba Qasem (north-west), another small tomb with a conical tower, bears the date of 1340. The larger chamber, with a handsome rib pattern on the interior of its dome, is believed to have been the tomb of a Sunni theologian called Baba Qasem; inscriptions bearing the names of the early Caliphs Abu Bekr, Omar and Othman prove its Sunni origin. The date of the Madrasseh Imami, which adjoins Baba Qasem, has been a subject of lively controversy. Godard believes that it antedates the Sunni tomb by some fifteen years, viz. 1325, whereas some of the faïence mosaic, carrying the names of both the early Caliphs and the twelve Imams, must belong to the period of the tolerant Muzaffarids, i.e. after 1358. The floral designs in the madrasseh and on the portal of the Mausoleum are of particular interest as they are about the

earliest surviving examples in Isfahan of faïence mosaic breaking
away from geometrical patterns into floral motifs.

It was in the fifteenth century that floral design came into its
own. Strangely enough there is only one building in Isfahan
which can be definitely attributed to this period, and even that
has been extensively restored and enlarged. It is the Darb-i-Imam
(north-west), an irregular-shaped shrine with two domes containing the tombs of two sons of imams. The fifteenth-century
faïence mosaic is generally considered the finest work of its kind
after that of the Blue Mosque at Tabriz, by reason of its flowering
design and harmonious colouring. In the large bare courtyard
which surrounds this shrine there is a tomb surmounted by a lion
which wears the face of the occupant, moustache and all. This
bizarre form of portraiture is unusual, but it is quite normal in the
Bakhtiari country west of Isfahan to find gravestones in the form
of stone lions. They were accorded as a mark of honour to those
who had achieved distinction in the tribe.

Two buildings in Isfahan belong to the Safavid period before
Shah Abbas, and they are close together just south of the Friday
Mosque: the Mosque of Ali (1521) and the Haroun-i-Vilayet
(1512) (both north-west). The first is a good straightforward
example of the four-iwan plan, but is singularly plain and rather
featureless. The Haroun-i-Vilayet on the other hand is a large
straggling building with a wonderful doorway of mosaic tiles
leading into the shrine. Pope says of it that the spandrels contain
exquisite curves which could not have been drawn by the greatest
illuminator, while the fluttering cloud bands in the tympanum
over the doorway are as fine as those in the finest carpets. The
shrine is much frequented because it is said to offer a cure for
sterility; it has been added to and much restored.

We come at last to Shah Abbas and the Golden Age. We
emerge from mud-walled alleyways filled with refuse and the
dark caverns of the bazaar where coppersmiths clank, printed
textiles flutter, and blindfolded camels walk round and round
grinding cotton seed, into the dazzling sunlight and space of the
great Maidan, with its breathtaking silhouette of blue domes
against brown mountains. There is nothing else like it in Iran,

this assembly of splendid buildings constructed more or less simultaneously according to a preconceived plan, this harmony of design and concentration of colour. We have seen what purposes the Maidan served in its heyday; today, despite traffic, it is a relatively quiet open space standing a little aside from the teeming life of a busy city. Some complain that its original character has been lost in recent years by the construction of a garden and the planting of trees on the square. These carpings seem to me pedantic. The landscaping is well done; it has not diminished the scale of the place or detracted from its grandeur, but it has made the Maidan a pleasanter spot to linger in on warm summer evenings, away from dust and heat; and surely it is the Isfahanis who should have the first claim on its enjoyment?

The two mosques facing the square are alike in spirit, but utterly different in form. The smaller, Sheikh Lutfullah, was built by Shah Abbas between 1603 and 1618 in honour of his father-in-law. In size it is relatively modest: a flattened dome rests on a square dome chamber and is reached by a corridor which runs diagonally from the entrance portal on the Maidan; that is all. There is no courtyard, no iwan, save the entrance portal, no vaulted galleries, no open space; everything is within. The whole interior is covered above dado level with mosaic tiles of extra-ordinary brilliance; all is colour, light, motion; every detail is perfect. The use of unglazed tiles as background to the floral pattern, both on the dome and within, spares the eye a surfeit of colour and glaze and sharpens the impact of the pattern. This building, more than any other in Iran, moved Robert Byron to that combination of eloquence and sharply defined description which is peculiarly his own. Of the dome, he says: 'Round a flattened hemisphere made of tiny bricks and covered with prawn coloured wash runs a bold branching rose tree inlaid in black and white. The genius of the effect is in the play of surface. The inlay is glazed. The stucco work is not.' Of the interior: 'If the outside is lyric the interior is Augustan. A still shallower dome about seventy feet in diameter swims above a ring of sixteen windows. . . . The dome is inset with a network of lemon-shaped compartments which increase in size as they descend from a

formalized peacock at the apex. . . . Each arch is framed in turquoise corkscrews. The mihrab . . . is enamelled with tiny
flowers on a deep blue meadow. Even the pattern of light
through the thick window traceries is inconstant, owing to outer
traceries which are several feet away and double the variety of
each varying silhouette.'

The Royal Mosque, the Masjid-i-Shah, the vast pile at the
southern end of the Maidan, is in design and conception the most
majestic expression of Persian Islamic architecture at the crown
of its most sumptuous and triumphant era. The scale is stupendous,
the plan ingenious.

This enormous building was started early in the seventeenth
century – the exact date is disputed – and not finally completed
until after Shah Abbas's death in 1628. Nevertheless it was built
in a hurry. The Sophy was, it seems, constantly nagging at the
architects and builders to get it finished. They were pressed to
proceed at once on the foundations. The architect, one Abul
Qasim, is said to have warned the Shah against the dangers of
subsidence, but he brushed these warnings aside. Thereupon, the
story goes, the architect disappeared for five years, having taken
careful measurements. When he emerged from hiding, he discovered that his fears had been fully justified. He reported this to
Abbas and was forgiven. The same hustle prompted the use of
haft rangi (coloured tiles) in the place of kashi (mosaic tiles)
throughout the building except for the inscriptions and the
entrance portal, the earliest part of the Mosque. As a result the
decorative work does not compare in delicacy or refinement with
that of Sheikh Lutfullah or many earlier buildings. Nevertheless
the total effect is overwhelming.

Once inside the great portal, whose massive dado of Ardistan
marble with finely carved corner columns leads the eye upwards
to glistening stalactites of mosaic, the enchantment takes effect
and critical faculties are dulled. Only prejudice bred of too much
knowledge could fail to succumb to those encircling walls of
dazzling blue, those soaring minarets, their reflections in the tank
of the great court, or the deep shade of the iwans which reveal
man's pigmy stature. For all its reckless riot of colour, the Royal

Mosque, by sheer weight of mass and contrasts of light and shade, is awe-inspiring; the hand may be the King's but the glory, there can be little doubt about it, is to God.

When we turn to the secular buildings adjoining the Maidan the difference is apparent at once. There is a startling contrast between the perfection of form of the two great mosques and the ungainly bulk of the Ali Kapu or the quaint absurdity of the Chehel Sutun. It seems almost incredible that buildings on the one hand so perfectly proportioned and on the other so primitive should have been built at the same time under the inspiration of the same monarch.

It would be tempting but misleading to attribute the difference to the powerful influence of Islam, to suppose that the best was reserved for the glory of Allah. The truth I fear is less flattering, and discloses the underlying weakness of Safavid architecture, skilfully concealed under its veneer of virtuosity. The days of innovation had long passed; Safavid architects were content to follow stereotyped forms, however brilliantly they might conceive and execute them. The daring that lies behind the Gunbad-i-Khaki in the Friday Mosque or the Oljeitu mausoleum at Sultaniyeh had long since departed. But in the case of religious buildings, and caravanserais and even bazaars followed the same conventions, they were the heirs of a magnificent tradition stemming from the Sassanian arch and the Seljuk dome. The tradition for secular buildings was entirely different; its characteristics were wooden columns and flat roofs, and the prototype not Sarvistan but Persepolis. It is astounding that the architectural discoveries of the Sassanian tradition were not more generally applied; yet there seems little doubt of the gulf.

Though the Ali Kapu looks like a grandstand, and indeed served as one, it was in fact a royal residence as well. 'That brick boot-box', Byron called it; and it is difficult to cavil at the comparison. It is a very tall rectangular building of five stories; the façade facing the Maidan carries an enormous balcony, covered with a wooden roof supported by very tall wooden columns, the height of the third and fourth stories combined. This terrace is the talar, or royal enclosure, from which the

Safavid kings watched the ceremonies and sporting events in the
square below. From it, or even better from the floor above it,
one can still obtain the finest view of the Maidan, the Royal
Mosque, the Sheikh Lutfullah dome, the town prison behind,
and indeed of the whole layout of the city with its mud domes,
blue-washed porticoed colonnades looking into private gardens,
and its battery of minarets on the north-eastern horizon. The
interior of the roof is embellished with marquetry. Behind the
talar is the throne room which was used as an audience chamber;
it is decorated with wall paintings of the period in which European influence was strong. For the rest, the interior of the Ali
Kapu is at once quaint and complex. A most involved system of
winding stairways leads from one floor to another and on all
floors there are wall paintings of much charm, with on the top
floor a central hall (under repair in 1971) containing porcelain
chambers, that is to say, niches of various shapes fitted into the
walls, as if for flasks of wine.

The Chehel Sutun is a grander affair. The park in which it
stands has been well preserved, and in front of the columned talar
there is a large tank. The name of the palace, Forty Columns, is
often explained by reference to this tank. There are in fact only
twenty columns in the portico; reflected in the water they make
forty. Or it may have been a traditional attachment to the
number forty, to be seen also for instance in the case of the
Chehel Dukhtaran, without any precise statistical connotation.
As with the terrace of the Ali Kapu, the vast wooden ceiling of
the talar is inlaid with marquetry. The slender columns are of
chenar (oriental plane) encased in wooden panels with stone
lions at their base. The interior is covered almost from head to
foot with wall paintings which have progressively been uncovered
and restored over the last twenty years – though the effect of
deliberate vandalism by later dynasties cannot be altogether
effaced. The smaller rooms are decorated with delicate floral
and bird designs, together with some figure paintings in the style
of miniatures. The reception hall, dominated by vast historical
frescoes showing battle scenes and royal receptions, contains
in a lower register an attractive collection of such miniatures,

and it was no doubt to these that Pietro della Valle referred when he wrote of 'men and women in lascivious postures including a number wearing hats and intended to represent Europeans'. There are also figure paintings on outside balconies, including one on the south side resembling Charles I.

The Chehel Sutun frescoes provide an exotic contrast to the rather rugged structure, a contrast which can be most fully appreciated by a visit to the roof of the building, where a forest of massive timbers in marvellous preservation shows that Safavid palace-builders, for all their adherence to an uncouth convention, were technically accomplished.

The architects of the period had moreover another string to their bow – bridge-building. Here again there was a good Sassanian tradition: embellishments were added according to the taste of the age. The bridge of thirty-three arches, known as the Pul-i-Allah Verdi Khan (named after Abbas's general who also gave his name to a sanctuary in the shrine at Meshed), was built about 1620. It carries the Chehar Bagh across the Zaindeh Rud, which is over three hundred yards wide at this point. In design and ingenuity however it is surpassed by the Pul-i-Khaju (1660) which crosses the same river about half a mile farther down-stream. With one exception this is the last of the great monu-ments of Isfahan, and it is perhaps the most remarkable of all Safavid buildings. In the Sassanian tradition, it is not only a bridge but a weir. It rests on twenty-four enormous piers of masonry divided by narrow channels in which the water, when required upstream, can be dammed. Each of these channels is covered by a broad pointed arch, with geometrical tiles in the spandrels. An arcade runs over these arches, giving two arches in the upper tier to each arch below. The roadway is at the level of the upper tier, every fourth arch being open to give access to it. In the centre of the bridge there is a hexagonal projection constituting a sort of pavilion, with small iwans facing outwards, decorated in mosaic. On the downstream side of the bridge steps descend to the river, in summer a favourite washing place, while in spring boys dive into the swirling current. The pedestrian can walk across the bridge at the level of the bottom of the lower tier

of arches; he can also pass inside each arch to the other side of the
bridge, and there is a series of low vaults running within each
arch along the whole length of the bridge. The sides of the upper
tier of arches, on each side of the bridge, are pierced by smaller
round-headed doorways, providing a footpath looking outwards
beside the road but separated from it save by the gap in every
fourth arch. It is an astounding construction, ingenious, practical
in the highest degree and at the same time lovely to behold.

The remaining Safavid buildings of Isfahan can be described
more briefly. The Mosque of Maqsud Beg (1603, north-west,
near the Maidan) has a fine tile mosaic doorway and mihrab.
The Imamzadeh Ismail (1634, north-west, adjoining the Chafa
Mosque) was restored by Fath Ali Shah. The Mosque of Hakim
(1654, north-west, reached through the bazaar) has a mihrab of
blue and yellow tiles and a good mimbar; it was built by a royal
doctor who fell from favour, migrated to the court of the Great
Mogul and worked there to such good effect that he was able to
transmit the funds for the construction of what is consequently
known as the doctor's mosque.

Two Julfa churches also belong to this period. The Cathedral
of St Saviour, built between 1606 and 1654, is a plain square brick
building surmounted by a dome. The interior is richly furnished
and carpeted, and covered from head to foot with wall paintings
of no great artistic value, mostly representing scenes of revolting
torture or massacre. Here and in the Church of Bethlehem (1627)
there is some good tilework. There is a museum of Armenian
manuscripts, paintings and other objects in the grounds of the
Cathedral, as well as a large library.

Of the two late Safavid palaces, we have already referred
briefly to the Hasht Behesht (c. 1670, south-west). This is now
being restored, and although its surroundings have lost most of
their charm the palace itself with its high balconies and fascinating
decorations – mainly birds and beasts – remains a splendid tribute
to the art of the late Safavid period and when completed may
well be seen to rank among Isfahan's major glories.

The Talar Ashraf (c. 1650, south-west) stands off the avenue
just to the west of the Maidan. Its exterior comprises in effect

three low iwans in a row. As the seventeenth century wore on
the iwan arch tended to flatten out and get lower, rather like the
transformation from Early English to Perpendicular in English
church architecture. The interior is used as an office by the
Ministry of Education. One is admitted by arrangement, and
hesitates to linger too long. The floral wall paintings round the
gold-rimmed vaulted stalactite roof are singularly interesting and
in excellent preservation. They are fuller, more florid, more
exotic than the Chehel Sutun wall paintings. If they lack their
delicacy, they show unbounded energy and an unfailing sense of
design. There is something curiously late Victorian about them.
Like Qajar tilework they would repay authoritative study.

Finally, we come to the last Safavid building and one of the
loveliest – the Madrasseh Mader-i-Shah (1706–14, south-west).
Sandwiched between a tobacco warehouse now a bazaar and a
vast caravanserai now converted into a luxury hotel, the madrasseh encircles a cool garden, a haven of peace. It is perhaps
more atmospheric than any other building in Iran except the
shrine at Mahan. A splendid embossed silver door opens from
the Chehar Bagh into a portal covered with geometrical mosaic
tiles. Facing the avenue too, is a charming dado of haft rangi in
yellows, browns and tomato red – presumably Qajar. The courtyard with its pollarded chenars, neat flowerbeds, cool tank and
flowing stream is sheer delight. The sanctuary, to the right, is
smaller and more graceful than that of the Royal Mosque. The
interior of the dome is decorated with a scroll design in mosaic
tiles which, observes Pope, resembles the Dome of the Rock at
Jerusalem. The exterior of the dome, covered with a flowing
design of mosaic tile on a pale blue ground, is precisely in the
tradition of a hundred years earlier but achieves a lightness and
grace which make it the equal of its predecessors, or perhaps even
a trifle lovelier than they. Essentially a conventional building, the
madrasseh has little to show that it belongs to a later century
except perhaps rather greater preponderance of geometrical tilework and the use of more varied colours, including black. It was
only finished six years before the Afghan onslaught; but how
satisfactory that it has survived in all its perfection.

We have now covered the monuments of Isfahan and Julfa chronologically and in some detail; in greater detail perhaps than the reader who is not also a prospective sightseer will be able to stomach. But the oasis of Isfahan, which on the map is shaped like a centipede in motion with Isfahan and its surrounding greenery at its apex, is richer in Islamic monuments than any other area of comparable size in the country. Enough has already been said about the Shaking Minarets, and the Zoroastrian fire temple above them, on the way to Najafabad (west). A few miles downstream from the city, best approached by a shady road starting from the Pul-i-Khaju on the south bank and known by the charming name of Dalan-i-Behesht (the Passage to Paradise), is the Shahrestan bridge, of great antiquity if uncertain date. The massive rounded piers on which the bridge rests may well be of Sassanian origin. The pointed arches between them are probably Seljuk, but the most distinctive feature is the smaller, irregular-shaped arches immediately above the piers, obviously designed to admit the maximum flow of water when the river is in spate; Pope suggests that the concept of these is Roman. Four miles to the east of Isfahan is the curious Safavid monument known as the Imamzadeh Shah Zaid, containing frescoes portraying figures, most unusual in a religious building and dating from the latter half of the seventeenth century. Farther downstream again there are the interesting remains of what appears to have been a fairly elaborate if abortive Mongol housing project. They consist of the ruins of three unfinished mosques, all built about 1325 apparently to serve the needs of a kind of overflow community, or satellite town, which the Il Khanids tried to establish there. That of Dashti consists of a square dome chamber and monumental portal. The mosque of Kaj was built adjoining a pre-existent mud brick structure with an iwan. That at Eziran comprises a square dome chamber with flanking corridors and a forecourt. It is believed to have possessed a lustre mihrab, now removed. Farther downstream again at Ziar, some thirty miles from Isfahan, there is a particularly fine late Seljuk minaret (c. 1120) ornamented with geometrical designs in glazed brick and several kufic inscriptions. At Barsian nearby, on the left bank of the

river, is a ruined mosque with minaret dated 1098. At Varzaneh
still farther downstream there is a very large Friday Mosque of
1444 but with a Seljuk minaret, and decorated with tile mosaics
closely related to those on the portal of the Winter Prayer Hall in
the Friday Mosque in Isfahan. There is a magnificent mosaic
faïence mimbar. At Kuhpayeh to the north on the road to Nain
there is a domed Mongol Mosque with an interesting cusped
squinch and a mosaic faïence mimbar that may have served as
model for Varzaneh. Finally some six miles north-east of Isfahan
at Hafshuyeh we have one of the few perfect four-iwan Mongol
Mosques with a stucco mihrab in the ruined dome chamber of
the same quality as that of Pir-i-Bakran (see below).

In the other direction, that is to say upstream and south-west
just off the Shahr-i-Kord road at a distance of some twenty miles
from the city is the village of Ashtarjan, with a Friday Mosque
dating from 1315. This is a good example of Mongol decorative
work which has suffered from being applied to a somewhat
hastily constructed building, much of which is in mud brick. It
consists of a dome chamber with a court surrounded by prayer
halls, with a north portal not in the centre of the court. There are
extensive polychrome decorations in the dome chamber, and a
large plaster mihrab with a half-octagonal head filled with stalactites and outlined by rope moulding. The brick vaulting of the
prayer halls, the winter prayer hall below ground to the right of
the entrance and the diagonal corkscrew bands of kufic on the
broken minarets, are all unusual features of this mosque.

But the outstanding building in the neighbourhood of Isfahan
is in the village of Linjan, some fifteen miles to the south-west of
the city turning left off the Shahr-i-Kord road. This is known as
Pir-i-Bakran, and takes its name from an old Sufi theologian
named Bakran who selected this spot, adjoining an existing dome
chamber, as a place of retreat where he also preached or held
classes. As his reputation, and the number of his pupils, grew, he
appears to have decided upon the building of an iwan, to the
south of the dome chamber, to provide shelter for his flock.
Bakran died in 1303 when the decoration of the iwan was still
incomplete, and shortly thereafter the building was converted

into a monument for the saint. His tomb was constructed at the rear, or northern end, of the iwan, adjoining the old dome chamber. The southern end of the iwan was blocked with a screen wall against which was placed a mihrab exactly oriented towards Mecca. An entrance to the tomb was provided at the end of a corridor to the east of the iwan.

Without some knowledge of this curious history, Pir-i-Bakran is a confusing little building, and its plan completely incoherent. Its distinction lies in its parts rather than its whole. The entrance doorway has a fine stucco inscription. The splendid plaster mihrab, consisting of a pointed arch recess of semi-circular plan within a second pointed arch, is polychromed in red, white and blue. The flanking walls are covered with glazed tiles. The screen wall which divides the iwan proper from Bakran's tomb chamber is constructed of large octagonal tiles pierced with a centre opening. There is a gallery above the tomb chamber, and above it a vault of brick stalactites faced with simulated brickwork in plaster, so characteristic of the period. The main feature of the little dome chamber in the rear of the sanctuary is a projecting rock with a hole in it which by tradition is the hoof mark of Ali's horse. Pir-i-Bakran, for all its chequered origin, has been able to withstand the ravages of time more successfully than many of its grander contemporaries because it is built largely of stone. This, and the conception of an open iwan not connected with a mosque, reflect the persistence of the Sassanian tradition of building in Mongol times. Its dusty surroundings, and the little village of Linjan with its duck pond, can have changed little since Bakran's day.*

Well beyond the bounds of the Isfahan oasis, some 120 miles on the mountain road to Hamadan, there is the town of Gulpaigan. This possesses a Friday Mosque which must be unique, consisting as it does of a Seljuk dome chamber and a Qajar court on the four-iwan plan with nothing, chronologically, in between. The sanctuary was erected by Malik Shah's son about 1106, and like the dome chambers of the Friday Mosque at Isfahan is constructed entirely of brick. It consists of a dome resting on a square base, with broad and heavy squinches. Though later in

* No longer true (1978).

date it cannot compare for energy or grace with the small dome
chamber (Gunbad-i-Khaki). Pope calls it 'baroque . . . a masterpiece of pessimism . . . an expert balance of movements in
themselves ungainly. . . .' But for those whose imagination has
been fired by Seljuk construction and brickwork, Gulpaigan is
well worth a visit. There is also a minaret with good brickwork
probably Seljuk in the main street.

On the road from Gulpaigan to Dalijan (between Saveh and
Isfahan) is Mahallat, home town of the Aga Khan's family and
one of the prettiest towns in Iran. The Friday Mosque has an
upstairs prayer hall in a timbered portico; and a house owned by
the Agha Khan, with a columned portico and floral painted niche
and ceiling, is worth a visit.

A turning to the left off the Gulpaigan road some sixty miles
from Isfahan leads through the heart of tribal country to some of
the highest mountains in the Zagros range, popularly known as
the Bakhtiari mountains. Here on the eastern side of the great
snowy parapet known as Zardeh Kuh (15,000 ft) a huge cascade
of water gushes from the rock, several hundred feet above the
valley floor; above it you can peer through holes in the rock, like
those in the pipes of an organ, to see this enormous water table
which differs from many others in these dry mountains only in
that its side has split open and it does not need to be drained away
by man-made channels. This is the source of the Kuh-i-Rang
river, and is a spot of some economic and historical interest, as
well as great scenic beauty. The interesting thing about the Kuh-i-
Rang river is that though it rises – the word is singularly inept –
east of the highest mountain in the Zagros, it flows south and then
west, becomes the Karun, and finally finds its way into the Shatt
al Arab at Khorramshahr. Like all the westward flowing Zagros
rivers, it contains a great deal more water than those which flow
eastward. It is moreover the Kuh-i-Rang's good fortune that its
upper valley is bounded on the east by a relatively low ridge
(about 9,000 ft); and just over that ridge there is another valley,
formed by the upper waters of a stream which flows east, and
ultimately becomes the Zaindeh Rud, the biggest river of the
plateau, and the source of all fertility for the great oasis of Isfahan.

In fact, without the Zaindeh Rud Isfahan would not exist; as it is the flow of the Zaindeh Rud, with its great seasonal fluctuation, is scarcely enough for Isfahan's needs. Is it surprising, therefore, that the Isfahanis should have cast longing eyes on the plentiful waters of the Kuh-i-Rang, dramatized for them by this tremendous half-open water table and waterfall? It was in the time of Shah Abbas that the idea was first conceived of cutting a section out of the low ridge which divides Kuh-i-Rang from Zaindeh Rud; signs of that unfinished project can still be seen on the summit of the ridge. Today this Safavid dream has been fulfilled, but in a different manner: on the Kuh-i-Rang, some four miles below the source, there is a small reservoir; this is connected with a tunnel under the ridge out of which Kuh-i-Rang water pours into the seasonally parched bed of the Zaindeh Rud, bringing great benefit to the city of Isfahan and its wonderfully fertile oasis.

To the south, a modern highway leads to Pasargadae, Persepolis and Shiraz (see Chapter Ten) past splendid pigeon towers, a superb Safavid caravanserai at Mahyar, and the strange rock village of Yazd-i-Khast, a ruin towering over a gully, which has attracted the attention of travellers from the earliest times.

CHAPTER TEN

South of the Desert

To the untutored Western eye, the Iranian plateau is virtually all desert. But the great basins to the south and east of Tehran, into which the streams of the eastern Elburz and south-eastern Zagros drain and disappear, have a peculiar intensity of barrenness which distinguishes them from the semi-deserts on their fringes. A straight line drawn from near Varamin to the point where Iran, Afghanistan and Pakistan meet crosses some of the most impassable tracts of country in South-west Asia outside Arabia. There are few settlements in this region and in effect only three tracks across it: Shah Abbas's Sang Farsh (stone carpet) from near Kashan to Firuzkuh across the western side of the Dasht-i-Kavir; the road, just motorable, from Yazd to Tabas which for the most part clings to the low ridges between the Dasht-i-Kavir and the Dasht-i-Lut; and the track from Kerman to Birjand which bisects the Dasht-i-Lut. This forbidding block of sand, salt and swamp has determined the direction of the eastern trade routes: the road to Turkestan and China keeps to the north of it, through Damghan and Khorasan; the route to India, the old spice road, lies to the south. Along this road, at the call of the camel rather than the qanat, there sprang into existence a number of ancient towns which flourished particularly in early Islamic times. No part of the country is more essentially Iranian, none has better retained the ancient customs and traditions of settled life on the plateau. Here are no Turks, Arabs, nomads, royal palaces (with one exception) or green pastures; it is the land of mud domes and wind towers, ab-ambars (water tanks) and caravanserais, walled villages and rare oases, Zoroastrian dakhmés (towers of silence) and Shi'a nakhls (wooden structures carried in Moharram processions).

Trade rather than fertility fostered settlements along this road, but the three places – Kashan, Yazd and Kerman – which have grown to the stature of cities all lie at the foot of snow-covered mountain ranges which proliferate water.

Nowhere is one more conscious of water, both its presence and its absence, than at Kashan. At the entrance to the town from Tehran, a road leads uphill to the right, between a strip of cultivation on the left and sandy undulations on the right. From the first rises the glistening blue cone of the Tomb of Abu Lu Lu, a local Shi'a whose merit derives from his having allegedly murdered the Caliph Omar in 664. The building probably dates only from the sixteenth century and has been recently retiled.

After four miles the road ends at the gate of the most surprising garden in Iran, the Royal Garden of Fin. Surrounded by a high wall and entered through a monumental doorway, it is traversed by a whole series of clear, fast-running streams; the water flows through marble channels and basins flanked by avenues of giant cypress, or under the archways of pavilions constructed by Shah Abbas and 'improved' by Fath Ali Shah. Some Safavid wall paintings are still visible, and the place is well tended.* There is a fascinating series of small rooms in the south-east corner of the garden which formerly served as the royal hammam. It was here that Mirza Taqi Khan, Nasr-uddin Shah's vizier, was murdered on his master's orders in 1852. Outside the garden, in the direction of the mountains, is the explanation of this splendid outburst of rare fertility, a large swimming pool built over a powerful natural spring. There is no more refreshing midday halt for the weary traveller in all Iran.

Moreover, as he swims round in this pure water, which is cold even on the hottest day, or watches the boys of the village diving for rials, he can also indulge in historical reflection. This is the oldest life-giving spring on the plateau. On the way up to Fin, he will have noticed the sandy mounds and depressions on

* But vulgarized by modern lighting (1978).

the right-hand side of the road. They mark the site of Sialk, where objects have been discovered dating back to before 4000 B.C., according to the researches of Dr Ghirshman, who worked here for many years between the two world wars. His excavations, of prime importance to the archaeologist, have enabled him to trace the successive stages of civilization during the three or four thousand years for which this site was inhabited. The first settlers lived in huts constructed from the branches of trees; their primitive pottery was in imitation of basketwork, their instruments of stone; they were buried lying hunched up on their sides, under their houses. At a higher level have been found traces of oval mud-brick of which houses were then made; red paint, a mixture of red oxide and fruit juice, with which the walls were decorated; and pottery, turned on a simple wooden device and painted with stylized animals. Higher still, relating to what is known as period III (4000–3000 B.C.) we come to rectangular bricks, more elaborate pottery turned on a wheel, and traces of metal-working. The houses were painted white; an increasing number of precious objects were laid beside the dead. This period seems to have ended with fire; in the succeeding one, monochrome pottery replaced painted ware, and cylinder seals appear – the only examples of writing yet found on the plateau earlier than the Achaemenian period. After this there is a long gap in the story, but sometime before 1000 B.C. the site appears to have been occupied by Indo-European invaders, Iranians, who constructed a fortified town and a palace of sun-dried brick and stone in the area known as Necropolis B. The painted ware with long beaks showing human figures and animals in movement, which can be seen in the Tehran museum and the Louvre, dates from this period. The Iranian dead were no longer buried under their houses but in vast separate cemeteries. Sometime about 800 B.C. a disaster, perhaps an Assyrian invasion, seems to have overtaken Sialk. As a result it was completely abandoned, and has never been inhabited in historical times.

After the delights of Fin and the revelations of Sialk, Kashan itself is something of a disappointment, somehow lacking the vitality and glamour of its sister cities. This was not always so.

In its great days, both before and after the Mongol invasion, it was one of the leading centres of artistic life. In the twelfth century it was with Rayy the foremost producer of pottery in Iran. After partial destruction in 1221 it experienced an extraordinary revival, and became the home of lustre faïence. What killed this essentially Kashani industry was the evolution of the mosaic tile known in Persian as kashi. But the triumph of the kashi from about 1400 did not spell the downfall of Kashan. The city also possessed a flourishing textile industry, particularly famous for its velvets, and this in time influenced the output of a superb series of carpets in the sixteenth century. Moreover, carpet-weavers from Kashan carried the city's fame to other centres – the Ardebil carpet, for instance, is the work of one Maqsud Kashani. The city enjoyed great prosperity under the Safavids. Shah Abbas at his special request was buried here beside an ancestor, and Abbas II celebrated his accession in Kashan. It was only with the Afghan invasion that decay set in; an earthquake in the latter part of the eighteenth century accelerated the process. Sir John Malcolm, visiting Kashan in 1810, said that no city could present a more uninviting prospect. Since then there has been some recovery.

For a city with such a record of artistic achievement, Kashan is singularly lacking in ancient buildings. There are two Seljuk minarets, one attached to the otherwise uninteresting Friday Mosque. The Maidan Mosque in the bazaar is Timurid, dating from 1463. The tomb of Shah Abbas I adjoins the older mauso-leum of Habib ibn Musa. There is a large Qajar hammam in the bazaar, but it does not compare with those of Kazvin or Kerman. In the centre of the town, in a maze of narrow alleys, is the Khaneh Burujerdi, a somewhat neglected Qajar mansion with amusing European-style wall paintings. Also worth visiting are two other nineteenth-century buildings, the Masjid-i-Agha Bozorg and the Madrasseh-ye-Sultan'i, the former with some good tile work.

North of Kashan, at Ravand, a road crosses the mountains to Dalijan, passing by the ancient carpet centre of Joshagan and the village of Neisar where there is an early Sassanian fire temple which throws a valuable light on the construction of a domed building on a square base. Godard takes 'this admirable little building, the most instructive of Sassanian monuments at present known' as a peg on which to hang a revealing architectural essay. The temple is built without wood, but simply of local stone, plaster and reeds; the four archways through which it is entered lean slightly inward to support the weight of the dome. At the four corners of the interior an early primitive squinch is visible. Walls of great thickness are designed in part to secure what Godard calls a 'service platform' at the level of the top of the arch and below the dome from which the latter could be constructed.

Half way to Dalijan on this same road is the Shrine of Sultan Ali (son of the Fifth Imam) at Ardehal, with Safavid tiles and early carved wooden doors. This is the scene, at the end of October, of a carpet-washing ceremony (Jashn-i-Qali Shui) considered by some to date from pre-Islamic times.

Another place of interest near Kashan is Qamsar, some twenty miles down the asphalt road to the south-east. This is the main centre after Shiraz for rose water production and should be seen in May when the roses are in bloom. On the way is an ingeniously designed Safavid caravanserai which according to Morier once carried an inscription saying that it was erected by Mir Sakee, one of Shah Abbas's generals.

Between Kashan and Yazd there are three small towns of special interest – Natanz, Ardistan and Nain. Natanz lies at over five thousand feet in a fertile valley open towards the south, a straggling place half hidden in orchards. The principal monument, identified from a distance by its tall minaret, is one of those complicated groups of buildings in which the early fourteenth century seems to specialize (cf. Bastam, Pir-i-Bakran). It comprises the Friday Mosque (1304), the tomb of Sheikh 'Abd as-Samad al Isfahani (1307), the entrance to a khanaqah or convent (1316), and the minaret (1324). A simple entrance leads into a corridor which divides the convent from the mosque. To the left is the building on which the minaret is constructed; beyond it, facing outwards, is the severely damaged convent portal, decorated in glazed faïence and unglazed terracotta. To the right is the tomb, entered through the mosque behind it, a small open courtyard on the four-iwan plan. Architecturally the mosque is not remarkable; its most curious feature is the square hole in the middle of the court, in which steps lead down to the qanat which flows below, and in which fish are sometimes clearly visible. The tomb consists of a high, forty-foot dome on a small octagonal base. Braided colonettes on each of the eight angles complete the sense of loftiness. The interior of the dome is filled with multiple plaster stalactites, dazzlingly white. Its lightness is enhanced by windows grilled with faïence, which pierce the squinches. Natanz is also the site of a ruined Sassanian fire temple and possesses a good Huseyneyeh. The adjoining street of potters is also worth a visit.

Two miles or so east of Natanz is the village of Afushteh, where there are a number of interesting though mostly ruined buildings of Timurid or Safavid date. And at Abyaneh, to the west, there is a Maidan Mosque with an unusual mimbar and mihrab of carved wood dated 1073.

South of Natanz the road forks left for Ardistan and right for Isfahan. A few miles in the latter direction, on the left is Tajabad, a large walled garden rather than a village, with three ruined Safavid buildings: a pavilion with remains of frescoes and an ornamental water-channel, a rose water distillery and a hammam. Local legend has it that Shah Abbas carried out military manoeuvres nearby in the summer and joined his wives in the pavilion in the evenings.

At Ardistan we are back on the edge of the desert. The town has withered, leaving, in a fair state of preservation, a Friday Mosque which contains some of the finest Seljuk brickwork outside Isfahan, and is one of the earliest buildings constructed on the four-iwan plan. The dome chamber is superbly illustrated in Pope's survey; the stucco inscriptions of the entrance iwan and the plain exterior in Morris, Wood and Wright's *Persia*. The small ruined Mosque of Imam Hasan has a portal, two minarets and a stucco mihrab. At Zavaré, eight miles north of Ardistan, in itself a most attractive little town, are the first dated mosque on the four-iwan plan in Iran, the Friday Mosque (1135), the Pa-Menar Mosque (probably Il-Khanid) with stucco work compris-ing six mihrabs, probably of earlier date, together with a fine Seljuk minaret, two Takiehs, a winter prayer hall and a worth-while bazaar. And fifteen miles to the east, off the track to Anarak, there is a remarkable decaying Qajar mansion known as Chehel Situn above Surangabad village.

Nain is an ancient town built over a hilly site which may partly comprise its own ruins; it gives the impression of a place sinking slowly into the desert. A maze of narrow streets, now intersected by modern avenues, lead past the Farah-Khané, a Safavid house recently restored, to the Friday Mosque, one of the oldest mosques in use in Iran, dating from the middle of the tenth century. Like the earlier but ruined Tari Khaneh at Damghan it consists of an oblong court surrounded by lofty and occasionally buttressed porticoes of slender proportions. These arcades are three bays deep except on the north-east. Some of the piers, which may have been too slender for their height, were rebuilt possibly in Seljuk times, but the round piers are original. Both the columns and the insides of the arches are loaded with a rich encrustation of stucco ornament. The stucco mihrab on the qibla wall is in a terrible state of repair, its base blackened by fire or lighted tapers; but its beauty can still be appreciated. Its theme, Pope tells us, is fertility. It conjures up a rich vision of succulent objects rarely seen in desert towns – entwining vines, colossal blossoms, pendant fruit. Stairs lead from a corner of the court on to the gently vaulted roof, and it is from here that the best view is obtained not only of the tumbling town but also of the lofty and unusual minaret – an octagon on a square base with a round top. At Muhammadiyya 3 km to the east of Nain there are two small mosques noted by Godard, one of which, the Sar-i-Kucha, contains a very fine painted kufic frieze running round the whole interior.

On first blush, Yazd may seem to have little to recommend it. It is built on a flat site in a particularly dusty and torrid plain; its summer climate is one of the most disagreeable on the plateau. Unlike most Persian cities it has little vegetation round it, is

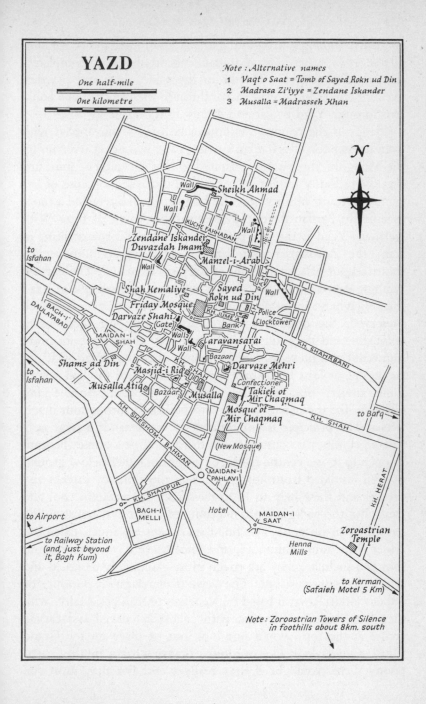

YAZD

One half-mile

One kilometre

Note : Alternative names
1 Vaqt o Saat = Tomb of Sayed Rokn ud Din
2 Madrasa Zi'iyye = Zendane Iskander
3 Musalla = Madrasseh Khan

N

Wall · Sheikh Ahmad
Wall
KUCHE FAHHADAN
Wall
Zendane Iskander
Duvazdah Imam
Wall · Manzel-i-Arab
to
Isfahan
Wall
Shah Kemaliye
Sayed
Rokn ud Din
Wall
Friday Mosque
BAGH-I-
DAULATABAD
Darvaze Shahi
(Gate)
KH. JUMEH
Police
Clocktower
Bank
MAIDAN-I
SHAH
Wall
Caravansarai
KH. SHAHRBANI
Wall
Bazaar
Shams ad Din
Darvaze Mehri
to
Isfahan
Masjid-i Riq
Confectioner
KH. SHAH
Musalla Atiq
Bazaar
Musalla
Takieh of
Mir Chaqmaq
KH. SHESHOM-I BAHMAN
Mosque of
Mir Chaqmaq
KH. SHAH
to Barq
(New Mosque)
KH. HERAT
MAIDAN-I
PAHLAVI
to Airport
KH. SHAHPUR
BAGH-I
MELLI
Hotel
MAIDAN-I
SAAT
Zoroastrian
Temple
to Railway Station
(and, just beyond
it, Bagh Kum)
Henna
Mills
to Kerman
(Safaieh Motel 5 Km)

Note : Zoroastrian Towers of Silence
in foothills about 8km. south

singularly lacking in trees and gardens, and looks, and is, perenni-
ally short of water. The mountains round about are completely
devoid of vegetation. Thanks to the wide, drab and practical
avenues which Reza Shah drove through the old city, one could
pass through Yazd by car and dismiss it as dull.

'Happy is the country without a history' – this applies with
even greater force to Iranian towns. Yazd was never overrun by
the Mongols. She has never aspired to be the capital of Iran; nor
was she seriously fought over by rival dynasties. Because of her
central position and her peaceful history, she has retained a more
specifically Persian flavour than any other town of Iran. With
Kerman, Yazd is the last real stronghold of Zoroastrianism in
Iran; the Zoroastrian population here numbers some seven
thousand out of a total of about sixty-six thousand. The narrow
winding streets are longer, cleaner, and more picturesque in Yazd
than elsewhere; the walls which bound them are generally well
preserved, the doorways and courts leading off them often
colourful, and the mud arches which span them are both more
numerous and more solid than in any other city. Yazd is, if not
the home, at least the happy hunting-ground of the bad-gir, or
wind tower, that peculiarly Iranian invention (simple and
effective like the qanat) which is to be found throughout desert
Persia. The principle is not difficult to understand: a large per-
forated chimney is constructed in the middle of a house; beneath
it, open to it, is a central room, or zirzamin, either below ground
or well insulated from hot air outside; the chimney catches any
breezes and these help to keep the air in the zirzamin cool and
fresh. But the bad-gir is often a thing of artistry far transcending
its utilitarian purpose. The finest specimens are much taller and
wider than house chimneys, and since there is no worry about
soot and suchlike, they are much more elaborately designed and
artistically self-conscious. The *genre* is unashamedly Gothic, or
rather Gothic Revival based on Venetian prototypes. Many, with
their long narrow openings with delicately curved and carved
arches at the top, would not look out of place on the Grand
Canal. Others look like outdoor organs; what a mighty caco-
phony there would be if they really were! For they must run

into hundreds in Yazd alone. Seen from the roof of the Friday Mosque, they dominate the skyline in at least three directions.

Another feature of Yazd, to be seen still in some old houses and also in the Church of St Simon the Zealot at Shiraz, are coloured glass windows framed in wooden tracery, some round, some rectangular, in geometrical patterns reminiscent of faïence mosaic.

The bazaars of Yazd are beyond question the most colourful and most bustling in Iran. They are smaller than those of Tabriz and less imposing than those of Isfahan; but in picturesqueness, variety and animation they have no rival.* But the visitor will regard this judgment as eccentric unless he knows where to look, for the geography of Yazd is rather perverse. The main artery of the city is the Khiaban-i-Pahlevi. Half way down this, on the right (east), stands one of the most prominent monuments of Yazd, the Takieh of Mir Chaqmaq, an enormous Qajar gateway with two very tall minarets. This is known as the Entrance to the bazaar. But there are three bazaar areas in Yazd, and all of them are to the left (west) of the Khiaban-i-Pahlevi. One, known as the Old Bazaar, lies to the north of the Friday Mosque in the same ancient quarter as the shrine of the Duvazdah Imam. This is picturesque, but small, and anything but animated. I remember principally a small vat for dyeing cotton yarn, of which my French companion remarked, very accurately: 'Il y a un odeur ici qui n'est pas très sympathique.' The other two lie on each side of the Khiaban-i-Shah, which runs west from the Khiaban-i-Pahlevi. That to the north is fairly animated but not particularly picturesque. Here are large warehouses and expensive carpet shops. It is in the bazaars to the south of the Khiaban-i-Shah that Yazd really comes to life. There are crowded alleys thronged with green-turbaned sayyeds and Zoroastrian women with their red and green chadors. There are bearded carpet vendors sitting crosslegged on their platforms; bales of brightly coloured cotton hang from the stalls; in places the clang of the copper-workers is so loud that it is impossible to speak. Everyone seems hard at work, buying, selling, shouting, hammering; one is bustled aside by men or donkeys carrying their burdens from warehouse to

* Written in 1961. See Annex, note 6.

stall or from stall to lorry. The Yazdis are famous throughout
Iran for their industry and here, uninhibited, it is on full display.
In addition, these bazaars offer other, unexpected delights. There
is a charming little maidan across which any morning you are
bound to see a procession of camels, their bells clanking even
above the din of the coppersmiths. There are numerous vistas
down into entrancing courtyards, such as the newly restored
Madrasseh Khan, which has two courts on different levels, or the
Central Police Station, formerly the headquarters of the Imperial
Bank of Iran, approached through a monumental doorway, a
charming nineteenth-century building which still retains much of
its Imperial glamour. For the colour photographer, in particular,
these bazaars of Yazd are an intoxication.

Yazd is famous for the vivacity and industry of its inhabitants.
Edward Browne said that their sing-song drawl reminded him of
Northumberland; and they certainly appear to have, improbable
as it seems in this stifling climate, a north country addiction to
work. It is certainly they who have made Yazd what it is – a
busy banking and commercial centre and a hive of small-scale
industry, which is the envy of many other cities of Iran.

It may be thought that Yazd, being a matter-of-fact, workaday
town, is not rich in ancient monuments; and it is true that the
city has no more benefited from royal patronage than it has
from nature; here are no palaces, no stately gardens, no Imperial
follies. What Yazd has, she owes to herself; but in the Friday
Mosque, the Duvazdah Imam shrine, the Vakt-u-Saat, the Mir
Chaqmaq Mosque and the mausoleum of Shams-ad-Din she can
boast buildings which each in their kind are among the finest in
the country. And the city walls, largely built by Timur, are the
most beautiful and best preserved of that epoch in Iran.

The Duvazdah Imam, deep in the ancient northern quarter,
was built in 1037, ten years before the Seljuk conquest. It is a
small square building covered with a low dome supported by
trefoil squinches of a strong simple form, the prototype of many
more complex developments of the Seljuk and later periods. The
plain whitewashed interior is relieved only by an arched recess
for the mihrab, above which is a red stucco panel (now darkened)

with a fine flowing unmistakably Iranian design in the 'quilted'
style; what Pope calls 'the great sunburst pattern within the
dome, composed of overlapping finger-like rays painted in blue,
white, red and green on a white ground' has disappeared.

The monument known today as Vakt-u-Saat (Time and the
Hour), in fact the tomb of Sayed Rokn ud Din, dates from 1325
and was originally part of a group of buildings which included a
madrasseh and a well-equipped observatory. It stands just to the
east of the Friday Mosque and was originally approached through
a large iwan with elaborate stucco ornament, but this has almost
wholly disappeared. The decoration of the square, domed interior,
though now sadly dilapidated, must in its day have ranked with
the finest fourteenth-century work and bears comparison with
that of the shrine of Oljeitu at Sultaniyeh. The dome in particular
is painted with rich medallions which include kufic lettering and
whose sunburst pattern resembles a great circular carpet. The
side walls and mihrab are decorated with relief patterns, once
polychromed and gilded.

The Friday Mosque, which was founded in the twelfth century
but was rebuilt between 1334 and 1365, is perhaps the finest and
certainly the best preserved building of that period in Iran. It is
outstanding both for the originality of its design and for the
details of its ornamentation. It is also a model of cleanliness and
brightness which many other Friday Mosques might well emulate.

The plan is unusual. The main court is elongated, with twelve
plain arches on each side dominated to the south by the iwan of
the sanctuary and to the east by the vast entrance portal. The
latter, an exceptionally high narrow iwan, is crowned by two
tapering minarets; it dates in part from the fourteenth and in part
from the early sixteenth century, is the most prominent building
in Yazd, and has a soaring grandeur unlike any other doorway in
the country. But it suffers somewhat from having had buildings
in front of it torn down, and standing as it now does at the end
of a newly constructed street ravaged by modernization its height
appears disproportionate to its width and its slender minarets
seem almost ready to topple.

The great south-west iwan serves as the threshold to some of the most exciting manifestations of Persian Islamic architecture. This iwan, unlike the portal, is remarkable not so much for its height as for its depth. Its sides, each with two double rows of arcades, are covered in rich blue, green and white faïence mosaic. The dome chamber behind it is brilliantly lighted from great vaults covering a gallery on the two sides; the qibla wall is tiled with plain geometrical designs which throw the splendour of the mihrab into relief. This mihrab is of unusual height, contained within a great rectangular frame formed by a superbly executed kufic frieze. The panel above the arch is filled with an exquisite flower pattern in faïence mosaic, broken by three medallions, one embossed. Within the arch is a powerful stalactite vault, richly tiled, and the square medallions on the lower wall space are framed in a striking and unusual setting of brilliantly decorated but unglazed brick.

The glories of the Friday Mosque do not end with this mihrab. There is the interior of the dome, with its animated catherine-wheel of blue and unglazed brick, a triumphant example of design appropriately applied. There are, on each side of the sanctuary, large whitewashed transverse vaulted halls unique of their kind. These are spanned by arches between which arched windows open to the side walls, giving a sense of both architectural lightness and brilliant lighting which is truly impressive. In the oratory on the north side, says Pope, 'the principle of the transverse vault is carried to a perfection not surpassed in any other building in Persia'.

Finally, the roof of the Friday Mosque, which can be easily reached by a stairway in the south corner of the court, provides a superb view not only of the squat dome and the portal but over the whole city, with its cupolas, wind towers and crumbling walls against a dramatic backdrop of jagged mountains.

There are two other monuments of the same period which are worthy of attention. The Mir Chaqmaq Mosque, near the so-called Entrance to the Bazaar (p. 215), was built in the mid-fifteenth century by an officer of Shah Rukh; it contains some good geometrical tilework of the period, and has a curious dome with a cornice which Robert Byron likens to the brim of a hat.

The mausoleum of Shams-ad-Din, in the south-west quarter (c. 1365), has a charming court, remarkable polychromed and gilded stucco reliefs, and a delicately carved stucco mihrab.

Other buildings in Yazd worth passing mention are the Mosque of Shah Abul Kassem near the Duvazdeh Imam with a stucco minaret of the twelfth century, and four mud-brick mausolea with painted plaster inside named Boq'a Shah Kemali, Madrasseh Ziya'a, Gunbad-i-Shaikh Ahmad and Huseyniyeh Hasht.

When we tire of architecture, Yazd has other curiosities. There is the Zoroastrian fire temple on the Kerman road, endowed by Bombay Parsees, where in a central room the everlasting fire is guarded by a priest who walks and intones almost continually. On the foothills to the south-west are two tombs of silence, approached by long wide stone stairs, where the Zoroastrians expose their dead in great enclosed cylinders of stone, to which Gentiles may not penetrate. There is an enormous burst of beehive domes, also on the Kerman road, each of which contains a press for grinding henna, once operated by blindfolded camels. In at least one square in Yazd, and in many of the surrounding villages such as Taft, large openwork wooden structures are to be seen, with lotus shaped sides and open ends. Known as nakhl, they are used for processional purposes during Moharram, covered with black bunting and carrying mourning banners. Along the Kerman road are several caravanserais of which the most interesting is 45 km from Yazd at Zein-uddin, circular and well fortified with five turrets and a recessed entrance.

Behind the sun-baked dusty valley in which Yazd lies, there rises a serrated ridge, grim and tremendous, in which projecting rocks assume fantastic shapes. To look at these mountains one might say that life and they were a contradiction in terms, so dry and brown and brutal do they appear. I have driven into them in April, when if ever they should be green, and the lower slopes showed few signs of life; not a blade of grass, only miserable tufts that never knew flower or leaf and look to have no purposeful existence. And then, suddenly, comes the miracle, so typical of the plateau: a densely wooded, intensively irrigated, thickly populated valley which coils like a snake for ten miles round the base of the great mountains of Shir Kuh (13,370 ft) and Barf Khaneh, or Snow House, giving way at the last to rocky slopes flecked with asphodel, which run right up to the base of the snows. The valley of Deh Bala, the Upland Village, a favourite summer resort of the Yazdis, is one of the great surprises of Iran. It is also something of a sporting centre, for again contrary to expectation mouflon, ibex and gazelle flourish in these remote unearthly hills.

To the south-west of Yazd, nestling beside a piece of desert of its own, is the ancient town of Abarquh, a port of call on the little-used road from Shiraz and Persepolis to Yazd. 'Grosse agglomération d'aspect misérable' is the Guide Bleu's unkind comment; but it is indeed a sad place. A huddle of buildings, mostly half or wholly ruined, are strung out where desert and foothills meet, with more houses, it seems, than inhabitants, and scarcely a green patch anywhere. But in Mongol times this was a flourishing city, and among its ruins are several interesting monuments. The Friday Mosque (1337) consists of four iwans with flanking arcades, a five-bay prayer hall and a plaster mihrab of simple design but first-class craftsmanship. Another mosque or madrasseh with two minarets, the Nizamiyeh (1325) is almost entirely ruined. On a little hill to the south of the town stands the interesting Gunbad-i-Ali, an octagonal tomb tower built entirely of stone and rubble with a heavy projecting cornice and dating from 1056.

The road from Abarquh to Yazd launches immediately out on to the vast salt flats, on which it is easy to drive when it is dry, but which are often impassable in spring. Beyond them the road curls round the southern flank of the mountains overlooking Yazd, passing beside some enchanting walled villages. The landscape is dotted with rocky promontories, like some rash on the moon; at their feet is a long, even, sandy slope running down to the bottom of a valley or over the horizon. This particular type of scenery is the hallmark of dry country; in areas of heavier rainfall, Fars or Azerbaijan, for instance, the slopes are furrowed, the spaces between the ranges are lower, and the curious unmistakable flat tilt of the desert country round Yazd is, literally, washed away and transformed into undulations. After a time as one travels it is possible to guess the amount of rainfall not only by the vegetation, which is often deceptive, but by the lie of the land, which is infallible.

First impressions are not always just. I arrived in Kerman in a dust-storm with visibility down to about fifty yards, and within an hour was listening to the Swiss Ambassador playing 'O God our help in ages past' on the harmonium of the Protestant Mission Church. Yet Kerman by reputation has the clearest, driest, finest year-round climate in Iran, and it would be hard to imagine any place further in spirit from the world of Calvin or John Knox.

Kerman is the last, and in some respects the loveliest, of the great desert towns. Unlike the others it stands high (5,600 ft) and is protected from the Dasht-i-Lut by a great arc of mountains, containing the highest peaks on the plateau outside the main Elburz and Zagros ranges. These mountains provide a good supply of water, and the plain of Kerman is intersected by the longest qanats in the world. The town itself lies immediately at the base of a barren rocky spur of these mountains, and the well-preserved walls of the medieval city still look a formidable and impressive barrier between the hills and the plain. The gardens of Kerman, though less famous than those of Shiraz, are of singular beauty, their vistas of cypress and umbrella pine hidden away behind turreted or massive brick doorways which suggest opulence. Kerman is unique among Persian towns in that it was sacked, not by the Mongols, but in 1794 by Aga Mohammed Qajar in pursuit of Lutf-Ali Khan, the last of the Zend dynasty. For having befriended this unhappy refugee, twenty thousand Kermanis were, it is said, sold as slaves and twenty thousand others blinded. Thus the neglect of the Mongols was amply repaid by this savage contemporary of George Washington. Structurally, however, Kerman to a remarkable extent escaped; and as Aga Mohammed's successors later did something to beautify the city, it has in fact more to offer in the way of ancient buildings than its history might suggest. The city is divided into

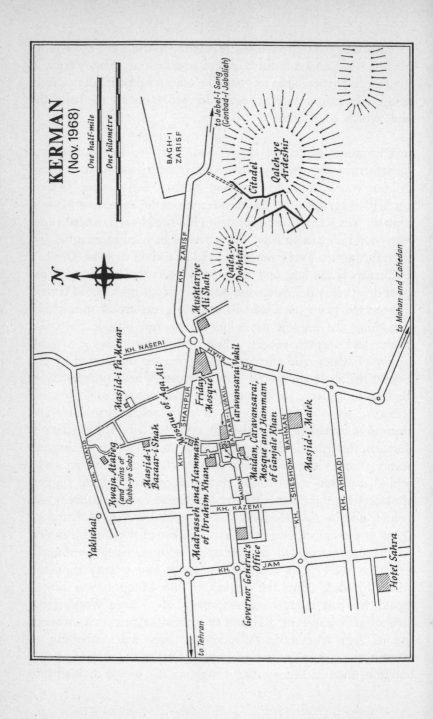

KERMAN
(Nov. 1968)

One half-mile

One kilometre

N

BAGH-I ZARISF

to Jebel-i Sang
(Gonbad-i Jabalieh)

KH. ZARISF

Qaleh-ye Ardeshir

Citadel

Qaleh-ye Dokhtar

Mushtariye Ali Shah

KH. NASERI

Masjid-i Pa-Menar

Mosque of Aga Ali

KH. SHAHPUR

KH. SHAH

Friday Mosque

Caravansarai Vakil

KH. VAKIL

Kwaja-Atabeg
(and ruins of
Qubba-ye Sabz)

Masjid-i
Bazaar-i Shah

KH. BAZAAR

Maidan, Caravansarai,
Mosque and Hammam
of Ganjale Khan

Madrasseh and Hammam
of Ibrahim Khan

KH. VALIAHD

Yakhchal

MAIDAN

KH. KAZEMI

KH. SHESHOM BAHMAN

Masjid-i Malek

KH. AHMADI

Governor General's
Office

KH. JAM

to Tehran

Hotel Sahra

to Mahan and Zahedan

11a. (*above*) KERMAN: Caravanserai Vakil (Qajar period), with wind towers of glazed tiles (*p. 225*) 11b. (*below*) KERMAN: Doorway of Pa-Menar Mosque, showing fourteenth-century tilework (*p. 223*)

12. BAM: Ruins of the old town from the citadel, with the new town beyond (*p. 228*)

four sections by avenues which intersect near the Friday Mosque
and it may be helpful to know in which of these sections the main
monuments lie. Many can only be approached through a maze
of narrow streets, for which a police or other guide is essential.

The oldest, reputedly Sassanian, is the citadel, popularly known
as the Qaleh-i-Ardeshir (south-east section). It is largely ruined,
but commands a fine view over town and plain.

The Jebel-i-Sang (north-east), or Stone Mountain, is a Seljuk
dome remarkable for its powerful stone construction, and one of
the oldest double domes in Iran. It is thought possible that the
outer dome was unfinished when the Ghuzz Turkomans sacked
Kerman in 1186. The purpose of the building is a mystery. It is
not oriented towards Mecca, and by popular tradition is of pre-
Islamic origin. This cannot be true, but the possibility that it
served some Zoroastrian rite cannot be excluded.

The Khwaja Atabek tomb (north-west), ascribed to the middle
of the twelfth century, is an empty shell, one of its sides having
disappeared in a recent earthquake, carrying the dome with it.
But enough of the carved stucco with which the interior was
covered remains to show that it was a fine example of Seljuk
workmanship. It is of curious plan, being octagonal without and
rectangular within, which made the walls very thin.

The vast, plain and austere Masjid-i-Malik (south-west), much
restored, contains three Seljuk mihrabs and a minaret of the same
period. There is some good vaulting in the Masjid-i-Bazar-i-Shah
(north-west) the main court of which is a Qajar restoration, and
some lovely mosaic tilework of the fifteenth or sixteenth century,
with stalactite vaulting, in the narrow doorway of the little
Masjid-i-Pa-Menar (north-west; see illustration facing p. 206).
The Qubba-i-Sabz has a Timurid façade.

The Friday Mosque (south-west) is one of the main glories of
Kerman. It is approached down a stairway which leads into a
long narrow court, in the centre of which is a pleasant pool. At
the far end stands the main portal, a masterpiece of fourteenth-
century architecture with later tilework, but what first catches
the eye is the saucy gold clock tower which tops it, a recent
addition to replace the fallen minarets, charming in its way but

more suggestive of the stables of an English country house than of an Islamic place of worship. It should not deflect attention from the details of the tilework of the portal: the fine geometrical work in the three ogival panels on each side of the entry, the twisted blue sugar-candy arch and the flowered tilework above it, the mosaic tiles in relief on the interior sides of the doorway. This leads into a domed vestibule which retains its original ceiling – a fascinating pattern formed by glazed geometrical bricks with a centre of mosaic tiles. Beyond lies the great court, regularly built on the four-iwan plan, with more fine tilework in daring colours on the south iwan and again in the sanctuary behind it. The mihrab and tiling date from the middle of the sixteenth century, when the mosque was extensively restored.

An interesting Safavid complex is the large arcaded square in the middle of the bazaar, known as the Maidan-i-Ganj Ali Khan (south-west). On the north side of this square is the Zarrab Khaneh or Mint; to the west an ab-ambar with remains of paintings and stalactite work inside the dome and some good Safavid tilework; to the south a large and handsome hammam and to the east a building known as a caravanserai, but possibly in fact a madrasseh, with small mosque attached. Both the latter were being restored in 1970, and the hammam being turned into a museum. In the hammam entrance are painted stalactites and inside a splendid marble door frame, carved in low relief with a pattern of storks, while in the second chamber are two translucent alabaster panels. The doorways of the so-called Caravanserai Mosque have mosaic panels (when last seen in poor condition) representing the figure of an angel with phoenix, dragon and lion, humorously designed and executed with great refinement.

Other noteworthy buildings date from the early Qajar period. The finest are the Hammam and Madrasseh of Ibrahim Khan (south-west), which adjoin on a square off the bazaar. The bath (men only), an elaborate series of domed and arcaded rooms, is filled with wall decorations including scenes from the life of Rustam, and dating from the reign of Karim Khan Zand.* The early Qajar

* Reported (1971) as being restored as a museum.

madrasseh is an example of the art of that florid period at its best. The large entrance, with its gay clock tower and its riot of tiles portraying peacocks, white wader birds and bowls of pink, yellow and blue flowers, is quite irresistible. It leads into a quiet courtyard, shaded with cypresses and pines, adjoining which is a fine Qajar house. The exuberant flowerbeds match perfectly the flowered tiles which surround it, and there is a small room on the north side of the court tiled with irises and roses and containing some excellent plaster work. The garden is overlooked by a bad-gir or wind tower covered with blue tiles, which seems to be a speciality of Kerman. There are two other good examples in the Caravanserai Vakil, another Qajar structure near the bazaar. A court of lesser charm is that of the Mushtariye Ali Shah (south-east), a pious foundation near the Friday Mosque, dominated by three bulbous domes, two blue-tiled, whose varying shapes in close juxtaposition seem at once humorous and irresponsible.

It is these gay, modest, carefree buildings which somehow epitomize the peculiar atmosphere of Kerman. At the opposite pole is the grim austerity of the Jebel-i-Sang. Like the surrounding mountains that smile only at dawn and sunset, it breathes the spirit of the desert, harsh and uncompromising, calling for strength, austerity, endurance. The other Kerman eyes the desert at its doorstep and laughs in its face; the blue domes, the tiled wind towers, the flowery courtyards, the languorous gardens, the carpet-weavers singing at their looms, the flashing eyes in the bazaar – they are one great act of defiance. No other city in Iran has quite this spirit, compounded of playfulness and poverty, gaiety and grace. No other city, moreover, has such clear air, such dazzling colours or such brilliant horizons. I know someone who, after living here for some years, moved to Isfahan and found it damp. The stars, they say, shine brighter in Kerman than anywhere else in the world.

A modern highway now links Kerman to Bandar Abbas (p. 292) reopening communications between Central Iran and the Gulf through Sirjan, 16 km south-east of which are the remains of old Sirjan the largest city of Southern Iran in the tenth century. To the south-east of this road, some forty miles from Kerman is Nigar, where there is a remarkably beautiful Seljuk minaret with a kufic inscription dated just before the Mongol invasion – a Seljuk outpost in time as well as space. But the Mongol invasion is like yesterday compared with the age of another monument in this direction. Eighty miles east of the Bandar Abbas road and 156 miles south of Kerman is an archaeological site of outstanding interest. The 65-foot mound of Tepe Yahya, where an American-Iranian mission financed by Harvard, Ford and National Science Foundations had been working for some years, yielded in 1970 inscribed tablets recording economic, transactions, thought to date from about 3200 B.C., in the same writing as that on proto-Elamite tablets found at Susa. Blank tablets nearby suggest that they were actually inscribed at Yahya; while the discovery of a steatite quarry and unfinished bowls suggests a source for the steatite ware found in various sites in Mesopotamia. These finds indicate the existence of an urban and literate civilization in South Iran at a period when it had hitherto been presumed to exist only in the Tigris-Euphrates basin. There have also been discovered impressive Achaemenian remains including a bakery and a pottery and there is now ample evidence that this part of South-eastern Iran was neither in pre-historic nor later times a cultural backwater.

Anyone setting out from Kerman in a south-easterly direction would assume after a glance at the map that he was launching irrevocably into the wilderness. The cities of Iran lie behind; ahead, beyond those barren mountains, is the Dasht-i-Lut, an endless salt waste where high spring winds whip sand over the road and camels, caravans and even cars are buried, sometimes for days, sometimes for good; the next town is Karachi, some twelve hundred miles away; on no other road in Iran does one have quite the same sensation of moving off the edge of the world.

But Iran is nothing if not a country of surprises; and at Mahan, some twenty miles south-east of Kerman, she plays her most splendid practical joke on the unsuspecting traveller. For here, in a green valley flanked by snow-capped mountains, at over six thousand feet and in a setting of incomparable clarity

and peace, stands the most ravishing single group of buildings in
Iran.

It is the shrine of Nureddin Nimatullah, a Sufi divine and poet
who died at Mahan in 1431. The earliest buildings on the site
date from a few years after his death. The shrine was considerably
enlarged and beautified during the reign of Shah Abbas, and
there were numerous additions and embellishments in the 1840s.
The result may appear something of a jumble to the architectural purist. But the styles of the different periods, though
clearly distinguishable, harmonize remarkably well; and there is
nothing of a jumble about the splendid symmetry of the plan,
whose courts, iwans, and central dome chamber surrounded by
subsidiary rooms reproduce faithfully the ground plan of the
Sassanian palace at Firuzabad. Moreover, as a result of attention
from successive dynasties and patrons, the shrine has been worked
upon, tended, swept and watered through the centuries with
loving care.

A long garden court lined with recesses, to which modern
tilework is now being added, leads through an east door with
sumptuous bone inlay in floral design to the main court which
adjoins the shrine itself. Here indeed is Paradise. A cooling stream
flows perpetually through this little garden, in the centre of which
is a cruciform tank with an octagonal basin, the whole shaded by
eighteen majestic cypresses and eight umbrella pines. On the far
side flashes the brilliant blue of the Safavid dome and the two
Qajar minarets which flank the main iwan. The tilework here is
Qajar, and its boisterous yellows, pinks and blues, and the
riotous floral designs, harmonize perfectly with this garden
setting.

The main building consists of a central chamber, in which the
shrine itself rests, surmounted by a dome on an octagonal base,
and surrounded by domed halls. The passage on the east, which
has five small domes, is believed to date from the early nineteenth
century; the hall to the west, covered only with three domes, is
the main example of Safavid work in Mahan. Here are to be seen
the famous doors from India with Chinese designs; a lovely grille
of faïence mosaic over the doorway leading into the dome

chamber; and a series of plaster medallions with rich and heavy
floral designs, presumably dating from the late seventeenth
century, for they recall the 'Victorian' style of the wall paintings
in the Talar Ashraf at Isfahan. .

The light painting on the interior of the main dome itself dates
from the foundation of the shrine in 1437, the tiles of the exterior
from the time of Shah Abbas.

To the west of the main building are two further courts, the
first unadorned, save for four cypresses, the second decorated
with geometrical tiles and dominated on the west by a Safavid
iwan to which have been added two rather gaudy Qajar minarets.
It is from the bays and roof of this iwan that some of the finest
views of the shrine may be obtained. The great central dome
rises above a cluster of subsidiary latticed octagonal domes in the
manner of a Byzantine church. The pair of minarets behind, and
the cypresses in the foreground, accentuate the upward surge and
carry the eye on to the glistening mountain range beyond. A
scene which lacks nothing in perfection of composition is further
enlivened by the colouring – the brilliant blue of dome and sky,
the deep green of the cypresses and the dappled emerald of the
trees in the village, the resonant brown of the brickwork, the
flash of the snows, the incredible clarity and translucent quality
of the air. No place in Iran spells quite this peace and contentment.

Two or three miles to the south of the shrine, and clearly
visible from the minarets, is a large walled garden with a pavilion
at either end and a watercourse in poor condition down the
centre. This is known as the Garden of the Farman Farma, and
belonged to Firouz Mirza the son of Mohammed Shah when he
was Governor of Kerman about 1880.

South-east from Kerman, beyond mountains which enfold a
valley of roses, lies the desert, forbidding and immense, with
spring gales more cruel than the sea; in winter calm or summer
heat the very distillation of deadness. The road lumbers on to
Bam, an oasis and former frontier post of Kerman province,
frequently sacked by Afghans and Baluchis, and the scene of the
last Zand stand in 1795. The ancient citadel and what lies below

it are Iran's most photogenic ruin (see Plate 12 opposite p. 207). The walls are still in good preservation. There is only one entrance to the town. The mosque has been repaired and appears to be in use. There is also a caravanserai and hammam and, in the new town built outside the walls after 1850, a TAC hotel. The oasis with its date palms, orange trees, eucalyptus and oleander is seen at its best in mid-winter.

Fifty miles east of Bam, on the edge of the Dasht-i-Lut, stands the ancient minaret of Milar-i-Naderi and beyond that is Zahedan, capital of Persian Baluchistan, airport and rail-head yet little more than a village engulfed in desolate wastes. To the south is the Bampur valley, where Aurel Stein located many prehistoric sites, one of which at Bampur itself has recently been excavated under the aegis of the Royal Asiatic Society and has yielded extensive pottery finds from six periods ending about 1900 B.C. To the north lies the once fertile and fruitful province of Seistan a wheat-growing region which thrived on the swamps of the Helmand river, and whose richness today lies above all in its prehistoric and archaeological remains. For instance Shahr-i-Sokhte, discovered by Sir Aurel Stein in 1916 and excavated by the Italian Archaeological Mission in the 1960s, bears traces of four phases or layers of residential construction, before and including the Bronze Age, and the place appears to have been a centre for the production of alabaster vessels and hard stone, especially lapis lazuli, cornelian and turquoise.

Near the Afghan border, crowning a basalt rock rising from the shallow lake Hamun, is the most remarkable monument of Eastern Iran. The Kuh-i-Khwaja, or Hill of the Lord, has long been a Zoroastrian holy place. Here Zoroaster himself is believed to have taken refuge, and its summit is crowned by a ruined fire temple. On its southern flank are the ruins of a great palace originally constructed in Parthian times, and rebuilt and enlarged under the early Sassanians. It is a melancholy if formidable ruin, but the Doric half columns of the earlier building are still visible, and there is some fine stucco ornament. On the walls of a long gallery behind the main courts were once splendid painted panels of Parthian date, in subtle and mellow colours, representing kings and queens, spectators and gods, horses and leopards, flowers and acanthus leaves (they were brought to Tehran before the war by Sir Aurel Stein, but when opened were found to have crumbled to dust). These ruins show that, even at this dead point in history, and as it were at the end of the world, Greek influence was still alive and native talent abounding.

CHAPTER ELEVEN

Fars

The province of Fars, which straddles the southern end of the Zagros range between desert and Gulf, is the cradle of Persian history and poetry. It is a country well favoured by nature. High mountain ranges provide water and pasture for the tribes; the valleys, blessed with higher rainfall than in the interior of the plateau, yield corn and citrus fruit; the lower hillsides are terraced with vineyards. Relatively mild winters and cool summers combine to provide a climate of almost Mediterranean perfection; every element conspires to make this region what it is, the birthplace of a civilization. We need no longer speak of Iran; this is Persia itself.

In a historical sense, Fars has a flavour entirely of its own. If Media belongs to prehistory, the desert towns to early Islam, Azerbaijan to the Mongol period, Isfahan to the Seljuks and Safavids and Tehran to the present, Fars is essentially pre-Islamic, but spiced with a dash of medieval poetry and eighteenth-century politics. We have here not only the greatest surviving glories of the Achaemenian period, but also the great preponderance of Sassanian remains. The hold of Islam, by contrast, seems more slender. Fars wore the Arab conquest rather lightly. It escaped destruction both by the Mongols and by Timur. Saadi and Hafez brought renown to Shiraz while other parts of the country were being reduced to rubble and ashes. A prosperous but not pre-eminent province of the Safavid Empire, Fars flourished in the eighteenth century under the firm and wise rule of Karim Khan Zand, at a time when the rest of the country languished. If its later history has been somewhat stormy, this is

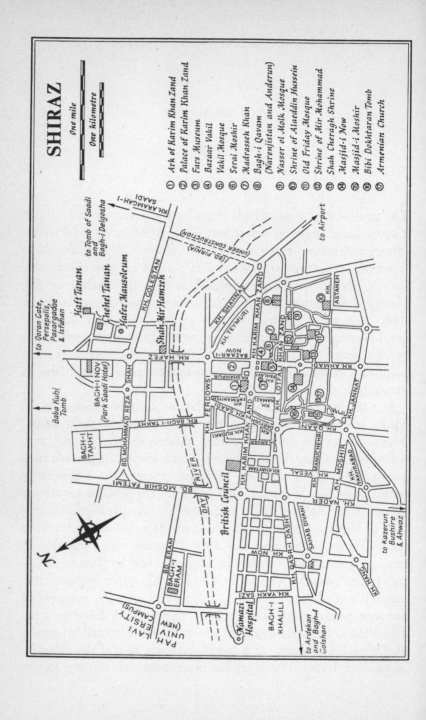

SHIRAZ

One mile

One kilometre

① Ark of Karim Khan Zand
② Palace of Karim Khan Zand
③ Fars Museum
④ Bazaar Vakil
⑤ Vakil Mosque
⑥ Serai Moshir
⑦ Madrasseh Khan
⑧ Bagh-i Qavam
   (Narenjistan and Anderun)
⑨ Nasser ol Molk Mosque
⑩ Shrine of Alaeddin Hussein
⑪ Old Friday Mosque
⑫ Shrine of Mir Mohammad
⑬ Shah Cheragh Shrine
⑭ Masjid-i Now
⑮ Masjid-i Moshir
⑯ Bibi Dokhtaran Tomb
⑰ Armenian Church

to Tomb of Saadi and Bagh-i Delgosha

KH. ARAMGAH-I SAADI

(UNDER CONSTRUCTION)

(Bd. PIRNIA)

to Airport

Haft Tanan

Chehel Tanan

Hafez Mausoleum

to Qoran Gate, Persepolis, Pasargadae & Isfahan

Baba Kuhi Tomb

KH. COLESTAN

Shah Mir Hamzeh

KH. SHAHRA

KH. TEYMURI

KH. HAFEZ

BAZAAR-I NOW

KH. SHAHPUR

KH. KARIM KHAN ZAND

KH. KARIM KHAN ZAND

KH. AHMADI

BAGH-I NOV
(Park Saadi Hotel)

BD. MOHAMMAD REZA SHAH

KH. FERDOWSI

KH. BAGH-I TAKHT

KH. PAHLAVI

KH. LOTFALI

KHAN ZAND

KH. NAMAZI

②

⑦
⑥
⑤

⑧

⑨

⑩

ASTANEH

KH.

BAGH-I TAKHT

RIVER
(DRY)

KH. RUDAKI

KH. DARYUSH

KH. SAADI

British Council

⑭

KH. NAMAZI

KH. FARMANFATEH

⑬
⑯

KH. JANNAT

⑰

KH. QAAN

BD. MOSHIR FATEMI

KH. KARIM KHAN

KH. KHAYYAM

KH. ANVARI

KH. MOSHIR

KH. VESAL

KH. MANUCHEHRI

KH. NADER

KH. FAKHRABAD

BD. ERAM

BAGH-I ERAM

KH. QASR-I DASH

KH. MON

KH. SAHAB DIVANI

KH. YAKH SAZI

BAGH-I KHALILI

Namazi Hospital

PAHLAVI UNIVERSITY (NEW CAMPUS)

to Ardekan and Bagh-i Golshan

to Kazerun Bushire & Ahwaz

KH. HANA

largely due to the predominance of the powerful tribes who roam its ranges, particularly the Qashgais. Fars thus presents many elements of contrast: exceptionally rich vestiges of ancient civilization; a well-planned sophisticated capital of great natural beauty; and a countryside shared by settled peasantry and hardy independent nomads.

Shiraz, by tradition the city of roses and nightingales, cypresses and wine, bulbous domes and terraced gardens, has I suppose been more extolled in poetry and prose than any other city of Iran. Hafez sang,

> 'Right through Shiraz the path goes
> Of perfection
> Anyone in Shiraz knows
> Its direction.'

'Defended by nature, enriched by trade and by art made lovely . . . a more delightful object can hardly be than what this city yields the eye from the neighbouring mountain,' declared Herbert; 'Here,' proclaimed John Fryer, 'grow the loftiest cypresses in the universe.' He was particularly impressed by the houses, whose porches and gatehouses were beautifully adorned, and by the gardens 'under whose shady Bowers we were feasted from the Heel of every day till Midnight by the interchangeable solicitations of our Christian friends'.

Shiraz is fortunate in its site. Few approaches could be more dramatic as the visitor descends the last pass on the road from Isfahan, and sees the town, its blue domes sparkling, framed by the arch of the Qoran gate. The pass is called Allah-o-Akhbar (God is Great), because legend has it that generations of travellers have stood there and thus expressed their wonder at the view below.

A friendly range of pinkish hills protects Shiraz from the north and south; fertile valleys open up to the west; only the wide dry plain and salt lake to the east give a hint of desolation. A kind of cosmopolitan breeze seems to have blown over this city, bringing it into touch with distant lands, like Spain or India, and exotic plants and thoughts; it has a gentle glow, an inner calm, a sort of lush contentment quite alien to life on the rest of the plateau. The great gardens with their high whitewashed walls and deep shades and cool water channels and ungainly houses with mirrored balconies and curvilinear gables, are an unfailing source of delight; and the Avenue Zand, built by Karim Khan and running west from the citadel, wide enough to have served once as a polo ground, is the most sumptuous street in Iran. Shiraz seems designed for a life of lazy contemplation and lingering indolence.

It is above all a town of the eighteenth and nineteenth centuries, as characteristically so in Persian terms, though not in size or quality of architecture, as Brighton or Bath are of the Regency in England. Those who come in search of magnificent works from the great periods of Persia's past will inevitably be disappointed. 'Its architecture and other signs', wrote Pietro della Valle in 1602, 'plainly show it to be the work of Muslims who are incurious architects. Inside is nothing of beauty or importance.' For two centuries more it remained a provincial centre until in 1759 Karim Khan Zand, emerging victorious after eleven years of fighting, decided to build a new capital here. His ambitions were grandiose. He wanted Shiraz to rival Isfahan as it had done during the great days of the Safavid Empire. But such dreams were beyond both his power and his purse, and much of his legacy was also destroyed in the earthquakes of 1823 and 1852 that levelled almost all of the old town. What has survived is light-hearted, vigorous if sometimes clumsy, but certainly a welcome departure from the tired formula of the later Safavid period. The new style is particularly evident in tilework and wall and ceiling decoration where the designs have become more naturalistic and the colours softer, the Safavid preponderance of deep blue giving way to greens, pinks or pale blues often used on a white ground. Increasing use was made of oil painting and also of rich mosaic mirror work, both popular under the later Qajar dynasty. The Zand achievement, however, is still largely unappreciated.

The most important building put up under Karim Khan Zand is the Vakil Mosque, completed in 1773, and the only major example of ecclesiastical architecture in Iran dating from the second half of the eighteenth century. It is a two-iwan mosque, with a large pillared hall behind the south iwan – a reversion to the earlier tradition of Nain and the great dome chamber of Isfahan. There are five rows of twisted stone columns, all monoliths together with their five acanthus capitals. Both the carved marble skirting and the predominantly green tilework, with naturalistic designs of flowers and trees, are excellent examples of Zand work. Leading to the left of the mosque is the Vakil bazaar, strongly built on the traditional pattern of covered bazaars.

Of Karim Khan's own dwelling, the Arg or Citadel now houses the prison and police headquarters, and is impossible to visit (though it is possible that one day it may be turned into a museum). Nearby, behind the Post Office, and sadly dilapidated, is what remains of his palace. This is a pavilion typical of the period, with a central columned reception hall, or *talar*, and a decorated ceiling. Originally this opened directly on to the garden but it has now been glassed in. Tiles would have adorned the gable above. Outside a carved stone dado depicts a scene from the Shahnameh of Firdausi. The garden has all but gone, though the T-shaped pool still exists, incongruously flanked by modern buildings. The gardens were once extensive, and included the pavilion that now houses the museum, on the other side of the extension of Khiaban Zand. Karim Khan was buried there, but his body was removed by the ruthless founder of the Qajar dynasty, Agha Mohammad, and placed beneath the entrance stone to his apartments in the Gulestan Palace in Tehran. The pavilion is octagonal, with panels of excellent Zand tiles depicting birds among intertwining trees in delicate colours. Within, the stalactite ceiling and upper register of the walls are covered in carefully restored paintings of floral arabesque and birds. In some of the niches are interesting examples of eighteenth- and nineteenth-century oil paintings. Other exhibits include little bird and flower drawings by the nineteenth-century Shiraz painter Lutf' AliKhan, and some Seljuk pottery.

But it is above all in the gardens and houses of Shiraz that the atmosphere of the period is best caught. These were the houses of opulent princes or merchants, architecturally idiosyncratic perhaps, but with undeniable charm. The gardens are not European in style; Edward Scott Waring, who visited Shiraz in 1802, commented: 'The gardens about Sheeraz are much celebrated; but the striking uniformity of long walks and narrow alleys is sure to displease European taste. You may, perhaps, walk a quarter of a mile, and on either side not have a view of a few yards. Yet the Persians delight in these gardens; anything delights them; and a running stream makes them almost frantic.' Over No Ruz (see p.37, footnote) they are at their most crowded, as Iranians flock down to Shiraz; April and May are quieter months and the gardens are richer in flowers.

To the north-east of the town, near the tomb of Saadi, and perhaps the most romantic, is the Bagh-i-Delgosha, where one walks through avenues of orange trees with glimpses of arid mountains in the background. In the middle stands a pavilion, curiously reminiscent of seventeenth-century Italy. It was built during the reign of Karim Khan though its foundations go back earlier, and it has been restored since. It is square fronted, with columned *talar* and painted ceiling, and flamboyantly carved stucco door frames and pediments. Inside the large central chamber is cruciform in shape, and deliciously cool, with a well beneath, and a lantern serving as a *bad gir*, or draft conveyor, above. Upstairs, in the winter room over the *talar* are beautifully inlaid doors, and pretty mirror work surrounding the fireplace. A charming little room off the well downstairs has walls of inlaid mirror work patterned like contemporary tilework or painting.

To the west, behind the tomb of Hafez, and situated at the foot of the mountains is the garden known as the Haft Tan, or Seven Bodies, after the holy men of that number said to be buried in the tombs there. It is a small walled enclosure, with a pavilion lying at the northern end, again probably built during the reign of Karim Khan. In the *talar* are delightful paintings, arabesques of trees and birds, similar to the tiled panels on the Museum pavilion, while in the niches are amusing religious paintings; that of Abraham about to sacrifice Isaac, restrained by a jaunty angel, is particularly splendid. Above are small insets of landscape and mythology and in the centre, a curious European of Restoration appearance, dressed in Persian clothes. In front is a pool full of gold fish, and beyond, the garden, with orange trees and immense, bowed umbrella pines. Across the road is the garden of the Chehel Tan, or Forty

Bodies, which the laying of concrete paths has alas deprived of its charm.

The Bagh-i-Takht, lyrically described by European travellers in the seventeenth century, and identifiable with a site where a garden was made in the eleventh century, is now in a ruinous state. Two of the former four pavilions have gone, and the terraced garden that leads down to a pool is quite bare. It is now army property, and therefore difficult to visit, but it stands out clearly at the foot of the mountains, above Boulevard Mohammad Reza Shah.

To the north-west, lying in front of the new Pahlevi University, the library of which dominates the hill behind, is the recently restored Bagh-i-Eram. The gaily coloured tilework dates from the reign of Nasr-uddin Shah (1848–96), which indicates at any rate a major restoration at that time, though the date of its foundation is uncertain. The garden is one of the largest in the town, with water courses lined by cypresses, umbrella pines and orange trees. The house is not open to the public, but permission to visit the garden is obtainable from the tourist office on Moushir Fakmi St.

The Bagh-i-Khalili, in the west of the town, near the Nemazi hospital, was laid out by the father of the present owner about fifty years ago. The pretty little verandahed pavilion is traditionally Persian, but the garden is laid out on more European lines, with intimate arbors and bowers of wisteria and the tiny yellow rose known as Shower of Gold, or Lady Bank's rose (out in April), a profusion of various coloured Bougainvillaea, and of course the roses for which Shiraz is famous.

Farther south, and perhaps the most elegant of the houses, is Afifabad, or the Bagh-i-Gulshan, built in 1863. Again army property, it is being restored as an officers' mess, and is difficult to get into, but a glimpse through the classical Persian gateway down to the principal pavilion reveals a surprising contrast to the other houses. The façade is comparatively sober, and has an arcade running all round it, reached by a flight of steps up to a double-columned portico.

A hotel (the Park Saadi) lies on the site of the Bagh-i-Nou, but all that remains from the original is probably the carved stone frieze with scenes from the Khamseh of Nizami, on a pavilion of more recent date, and the pool in front.

In the south-east of the town, on Khiaban Lutf'Ali Khan, is the Bagh-i-Gavam, consisting of two houses built in the late 1870s. The largest, to the right, is known as the Narangistan (Orangery) and now houses the Asia Institute. It is entered through a chamber in a blank arcaded wall, facing the street. Inside, this building has a verandah on either side, which served as a kind of waiting-room to the offices behind, and is decorated with scenes from Persian mythology, in tilework. In the central niche are three almost life-sized servants carrying pears, wine and sherbet (fruit juice), while beneath a dado are shown representatives of the Tributary Nations from Persepolis. The pavilion at the other end has a *talar* (usually covered by a canvas sheet) which is lavishly decorated with mosaic mirror work, and at the back a small room where the head of the family sat in state in an interior that has been described as similar to an enormous gaudy jewel. To the right is a room currently used for conferences, which is entirely painted, and the window-frames filled with coloured glass. On the other side of a narrow alley lies the anderun, or women's quarters, a charming, intimate court-yard, built on all four sides with delicate columned veran-dahs decorated with somewhat baroque stucco, others with mirror work on a coloured ground, and generally flamboyantly painted ceilings, with insets of European scenes. Beneath lie the summer quarters, deliciously cool, and lit by stone grills at ground level.

Of old Shiraz, the Friday Mosque was founded in 894, but only some stonework and the acanthus design in the mihrab (which is now in a modern annex to the right, and often locked) survive from this period. The most unusual feature is the square, turreted buil-ding, known as the Khoda Khaneh, built in 1351 in imitation of the Kaaba at Mecca, in the centre of the court. This mosque now forms a religious complex with the Shah Cheragh and Mir Moham-mad Shrines, which lie at opposite corners of a large open space. The Shah Cheragh dates from 1349, though what is visible is en-tirely a Qajar restoration, and the onion shaped dome was torn down and rebuilt in 1959. A new minaret is in the process of construction. The Mir Mohammad is a smaller, also much restored shrine, with a similar dome. Both are held in great veneration and it is advisable to retire if entry is discouraged. Also much venerated is the Sayd Alaeddin Shrine in the south-east of the town. With its honeycomb-patterned dome this has also undergone many changes. The most unusual is a curious free-standing minaret of recent construction, looking somewhat like a campanile. Outside the Shah Cheragh, across the square on Khiaban Ahmadi is the New Mosque, built in the early thirteenth century, and said to be the largest mosque in the country. It was badly damaged in the earthquake of 1852 and has been much restored, though it retains a certain grandeur in its simplicity.

A little way to the west, through a maze of narrow streets, is the so-called Armenian Bazaar, and nearby, a dome chamber known as the Imamzadeh Bibi Dokhtaran, which was said to have been founded in Timurid days. The present building is of little architectural interest, but it is well worth climbing on to the roof for the excellent view it affords over the town, with tantalizing glimpses down into little decorative courtyard houses and tiled gables, as well as over the main mosques. In this bazaar is a small Armenian church, said to date from 1662, with several European tombs. Nearby is the Masjid Moshir which has good examples of floral Qajar tilework, and a pretty entrance chamber with a grill looking into the court. Close to this is a Huseyneyeh of the same name.

The Madresseh Khan, on the other side of Khiaban Lutf'Ali Khan, was built in the early seventeenth century, but all that remains from that date is the entrance hall (dated 1615) with tilework radiating from a central medallion, some of which has been rather badly restored in paint, and stalactite mosaic over the entrance outside, where an inscription states that Nasr-uddin Shah carried out restoration work towards the end of the nineteenth century. The interior is currently being restored.

Further east on this street is the Nasir-ul-Mulk Mosque, dating from the second half of the nineteenth century, and worth noting for its tilework.

At the bottom of the Vakil Bazaar is the Serai Moshir, a Customs House also built in the second half of the nineteenth century and now restored as a tourist attraction, with a traditional style Persian tea-house and boutiques, selling among other things, Persian handicrafts. It is built in typical courtyard plan, with rooms on two levels, and orange trees and a pool in the centre.

In recent years Shiraz has again been enjoying a boom made possible by the economic development in the area and faster and better communications. It is also becoming important as an educational and cultural centre. New buildings went up in Shiraz in the 1950s at a faster rate than anywhere else in the country except Tehran. Of the modern additions to the sights of the city, the following are noteworthy. The reconstructed tombs of Hafez (1936–38) and Saadi (1952–53) stand in gardens to the north-east of the city. The first, with some of the poet's best known lines carved in relief, lies under a somewhat ornate cupola approached across an impressive colonnade; the setting is delicious and in spring and early summer the garden is a riot of flowers. Saadi's tomb shelters in a spectacular position at the base of the mountains; it consists of a high portico, with dome behind and lateral colonnade. The beautifully kept and colourful garden contrasts brilliantly with the somewhat severe building. Behind the colonnade are steps leading down to a clear underground spring full of fish reputed to be sacred to Saadi. To the west of Shiraz, at the far end of Zand avenue there is the large and excellently equipped Nemazi hospital. The new Pahlevi University, built of yellowish brick, is dramatically sited in the side of a hill to the north-west of the town. And behind a high wall in the eighteenth-century quarter to the south of Khiaban Zand is a remarkable Christian church dedicated to Saint Simon the Zealot. This building, which was erected shortly before the Second World War under the personal supervision of the Reverend Norman Sharp of the Church Missionary Society, is a skilful blend of Christian and Islamic architectural forms. A copy of the first complete translation into Persian of the New Testament made in Shiraz in 1811, is housed here.

All the charms of Shiraz however must not deflect the visitor from Persepolis, the nearby Royal Tomb and Sassanian rock carvings of Naqsh-i-Rustam, or the tomb of Cyrus the Great at Pasargadae.

Unlike some of the monuments described in this book, Persepolis has been much visited and written about. I shall aim merely at drawing together threads of information which may be useful to the visitor.

Persepolis was an artificial creation of Darius, extended by Xerxes and used by his successors until the time of the invasion of Alexander, when it was burnt. Darius may have found Cyrus's capital at Pasargadae too remote, or bad for communications, or rather old-fashioned in its lay-out; or he may have just wanted a place of his own. Anyhow, he decided to build a brand-new, more up-to-date and more concentrated Palace Complex. He presumably chose the site partly because it adjoined the city of Istakhr and overlooked the wide plain, and partly because it was a handy place for getting good building stone out of the adjacent Kuh-i-Rahmat. That it faced south-west, was backed by a low range of stony hills, and became disagreeably hot in summer mattered little to Darius and his successors, who used it in spring and autumn only and spent their summers at Ecbatana (Hamadan). And no one else really had to to be considered. For – and this is something to be constantly borne in mind – the platform and what was built on it were for the court and nothing else. It was essentially a Royal Enclave. There was no town, no large-scale place of worship, no normal life on the terrace. It was designed to house the king, his harem and his court, and to provide an appropriate setting for the constant round of royal ceremonial during a few months in the year only. It is still possible to form a good idea of what court life was like, and what went on in the various buildings, from the carvings which have survived on walls, doorways and staircases. When we consider that Darius had an empire to run it is remarkable how much he managed to accomplish in so short a time. And Xerxes ran him close.

Thanks to the researches of scholars and the attentions of travellers, a good deal is known about the history and purposes of the royal platform. It has recently been discovered that the Achaemenians called it Parsa; but it was better known perhaps by successive nicknames. In the fourteenth century and for some five hundred years thereafter it was known as Chehel Minar, the Forty Minarets

– an understandable if misleading appellation. The modern Persian calls it Takht-i-Jamshid, the Throne of Jamshid, but this, of course, is a fancy name drawn from legend. Persepolis is the name by which we think the Greeks called it, but there is something odd even about that. For as Curzon points out, correct Greek for 'the City of Persis' – and it never was a real city – would have been Persopolis; he even suggests that Persepolis may have been a name evolved in rather bitter joke based on the Greek word περσις meaning destruction, after it had been allegedly burnt under Alexander's nose.

The approach to Persepolis from Shiraz lies first over a range of rolling hills, and then across the fertile Marvdasht plain. Near the bridge where the plain begins is the ancient Band-i-Amir, a tenth-century dam which has come down to us as the 'Bendemeers Stream' of Thomas Moore's poem. This region is rich in ancient remains, the oldest, Darvazeh Tepe known to have been occupied from 2100 B.C. to 1800 B.C.. No less than nine prehistoric mounds dating back to the sixth century B.C. were excavated in the 1960s by Professor vanden Berghe who also discovered a damaged rock relief at Guyum (30 km north-west of Shiraz) portraying Bahram II identifiable by a special crown similar to that on his coinage.*

A first view of Persepolis, seen from the south-west, is disappointing. An obscure row of thin factory chimneys, hardly distinguishable from the low Kuh-i-Rahmat behind, appears at the end of the road. 'There are few visitors,' Curzon noted, 'who are not disappointed with the first *coup d'oeil*.' It must have been from the north-west that Herbert was reminded of Windsor Castle seen from Eton; even so, however, the comparison appears singularly inept, and one is tempted to remember that he was writing for readers few of whom would have the chance to test his veracity.

The Shiraz road leads straight past a modern hotel, and then reaches the foot of the great entrance staircase. Here expectation and excitement begin to mount. The great stone blocks of which the terrace is composed strike a note of massive solidity; the height of the wall (fify-nine feet sheer at its greatest extent on the east

* See Annex, note 7.

side) cannot fail to impress. The size of the columns far above, so miniscular when seen from the distance, can now be grasped.

Our sense of scale is sharpened as we climb the stairs. These are a double flight, constructed of huge stones and so beautifully proportioned that a horseman can ride up or down them with ease. Since staircase building is an art of which we have learnt nothing and, it often seems to me, forgotten something since 500 B.C., I append the measurements and other details for the benefit of future practitioners.*

There are sixty-nine steps in each first flight and forty-two in each second flight. The stone landings at the turn of each staircase occupy an area of 192 square yards. One climbs each step with a sense of awe. Massive, rugged, devoid of ornament, designed perhaps to terrify but not to tire, the entrance staircase was the main means of access to the platform; no doubt prisoners and petitioners, tribesmen to render homage and soldiers to guard the palaces used it far more frequently than the king.

It is only when we reach the top of the stairs that the vast size of the platform (325 by 487 yards) begins to impose itself. It runs far more deeply north-east into the hillside than could have been imagined from below.

The ruined gateways facing the top of the stairway are thought to have belonged to an entrance hall measuring eighty feet square which may have been used for important ceremonies in its own right, for a beautifully carved bench and throne seat – the only fixed throne seat in Persepolis – stand within. The outer doorway is flanked by winged bulls, the inner one by similar winged monsters with human head and bull's body. An inscription states that this building was constructed by Xerxes.

To the right of the entrance stairway, on a raised platform approached by carved monumental staircases to the north and east is the Apadana or palace of audience of Darius. The central portion of this square building, flanked by porches on the east, west and north, alone measures 195 feet square. The Apadana had six rows of six columns some sixty feet in height, and each porch had twelve columns. Several of these survive. This is

* Length of each step, 22½ feet; width, 15 inches; height, 4 inches.

the outstanding building of Persepolis and, on account of its
staircases, one to which the visitor will return again and again.

To get bearings of the buildings south of the Apadana it is useful
to climb to the top of the unexcavated mound immediately beyond
it. That to the west of the mound, on somewhat higher ground, is
the small private palace of Darius known as the Tachara (winter
palace), with windows giving a fine view towards the south. Like
all other Persepolis buildings, this had a square plan, but only three
rows of four columns (which accordingly were not properly centred) plus two more rows of four in a porch to the south. It was
probably intended to be oblong; then the plan was changed.
Though begun by Darius, it was only finished by Xerxes. The
columns, and possibly the capitals also, were of wood. The stonework of doors and windows has remained in good condition.

Immediately to the east of the mound, and south-east of the
Apadana, is the small building known as the Tripylon. This consisted of a small room with four columns only, with porticoes of
equal width opening through narrow doorways to the north and
south; the north portico is approached by a small monumental stairway closely adjoining that of the Apadana. The Tripylon was certainly not a palace; it was either the main hall giving access to the
other palaces, or a kind of military headquarters.

To the east of the Tripylon and the Apadana is the Hall of a
Hundred Columns. This measured some two hundred and forty
feet square, but it was considerably lower in height than the Apadana, on which it was modelled. This hall, built as an audience
chamber by Xerxes and completed by Artaxerxes, must have been
uncommonly dark. Perhaps this was intentional, as adding to
the mystery surrounding the monarch. Herzfeld is horrid enough to
suggest that Alexander chose this hall for destruction because it was
so ugly. It is by no means generally accepted that Alexander destroyed Persepolis by fire deliberately.* Perhaps the problem will
never be resolved. But the main body of the evidence, such as it
is, is to be found here, in the Hall of a Hundred Columns. It was
originally excavated by workmen of Ferhad Mirza, Governor-
General of Fars, under the superintendence of a Dr Andreas in
* cf. p. 15 and Annex, note 2.

1878. Well over an inch of ashes was found under the débris. The marble columns were blasted by heat, suggesting that the hall must have been filled with combustible material. If the fire was not an incendiary one, started in several places at once, it must have spread with great force, for the Hadish or Private Palace of Xerxes, some hundred yards away to the south-west, also shows signs of considerable damage by fire.

This is the hall with thirty-six columns to the south of the mound, also standing on high ground, with small rooms leading off it to east and west, and an entrance hall to the north. To the south there was a balcony, with a stone balustrade, overlooking the anderun, or Queen's apartments, below.

These extended over a large L-shaped area at the southern extremity of the platform. Part of the site is now occupied by buildings used to house the Archaeological Mission working there; the former reception hall has been reconstructed, with a museum which contains a number of bronze, earthenware and other objects found locally. Between the anderun and the Kuh-i-Rahmat, and to the south-east of the Hall of the Hundred Columns, are the remains of the Treasury Buildings begun by Darius and continued by his successor, occupying an area in excess of twelve thousand square yards. Behind, on the rock face of the Kuh-i-Rahmat, are the tombs of Artaxerxes II and Artaxerxes III.

There is evidence that the planning of the buildings, though executed by successive monarchs, was conceived as a whole. This is shown not only in the relationship of the various palaces to each other, but also in the arrangement of watercourses, which correspond exactly to the walls of buildings subsequently erected from the roofs of which they were partly fed. Underground channels extend for more than a mile under the platform; they are in places wide enough for two men to walk abreast, and we are told by Curzon that Sir John Chardin walked in them for thirty-five minutes 'till compelled to retire by the terror of his attendants'. They are not on the ordinary tourist run today.

Another feature of the buildings was that while the foundations, staircases, bases, windows, doorways, and many of the columns of the main palaces were of stone, the roofs were of wood and the walls of brick. Thus, even had there been no fire, it is inconceivable that any single building could have remained intact. What is surprising is that so much has survived so well. This is due in part to the quality of the stone, a calcareous limestone from the Kuh-i-Rahmat behind. But the columns were of stone, Herzfeld thinks, only when large enough tree trunks were not available. Wooden columns invariably had stone bases and many were fluted; although the tori (the small rim separating the main columns from the bases) were invariably smooth, the bases were bell-shaped and ornamented. At the head of the columns, whether of wood or stone, were found either impost blocks in the form of animals, or complex capitals carved in two or even three tiers like the leg of a piece of Victorian furniture. The first were used in the Apadana, the porticoes, the Tachara, Hadish, harem and smaller buildings, the latter at the main gate in the Tripylon, the Hall of a Hundred Columns, and in the interior and northern portico of the Apadana.

For many the greatest interest of Persepolis will lie not in the plan, constructional methods or purpose of the buildings, nor yet in the magnificent setting, but in the carvings on staircases, and doorways. These have been marvellously preserved – in one case one might say miraculously, for the great eastern approach to the Apadana, which alone is complete and undamaged, was covered by sand and rubble blown down from the Kuh-i-Rahmat for close on two thousand years. Apart from the functional sculpture – the two-headed animal capitals, the floral ornamentation of the columns, and the colossi on the entrance hall, and the symbolic designs – the winged sun-disk, symbol of Ahuramazda, or the combat between lion and bull – the stone decoration of Persepolis aims to portray scenes which took place at the spot where they occur. Thus, at the entrances to the Private Palaces we find the King being moved about under a parasol. In the audience halls he appears on the throne, a servant with fly whisk made from the tail of a wild bull in the background. The stairs of the smaller palaces portray servants carrying dishes, napkins or incense burners according to the use of the room. Between the bedrooms of the

Tachara Babylonian eunuchs are represented. Finally, and most obviously, the great staircases portray those who passed up them or patrolled them, the tributaries of Empire, spectators at ceremonies, sentries and guards. It is the well-preserved eastern stairway which the modern visitor will wish to study in most detail. On the north side of the stairway are guards standing at attention in the three registers. These are Susian regiments, their head-dress a kind of Arab agal, ninety-two identical figures. Behind at the top are men carrying the royal dais and a throne; others lead the King's saddle-horse and two empty chariots. Below and behind are two registers of Median and Persian officers, alternating; the Medes with lances, bows encased and daggers in scabbard, the Persians with shields or bows and quivers. On the south side the visitor will see that there are eighteen panels in three registers, together with five more on the outer ascent – a total of twenty-three in all. Each panel portrays the tributaries of the countries included in the Empire, escorted by a Mede or Persian, bearing an appropriate offering. Every scene is divided from the next by an exquisitely chiselled cypress tree.

The attribution of precise topographical identification to each of these tributaries has, not unnaturally, been a subject of scholarly controversy, and E. F. Schmidt of Chicago has recently discovered inscriptions above one of the tombs at Naqsh-i-Rustam which may provide further clues or cause previous attributions to be revised. In the list below which starts with the uppermost register and reads from right to left. I have followed Dr R. D. Barnett (*Iraq*, Spring 1957, Vol. XIX p. 65) Keeper of the Department of Western Asiatic Antiquities at the British Museum, who differs only slightly from Herzfeld and Schmidt (before the latter's recent discoveries); where differences occur I have shown the Herzfeld and Schmidt version in brackets. I have added a description of the gifts in some cases by way of local colour and as an aid to identification.

Top register: Medians, Susians, Aryans (cups and skins) Arachosians (camel), Egyptians (bull), Parthians, Sagartians.
Middle register: Armenians (horse, vase), Babylonians (humped

bull), Lydians (Cilicians) (skins, two rams), Scythians (long
pointed caps), Gandharians, Chorasmians (Sogdians).

Bottom register: Sogdians (Syrians) (chariot drawn by two horses),
Cappadocians, Ionians, Bactrians (two-humped camel), Indians, (offerings in baskets suspended by pole from the shoulder).

On the outer stair: Skudrians, Arabs (dromedary), Drangianians,
Libyans and Ethiopians (giraffe).

As a historical record of the extent and variety of the Persian
Empire the great procession is undeniably impressive. Opinions
vary as to its artistic merit. Some find it stiff, static and repetitive,
the figures too alike, the clothes and gifts insufficiently differentiated, the whole effect monotonous, the animals alone with real
vitality. By any standards they are indeed irresistible. As for the
effect of the whole, it must be remembered that the purpose was
not to display individuality. It was to convey the feel of a vast
ceremonial. Those who came to pay tribute were in the eyes of
the monarch not so much persons as symbols. Their representations in stone has perhaps diminished the element of flesh
and blood and increased the symbolism. The rhythm of the
procession, broken by animals, attendants, chariots and cypresses, is
exquisitely conveyed. The detailed portrayal of dress, folds, individual tributes, harness, muscles, the flesh of animals, is admirable.

The road which curls round the northern end of the platform
leads to Naqsh-i-Rajab and Naqsh-i-Rustam. The first lies in a
rocky recess just to the right of the road about two and a half
miles from Persepolis. 'So snugly hidden is this rock-nook,' says
Curzon, 'and so littered are its approaches with loosely piled
boulders that four travellers out of five would probably pass it
unobserved.' There are two Sassanian carvings to the right of the
little gully and one on the left. The first represents Ardeshir
(according to Curzon) or Shapur (Herzfeld) being invested by
Ormuzd, both mounted; Herzfeld observes that the scene lacks
realism, for the wind is blowing their garments in opposite
directions. The second carving on the right portrays another

investiture, this time certainly of Ardeshir, in which both par-
ticipants are on foot; there are diminutive figures, one of whom
is naked, between them, and what appear to be two women behind Ormuzd.* The sculpture on the left, which is the largest
and best preserved, shows Shapur on horseback followed by
nine nobles or conceivably sons, almost certainly including
Shapur's heir Hormuzd.

Naqsh-i-Rustam lies off to the left of the main road under a
mountain ridge. This was the spectacular site overlooking the city
of Istakhr chosen by Darius and his three immediate successors for
their rock-tombs and subsequently adorned with seven bas-reliefs
by the Sassanians. Nor is this all, for there are the remains of an
Elamite carving, showing the site was used (probably for religious
purposes) before Darius, twin fire altars, and a square stone building, popularly known as the Cube of Zoroaster, the purpose of
which has given rise to livelier archaeological controversy than
any other structure in Iran.

The Cube stands some fifty yards back from the rock-face,
opposite the tomb of Darius II. It is built of massive blocks of
white stone, measures eight yards square, and is nearly forty feet
high. On three sides the upper face of the building is relieved
from monotony by six slabs of black stone false windows, while
on the fourth side a stairway, partly ruined, leads to a massive doorway which gives access to the only room in the interior of the
building. The lower walls bear inscriptions in Pahlevi and Greek,
which date from Sassanian times. The construction is immensely
sturdy, the proportions exquisite. There is no doubt that the Cube
was built in the Achaemenian period, probably in the time of
Darius; the ruins of a building of similar construction and proportions are to be found at Pasargadae.

The controversy relates not to its period but to its purpose.
Over the last century or so, this has been the subject of the wildest
conjecture. It has been called the Royal Treasury, a chamber for
embalming and preparing royal corpses, a deposit for the kings'
bodies, the tomb of Hystaspes, and the place where royal standards were kept. Nowadays there are broadly two schools of
* See Annex, note 8.

thought. Dr Ghirshman is convinced that it and its counterpart at
Pasargadae were fire temples. Herzfeld and Mr Sami aver that
they were royal tombs. The first view is supported by the relative
proximity of fire altars – it is argued that the eternal fire must
have been kept in a nearby building – and by the Sassanian inscriptions of Shapur and his high priest Kartir which point to the continued important religious associations of the building. From the
other side it is maintained that the massive doors, which could be
closed from within, preclude the idea of a fire temple; that the
later inscriptions prove nothing about the original functions of the
place in Achaemenian times; that blind windows would be more
appropriate to tombs; and that at any rate two of Darius's predecessors are, sepulchrally speaking, unaccounted for. According
to this school of thought, the Cube is the tomb either of Hystaspes,
Darius's father, or of Cambyses, and if the former, the comparable building at Pasargadae might be Cambyses's tomb. I make no
attempt to take sides in this controversy, merely warning the reader
of the many pitfalls which surround him though there is increasing support for the fire temple theory (see p. 256) and recent
evidence of another sanctified enclave at Imamzadeh five miles
away.

What are unquestionably tombs stand on the rock face opposite in awesome majesty, deeply incised into the smoothed
pinkish surface some thirty feet above the present ground level.
They are cut in the form of a broad cross, sixty feet by seventy-two
feet. The upper panel, intensively carved, is divided into two
sections. The lower of these comprises two rows of seventeen
figures each, with arms uplifted, supporting a platform or throne.
Above them is the King, on the left, facing Ormuzd, with a fire
altar between them. In the transverse arm of the cross, below a
heavy cornice, four bull-headed half columns rise to give the
semblance of a façade of an Achaemenian palace. In the centre is
a small doorway which leads into the tomb chamber itself. The
walls between the columns, and the lower panel, are completely
bare. The scale, the symmetry and the simplicity are profoundly
impressive. The tomb chambers are bare, save for the plain
sarcophagus itself; they are difficult of access, being approached

only by two metal ladders set against the face of the rock. The
legend goes that Darius's parents fell to their death when visiting
his tomb. From left to right the tombs belong to Darius II,
Artaxerxes I, Darius I, and Xerxes.

Below and to the left of the royal tombs are the Sassanian bas-
reliefs.* For some, whatever their historical or artistic merit
they merely diminish the austere splendour of the tombs. One
feels that the Sassanians, however entitled to their say, might have
said it somewhere else. Starting from the right, the first is an
inferior carving, thought to represent Narseh, Bahram II's uncle
and successor, receiving the crown from the goddess Anahita,
with a child between them. This relatively late work has not
had a good press. Herzfeld points out that the goddess has the
neck of a prize fighter, while her ear is in the wrong place.
Byron describes her 'municipal crown piled high with sausage
curls', and draws attention to the King's muslin cowboy trousers.

The second relief below Darius's tomb shows two scenes of
equestrian prowess and represents Bahram II.

The third, between Darius and Artaxerxes, is perhaps the most
famous of the Naqsh-i-Rustam reliefs. This no doubt is what
Josefa Barbaro called 'a great image on horseback, seeming to be
of a boisterous man who they say was Samson'. It is in fact an
enormous representation of Shapur I; the kneeling figure on the
left is a Roman Emperor (Philip or Valerian), the man standing
between them being the other. The captives wear Roman dress;
the laurel wreath indicates their Imperial status. If it were not for
the occasion, one would say that Shapur was almost overdressed.
His crown surmounted by a globe, looks intolerably uncomfortable. But there is human pathos in the Emperor's outstretched
arms, even if his face shows no trace of emotion.

The fourth carving, below Darius II, and the fifth, a little further
on, again show equestrian combats; the horses are bigger than they
ought to be, but the scenes have spirit.

Number six is carved on a curving corner site. Round the
corner on the right is a dim shallow figure, an Elamite priest, and

* These, and other Sassanian reliefs (except for those on the west side of the
Bishapur valley, see p. 258) can only be seen in sunlight before 9 a.m.

to the left a crowned female head – the oldest things in Naqsh-i-Rustam. Any other Elamite traces have been effaced by the Sassanian reliefs, which represent Bahram II receiving homage from eight subjects wearing lofty caps or tiaras, and heavily bearded.

The seventh panel is another portrayal of the investiture of Ardeshir by Ormuzd. Both are mounted, and the horses, with heads touching and one leg raised, make a pleasantly symmetrical pattern. Ormuzd, on the right, holds a sceptre in his left hand while his right hand grasps the circular hoop or cydaris, which Ardeshir receives with his right hand. Behind the King stands a servant with a fly-flap; his expression and gesture are suitably obsequious. Reaching the end of this portrait gallery in stone we may well feel, with the normally indefatigable Curzon, that 'there are a clumsiness and ponderous stability about the forms and movements, except in the panels of equestrian combat, that produce a sense of fatigue' (see plate 15a).

A well-conserved pair of Sassanian fire altars carved out of a rock stand round the corner beyond the seventh panel, in a commanding position overlooking the plain.

Cyrus called it Pasragada; the Greeks and Romans Pasargadae; to the Moslems it was Takht-i-Mader-i-Suleiman, the throne of the Mother of Solomon, who still gives her legendary name to the adjoining village. But there the resemblance to Persepolis ends. The nature of the site, the scale and layout of the buildings, certain of their architectural features, the materials used, the ornamentation and taste, are all in marked contrast.

The site of Cyrus's capital lies about forty miles from Persepolis along the road to Isfahan, cutting through a high ridge of pastoral country frequented by· migrating Qashgai and Khamseh tribes. At length the road emerges on to the wide grassy plain of Murghab (water bird) encircled by vast ranges; Pasargadae lies three or four miles to the left and is accessible by a well-marked tarmac road.

We are at a height of over six thousand feet. The air is light, the mornings are cool. The gently rolling plain, and the mountains which bound it, are green in spring and, briefly, carpeted with flowers. The majestic calm of this pastoral scene is enhanced by a sense of history. Here Persia was born, here its founder lived and was buried, here Alexander came to avenge the destruction of Cyrus's tomb; here silence, broken only by the bleating of sheep, the flapping of eagles and the occasional laughter of children, has reigned for over two thousand years.

It did not look like this in Cyrus's day. Palaces, glistening white, stood well apart from each other, spaced out among the trees and flowing water channels. Strabo in his *Geography* describes the tomb of Cyrus as 'a tower of no great size, concealed beneath the thicket of trees'; recent excavations have proved the existence of ample watercourses. It is easy to imagine that there was a friendly, sylvan simplicity about Cyrus's headquarters which was not grand enough, or suitably forbidding, for Darius and his successors.

Much valuable excavation has been undertaken in the last twenty years, first by the Iranian Archaeological Service under the direction of Mr Sami and since 1961 by Mr David Stronach, Director of the British Institute of Persian Studies. They have uncovered the remains of two palaces, an entrance hall or gatehouse, a bridge and two garden pavilions, studied the stone tower known as the Zendan-i-Suleiman, done extensive work on the citadel or Takht-i-Suleiman, and investigated the more distant mound to the west which Herzfeld thought was the base of a temple.

Cyrus's tomb was so strongly built that we can see it much as Alexander saw it. From a stone base measuring about forty feet square, six tiers of massive stone steps rise to form the foundation of the tomb chamber itself, entered through a low narrow doorway, and measuring only eleven and a half by seven feet. The tomb is capped with a gabled stone roof, thirty-five feet above ground level. At the highest point of the tomb façade, above the doorway, David Stronach discovered in 1970 a hitherto unnoticed sun-disc. Some of the original twenty-four triangular rays that once surrounded the disc can still be seen from ground level when the boss is lit by a side light. This enigmatic symbol is presumed to be connected with the religious beliefs of which hitherto little has been known of Cyrus himself, lending qualified support to the view now developing among scholars that he may have already become a follower of the reforms introduced by Zoroaster into the old Iranian Mazdean religion (see p. 256 below).

Of the other buildings, by contrast, so little remained above ground that they have had to be rescued from oblivion. A slender stone column, a corner pier with trilingual inscription, and two uninscribed piers in the Palace of Audience; elsewhere a winged figure on a doorway and a second inscribed pier from the Private Palace; these were all Curzon saw in 1887. But recent excavations have disclosed the ground plans and interrelationship of the Imperial precinct. Unlike the square buildings of Persepolis, Cyrus's palaces were oblong and surrounded with colonnaded galleries. At Persepolis the stone used was a hard bituminous dark grey limestone; the Pasargadae stone, coming perhaps from the mountains of Sivand, consisted of black and white limestone used in deliberate contrast and with telling effect. All the Pasargadae columns were of white stone. Those at Persepolis which were of stone had vertical flutings; the base of the shaft, or torus, was smooth, but rested on a circular plinth, generally carved with bell-like ornament. The white stone columns of Pasargadae were smooth and slender, but the tori of the Private Palace had horizontal flutings, and the plinths were double, rectangular and undecorated, though the lowest section was of black stone. I have more than a suspicion that the Pasargadae palaces were exquisitely proportioned, graceful, full of light but bare of decorative detail, while those of Persepolis were oppressively large, clumsy, drab and overloaded with ornament; that Pasargadae charmed where Persepolis impressed.

The Palace of Audience covered a total area of 183 by 147 feet. The central hall measuring 106 by 72 feet had two rows of four columns of white limestone, one of which, to a height of 36 feet, is still standing. The floor consists of two layers of stone, the upper layer being well cut, laid and polished. The capitals were of white limestone; part of the plinth black. A remnant of carving from the base of a doorway shows a bull's hoof and the tail of a fish covering the leg of a man; in another there are two bare human feet, excellently carved, and the sinister claws of a lion-demon.

3. PERSEPOLIS: Doorway in the Palace of Darius. The carving represents the King overcoming a winged beast (*p. 243*)

14a. PERSEPOLIS: The fallen bull (*p. 246*)

14b. PERSEPOLIS: Detail of carvings on the Eastern Stairway (*p. 247*)

The Private Palace consisted of a central hall measuring 102 by 73½ feet, with thirty stone columns with double square plinths, the lower black, the upper white, and a torus with horizontal flutings which Stronach calls among the finest ever produced in Iran and unique outside Greece and Ionia. The stonework throughout is exceptionally fine, the black stone door jambs and the carefully cut plugs inserted in imperfections in columns and floor stones being particularly noteworthy. All these features point to the conclusion that the Private Palace was started later than the neighbouring buildings and was probably only completed in the reign of Darius.

What was once thought of as a third palace is now believed to have been little more than a gatehouse, with winged bulls guarding the entrance. It measured 87 by 71 feet, was supported by eight columns, of which no trace remains, and apparently had no galleries. But here, on the eastern jamb of the northern chamber, is the most complete bas-relief at Pasargadae and one of the oldest pieces of Achaemenian stone carving extant. Described by Morier, drawn by Ker Porter, and observed by Flandin and Dieulafoy to say nothing of Curzon, it represents a figure in profile with outstretched hand, four wings, two reaching above the head and two others nearly down to the feet, tight-fitting Elamite robes, and an elaborate Egyptian or Phoenician crown supported on two twisted horns.

One hundred and fifty yards west of the gatehouse an isolated white limestone block has proved to be part of the buried foundations of a bridge over the principal watercourse. The partly excavated remains consist of two opposed limestone side-walls with five rows of three columns between them. The remains of yet another building believed to be a garden pavilion have been discovered one hundred and twenty yards north of the Palace of Audience; it rested on a rectangular platform and lay on the route between the two palaces in the midst of the garden.

The ruined Zendan stands to the north of the Private Palace. It seems to have had many points of resemblance with the Cube of Zoroaster (see p. 249) of which it was the progenitor, just as the Zendan itself bears traces of its descent from Urartian and Median tower temples. Indeed, since Darius built a virtual replica of the Zendan – viz. the Cube – it may well be possible that Darius and Cyrus shared the same religious beliefs and that Cyrus himself was already a devout Zoroastrian. However this may be, it seems more probable that the purpose of these buildings was religious rather than funerary, and that they were used to store religious documents or house the sacred fire, the chief difficulties about the latter being to find an explanation for the absence of blackening of the roof at Naqsh-i-Rustam (the Zendan has no roof) and of ventilation in the interior of the building (cf. p. 250).

Some nine hundred yards to the north of the palaces stand the remains of the great stone platform popularly known as the Takht-i-Mader-i-Suleiman. The quality of the masonry, deriving much from Ionian and Lydian models, suggests that Cyrus intended to build a further palace on the summit. The huge white limestone blocks, once held together with metal clamps, of which the platform is constructed, are the only known example in Achaemenian architecture of rusticated masonry. Recent excavations have disclosed two staircases, one unfinished and with no signs of wear, a columned hall on the west side, streets running on the north-west and south sides, residential accommodation (including a bathroom) and magazine rooms to the east, and a parade ground in the centre. Furthermore, on the south-east part of the site, there has been found a tablet recording Xerxes's attack on the cult of Daeva and praise of Ahuramazda (cf. p. 36) together with coins of the Seleucid period. From all this (and more) it is currently deduced that the platform was intended for the site of Cyrus's Palace; that this was never finished but a fortified building was erected in its place, possibly under Darius or Xerxes; that a great fire occurred there but after 280 B.C. and cannot therefore have been the work of Alexander; and that there was a short-lived occupation in the early Islamic period.

Away to the west of the citadel lies the so-called sacred precinct, comprising a mound and a pair of limestone plinths which werec probably fire altars. The mound covers a carefully built mud-brick platform of later date; no trace of the base of any building such

SHAPUR (BISHAPUR) 257

as a temple has been found, and Stronach suggests that the platform might have been a stage for sacrificial rites, a vantage point for viewing ceremonies, or have supported an additional fire-altar.

However this may be, the glories of Pasargadae belong preponderantly to the reign of the Great King whose 2500th anniversary was celebrated in 1971.

Shapur, or Bishapur, the Sassanian capital, lies north of the old road from Shiraz to Bushire about fifteen miles beyond Kazerun. It can be reached in less than three hours from Shiraz along the modern highway to Ahwaz, passing through mountainous country and then descending dramatically into a wide park-like valley of ilex groves and white limestone walls. Lying at an altitude of eight hundred metres (2,500 feet), exposed to blasts of hot air from the Persian Gulf, yet in an area of relatively heavy rainfall, Bishapur is generally at least 10° F. warmer than Shiraz, while the surrounding countryside, except in high summer, gives an impression of greater luxuriance.

The large city of Bishapur, which flourished from early Sassanian to early Islamic times, stood like Istakhr on a plain near a river valley whose rock walls were decorated with bas-reliefs depicting royal triumphs. But whereas the palace area at Persepolis stands in isolation round the corner, so to speak, that at Bishapur lies between the city area (largely as yet unexcavated) and the gorge, and near to both.

The main excavated buildings are a fire temple well below ground level, and three buildings of the adjoining palace – a great hall, a court and an iwan. The fire temple, one wall of which remains standing to its original height of forty-five feet, consisted of a square room surrounded by corridors and water courses. It was constructed of well-dressed stone and the roof was supported by protomes of kneeling bulls. It was approached from the palace by a stairway of twenty steps, covered with a barrel vault. There was a small room adjoining the temple in which the sacred fire was kept. Ghirshman suggests that the cult of water, personified by Anahita, may have been practised here as well as the cult of fire.

Shapur's palace was built, like that of Firuzabad, of rubble. It was a cruciform building, with four iwans which served as an audience chamber. The large open court to the west of the palace had a floor covered with mosaics, of which some traces remain. On the other side, giving access to the galleries of the audience chamber, was a triple iwan eighty feet across, decorated with rich stucco ornaments, while the floor was covered with mosaic panels representing portraits of both men and women – including a court lady fanning herself, courtesans, and a naked musician playing a stringed instrument. This mosaic pavement, clearly influenced by Graeco-Roman traditions, is unique in Iran; some of the panels have been well preserved and can be seen in the Tehran Museum.

The remains of a further palace, to the east, have been partially excavated, also the city wall; and some way beyond the fire temple a votive monument, consisting of two columns and bearing an inscription which tells us that it was erected by Shapur I in A.D. 266, has been uncovered. An Iranian archaeological mission has, since 1968, exposed both part of the northern perimeter wall and remains of Islamic buildings, including a tall stucco crenellation whose decoration closely resembles that of Sassanian mouldings.

For most visitors, however, the main attractions of Shapur lie in the gorge. Few archaeological sites in Iran compare with this in the beauty of its setting. The valley bottom is thickly wooded with orange and lime; a cool clear stream, its deep pools shimmering with fish, flows over a sandy bed; no pleasanter place for a bathe or picnic can be imagined.

Just above one's head, four of Shapur's six masterpieces of Sassanian art are chiselled on the cliff face. Access to them has recently been greatly improved by the construction of paths and by clearance of the immediate foreground, so that they can now be easily seen and readily photographed (afternoons preferable). They stand high on the rock, above a water channel which has been constructed in part of the rock face.

The first carving (proceeding up the left side of the valley) represents a triumph over the Romans. The scene is portrayed in four registers on a concave wall. The figures are more numerous than on any other Sassanian panel, but most of them are less than life-size. In the middle of the third panel an enormous Shapur on horseback looks down on two diminutive Romans, one standing and one kneeling, as well as on a corpse, while a cherub – the first example in Sassanian sculpture and clearly attributable to Western influence – floats overhead.

The second relief portrays Bahram II receiving the submission of an Arab tribe, led like the tributaries at Persepolis by a Persian usher and followed by horses and camels. This panel has been badly defaced by an old water channel. Herzfeld suggests it may have been deliberately cut by Narseh, Bahram's successor and rival.

Some colour is lent to this view by Herzfeld's discovery that on the next panel, representing the investiture of Bahram I, Narseh has written his name over Bahram's. This is perhaps the high-point of Sassanian rock-carving; compared with earlier sculptures, the symmetry has softened, there is greater variety of relief and the portrayal of figures is more realistic. The water-channel here only cuts off the legs of the horses, and recent excavation below it has uncovered the recumbent, corpse-like figure of what might be a Roman soldier.

The fourth relief on the west bank is of Shapur II, and is in a clumsier style. The King is seated in the centre, wearing a double crown, his legs wide apart, his left hand on his sword, his right holding a lance. On the left above, are a row of courtiers; below, Persian soldiers with the King's horse. On the right are chained and wounded prisoners, a bearded gentleman with his back to the audience balancing a decapitated head in each hand, and other characters including a boy riding a diminutive elephant.

On the other side of the valley are two carvings, which are far more accessible because a motorable track passes just below them. The first is a combination piece: Shapur I is at once being invested by Ahuramazda and receiving the submission of a Roman Emperor probably Philip the Arab who was defeated in 244, two years after Shapur's coronation and during the period when he reigned jointly with his father Ardeshir. The panel is unhappily badly damaged, but both the facial expression and the posture of the fallen Emperor are well portrayed.

The second and last of the Bishapur reliefs is a panel in two registers, with Shapur receiving Valerian's submission in a larger compartment centred between the two. The composition as a whole is stiff and unconvincing.

The track past the last two bas-reliefs ascends the valley above the gorge. Where it widens, about four miles upstream, a series of caves can be seen at the summit of the flat-topped ridge to the left. In one of these, whose sides have been planed to receive reliefs which were never begun, stands a giant statue of Shapur I carved from a stalactite. The *Blue Guide* observes that the excursion to the cave belongs to the speleologist more than to the archaeologist. Either should be warned that the climb is an exceptionally stiff one.

Some sixty miles south-west of Kazerun in a remote upland valley is a very small well-preserved tower more primitive in construction than the Zendan at Pasargadae, and unlike it apparently a tomb, probably dating from the first quarter of the sixth century B.C. The rough country north-west of Bishapur, between there and the Khuzistan border, through which ran the Royal Road from Persepolis to Susa, is full of ancient sites. Near Nurabad twenty-five miles from Bishapur on the way to Fahliun there is a square stone tower, the Mil-i-Azdaha, which has many similarities with those at Naqsh-i-Rustam and Pasargadae and is therefore probably a temple for guarding the sacred fire. But it has no blind windows and the stones are joined not by iron clamps but with plaster, mortar which suggests Seleucid or Parthian construction. Fifteen miles north-east of Bishapur is Naqsh-i-Bahram, with a Sassanian relief on a rocky bluff. The region of Fahliun to the north has several monuments of interest – two miles to the east, an early Islamic bridge; four miles to the west, at Djin-Djin, an Achaemenian royal pavilion of which the bases of the columns are still visible; at Tulaspid, a few miles farther on, some Elamite ruins; ten miles north-west of Fahliun, near the village of Setalun, at the top of a high rock overlooking a gorge, at a place identified by Herzfeld as Kuran-gun, an Elamite bas-relief representing two divinities, one of whom appears to be emptying a vase of water on the heads of his worshippers; and south-east of Fahliun, on a summit three throusand feet above the plain, an Islamic fortress known as the Qaleh-i-Sefid, the White Castle. Beyond Tulaspid again is an impressive rock tomb known as the Da-u-Dokhtar, with four half columns carved on the face of the rock and a central doorway as at Naqsh-i-Rustam. Herzfeld considered it to be the tomb of either Teispes (see p. 10) or Cyrus I; vanden Berghe attributes it to Teispes for it was in the centre of his kingdom. Though all these places are at the moment difficult to reach, access will become easier when the road from Shiraz to Ahwaz is completed.

South-east and west of Shiraz, too, the country is rich in early remains. Firuzabad, now the winter headquarters of the Qashgai tribe, and once the capital of Ardeshir I, lies in a plain in the midst of attractive scrub-covered mountains some seventy miles from Shiraz. The final approach is made through a long gorge commanded by a Sassanian castle known as the Qaleh-i-Dukhtar, which according to Ghirshman may well have been Ardeshir's first headquarters. Half castle, half palace, it is strongly built on a narrow spur of rock four hundred feet above the river, which hems it in on three sides. The mouth of the spur is closed by a massive semi-circular bastion seventy feet high, behind which rises a square hall surmounted by a dome sixty feet high and open on three sides. On two sides great arches open on a view of mountains and the gorge below, and the third opens on to a long barrel-vaulted iwan. From these two buildings, which between them formed the audience hall and antechamber of Ardeshir, the castle drops in a series of terraces towards the point of the spur overlooking the river. Half way down are thick walls within which sloping ramps, wide enough for a horse, run up through two floors. Ruined as it is, this pile rivals the medieval castles of Europe, which it anticipated by a thousand years.

A little farther along the gorge, on the far side of the river, are the remains of a Sassanian bridge and a rock carving showing the crowning of Ardeshir by the God Ahuramazda. Farther on, almost at the point where the gorge emerges into the plain, is a vast (20m.) rock carving showing the defeat of the Parthian King Artabanus V by Ardeshir and that of the Parthian Vizier by Ardeshir's son Shapur. Across the river from the road, and carved in faint relief, it is difficult to detect but well worth the search for its spirited pictures of the two monarchs in armour and their supporters charging full tilt at each other.

In the plain itself, near the mouth of the gorge rises the great mass of Ardeshir's palace, dating probably from the time of his triumph. A visit to the palace involves wading across the river and a walk through a thicket of myrtle. Built in front of a circular pool fed by a spring, the palace is three hundred and forty feet long by one hundred and sixty feet wide, and the walls are thirteen feet thick. It consists of the remains of a barrel-vaulted iwan followed by three square domed chambers side by side. The central dome, about sixty feet high, is in a good state of preservation, and one can walk up to the galleries and eventually on to the roof of the building. Almost the only decoration consists of Egyptian-style pediments over the doors of the hall, which the young dynasty copied from Persepolis – possibly in an effort to identify themselves with the Achaemenians.

Built of rough stone masonry, Ardeshir's castle and palace lack surface charm, but they have the strength which is the hallmark of Sassanian art and their square domed halls represent a landmark in the history of architecture. The manner of their construction, half-cones made of brick rising from square corners, has no known antecedents west of Persia. Greek and Roman domes were constructed on quite different principles. Byron declares that the Palace of Ardeshir saw the birth of the squinch and the solution of the problem, which had defeated European architects, of putting a dome on a building of any shape. Domed halls and iwans between them also provide the two essential forms from which the glorious development of Persian Islamic architecture was to be built up.

Farther on in the plain, a little beyond the modern village, lie the remains of the city of Firuzabad, a great circular ditch and earthwork over a mile in diameter. In the centre of the old town there stands a ninety-foot tower, locally called the Minar (minaret) which is in fact a Sassanian fire temple. Traces of a spiral staircase which lead to a roof where the scared fire burned in the sight of the faithful are still visible.

An ancient road once ran from Firuzabad to Siraf on the Gulf
(see p. 290), and near this road stands the Sassanian fire temple
complex of Kunar Siah, the best preserved example of Atashgah
and Chahar Taq in a single enclosure (cf. pp. 50–51).

West of Firuzabad lies Farrashband where there are two more
Sassanian fire complexes, T. Jangi and Khurma Yak; while at
Buzpar to the south-west, Professor vanden Berghe discovered in
1960 a limestone tomb which at first sight bears a remarkable
resemblance to that of Cyrus at Pasargadae; but it is simpler and
less than half the size. It is thought to be the tomb of one of Cyrus's
ancestors, perhaps his Persian grandfather (not Astyages! see p. 10).

Eastwards the road from Shiraz leads to Sarvistan, Fasa and
Darab. Six miles south of Sarvistan village are the remains of another Sassanian palace, attributed by Herzfeld to Bahram V (420–
40). Built of rough masonry, it is chiefly of interest to students of
architecture. But like so many of Persia's early monuments it also
has a beauty born of a skilful use of natural features. Situated a
mile or so in front of a prow-like cliff at a point where two broad
valleys join to form a vast empty plain, it could well have been a
hunting lodge for King Bahram Gur (the Wild Ass). The plan
is not dissimilar from that of Firuzabad – iwan, dome, court –
but there are significant differences. The building has several
entrances – perhaps the need for strict security had diminished;
one lateral entrance, leading into a large subsidiary iwan to the
north of the dome, has assumed particular importance. The main
iwan, on the west, is shallower than the earlier model; the domed
room is larger. Finally the vaulting is more involved and intricate,
suggesting a considerable evolution in architectural techniques in
two hundred years.

Between Sarvistan and Fasa, near the village of Miangol, there
is a fire temple, and above it a Sassanian fortress – another Qaleh-
i-Dukhtar. Near Fasa itself are the remains of a fortress, the
Qaleh-i-Gabri, and of a Sassanian or early Islamic dam. Situated
in a well-watered plain entirely surrounded by cliff-like mountains, Darab was an important Sassanian town, like Firuzabad
circular in plan and with four gates. Its ditch and earthwork,
which is forty feet high in places, still have a grand air, but inside

little remains beyond traces of an aqueduct and of a fortress on a hillock in the centre of the town. At the foot of the mountains close to the town, there is a colossal Sassanian rock carving, long believed to depict the triumph of Shapur over Valerian but now thought to celebrate Ardeshir's victory over unidentified Western foes (see article by Georgina Herrman in *Iran* VII for this and an admirable account of the Ardeshir and Shapur rock carvings generally). The carving is beautifully sited on a small cliff at a point where a spring gushes from the rock to a vast pool, a type of site much favoured by the Persians through the centuries for their memorials.

Also close to the town is a small mosque carved out of an outcrop of rock. It is built in the form of a Greek cross, with flanking aisles and a large light shaft at the crossing. The only form of decoration consists of three inscriptions in the rock surface, one of which bears the date 1264. Wilber suggests that the building may have been either a fire temple or more probably a Christian church.

Beyond Darab, on the way to Bandar Abbas, lies Fing, and between here and the coast in a remote valley at the base of a limestone ridge Professor vanden Berghe discovered in 1957 two square buildings of local stone, a hundred and fifty feet apart, one an atashgah and the other a chahar taq, the first of these complexes to be identified (see p. 51). The siting of these buildings far from other Sassanian remains is of interest. The place is known as Tang-i-Chak Chak.

South from Fasa a gravelled motor road winds down to Jahrum, on oasis town whose attractive old houses nestle among groves of date palms, and on across broken country to Lar, sixty miles to the west of which is Khonj, with two Timurid mosques. This was the route from the Gulf coast followed by seventeenth-century travellers from Bandar Abbas to Shiraz. Fryer, who did it twice in each direction, saw at Jahrum, where there are the remains of two forts, 'a Coloss more than sixty feet high and thirty in circumference raised to some departed saint and overlooking many humble tombs' – perhaps a reference to the tower of the Qaleh-i-Gabri and its surrounding ruins. Fruit was plentiful here; he mentions excellent dates, stoneless white grapes, and sunburn ointment made from ground seeds, and 'in the adjoining plain, liquorice growing wild and several plashes where flourished lascivious shrubs'.

Of the ill-fated Lar, gravely damaged in the 1960 earthquake, but already before that something of a ghost town withering for lack of water, he gives an enthusiastic account. The setting was attractive: the road ran along a valley 'in which husbandmen had planted their cottages on each side of a gliding brook, here and there beset with tamarisk trees'. In the town itself he was much impressed by the Governor's palace with 'stately apartments, lakes and gardens equal to the Roman pride in its age of Wantonness', an Exchange (Bazaar) of polished stone, and the princely houses of the merchants. Herbert, too, some fifty years earlier had had a rousing welcome at Lar, and Pietro della Valle, though he arrived there in tragic circumstances and was aware of the bad reputation of its water, sang its praises and admired the construction of its wind towers. Moreover, he says the town was almost entirely given over to intellectual pursuits; nowhere had he found so many learned men and distinguished scientists as at Lar.

CHAPTER TWELVE

Khuzistan and the Gulf

The south-eastern tip of Mesopotamia has, throughout its chequered history, generally been under Persian sovereignty. Its present name, Khuzistan, has roots deep in the past. The Khuzis were a tribe of Elamite origin who settled in the province (then known as Susiana) under the Sassanians. In the seventeenth century it was known as Khuzistan or Chusistan; its nineteenth-century name of Arabistan was acquired by reason of its predominantly Arab population, but in defiance of its history.

Khuzistan forms a triangular-shaped wedge betwen the Iraq border to the west and the Bakhtiari mountains to the north-east; its base is the head of the Persian Gulf. Though it includes a considerable area of Zagros foothills, Khuzistan is mostly flat; a large part of the plain is desert. For much of the year the climate in insufferably hot. But Khuzistan has been the richest province of Iran and is well on the way to becoming so again.

The modern explanation is oil, communications and water. The rich oil deposits discovered in 1908 by the predecessor of the Anglo-Persian Oil Company all lie in or near the hilly region to the east of Khuzistan between Lali in the north and Gach Saran in the south. The large town of Abadan has grown up round the refinery in the south-west corner of the province. The ports of Khorramshahr and Bandar Shahpur are linked by railway with the interior. A fourth port, Bandar Mashur, has been constructed, half way between Abadan and the mountains, specifically for the export of crude oil, followed in the 1960s by the large-scale development of Khang Island (see below).

Oil, however, does not explain former glories. The existence of oil at Masjid-i-Suleiman was, it is true, known to the ancients, but they used it for religious ceremonial rather than for commercial ends. The wealth of Susiana was based on communications and, above all, water. Three great rivers like the branches of a tree converge on central Khuzistan. The Karkheh flows down from the mountains of Luristan. The surging Diz, whose gorges provided the route for the trans-Iranian railway, rushes down from the northeast. The mighty Karun pursues its circuitous course from the east to join the Diz some twenty-five miles north of Ahwaz. In the heart of Khuzistan these three rivers flow for a long time side by side; but whereas the Karkheh loses itself in the swamps of the western desert, never to reach the sea, the Karun, with the Diz, flows on to join the Tigris and Euphrates (jointly known by this time as the Shatt-al-Arab) at Khorramshahr on the Iraq frontier.

The original mouth of the Karun was the Khor Musa, a deep inlet with excellent anchorage where the ports of Bandar Mashur and Bandar Shahpur are now situated. The main volume of Karun water flowed this way until, it seems, the eighteenth century. At a much earlier date, according to one legend, in the time of Alexander, a channel known as the Haffar or dugout was constructed connecting the Karun with the Shatt-al-Arab. This was apparently enlarged in the fourteenth and fifteenth centuries by successive floods. Moreover at some stage unspecified the main natural flow of waters issuing from this cut did not join the Shatt at Khorramshahr at all but ran to the east of Abadan Island, emptying into the Gulf through the estuary known as the Khor Bahmanshir.

Nor did the Karkheh always disappear into the desert. It may well have followed something like the present course of the lower Karun. The reason for all these changes is simple. The delta of the great rivers of Mesopotamia is constantly extending itself further into the Gulf. 'The level plains at the foot are the flesh washed off the bones in the form of pure silt,' wrote young Arnold Wilson in a letter home in 1908. Seaward Khuzistan is thus both new and fluctuating. The site of Abadan itself may well have been swamp in prehistoric if not in Achaemenian times. The delta is no place to look for ancient civilizations.

The country north of Ahwaz, where Karkheh, Diz and Karun flow side by side, is, however, a different matter. This region enjoys what is by Iranian standards an abundant rainfall – that is to say an average of fifteen inches a year as compared with nine in Tehran and five in Isfahan. Allowing for the risk of a dry year, dry farming is possible; some of the most favoured tribal pastures, those of the Bakhtiari, are in this area. These plains were the bread-basket of the Achaemenian empire. In Sassanian times, tremendous irrigation works were undertaken. There was a dam, long disused, on the lower Karkheh. Even the little Chaour which flows past Shush is said to have had twenty stone dams. After the Arab con-quest oranges and sugar cane were grown in this region. The ruins of Susa, Choga Zambil, Shushtar and Dizful bear witness to past greatness and glories which in a new guise may now come again.

The economic transformation of Khuzistan derives not only from oil but also from water and power. The huge Mohammed Reza Pahlavi dam, on the Diz north of Dizful (accessible from Andimeshk and visible by arrangement), built in the 1960s in a dramatic gorge is the highest dam in Asia. It provides power to Khuzistan, and by overhead transmission to Tehran. It also con-trols enough water for an irrigation project south of Dizful and Andimeshk. Some 100,000 hectares of land are being made avail-able for large scale farming and food processing industries; it is claimed that any tropical crop can be grown in the summer and vir-tually any temperate crop in the winter. On the southern edge of the area at Haft Tepe a successful sugar cane industry has already been established hard by Choga Zambil. Thus past and present merge.

The great mounds of Susa, the modern Shush, conceal five thousand years of history, which patient excavation is only slowly unfolding. The most important archaeological site in Iran was only detected and identified by an English archaeologist, W. K. Loftus, in the 1850s. Even the site of the greatest city of the civilized world in 500 B.C. was unknown to Napoleon's contemporaries. His compatriots, Dieulafoy, de Margan, de Mecquenem and Ghirshman, the last three being members of the officially con-stituted French Archaeological Mission, have been responsible for vast labours and astounding discoveries. It was de Morgan who, at the turn of the century, arranged for the construction, high on the north-west mound, of the moated, battlemented castle which so easily identifies Shush from a distance. It was not intended as a work of art, nor as a projection of French culture, but for a severely practical purpose – to protect its archaeological inmates, and treasures, against marauding Arab tribes. Even in 1908 the road from Ahwaz to Dizful via Shush had not yet been mapped, because of the dangers of travel.

Susa was an inhabited site at the beginning of the fourth millennium – say about 4000 B.C. Pottery from this period is constructed of fine clay, beautifully shaped, and painted with stylized animal designs. After about 3400 B.C. there is a change, presumably the result of a conquest; painted pottery disappears and is replaced by monochrome red ware. When it reappears, about 3100 B.C., it is of somewhat inferior quality. Early in the third millennium a civilization arose at Susa which created its own writing – Ghirshman calls it proto-Elamite. The writing was ideographic and cannot yet be translated though the frequent appearance of numbers and additions suggests that it was used inter alia for accounting purposes. Towards the end of the third millennium a cuneiform script, believed to be of Akkadian origin, appears side by side with these early ideographs. This is thought to reflect several centuries of struggle between the Elamites who inhabited Susa and points east, and the Sumerian or Akkadian peoples who flourished in modern Iraq. About 2100 B.C. a temple of which the foundations have been discovered was erected to the honour of Inshush'nak, the Lord of Susa, a leading Elamite deity. The presence at Susa of the stela of Khammurabi, a Babylonian King who reigned about 1930 B.C., suggests an Elamite victory at that epoch. After a short period of domination by the Kassites, who were Caspian people of Indo-European stock, Susa enjoyed about 1300 B.C. a further prosperity under the Elamites. Three hundred years later it was seized by Nebuchadnezzar. The Elamites returned for a brief spell about 700 B.C. only to be finally extinguished by the Assyrian conqueror Assur-Banipal (Sardanapalus) about 645 B.C. The place was looted, the temple of Inshush'nak desecrated, and the city itself destroyed by fire.

The Assyrian domination was, however, short-lived. Darius made Susa the centre of his empire (521 B.C.). He made a citadel, surrounded the town with a wall of unbaked brick and a moat, and built a palace and apadana or throne room for himself. Clay tablets, discovered on the site of the palace, record how this building was constructed. Workmen and materials were brought from all over the empire. Local stone from Elam was worked by Ionians and people from Sardis. The gold came from Sardis and Bactria, but the goldsmiths were Medes and Egyptians. Timber was brought via Babylon from the cedars of Lebanon, but wrought by Sardians and Egyptians. Babylonians were responsible for the enamelled brick, Medes and Egyptians for wall decorations. Precious stones from Sogdiana and Chorasmia, silver and ebony from Egypt, and ivory from Ethiopia and Sind completed this extraordinary assemblage of talent and riches. The apadana was approached by a staircase similar in plan to that which we see at Persepolis. The predominant feature of the decorations was enamelled bricks representing winged bulls, lions and human figures, which are in excellent preservation at the Louvre. Susa surrendered to Alexander without resistance; he removed the treasure but did not damage the buildings.

Susa continued to flourish, though perhaps in relative decline, under succeeding dynasties. The Archaeological Mission has discovered a Parthian cemetery, the form of burial in a terracotta sarcophagus suggesting an intermediate stage between Achaemenian interment and Magian exposure. The city was damaged during the Parthian-Sassanian wars around A.D. 230 but was rebuilt by Ardeshir. Later it became the site of a Christian bishopric, but the prominence it gained thereby drew the wrath of Shapur II, who destroyed it. The foundations of a Sassanian palace, have, however, been discovered on the site. In the face of the Arab conquest, Susa surrendered without a fight. The city continued as an inhabited place, though in Islamic times the bulk of the population appears to have been in the area of the so-called Artisans' City, to the east of the site; Dr Ghirshman has here discovered the foundations of a colonnaded mosque on the Arab plan, as well as of three Islamic cities superimposed on each other. It was the Mongol invasion which gave Susa its death blow. For several centuries now it has been a dead city.

The site comprises four enormous mounds. That on which the castle is built is the ruin of the Elamite city. To the north-east is the so-called Apadana mound where Darius built his palace. Its foundation walls now exposed show clearly the outline of the various rooms; and column bases have been placed in position. In 1970 M. JeanPerrot, now in charge of the French Archaeological Mission in succession to Dr Ghirshman, discovered two foundation stones of grey marble, one in Elamite, the other in Akkadian' beginning 'I am Darius the great king', thus firmly dating the palace as having been built after his accession (522 B.C.). The stones have been removed to the Tehran Archaeological Museum and replicas put in their place on the Apadana.

To the east and south of the Apadana is the so-called Royal City, first inhabited by the Elamites but extended by the Achaemenians. Some years ago the French Archaeological Mission, in a large sample dig at the northern end of the mound, discovered, to start with, the foundations of nine cities superimposed on each other. They began with three from the Islamic period, followed by a gap of three inches, and then signs of devastation – ruins of houses, broken walls, numerous tombs. That this was the work of Shapur II was confirmed by the discovery of jars containing children's bodies but inscribed with Nestorian crosses. The Sassanian layer also contained evidence of a large room whose walls were covered with frescoes of hunting scenes. At the next level (Parthian) a bath-house decorated with mosaics and a bas-relief of Artabanus V were discovered. At the bottom level which has now been reached – but above the surrounding country indicating that the original site was a natural ridge – have been found the archives of a large land-owner named Temti Wartus who had financial dealings with Bahrein in the eighteenth to seventeeth century B.C. His house was apparently built on the ruins of smaller houses. The remains of a small temple have also been uncovered.

Beyond the Royal City to the east lay the so-called 'Artisans'

City, and here similar recent sample digs have uncovered, in the Islamic streets, the foundations of a very early mosque; in the Parthian layer, a large cemetery showing different forms of burial; and below this an early Achaemenian village, possibly one of the earliest *Persian* settlements in Khuzistan.

On the west bank of the little river Chaour the foundations of a palace with many column bases are now (1971) being excavated. It appears from inscriptions to have been constructed by Artaxerxes II or III.

For all this wealth of historical discovery there is not much to show on the spot. Yet few would fail to be moved by the sight of these rounded piles of rubble, still holding fast to many of their treasures and their secrets, in the midst of a relentless plain bounded on a clear day by the snow-capped peaks of distant Zagros.

And so we come to Choga Zambil, the modern name of an Elamite town and temple which was known as Dur-Untashi, after the Elamite king Untash-Huban by whom it was built about 1250 B.C. It was destroyed by Assur-Banipal some six hundred years later, though it appears to have been used for temporary shelter in Parthian times. It lies some twenty miles south-east of Susa, on the banks of the river Diz, and is now accessible only through the sugar project area (see p. 268). A desert track, impassable in wet weather, leads off the Ahwaz road a few miles south of Susa, crosses the railway at the little station of Haft Tepe (seven mounds) where the Iranian Archaeological Service under Dr Negahban is engaged in extensive and important excavations of the Elamite city of Tikni starting with tombs in the temple area. Suddenly, at the top of a rise, a great artificial mound, skilfully excavated, comes into view; the low buildings in the foreground are the residential quarters of the French Archaeological Mission.

The site was rediscovered by geologists prospecting for the Anglo-Persian Oil Company in 1935. It was identified by M. de Mecquenem, the then head of the Mission, but serious excavation did not begin until the winter of 1951. Dr Ghirshman made it the main scene of his labours for seven successive winters and what he uncovered there constitutes, beyond question, the most exciting archaeological exploration in Iran in recent years. The work was not without difficulties. It could only be undertaken between November and March, partly because of the climate and partly because the bulk of the labour – and over a hundred men have been employed at a time – had to be imported from the Zagros and was available only during the 'dead' agricultural season in the mountains. The Mission had to organize their supplies, no easy task in this remote spot, and to provide them with at least the minimum of social services. Tons of debris had to be removed from the site, and for this purpose a light railway track was built to connect Choga Zambil with the river Diz, in which the earth was dumped. Constant expert supervision was needed since on a site of such potentialities some find or clue of immense importance may be uncovered at any time and no sooner found than destroyed by a careless or ignorant workman. The highly delicate task of piecing together broken objects, reconstructing certain features of the buildings, and cataloguing inscriptions and pictorial finds such as cylinder seals had to be undertaken on the spot. It was inspiring to see Dr and Mme Ghirshman working together on this labour of love, which at the same time has much of the excitement of a detective story. One day, perhaps, they will write the full story,* describing in detail the discovery of every clue and the process by which these were fitted together to enable them to reach their conclusions. I shall simply state the conclusions they have reached, as I understand them, without trying to describe in any detail all the fascinating evidence on which they are securely based.

The town of Dur-Untashi was surrounded by a wall measuring 1,300 by 900 yards; the remains of these ramparts can be clearly seen. There was an inner wall, enclosing the sacred quarter; this was 440 yards square. At the centre of this inner sanctum, surrounded by temples and chapels, rose the ziggurat or sacred tower such as was found in every important city of Mesopotamia in this period. The remains of some twenty ziggurats have been discovered, but that of Choga Zambil is the largest of them all as well as the best preserved. The outer dimensions of the tower are about three hundred and forty-six feet square; it consisted of five

* See now Bibliography (1978).

storeys, surmounted by a temple, and its total height was about one hundred and seventy-four feet. The present ruin, which rises only a little above the height of the third storey, is over eighty feet above ground level; and that is impressive enough.

The ziggurat looked like a series of boxes, square in plan and rectangular in elevation, laid on top of each other, each smaller than the one below it; its profile was that of a stepped pyramid. (A scale model in balsa wood, constructed by Mme Ghirshman in the long winter evenings on the site, can be seen in the Louvre.) With the exception of the temple, the successive storeys were not built on top of each other but inside each other, so that every one had its own foundations at ground level. It was not a series of solid boxes on top of each other but a succession of hollow boxes fitting tightly into each other, the inner box always being taller than the one next outside it.

The first floor is only about three feet above ground level, and the second, which is nearly twenty-five feet above the ground, has a roof or platform twenty-five feet wide except on the north-east where it is thirty-nine feet. These were the first to be con-structed. They comprised a low building surrounding an open court. It was within this court that the central part of the building was later erected. How long after the third, fourth and fifth storeys were added is not clear. They appear to have measured thirty-nine feet in height and over twenty in width. The fifth, unlike the others, was not hollow but was covered with a terrace roof measuring approximately one hundred and fifteen feet square; it was on this terrace that the temple was built. The ziggurat was constructed mostly of mud brick but completely cased in baked brick; it is largely thanks to the quality of the latter that it has been possible to identify the form and construction of the building in such detail. On every floor, at eye level, there was a continuous row of bricks carrying a cuneiform inscription which had been found fifty years earlier, at Susa by Father Scheil. This has enabled the height of each floor and outer terrace to be accurately gauged.

Each face of the building had at its centre a monumental doorway surmounted by an arch at first floor level. Before the central part of the ziggurat was constructed, these doorways would have led into the interior court. They still give access, by means of lateral stairways, to the roof of the second floor. There is, however, no means of access from this platform to the upper part of the building. There is only one entrance to the third floor platform, by means of a stair which climbs steeply and straight inwards from the doorway on the south-west face. This has a lateral stair leading right-handed only on to the roof of the third storey. These are all extant. By careful researches into the depressions formed by watercourses in the upper part of the present structure, Dr Ghirshman has established that another stairway, doubtless similar in character, led from the third to the fourth and fifth storeys on the south-east side; and that the only entrance to the temple itself from the fifth storey was on the north-east face. This maze-like pattern of stairs and platforms was clearly deliberate. It seems reasonable to suppose that no one save high priests of the cult was permitted to go higher than the second floor platform, if that far. The procession of holy men entered the building on the south-west side, was hidden from view till it reached the third floor, proceeded along this to the centre of the south-east face, disappeared up another stairway, reappeared on the fifth floor, turned right-handed again and entered the temple itself on the north-east. There is ground for thinking that it was mainly in the open space facing the north-east side of the building that the public was permitted to congregate. Thus it is possible to envisage the scene: a large congregation filling the great paved square, watching with hushed attention for the moment when the priestly procession would appear at the left end of the fifth floor platform, some hundred and fifty feet above their heads.

The ziggurat was surrounded on every side by courts paved with square bricks. To the south-west, the side from which the priestly procession set out, there have been excavated on the far side of the court a series of four chapels separate from each other, entered only from the court, and bearing no kind of inscription. But a large number of animal heads and cylinder seals, showing feasting and hunting scenes, animals and geometrical subjects, presumably all votive offerings, have been found in them. On the north-west side were three larger buildings which have been identified as the temples of the gods Huban and Ishni-qarab and of the goddess Kiririsha. In the last was found, under a pile of more than a hundred clubs of marble, bronze, hematite, alabaster and chalk, most of them inscribed, a number of bronze objects including daggers, knives, decorated plaques, cups, vases, little animal figurines, and cylinder seals portraying banqueting scenes. Dr Ghirshman suggests that these objects were looted from various parts of the main buildings and hidden in the temple by the thieves. The temple of Ishni-qarab was surrounded by houses of the clergy, kitchens, workshops and warehouses. It seems likely that there was a flourishing industry for the manufacture of votive objects somewhere in the vicinity. The north-east side of the ziggurat differs from the others in several respects. The adjoining court was particularly wide. The surrounding wall is here broken by a monumental gateway almost, but not quite, opposite the monumental door on the north-east face of the ziggurat. A paved way, at a slight angle to the line of the ziggurat, leads from the one to the other. Opposite and for some distance to the right of the entrance, a sloping platform made of baked brick projects from the side of the ziggurat. This would have enabled a large number of people to reach the first floor of the building, without steps. It seems probable, therefore, that the principal public access to the base of the ziggurat was on this north-east side – the direction in which the doorway of the temple faced. Near the northern corner of the sloping platform was a circular column of bricks, probably an altar. The pedestal and niche of a similar construction in front of the main south-west doorway has been recreated under the direction of Mme Ghirshman.

The most intriguing problem of the ziggurat relates to what went on below the second platform. As originally constructed, it consisted of a low square round a large central court. Some twenty inches below ground level, Dr Ghirshman found a series of narrow rooms approached by tiny brick staircases from the second storey roof. These rooms varied in size on each side but had one feature in common: the walls were all meticulously lime-washed. On the north-west face there were seven rooms;

five were empty, one contained three big jars and about twenty
little ones, the seventh yielded packets of earth in three colours,
white, red and yellow. Similar rooms on the south-west face
were all empty. Under the north-east platform, however, which
was wider than the others, there were two rows of rooms in
parallel. The outer row resembled the others, staircase and all;
one contained over a thousand 'nails', that is to say votive objects
shaped like mushrooms, made of glazed earthenware and often
inscribed 'Untash Huban', another some two hundred and fifty
plaques of the same ware with projecting head, or base, shaped
like a nail. The inner row of rooms, however, was more puzzling.
There was no entrance from above. Instead each was provided
with a large doorway, some thirteen feet high, facing inwards,
that is to say towards the interior of the ziggurat or, before that
was built, the court. These doors had been blocked with great care
with baked bricks and the rooms themselves filled with baked
bricks. There was a narrow hole in the roof of each through
which the workmen who filled the doorways and rooms with
bricks could have eventually made their escape. It seems probable
that the blocking of these rooms was undertaken at the time when
the central part of the ziggurat was constructed, and that they
were the tombs of some divinities.

To discover what went on below the second storey platforms
on the south-east face involved another piece of detection. To the
right of the monumental doorway were a series of rooms entered
from the first floor platform through a baked brick arch. Here
were discovered the remains of the hinges of a swing door, pieces
of striped cylindrical glass used for decorative purposes, and
pieces of wood which formed part of the door itself. In the small
entry hall was an altar made of baked brick but plastered over.
The adjoining rooms, which were paved in brick and divided
from each other by wooden doors, showed signs of also being
used for worship; furthermore they had wooden ceilings. This
may explain why they were wider than similar rooms on the
other faces of the ziggurat (eleven and a half feet as compared
with less than seven). An inscription indicates that this suite of
rooms was dedicated to Inshush'nak.

Similar rooms were discovered to the left of the monumental doorway, but with no access from the outside. Profiting from his experience with the inner row of rooms in the north-east face, and guided by certain other clues, Dr Ghirshman looked else-where for an explanation of these rooms and found it in the form of an arched doorway twenty-five feet high, leading inwards from one of the rooms and sedulously blocked with baked bricks. He has called this complex the temple of Inshush'nak A, and con-siders that it can only have been used for worship up till the time when the central part ot the ziggurat was built.

The work of excavating the Elamite tower and its immediate surroundings has been largely completed. But one important problem remains. Brickwork which has been marvellously preserved for thirty-two centuries under the kindly protection of earth and sand, is now exposed to the elements and unless special steps can be taken to strengthen it, it is feared that the monument will rapidly disintegrate. To this problem Dr Ghirsh-man has lately given much attention, but it demands an effort and an expenditure which are beyond the means of the French Mission, and even the Archaeological Service of Iran.

Shushtar, which Arab invaders thought one of the wonders of the world and fourteenth-century travellers praised as prosperous and beautiful, is dependent for its livelihood on irrigation works that have broken down and is now actively in decay.

No one knows exactly when Shushtar was founded. According to legend it is the second oldest city after Susa, and probably existed in pre-Sassanian times. It was the scene of a series of fabulous engineering exploits under the aegis of Shapur I, was beseiged for six months during the Arab invasion and experienced a further wave of prosperity in Mongol times to which the lovely, broken, fourteenth-century minaret of the Friday Mosque still bears witness. The building was begun about A.D. 867 and has a prayer hall with massive columns and good Seljuk stucco friezes. Round the city are five shrines to Arab generals, who perished during the six-month resistance to their invasion. In the eighteenth century Shushtar was the scene of extensive fighting during the Afghan wars. Half the population perished in a plague in 1831-32. In the same year the great bridge was damaged, though subsequently repaired. In 1876 the plague broke out again. In 1885 an even worse flood wrecked the bridge. In 1928 some of the ruins were washed away in what has been called the worst flood within living memory. The construction of the trans-Iranian railway, which passed well to the west of Shushtar, was a further blow. When Arnold Wilson visited Shushtar in 1908 he described the town as 'picturesque, dirty and compact'. Less than fifty years later, the authors of the *Blue Guide* say, in phrases less measured than is their custom, 'Shushtar is a town which is declining every day . . . it is in the process of being abandoned. . . . It seems to be shrivelling up into a sickening grey shell compounded of sunbaked bricks and rubbish'.

Yet by any standards Shushtar is an extraordinary place. It stands on the left bank of the Karun, a few miles out on the plain below the last gorge. The town is built on a slight eminence at a point where the southward flowing river bends west. At this point a dam was constructed to divert about a third of the Karun into an artificial channel known as the Ab-i-Gargar which runs between high banks and forms the eastern boundary of the old town. Half a mile downstream another dam, the Band-i- Gargar, was built across this channel; water was drawn through rock tunnels starting above the dam on either side of the channel; even now it drives some thirty flour mills below the dam. Still farther down the channel is yet another dam, designed for irrigation purposes.

But the major works are on the Karun, or as it is known here, the Shatait, the natural river bed which forms the northern and western boundaries of the town. Below a citadel of indeterminate date known as the Castle of Salasil, two tunnels were cut, through which dammed waters flowed into another artificial channel, the Nahr-i-Darayan, which skirted the town on the west and irrigated a large area to the south. Across the Shatait some three hundred yards below the citadel was flung the greatest work of all – a combined dam and bridge, six hundred yards long and sixty-six feet wide, capable of raising the water level above it by six feet, built of dressed stone bound in cement and protected from erosion by an artificial stone bed in the river above

it, the stones linked with metal clamps. This stupendous undertaking, known as the Band-i-Qaisar or Valerian's bridge, was,
like all the other irrigation works at Shushtar, built under the
orders of Shapur I, and there may well be some truth in the
tradition that Roman prisoners captured when Valerian was
defeated at Edessa in A.D. 260 had a hand in the making of it.
Thanks to its excellent workmanship and repairs carried out in
the Middle Ages, this bridge-dam continued to serve its double
purpose for over sixteen centuries; it was not till the great flood
of 1885 that it was irreparably broken. It consists now of twenty-
eight arches on the left bank and seven on the right; dammed
waters no longer flow into the Nahr-i-Darayan. With the
collapse of Valerian's bridge, the fertile oasis which it watered has
withered; Shushtar too has crumbled. It may, however, be hoped
that with the general economic development of this rich province, of which it was so long the capital, the ancient city may
revive.

The sister town of Dizful, which lies to the north-west on the
banks of the Diz, has a similar, if less chequered career. Here too
there was a 'Roman' bridge and dam, over four hundred yards
long, with twenty-two arches and a corresponding number of
supplementary openings to take flood water; here too were
water mills built out into the stream; here too the bridge is
broken and irrigation has long since ceased; here too a canal was
built to furnish the town with water. At different times, Dizful
has been famous for its narcissi, its indigo, and for the manufacture of reed pens. Being nearer the trans-Iranian railway than
Shushtar, it has suffered less in recent years for its situation.

North and east of the great rivers rise first the foothills and
then the great central massif of the Zagros range. A series of
ridges run closely parallel, north-west and south-east, each
steeper, more rocky, more jagged than the last. In spring the
lower slopes are brilliantly green, flecked with tulip, anemone
and wild daffodil; for the rest of the year they are baked to a
dull brown.

The higher ranges are covered with scrub; the heights are
snow-covered for the greater part of the year. There are few

settled places save along the edge of the plain and in some of
the wider valleys; this is the country of the great Bakhtiari
migration. Except where bridges are available the raging torrents
must be crossed either by swimming or by raft. The rafts, known
as killik, are made of inflated goat-skins; men paddle them downstream loaded with women, children and flocks, haul them a
mile or so upstream on the far side, and then float them back to
the original starting point. It may take two or three days for a
large party to be conveyed across one of these streams; many
horses and cattle, which are required to swim, may be lost in the
process. But the ardours of the crossing are less than those of the
mountain passes, where the men of the tribe dig steps in the
heavy snow to enable a slow single file, donkeys loaded with
children or chickens, cattle driven by turbaned women, old men
who have trudged this way annually for fifty years, to climb to
ten thousand feet before descending to their summer pastures on
the upper reaches of the Zaindeh Rud. When a halt is called and
the black tents are pitched, the men of the tribe go off hunting for
pig or ibex, or, in their black vertical skull caps and baggy
trousers, engage in the tribal stick-dance, or ride at full tilt across
a meadow and, turning round a hundred and eighty degrees in
their saddles, practise firing behind them – the Parthian shot!

This country has been traversed for centuries. and there are
many ancient remains. At Masjid-i-Suleiman, where oil was first
discovered in 1908, stands a great platform, believed by Ghirshman to be of Achaemenian construction, by others to be Parthian,
approached by twelve staircases, on which was constructed the
only Parthian temple yet to be found in Iran, showing Elamite,
Iranian and Western architectural influences, as well as a sanctuary
in which a statue of a naked man holding a lion has been discovered
and which is accordingly believed to have been a temple of Her-
acles. The site has also yielded an impressive quantity of Parthian
statuary illustrated in *Iran* VIII. In the centre of a small plain at the
foot of the western slopes of the Mungasht there is a 'romantic
little fort' (Wilson) Kala Tul, and close by an Elamite rock carving.
Near Izeh (Malamir) are many rock reliefs; those of Shah Savar
and Hung-i-Nauruzi dating from the Shimash dynasty of Elam

(about 2000 B.C.) discovered by Professor vanden Berghe in 1962; the neo-Elamite reliefs and inscriptions of about 700 B.C. in the gorges of Kul-i-Farah and Shikaft-i-Suleiman whose processional panels and royal presence foreshadow Achaemenian sculpture; and a scene of a vassal presenting homage to Mithridates I (171– 138 B.C.) cut into the back face of the isolated rock whose front bears the Elamite relief mentioned above. The four full-face figures on the right are characteristically Parthian. At Shami, due east of Shushtar, was the Parthian temple at which the bronze statue now in the Tehran museum and other bronze objects were discovered. Near Shimbar, to the north, Layard identified a Pahlevi inscription at Tang-i-Butan or defile of the idols, where there are two Parthian rock reliefs. At Kuh-i-Tina and Taraz, to the north-west and north-east of Shimbar respectively, Professor vanden Berghe discovered two very worn Parthian reliefs in 1964. Most famous of all are the Parthian sculptures carved on detached rocks at Tang-i-Sarvak, thirty miles north of Behbehan. The subjects include a king on a camel and a horseman fighting with a lion.

Ahwaz, the modern capital of Khuzistan, lies on both banks of the Karun some fifty miles south of Susa. It owes its origin to the fact that the river can be more easily crossed here than for many miles above or below. Cyrus is believed to have built a bridge of boats here to effect the crossing on his annual migration route from Susa to Pasargadae. Shapur I constructed another great dam at this spot. It was washed away in the fourteenth century, though its foundations have been used for the construction of a railway bridge which crosses the Karun here on its way to Bandar Shapur. The prosperity of modern Ahwaz derives from its central position; railways from Khorramshahr and Bandar Shapur, and roads from Abadan, the oil fields and the north, converge here and Ahwaz may conceivably become the centre of an important new oil field. The town shows little evidence of antiquity.

Round Ahwaz only an occasional patch of green relieves the monotony of the flat sandy desert, but as we approach the mouths of the great rivers the desert is halted by intensive cultivation, with a strip of date-palm groves one to three miles wide. Seen from the air it is a narrow green ribbon flanking the muddy waterway; the trees stand rigid, neat, rectangular like troops on a parade ground. From below, they shut out the desert and the dust; a glimmer of green grass lines the irrigation ditches, and in the shade of the palms cows graze and little mud villages lie tucked away.

Khorramshahr, the principal port of Iran, lies on the right bank of the Karun cut at its junction with the Shatt-el-Arab; until the 1930s it was known as Mohammerah, and was the seat of a semi-autonomous sheikhdom. The ocean-going port is on the Shatt and consists mainly of docks and warehouses. The residential part of the town faces the Karun. Its long river front is shaded with spreading Bougainvillaeas and flanked with handsome country houses of mellow brick standing in lush gardens. The river, whether rushing past at the time of spring floods or flowing more gently at other seasons, is always a scene of animation – ferries and motorboats head upstream against the current to reach the other side, naval launches issue from the base near the junction with the Karun, turbaned Arabs with long grey or white garments punt high-prowed dhows or shout to their companions.

Across the Shatt from Khorramshahr is Iraq; across the Karun, over a new bridge, Abadan Island. This was formerly known as Jezirat-al-Khidr, after a saint who is said to have disappeared there. A shrine was built in his honour, and though the present building is of little antiquity, the anchor of the boat in which he is reputed to have arrived can still be seen, embedded in the dome. This is the only relic of antiquity that Abadan retains. Until the construction of the refinery and port in 1910, the island had only a few thousand inhabitants; today it possesses one of the largest and best equipped towns in Iran. The refinery stands on the banks of the Shatt about seven miles from Khorramshahr; the town has grown up all round it, particularly to the south. There are some pleasant, well-planned residential quarters, whose resemblance to Hampstead Garden Suburb is often a source of mild amusement to the foreign visitor. But on the whole Abadan reflects credit on its creators. The houses, constructed of local materials, blend fairly happily into the landscape. Their design is simple and unaffected. Trees and gardens have been skilfully used in the planning and show what can be done, when water is available, in a harsh climate and a setting almost totally devoid of any natural beauty.

The Persian Gulf, nowhere more than fifty fathoms deep, dotted with islands and rich in fish, pearls and oil, is Iran's foremost frontier and only sea-route. As an inland sea, it has a place in history second only to the Mediterranean; its reputation as one of the hottest spots on earth tends to obscure both its archaeological interests and its scenic attractions. A journey down the Persian side of the Gulf at any time between November and April can be a most pleasurable experience; the rugged coastline, broken here and there by bays and islands, with its forgotten villages, crumbling wind towers and dusty palm-groves, is a constant delight; by day we can watch with Fryer 'tropick birds resting themselves upon the drowsy tortoise supinely floating on the sea' or shoals of gambolling porpoises; at night, under a clear sky, the bows of the ship cut through calm waters sparkling brilliantly with plankton. With modern contrivances the notorious damp summer heat of the Gulf should be easier to overcome.

At Bushire modern seagoing vessels must lie some six miles offshore, in an anchorage exposed to the prevailing shemal or north wind, and discharge cargo and passengers by lighter. This, and the building of the trans-Iranian railway, have brought about the decay of the city. Once a prosperous place of sixty thousand inhabitants, it is now reduced to fourteen thousand.* Ten foreign consulates were once established there; when I visited Bushire in 1957, I was told that there was one foreign resident, a Russian maidservant.

The rise of Bushire dates only from the eighteenth century, but was then rapid. Nadir Shah developed it as a port and naval station. The East India Company transferred its principal factory there from Bandar Abbas in 1763 because, as their agent wrote, 'a Person there need have no connexions or caress anyone but the Sheikh himself'. In 1808 Bushire had four hundred houses,

* This was in 1958.

including nine great men's houses with wind towers, four Shi'a and three Sunni mosques, two hammams and two caravanserais. Shortly before this the British Residency for the Persian Gulf, an offshoot of the Government of India, had been established there, and remained until 1947 when it was moved to the opposite shore of the Gulf. Bushire thus has a far longer association with Britain than its opulent neighbour, Abadan.

No place could present a greater contrast. Bushire has been much maligned. 'The swamps surrounding the town render it particularly unhealthy,' says the *Blue Guide*. 'The streets are very narrow, irregular, ill-paved and filthy,' declares the *Encyclopaedia Britannica*. It is, needless to say, no health resort; and it has obviously fallen on evil days. But in the city itself there are a number of fine eighteenth- and early nineteenth-century buildings, with balconies whose blue shutters rattle in the wind. Moreover, for all its decay, the place has a solid, permanent air; this is due largely to the use of a delicately toned grey local stone, a conglomerate of shell and coral, quarried in the neighbourhood. In contrast to the low mud buildings of the plateau, the stone houses of the merchants are of two or three storeys, and the narrow streets have dignity and, still more important, shade. The former British Residency office, now the headquarters of the Ministry of Justice, occupies a fine position in the picturesque waterfront, and behind it is the former Anglican Church, closed since 1947; a notice showing the hymns sung at the last service was still in place ten years later, and on the roof is a bell bearing the inscription 'Political Resident 1865'.

The interior of the Bushire peninsula, too, has a certain wistful charm. It is dotted with large white country houses in, I suppose, an Anglo-Iranian style, with deep balconies and columns on their flat roofs which presumably carry awnings in the hot weather. There are gardens with stone parapets, banyan and acacia trees, and well-built stone walls. At least in winter, when the undulating wasteland is green, it is a park-like landscape, a mildly tropical version of Wimbledon Common. Since Niarchos, who sailed up the Gulf in 326 B.C. and came to 'a peninsula named Mesambria, wherein were many gardens and all kinds of fruit', no traveller as far as I know has ever written a word in its favour. James Fraser, who visited Bushire, admittedly in August 1821, found it 'difficult to convey an adequate idea of the parched and disgusting barrenness of the country around this place'.* Perhaps its long association with successive generations of British officials has stirred up in me some atavistic urge which warps my judgment. Perverse it may be, but in my mind the Bushire countryside remains a green, soft, friendly, vaguely feudal landscape, a surprising curtain-raiser to the tropical excesses and hellish ardours of the Gulf.

Even if Bushire is dying – and there is a chance of a modest revival – it has a seaward neighbour which is rapidly leaping into life. The island of Kharg, or Karag, does not figure very prominently in the history books. It is marked only on the more sophisticated maps. Standard works of reference ignore its existence. Until the mid-fifties only a minority of Iranians had heard of it. Yet today, in terms of both past and future, it is perhaps the most interesting island off the Persian coast.

Kharg lies some thirty miles north-west of Bushire, well off from the land. It is about five miles long and three miles wide, and though it only rises to some three hundred feet at the centre it has an indented and rocky shore, particularly on the west. It is well supplied with water and, by Gulf standards, fertile. Until the mid-fifties it housed a small penal colony and had in addition about three hundred inhabitants. who lived by agriculture and fishing. It has a little companion, Khargu, barely more than a sandspit, but reputed to possess a tree and two cows, as well as sheltering the occasional migrant fisherman.

In 1957 the Iranian Oil Consortium, faced with the need to find additional seaward outlets for their crude oil from the expanding field of Gach Saran, decided that the most practical solution was to build a pipeline to the coast near Ganaweh and thence underwater to Kharg. Gach Saran being some two thousand feet above sea level, oil would flow by gravity not only down to the coast and underwater but also into storage tanks to be constructed on a hill on the north-east side of the island. The project also involved the construction of a jetty half a mile long

* *Journey into Khorasan*, 1825.

15a. NAQSH-I-RUSTAM: Investiture of Ardeshir (carving No. 7); Bahram II
(No. 6) is on the right (*p. 252*)

15b. NAQSH-I-RUSTAM: The tomb of Xerxes; the entrance to Darius's
tomb is to the left (*p. 251*)

16a. PASARGADAE: Cyrus's tomb. 'Grudge me not this little earth that covereth my body' (p. 253)

16b. HORMUZ: Ruins of the Portuguese fort. 'This poore Citie is now disrobed of all her braverie' (p. 294)

in a bay on the same side of the island, at the end of which would
be a sheltered anchorage in water deep enough for the largest
tankers. Kharg can now handle a larger volume of crude oil than
any other port in the Gulf except Kuwait.

Only in the middle of the eighteenth century had Kharg
previously emerged into temporary prominence. One day a
former Prussian officer, Baron Kniphausen, then Dutch East
India Company agent at Basra, was summoned to call on the
Ottoman Governor. After an unduly long wait he was invited
into a room adjoining the Governor's office and was put under
arrest. After several days' detention he was told that he had been
'criminal with Turkish women and defrauding the Government
of its customs'. He subsequently discovered that his deputy had
been involved in some underhand dealings, and that he could buy
his freedom for one hundred thousand rupees. The Baron was a
man of resource. He persuaded the authorities, according to his
own account, to accept fifty thousand rupees by promising to
leave the country and suggesting that thirty thousand of the
balance should be borrowed from the deputy, who would be
left in charge. The offer was accepted. Kniphausen, having
secured the discomfiture of his deputy, shook the dust of Basra
off his feet for ever; he made a quick survey of Kharg Island, then
went personally to Batavia to clear his reputation with his
principals and persuaded them to sanction an agreement with the
Ruler of Bandar Rig, the Sheikh of Kharg, for the transfer of
sovereignty over the island to enable the Company to found a
new factory on the site. He returned in 1753, with the object,
inter alia, of holding up Turkish vessels until he had secured
repayment of the hundred thousand rupees; in this also he
succeeded. There were only about a hundred inhabitants on the
island at that time; labour had to be imported from both shores
of the mainland. A square fort, with four bastions each manned
with eight guns, was quickly built at the north end of the island
on a low point facing towards Khargu. A triangular strongpoint
was erected at the north-west point of the island. Between these
two Kniphausen constructed an esplanade, a small stone pier to
afford protection for shipping, and a number of houses for

Europeans, equipped with ventilators. Unfortunately for him the Dutch occupation was short-lived. Before Kniphausen's return from Batavia the worthy Sheikh of Bandar Rig had been murdered by his second son, Mir Muhanna, a notorious rascal who quickly made a reputation for himself as a highwayman by raiding caravans as they passed up and down the Bushire-Shiraz road. Next turning pirate, he occupied the miserable sandspit of Khargu and from that point of disadvantage somehow contrived to block the Dutch on Kharg and later, in 1766, to capture their fort. For three years Mir Muhanna ruled the island; the English from Bushire failed to dislodge him; Karim Khan, the Ruler of Shiraz, was more successful, and in 1769 Mir Muhanna fled to Kuwait. Under the Treaty of Finkenstein between Napoleon and Fath Ali Shah, designed to enlist Persian support against Russia, Kharg was ceded to the French in 1807; but as the Treaty was never put into operation, the French never occupied the island. Between 1838 and 1842, and again in 1856, Kharg was occupied by British troops, and for a short time in the former period the British Residency was transferred there from Bushire. It was even suggested that the British might purchase the island, but this came to nothing.

This was not the first suggestion of its kind. In 1758 the island was visited by a doctor of the East India Company, Edward Ives. He wrote as a footnote to his chapter on the subject: 'Is not then the island of Kharg as well upon the account of its situation for trade as for its pearl fishery, an object worthy of our East India Company's consideration?'*

Both Ives and Niebuhr, a German traveller after 1760, left interesting accounts of the condition of Kharg at this time. Taking a walk towards the south end of the island with Kniphausen and a Dutch ensign quaintly named Robinson, Ives passed through some agreeable fields of corn, and some gardens in which coleworts (? cauliflowers), beans and peas grew in profusion. Niebuhr observed grapes, figs, dates and other fruit. The principal tree then as now was the banyan; the hills abounded in a great variety of shells. Ives 'could not but notice' a large

* Voyage from England to India in 1758.

handsome building which some people said was the tomb of Mohammed the son of Ali. This he declined to believe; instead, he and Kniphausen stood before a tiled doorway, marvelling at the stone masonry, while the Baron pontificated on the possibility that it was a Portuguese chapel. Niebuhr wrote of an aqueduct with holes in the rock like chimneys. Ives noticed near the shrine 'a subterranean passage made for the conveyance of water'; and, in other parts of the island caverns hewn out of the solid rock and structures which appeared to have been appropriated to religious uses to judge by the fact that a crucifix had been discovered in one of the walls. Niebuhr discovered in one hole in the rocks a carving which might have represented the story of Rustam; but it was badly defaced, he suggested by Sunnites.

These accounts are as intriguing to the modern visitor to Kharg as Kharg today would be to Ives and Niebuhr. The modern port and jetty have been constructed not far from the old Dutch fort, of which few if any traces remain. Behind this, most probably on the same eighteenth-century site, stands the only village. Inland from the village and port, there is an extensive burial ground. Behind this runs a limestone ridge, on the sides of which are burial caves noticed by Herzfeld, some with primitive crosses carved on the exterior. Within are open tombs carved in the side walls, in sets of nine, and at the back a more elaborate sepulchre, with a bas-relief showing a man reclining on a couch, no doubt Niebuhr's 'story of Rustam'. This is similar to the carvings on certain tombs at Palmyra (Syria) and suggests that there may well have been a settlement of Palmyran merchants here in the second century A.D. when Kharg could have served as a transshipment point for Palmyra's flourishing oriental trade.

Above this low ridge, and to the north of the caves, is a bowl where the most noteworthy remains on the island are to be found. A large stone platform suggests the foundations of a Sassanian palace or shrine. Its upper surface is intersected by an elaborate system of shallow watercourses, and there are a number of circular depressions carved in the stone, about a foot across, which hint at some religious or ceremonial purpose, probably for receiving votive offerings. Nearby is the shrine of Imamzadeh

Mir Mohammed (1359) with its prominent pineapple cone with stalactite entrance portal in mosaic faïence; this is Ives' 'Portuguese chapel'. The whole of this area is still punctured with circular qanat holes, three or four feet in diameter, remarkable because they have been bored in the living rock to a depth of approximately eighty feet, presumably contemporary with the watercourses on the platform. For the Kharg massif is as it were the permanent well-head covering a perpetual fresh-water spring; and a water table, constantly refreshed from below, at an altitude somewhat above sea level is the source of the island's fruitfulness. It may seem staggering at first sight to encounter such a phenomenon in an island twenty miles off shore. Fresh-water springs in the Gulf are, however, by no means unusual; there are, for example, a number of them in the sea off Bahrain Island.

Serious research into the earlier history and monuments of Kharg has only recently been undertaken. Herzfeld's visit to the island in 1924 was brief and superficial. But as a result of the oil development Kharg has been visited several times since 1958 by Dr Ghirshman. In a monograph published in the *Revue Archéologique* he recalls that one of Alexander's companions found an island named Icarus near the head of the Gulf, where there was a temple of Apollo and an oracle of Artemis, and he suggests that this may well have been Kharg. He thinks it possible that the temple was located in the same bowl as the later Zoroastrian shrine – a holy place which retained its sanctity despite changes in religious cults. As for the tombs, he believes some to have been Zoroastrian, others Palmyran, and points out that though similar tombs have been found as far afield as Merv, these are the first to indicate the extent of Palmyra's maritime trade.

The history of the remainder of the Persian shore of the Gulf revolves principally round six places: Siraf, due south of Shiraz; the island of Qais, near the southern tip of the coast of the Persian Gulf proper; two Hormuzes and Bandar Abbas, in the great northern bay facing the tip of Arabia; and Jask, at the entrance to the Gulf of Oman. The story is of early trading centres moving eastwards down the Gulf, and later, foreign factories moving westwards up it.

Siraf was the principal port in the Gulf in the ninth century; Istakhri, who visited it about 950, describes it as almost as large as Shiraz. It was seriously damaged in an earthquake in 977, and thereafter rapidly declined. The site, on a narrow shelf backed by a limestone ridge, one of the hottest places on the Iranian shore of the Gulf, was extensively excavated from 1966–73 by the British Institute of Persian Studies whose finds are fully described in *Iran* Vols. VI, VII, VIII and IX (1968–71), required reading for any prospective visitor. These finds include: the foundations of a large 'congregational' type mosque built close to the sea on the ruins of an earlier, probably Sassanian, building, the mosque probably dating from the early ninth century but extended between 1024 and 1050; the foundations of large merchant houses, smaller dwellings and the plan of streets mainly of the tenth century; a shrine on a promontory built on the site of a much older cemetery in the late fourteenth or fifteenth century; a large industrial area adjacent to the sea, in which glazed ware and probably glass were made for export; a hammam and on the hillside a palace complex. Remains of Chinese and Far Eastern pottery also found on the site suggest extensive trade with Eastern Asia in this period; the wooden columns of the Great Mosque, described by Yaqut (1216), may well have been imported from East Africa; both illustrate the commercial importance of the city in its heyday and underline the historical significance of the recent excavations. On the hills behind the ruined city are enormous fields of graves, many with elaborately carved stone covers.

In the eleventh and twelfth centuries the island of Qais replaced its more ancient rival Siraf which by that time had decayed and was at least partly in ruins. Qais is a low, oblong island about eight by four miles, without a sheltered harbour. But water appears to have been plentiful and the island abounded in date palms and acacia trees. The town, in the middle of the north coast, was picturesque and contained houses of stone and plaster rising to seven storeys, with the appearance of castles. Seen from the sea the village of Qais, with its wind towers and flourishing gardens, is impressive even today. Bandar Lingeh on the mainland to the east was once a centre of the pearling industry but now lives largely by smuggling. Bad-girs, ab-ambars and decaying mansions recall its more prosperous past. There is a large Portuguese fort five miles inland.

Opposite the Musandam Peninsula, as the northern tip of Oman is called, the Persian coast recedes in a great circular sweep to furnish a scene of overpowering grandeur. Landwards, the monotonous rocky coast rising steeply from the sea breaks up to give a broken shore line; behind it rise, in fearsome majesty, tier on tier of craggy mountains on which snow can often be seen in midwinter. In the other direction the sea is riven with jagged islands of varying shades – black, red, brown and white – and grotesque shapes like the background to the more menacing landscapes of Hieronymus Bosch. The scale is so vast, and the setting so brilliant, that sailing up towards Bandar Abbas in favourable weather it is difficult to believe one is not approaching one of the great spectacular harbours of the world.

Maybe it will one day fulfil this expectation. With the completion of an asphalt highway to Kerman and the development of Kerman copper, the possibility of a tourist industry, and plans for building Iran's main naval base here, Bandar Abbas's fortunes are changing as dramatically as its face has changed in recent years, with wide boulevards and impressive new buildings. I set down here more for its historical interest than its topical accuracy my description of its decrepit yet captivating quayside in 1957.

'The Bandar Abbas waterfront has a style of its own. The two-storeyed houses with their arcaded balconies and wind towers stretching for a mile or two in each direction along an embankment overlooking golden sands are in the tradition, at least, of Georgian Brighton; but the pier, such as it is, is crowded with ladies whose appearance in any English south-coast resort would prompt telephone calls to the police. They are heavily veiled, their faces are covered with black masks hiding all except the eyes, and they move steadily, with precision and grace, carrying on their heads chromite slabs, or petrol tins loaded with chromite. The rest of modern Bandar Abbas is less striking – a little covered bazaar, a Hindu shrine, a former British Consulate, and a fish factory'.

It is small wonder that ancient mariners, entering this breathtaking bay, supposed instinctively that it must yield a good
harbour. The first settlement lay some way up the river, on the
north-east corner of the bay, near the modern village of Minab.
Niarchus calls it Harmozeia, declaring it 'a hospitable region rich
in every production except only the olive'. Marco Polo said that
Hormuz was a city of immense trade, renowned for the export
of horses to India, but 'a very sickly place' on account of the
tremendous heat of the sun. At the end of the thirteenth century
Hormuz was allegedly exposed to Tartar raids (in fact there is no
evidence that the Mongols got anywhere near the Gulf), and
in consequence a decision was taken to transfer the city to the
island of Jerun, which adopted the name of Hormuz. The
transfer, according to Ibn Battuta, had been completed by about
1355.

It was a curious, in some ways almost a desperate, step. Jerun
lay some five miles off the coast. It consisted largely of perpendicular precipices of oxide and salt, and was completely
without vegetation. All fresh water had to be brought from the
mainland. Yet here, for nearly three hundred years, flourished
one of the busiest and most glamorous markets of the Orient, a
city of fabulous wealth praised in legend and glorified in verse.

Early in the sixteenth century, not long after the rounding of
the Cape of Good Hope by Vasco da Gama, the Portuguese
appeared in the Indian Ocean. Albuquerque, soon to become
Captain General and Governor of India, decided that there were
three key points which it was necessary to hold to safeguard the
new Portuguese Empire: Goa, Aden, and Hormuz. He seized the
island in 1506/7 and again occupied it, this time without a fight,
in 1515. Hormuz remained in Portuguese possession for over a
hundred years. The Portuguese had a virtual monopoly in the
Gulf, and all their trade flowed through Hormuz throughout the
sixteenth century.

The early seventeenth century saw the rapid collapse of
Portuguese power in the Gulf. This was due to four causes: the
decline of Portugal; the growing strength of Persia under Shah
Abbas; the formation of the English East India Company, which

established a factory at Surat in India, in 1612; and a business miscalculation by which the Company imported far larger quantities of broadcloth than could be consumed in India. As a result of this error of judgment, they sent emissaries to Persia in search of further markets. Shah Abbas, interested in breaking the Portuguese monopoly, granted them a farman or royal order. An East India Company trading post was established at Jask in 1616; factories were opened at Shiraz and Isfahan. This develop-ment caused consternation in Hormuz. The Persians, growing confident, attempted a blockade of the island. In 1621 the Shah prevailed upon some Company vessels in Jask to join in an attack on the Portuguese, despite the fact that Britain was not at war with Spain, with which Portugal was then united. Qishm, the long island on the west of the bay, was first captured and two months later the Portuguese on Hormuz surrendered, in April 1622. Shortly thereafter the island was abandoned. Thomas Herbert wrote its epitaph in 1627: 'This poore place, not now worth the owning, was but ten years ago the only stately City in the Orient.' Today there is little left on Hormuz beyond the remains of a Portuguese fort, and some four hundred inhabitants who work the red oxide mines in the interior of the island.

The trading post was moved to the village of Gombroon on the mainland, which was renamed Bandar Abbas, the port of Shah Abbas. The East India Company, having obtained customs-free treatment in reward for their assistance with the capture of Hormuz, removed their factory in 1623 from Jask to Bandar Abbas, and there it remained until transferred to Bushire in 1763. The Dutch, who later helped to extinguish the last remains of the Portuguese fleet in the Gulf, established themselves there shortly afterwards. Tense rivalry soon developed. The Dutch secured a share of the silk trade; they refused to pay customs; and they captured the valuable spice trade. By the middle of the seven-teenth century they occupied the dominant position. Fryer, writing in 1676, left an interesting account of Bandar Abbas. He was charmed with the Persians, 'the most Courtly people of the East . . . an open, jovial and clear-complexioned Race of Mankind'. He was appalled at the climate. 'Nothing is left here

but a sensible Map of Purgatory, if that may please some to be a
Road to Paradise.'

Other travellers have spoken in equally disparaging terms.
'Nature seemed not to have designed that it should be inhabited,'
wrote Fitch. Herbert reported that in the hot season the inhabitants lay naked in troughs filled with water. Fraser later, in 1821,
described all the buildings as subject to 'rapid decay, the effect
probably of some acrid principle in the atmosphere'.

Inland, Fryer found two Indian temples, and tombs in which
he alleges religious men were burned alive with a stone of
Hormuz salt to stand on and another on the head. He writes of
villages consisting of 'Houses on wheels to be drawn up and
down at pleasure', and of palm trees used for roofing but leaving
'a flourishing Peruke of palms fit to be worn only by the greatest
heroes'. There were hot baths of salt which for both vomiting
and purging were more violent than vitriol and antimony. He
came to places perfumed with jasmine of all sorts, roses, violets,
primroses and other fragrant flowers.

But his most curious comment relates to 'Congo' (Kung*),
twenty leagues nearer the mouth of the Euphrates than Gombroon. Here, he says, 'there is a great plenty of what they call
Ketchery, a mixture of all together or Refuse of Rough Yellow
and Unequal which they sell by Bushels to the Russians, who carry
them overland to Archangel and dispense them through the
Northern Coast for Ornaments to their Fur Caps'.

The aim of this book has been strictly limited – to describe and
explain the country's past so as better to understand the more
vital subject, not touched on here, of its present and its future.
Yet even the modest task I have set myself has in some respects
defeated me. There are things which defy explanation; mysteries
which remain unresolved. But there are also consolations. Who,
for example, could have predicted that a tour of the Persian Gulf
would end at Archangel?

* Near Lingeh, opposite the western end of Qishm Island.

Annex to the Third Edition

Note 1, page 8

This dynastic treatment works well for most practical purposes from the Achaemenians onwards. There are, however, many references in my text (see, for instance, pp. 62, 157–8, 251–2, 256, 260, 269 *et seq.*) to earlier history or buildings. To make these intelligible some reference should be made at least to the Elamites and the Urartians – early peoples not dynasties.

The Elamites, a people with a distinctive culture, religion and language of their own, were the principal inhabitants of S. W. Iran from the third millennium until the middle of the sixth century B.C. (cf. also p. 269). During this long period, Elamite power, struggling with Babylon and Assyria, expanded and contracted considerably in both political and geographical terms, but evidence of Elamite culture, e.g. temples, inscriptions and rock carvings, can be found in many parts of an area stretching from well to the north of Susa south-eastwards to Naqsh-i-Rustam near Persepolis and the Bushire peninsula. Being the nearest thing to a civilized people that Cyrus absorbed, the Achaemenians paid the Elamites the compliment of using their language for their trilingual inscriptions. From about 1800 B.C. to 700 B.C., the Elamite rulers bore the title of King of Anshan and Shushan. Shushan is Susa or in modern Persian Shush; the identity of Anshan has till lately remained a mystery. For some recent light on it see note 7 below.

The Urartians were forerunners of the Medes who flourished in N.W. Iran, the modern Azerbaijan, in the eighth and seventh centuries B.C. The principal traces of Urartian culture to be found are in the form of hill forts and rock tombs, precursors of the Royal Tombs of Persepolis and Naqsh-i-Rustam.

Note 2, page 15

Robin Lane Fox, in his Alexander the Great (pp. 258–64) suggests that Ptolemy's account of the origin of the fire, namely that it was a calculated act of revenge, was a cover-up story. He maintains that the alternative explanation given by other contemporaries, namely that Alexander and his companions were taunted into a destructive revel by Thais, may have more truth in it than might be supposed – because, he says, there is independent evidence that Thais was Ptomely's mistress and bore him three children.

Note 3, page 38

Ormuzd or Hormuz(d) in modern Persian. The latest Zoroastrian thinking about the winged figure in Achaemenian and Sassanian bas-reliefs is that it is not, as hitherto assumed, Ahuramazda himself – it would have been unseemly to portray the deity in person – but his divine messenger Forouhar.

Note 4, page 172

Also in the same area to the east of the Darius inscription there is to be seen, close to the road, the dissolute figure of Hercules on the back of a lion – a statue of the Seleucid period – and two Parthian reliefs damaged by the superimposition of an XVIII c. addition. The caravanserai in the village to the south of the main road is also worth a visit.

Note 5, page 182

This description still held good for the most part until the 1960s. But now the Isfahan oasis, though still green and well supplied with pigeon towers, is being progressively industrialized and built over. The approach from the south, in particular, which formerly yielded a spectacular view of the city, has been transformed by the creation of a large defence area and the erection of flat blocks.

Note 6, page 215

Literally this may still be true. But many of the picturesque features described in this paragraph are now hard to find or – like the Zoroastrian costumes and the camels – have disappeared.

Nevertheless the curious visitor will still find much of interest in the area south of the Khiaban-i-Shah and also to the north of the Friday Mosque, particularly if he looks not for commercial stalls but for interiors where things are still being made – copper trays, givehs (rope-soled sandals), kalyan (hubble-bubble pipes), the dyeing of wool or the dramatic baking of flat bread in the fiery furnace.

Note 7, page 242
One of the largest of these mounds, at Malyan, has been extensively excavated by the University of Pennsylvania since 1971. There are strong indications of a large city with wide trading connections which flourished before 1000 B.C., with no sign of later or Achaemenian occupation; and archaeologists regard the evidence that this was the site of Anshan, the secondary Elamite capital (see note 1) as overwhelming. To reach Malyan it is necessary to leave the Shiraz/Persepolis road south of Zargan and follow a track, through Tell-i-Bayda, for 42 kms.

Note 8, page 249
Probably Ardeshir's queen and her attendant. Note how she holds her hand to her mouth as a gesture of respect. To the left of this relief and separate from it is the somewhat sinister figure of Kartir, High Priest to a number of early Sassanian kings.

Notes on Travel (1978)

Exchange rates (March 1978): £1 sterling = Rls. 135: $ U.S. 1 = Rls. 70. Visas are not required for British citizens visiting Persia for up to three months, but American visitors need one. Smallpox vaccination is essential, cholera advisable. Up to date TAB injections are also recommended. Hotel charges have risen steeply in recent years and a single room without breakfast in a good hotel in Tehran costs between Rls. 3000 and Rls. 4500. In most provincial centres costs are approximately half these levels.

Tehran is six hours' flying time from London and there are now non-stop flights from New York as well as from many European centres. A return economy fare from London to Tehran cost Rls. 72,000 or Rls. 110,000 first class. Return economy flights from New York cost Rls. 101,000 and from San Francisco Rls. 128,000. There are no cut-price charter flights to Iran, although cheaper 'excursion' rates are sometimes available. Iran time is normally 4 hours ahead of G.M.T.

Chapter Four

Tehran has a number of good hotels which, in the city centre, include the Park, the Imperial, the Sina, and the Kings. All the de luxe hotels (Intercontinental, Hilton, Arya Sheraton and Evin) are thirty minutes or more to the north. Shared taxis (orange) are cheap (not more than Rls. 50) and private taxis are available from Rls. 250 an hour. Most of the beauty spots mentioned in Chapter Four are less than two hours by car from Tehran.

Tehran museum opening times are (1978) as follows:

Archaeological Museum: 9 a.m.–1 p.m. and 3 p.m.–6 p.m., daily except Mondays and Fridays
Note. The Treasure Room is open only on certain days and in the mornings only.

Carpet Museum: 10 a.m.–5 p.m., daily except Saturdays

Negarestan Museum (Qajar paintings): 10 a.m.–6 p.m., daily except Saturdays

Crown Jewels (Bank Melli, Avenue Ferdowsi): 3.30 p.m.–6 p.m., daily except Fridays and Public holidays

Ethnological Museum: 9 a.m.–4 p.m., daily except Fridays and Public holidays

Golestan Palace: 9 a.m.–12 noon and 3 p.m.–5 p.m., daily except Fridays and Public holidays

Shahyad Monument: 9 a.m.–4 p.m., daily except Mondays and Fridays

Good Tehran restaurants include Xanadu, Bavaria, Chez Michel, Lautrec, The Cellar, the Restaurant Swisse and restaurants in the Hilton, Arya Sheraton and Intercontinental hotels. The Khansalar and Chez Farid specialize in Persian food. Up to date information about other restaurants and night clubs is available from the publication 'This Week' in Tehran and from the local press.

As well as the Bazaar, there are many shops selling Persian carpets, antiques and handicrafts on Avenues Ferdowsi and Manouchehri. Government-run and reasonably priced handicraft shops are located on Avenue Takhte Jamshid opposite the U.S. Embassy and on Avenue Villa above the intersection with Avenue Takhte Jamshid. There is also the Iran Carpet Company shop at 160 Avenue Ferdowsi.

Road travel has been greatly facilitated by the construction of asphalt highways between Tehran and Iran's major provincial towns. All are now complete except for the roads to Zahedan,

both from Mashad and from Kerman. The last links of both are
due to be completed during 1979. Except at the peak tourist
season of the Persian New Year holiday (21st March and two
weeks either side of this date) accommodation is easily available
out of Tehran. There are now around 50 hotels (mainly small, but
all having restuarant facilities) operated by the Iran National
Tourist Organization (Into) throughout the country, details of
which are available from Into Headquarters on Elizabeth Boulevard. Prices vary from approximately Rls. 800 to Rls. 2000 for
double room.

Chapter Five

There are three flights daily to Meshed, operated by both Iran
Air and Pars Air, taking one hour. The thrice-weekly high speed
train takes ten hours. By road Meshed is two days (600 miles)
taking the Caspian route through Amol, Gorgan and Bujnurd.
Tus, Sangbast, Nishapur and Turbat-i-Jam can be reached by car
from Meshed in the day.

Chapter Six

The only railway to the Caspian runs via Amol to Gorgan.
Babolsar can be reached from Tehran via Amol in about five
hours by road; other roads to the Caspian run via Rasht to Bandar
Pahlavi (seven hours) and via Karaj to Chalus (five hours). There
are daily flights to Rasht and flights by air taxi to Chalus and
Babolsar. There are now many good hotels along the Caspian
coast, especially at Ramsar, Bandar Pahlavi and Babolsar.

Chapter Seven

There are three flights per day from Tehran to Tabriz taking
one hour. The best hotel is the International. The road journey
(400 miles) is eight hours' exhausting drive. On the way there are
Into Inns at Qazvin and at Zanjan which is close to Sultaniyeh.
For the tour of Lake Rezaieh (425 miles) and for Ardebil (320

miles return) a car is necessary, although there are daily flights from Tehran to Rezaieh. There are Into Inns at Khoy, Rezaieh and Mahabad.

Chapter Eight

The road journey to Hamadan from Tehran takes about five hours; to Kermanshah about seven. There are also daily Iran Air flights to Kermanshah (forty-five minutes). Hamadan's principal hotel is the Bu Ali, bookings for which should be made through the Pahlavi Foundation in Tehran. Kermanshah has a motel on the eastern outskirts and the hotel Bisitun in the centre. Sanandaj, Khorramabad, Malayer and Nahavand all have good Into Inns.

Chapter Nine

There are six flights a day to Isfahan (forty-five minutes) and daily bus services. The road journey via Qum takes about six hours from central Tehran. There is a luxury hotel on the grounds of an old caravanserai (the Shah Abbas); other good hotels include the Kourosh, the Ali Qapu and the Irantour. There is an Into Inn on the Shiraz road two miles south of the city. Guided tours are available and it is possible to cover most of Isfahan's sights on foot, or with the help of cheap, shared taxis. Restaurants include the 1001 Nights, the Canary and the Shahrzad.

Chapter Ten

There are daily flights from Tehran to Kerman and Yazd. Yazd (430 miles) can be reached via either Isfahan or via Kashan and Natanz in a long day's drive. Three miles south of the town centre is the modern Motel Safayeh. In Kerman there is the new Asman hotel near the airport. There are Into Inns at Mahan (one hour's drive from Kerman) and at Bam, two hours farther on. Abarquh can be seen in the course of the nine-hour drive (only partially asphalted) from Shiraz to Yazd. There is an Into Inn at Sinjan.

Chapter Eleven

There are five flights a day (seventy minutes) to Shiraz from Tehran. Hotels in Shiraz include the Park, the Kourosh, the International, and the Into Hotel on the airport road. Private taxis can be hired for Rls. 1500 per half day (plus Rls. 250 per additional hour) at the airport.

At Persepolis (fifty minutes by road from Shiraz) there is the de luxe Hotel Dariush. Pasargadae is one and a half hours farther north along the road to Isfahan. The road journey from Isfahan to Shiraz taking in Pasargadae and Persepolis en route can be done in a day. Bishapur is some two and a half hours west of Shiraz along an excellent modern road; Jahrom, three hours south-east of Shiraz along an asphalt road, has an Into Inn, as have Fasa, Darab and Estehbanat. Firuzabad is three hours' magnificent drive to the south of Shiraz along a road more suited to four-wheel-drive vehicles.

Chapter Twelve

There are daily flights to Ahwaz (forty-five minutes) and to Abadan (one hour). At Abadan there is the International Hotel and at Ahwaz the Ahwaz Hotel. Shush, Choga Zambil, Dizful, and Shushtar can be visited from Ahwaz in a day. Iran Air has a daily service via Shiraz to Bushire (Into Inn) and to Kharg Island where arrangements for disembarkation and sight-seeing must be made in advance through N.I.O.C. Bandar Abbas (Hotel Gombroon) also has daily flights from Tehran and there is a good highway linking it with Kerman. The coast road along the Persian Gulf to Bushire is being improved but is currently only fit for four-wheel-drive vehicles.

General

Most large towns have Into offices which can provide local information about guides, transport, routes etc.

Iran Safaris Ltd (P.O. Box 492, Tehran) organize shooting and hunting expeditions for varying budgets, also photographic

safaris, fishing trips to the Caspian, and visits to desert carvan-
serais.

The best seasons for travelling are:

Azarbaijan and Khorasan:	early summer and autumn
Tehran, Isfahan and Shiraz:	spring and autumn
Yazd and Kerman:	early spring and late autumn
Khuzestan and the Persian Gulf:	winter
Caspian:	summer and autumn
Tribal areas (e.g. Fars, Lurestan, the Bakhtiari country):	migration times in March/ April and September/ October

Motoring conditions vary according to season, and mountain
passes in Azarbaijan, the Elburz and the Zagros are apt to be intermittently blocked by snow and/or landslides from December until
the end of March. It is advisable to take food and drink on a day's
journey, and drinking water should always be carried on summer
trips. Those making extensive tours are advised to carry emer-
gency camping equipment.

It is inadvisable to visit mosques and shrines, particularly in the
religious centres of Meshed and Qum, during Moslem festivals
and the months of Ramadan and Moharram. The dates vary each
year according to the Lunar calendar, so advice should be sought
in advance.

The quality of drinking water, and ice made from it, varies.
In almost all the major towns tap water is purified, but advice
should be sought in the more remote parts of the country. In
summer visitors should avoid fresh fruit and vegetables that have
not been carefully washed or boiled.

The national drink is weak tea, taken without milk, and offered
everywhere from bazar carpet shops to roadside chaikhanehs
(tea-houses). Yoghurt ('mast') is also extensively drunk mixed
with soda water when it is known as Ab-dough, and with chopped
cucumber ('khiar'), raisins, mint and nuts when it makes a delicious
cold soup called mast-o-khiar. A wide range of internationally-
known soft drinks (e.g. Coca Cola and Pepsi Cola, Seven Up,

Soda and Tonic water) is available cheaply, and there is a variety
of good local wines, beers and vodka. Other alcoholic drinks tend
to be imported and fairly expensive.

Persian caviar is of the highest quality but expensive (Rls.
5000–6000 per kilo), as are the locally-grown pistachio nuts
('pesteh', Rls. 600 per kilo). Excellent fresh fruit including peaches,
melons of all kinds, and citrus fruits are available cheaply during
the appropriate seasons. The staple diet is flat, unleavened bread
('noon') which varies in texture and taste throughout the country.
On the Caspian its place is taken by rice ('berenj'). There are many
delicious Persian dishes, either including rice, such as Fesenjoon
(walnuts, chicken or duck, and pomegranate juice), shirin pulau
(almonds, pistachios and meat) and albadu pulau (cherries), or
meat broiled over charcoal (lamb, chicken or fish kebab). Restaurants with European-type food can also be found in almost all the
towns of Persia.

APPENDIX II

Notes on Travellers and other Authorities

JOSEFA BARBARO (*c.* 1460). Venetian Ambassador to Uzun Hasan, White Sheep leader. Visited Naqsh-i-Rustam.

IBN BATTUTA (1304–78). Native of Tangier and extensive oriental traveller. He visited Isfahan and Shiraz about 1325 and paid at least three other visits to Persia thereafter.

EDWARD GRANVILLE BROWNE (1862–1925). Oriental scholar and Cambridge don who visited Persia in 1893 and never forgot it. His *Year Among the Persians* and *Literary History of Persia* are outstanding contributions to Anglo-Persian studies. Among English scholars, his name is uniquely revered in Persia.

SIR JOHN CHARDIN (1643–1713). A French Protestant jeweller. Visited the court of Shah Abbas II *c.* 1665 and again in 1672–75. Settled in London in 1681 and was later employed by the East India Company. Buried in Westminster Abbey.

RUY GONZALES DE CLAVIJO (d. 1412). Sent by Henry III of Castile as envoy to the court of Timur in 1403, travelling from Erzerum via Tabriz, Sultaniyeh, Tehran and Meshed to Samarkand. Author of *Historia del Gran Tamorlan*.

GEORGE NATHANIEL CURZON (1859–1925). Travelled extensively in Central Asia and Persia 1888–89. His *Persia and the Persian Question* (1892) is a documentary of astounding topographical accuracy tinted with purple patches and shot through with characteristic grandiloquence.

JOHN FRYER. Surgeon to the East India Company who visited South Persia and Isfahan 1676–77. Almost as colourful and comical as Thomas Herbert (*q.v.*).

DR ROMAN GHIRSHMAN (b. 1895). Has been engaged in pre-Islamic exploration in Iran and Afghanistan since 1931, notably at Sialk, Shapur, and Tchoga Zambil. Head of the French Archaeological Mission to Iran, with headquarters at Shush. Author of numerous works.

COMTE JOSEPH-ARTHUR DE GOBINEAU (1816–82). Secretary at the French Legation, Tehran, 1855, later returning as Minister. Proponent of racial theories later taken up by German scholars and distorted by the Nazis. Author of *Essai sur l' Inégalité des Races Humaines* (1853–55), *Trois Ans en Asie* (1859), *Souvenirs de Voyages* (1872), and *Nouvelles Asiatiques* (1876).

ANDRE GODARD (b. 1888). Former Director of Archaeological Service of Iran. Has made detailed studies of Sassanian and Islamic monuments in all parts of Iran.

JONAS HANWAY (1712–86). London merchant who attempted to revive Caspian trade 1743–45. Said to have been the first Londoner to carry an umbrella.

THOMAS HERBERT (1606–82) of York. Accompanied Sir Dodmore Cotton to Persia in 1627, travelling via Bandar Abbas, Ashraf, Kazvin and Kashan to Isfahan, where he remained till 1629. The most colourful and imaginative of early travellers to Persia.

SIR HENRY LAYARD (1817–94). Travelled in Persia 1839. Later excavator of Nineveh. Author of *Early Adventures in Persia, Susiana and Babylonia* (1887).

SIR JOHN MALCOLM (1769–1833). Sent by the East India Company as envoy to the court of Fath Ali Shah in 1800, and again in 1810. Author of a two-volume *History of Persia*.

JAMES MORIER (1780–1849), Diplomat. On the staff of Sir Harford Jones (Minister) 1810, and in 1814 himself Minister *ad interim*. Author of two *Journeys* (1812, 1817) and *The Adventures of Hajji Baba* (1824). A penetrating but tendentious observer of the Persian scene.

MARCO POLO (1254–1324). Son of Nicolo Polo, a Venetian who visited the court of Kubla Khan in Peking about 1260 and was sent by him as envoy to the Pope. He accompanied his father and uncle on a return journey to China across Persia about 1271 by way of Tabriz, Saveh, Yazd, Kerman, Hormuz, Tabas and Nishapur. About 1292 Marco, with his father and uncle, returned to Persia from Peking with a bride for Arghun Khan, who had died by the time they arrived; she married Ghazan instead.

SIR ROBERT KER PORTER (1777–1842). Artist and author. Court Painter at Petersburg, 1805. Visited Tehran 1814, studying costumes and antiquities and painting portraits. Author of *Travels in Georgia, Persia and Armenia*. British Consul to Venezuela 1826–41.

SIR HENRY RAWLINSON (1810–95). Reorganized the Persian Army 1833–39. Deciphered Bisitun inscription 1839–46. Minister to Persia 1859–60. Member of India Council.

ANTHONY (1565–1635) and ROBERT (1582–1628) SHIRLEY, of Wiston Park, Sussex. Went with Essex's blessing in 1598 to enter Shah Abbas's service and induce him to make common cause against the Turks and develop trade. Anthony returned to Europe as Shah Abbas's envoy in 1599. Robert, appointed Master-General of the Persian Army, was sent to Europe in his term by Abbas in 1608. Knighted in 1613, he returned to Persia thereafter and in 1627 accompanied Sir Dodmore Cotton as first English Ambassador to Persia. Died at Kazvin, 1628.

SIR MARC AUREL STEIN. Born 1862 in Budapest. Superintendent of India Archaeological Survey, 1910. Carried out extensive archaeological explorations in South-west Persia 1913–16 and after 1926. Author of *Old Routes of Western Iran*.

JEAN BAPTISTE TAVERNIER (1605–89). French Protestant geographer and diamond merchant. Visited Persia in 1632 and again in 1638, 1644, 1654, 1657, 1664 and 1667.

PIETRO DELLA VALLE (1586–1652). Roman traveller in the Orient. Visited Persia with his Syrian Christian wife in 1617–23. Took up residence at Isfahan while waiting to pay his respects to Shah Abbas, whom he finally ran to earth at Ashraf (Behshahr). His prolix *Viaggi* are admirably summarized in *Pietro's Pilgrimage* by Wilfrid Blunt (1953), including his moving account of the death of his wife, Maani, at Minab near Bandar Abbas in 1621.

SIR ARNOLD WILSON (1884–1940). Young Indian Army officer attached to Ahwaz and Mohammerah Consulates in 1908 for the purpose of protecting oil drilling operations. Explored and surveyed Luristan and Fars. In 1913 as assistant to Sir Percy Cox, Resident at Bushire, responsible for demarcation of Turkish-Iranian frontier. Resident Director of Anglo-Persian Oil Company (1921–26). His *Persian Gulf* (1928) is the best history in English of that region, and *South-West Persia* (1941) a vivid autobiographical fragment.

Bibliography

ARBERRY, ARTHUR J., *Legacy of Persia*. Oxford University Press, 1952
Shiraz: Persian City of Saints and Poets. University of Oklahoma Press, 1960
Oriental Essays. George Allen & Unwin, 1960

ARFA, GENERAL HASSAN, *Under Five Shahs*. John Murray, 1964
The Kurds. Oxford University Press, 1966

ARNOLD, SIR THOMAS W., *Painting in Islam*. Dover Publications, N.Y., 1965 (A reprint of the 1928 edition)

ATHAR-E-IRAN, *Annales du Service Archéologique de l'Iran*, Vol. IV. Enschede en Zonen, Haarlem, 1949

IBN BATTUTA, *Travels* (tr. H. A. R. Gibb). Broadway Travellers, 1928

BELL, GERTRUDE, *Persian Pictures*. Benn, 1947
Earlier Letters. Benn, 1927
Collected Letters. Benn, 1927

BELLONI, GIAN GUIDO (and Liliana Fedi Dall'Asen), *Iranian Art*. Pall Mall Press, London, 1969

BENJAMIN, S. G. W., *Persia and the Persians*. John Murray, 1887 (Mr Benjamin, Minister in Tehran 1883–85, was the first American representative to Persia)

BINNING, ROBERT B. M. (Madras Civil Service), *Two Years' Travel in Persia, Ceylon, Etc*. W. H. Allen, London, 1857

BLUNT, WILFRID, *A Persian Spring*. James Barrie, 1957
Pietro's Pilgrimage. James Barrie, 1953
(photographs by Wim Swaan), *Isfahan, Pearl of Persia*. Elek Books, London, 1966

BROWNE, E. G., *A Year among the Persians*. Cambridge University Press, 1926

A Persian Anthology. Methuen, 1927

A Literary History of Persia. T. Fisher Unwin, 1906

BUCKINGHAM, J. S., *Travels in Assyria, Media and Persia.* Henry Colburn, London, 1829

BYRON, ROBERT, *The Road to Oxiana.* John Lehmann, 1950

CAMBRIDGE HISTORY OF IRAN, Vol. I, *The Land of Iran.* ed. W. B. Fisher

Vol. V, *The Seljuk and Mongol Periods.* ed. J. A. Boyle. Cambridge University Press, 1968

CARSWELL, JOHN, *New Julfa.* Clarendon Press, Oxford, 1968

CHARDIN, SIR JOHN, *Voyage en Perse.* Amsterdam, 1711

Voyage de Paris à Isfahan. Paris, 1723

COON, CARLETON, *Seven Caves.* Jonathan Cape, 1957

COSTA, A., and LOCKHART, L., *Persia.* Thames & Hudson, 1957

CRESWELL, K. A. C., *Early Muslim Architecture.* Penguin Books, 1958

CRONIN, VINCENT, *The Last Migration.* Hart Davies, 1957

CULICAN, WILLIAM, *The Medes and the Persians.* Thames & Hudson, London, 1965

CURZON, G. N., *Persia and the Persian Question.* London, 1892

DUBEUX, LOUIS, *La Perse* (in the series L'Univers. Histoire et description de tous les peuples) Firmin Didot Frères, Paris, 1841

EASTWICK, EDWARD B., *Three Years' Residence in Persia.* Smith, Elder & Co., London, 1864

EDWARDS, A. CECIL, *A Persian Caravan.* Duckworth, London, 1928

The Persian Carpet. Duckworth, London, 1953 (reprinted 1960, 1967)

FRASER, JAMES B., *Journey into Khorasan.* London, 1825

Historical and Descriptive Account of Persia. Oliver & Boyd, Edinburgh, 1834

FRASER, JAMES, *The History of Nadir Shah.* A. Millar, London, 1742

FRYE, RICHARD N., *Persia.* George Allen & Unwin, London, 1968

The Heritage of Persia. Mentor (paperbacks), N.Y. 1966
(Hardback pub. Weidenfeld & Nicholson)

FRYER, DR JOHN, *A New Account of East India and Persia.*
London, Chiswell, 1698. Hakluyt Society Edition 1909–15

GAIL, MARZIEH, *Persia and the Victorians.* George Allen &
Unwin, 1951

GHIRSHMAN, ROMAN, *Iran.* Penguin Books, 1954
'Travaux de la Mission Archéologique Française de Susiane'.
Ars Orientalis, 1954
'The Ziggurat of Tchoga-Zambil'. *Archaeology,* 1955
Articles on Tchoga-Zambil in *Arts Asiatiques,* 1955–57
'L'Ile de Kharg (Ikaros) dans le Golfe Persique'. *Revue Archéo-
logique,* 1958
'The Island of Kharg'. *Iranian Oil Operating Companies,* Tehran,
1960

GHIRSHMAN, TANIA, *Archéologue malgré moi (Vie quotidienne
d'une Mission archéologique en Iran.* A la Baconnière, Neuchâtel.
Albin Michel, Paris, 1970

GIBB and KRAMERS, *Shorter Encyclopaedia of Islam.* Leiden,
1953

GOBINEAU, COMTE JOSEPH-ARTHUR, *Trois Ans en Asie.*
Grasset, 1923
Correspondance avec Comte Prokesch-Osten. Libr. Plon, 1933

GODARD, ANDRE, *Les Monuments de Maragha; Publications de la
Société des Etudes Iraniennes et de l'Art Persan,* No. 9, 1934
Articles on 'Les Anciennes Mosquées de l'Iran' in *Arts Asia-
tiques,* 1956
The Art of Iran. George Allen & Unwin, 1965

GRAY, BASIL, *Persian Painting.* Skira, 1961

GUIDE BLEU, *Moyen Orient.* Hachette, 1956

GUILLAUME, ALFRED, *Islam.* Penguin Books, 1954

HERBERT, SIR THOMAS, *Travels in Persia, 1627–29. A relation
of some years travaile begunne 1626 into Afrique and the greater
Asia.* London, 1652

HERODOTUS, *The Histories* (tr. Aubrey de Selincourt). Penguin
Books, 1954

HERZFELD, ERNST, *Iran in the Ancient East.* Oxford University Press, 1941

HILL, DEREK (and Oleg Graber), *Islamic Architecture and its Decoration.* Faber & Faber, 1967

HUOT, JEAN-LOUIS, *Persia Vol. I* (Archaeologia Mundia series). Frederick Muller, 1965

HUXLEY, JULIAN, *From an Antique Land.* Max Parrish, 1954

IRAN, *Journal of the British Institute of Persian Studies*, Vol. I, 1963, to Vol. XVII, 1979

IVES, EDWARD, *Voyage from England to India in 1758.* Pub. 1773

JONES, SIR WILLIAM, *Works.* 6 vols. London, 1799

JUVAINI, *World Conqueror* (tr. J. A. Boyle). Manchester University Press, 1958

KEPPEL, MAJOR THE HON. GEORGE, *Travels in Babylonia, Assyria, Media and Scythia in the Year 1824.* Henry Colburn, London, 1827

LAMB, HAROLD, *Persian Mosaic* (An Imaginative Biography of Omar Khayyám) Robert Hale, 1943
Cyrus the Great. Robert Hale, 1960

LANE, ARTHUR, *Early Islamic Pottery.* Faber & Faber, 5th imp., 1965
Later Islamic Pottery.

LE BRUYN, CORNEILLE, *Voyages.* (4 vols.) Gosse & Neaulme, The Hague, 1732

LE STRANGE, G., *Don Juan of Persia (A Shi'ah Catholic 1560–1604).* The Broadway Travellers series, Geo. Routledge & Sons, 1926

LEWIS, BERNARD, *The Assassins.* Weidenfeld & Nicolson, 1970

LINSCHOTEN, J. H. VAN, *Voyage.* Hakluyt Society, 1885

LOCKHART, LAURENCE, *Persian Cities.* Luzac, 1960

LUKONIN, VLADIMIR G., *Persia II* (Archaeologia Mundi series). Nagel Publishers, Geneva, 1967

MALCOLM, SIR JOHN, *Sketches of Persia.* J. Murray, 1828
Sketches of Persia. J. Murray, 1849

MALLOWAN, M. E. L., *Early Mesopotamia and Iran.* Thames & Hudson, 1965

MANDELSLO, JEAN-ALBERT DE, *Voyages Célèbres et remarqu-ables faits de Perse aux Indes Orientales par le Gentilhomme des Ambassadeurs du Duc de Holstein en Muscovie et Perse.* Amsterdam, 1727

MEEN, V. B. (and A. D. Tushingham), *Crown Jewels of Iran.* University of Toronto Press, 1968

MEHDEVI, ANNE SINCLAIR, *Persian Adventure.* Victor Gollancz, 1953
Persia Revisited. Michael Joseph, 1964

MORATH, INGE, *De la Perse à l'Iran.* Achile Weber, 1958
De la Perse à l'Iran, Conzett & Huber, Zurich, 1958

MORIER, JAMES, *Journey through Persia, Armenia and Asia Minor to Constantinople, 1808–1809* (Harford Jones Mission). London, 1812
Second Journey through Persia, Armenia and Asia Minor to Constantinople, 1810–1816 (Gore Ouseley Embassy). London, 1818

MORRIS, JAMES (and Roger Wood and Denis Wright), *Persia.* Thames & Hudson, 1969

NICOLSON, HAROLD, *Sir Arthur Nicolson, Bart., First Lord Carnock.* Constable, 1930

NIEBUHR, C., *Voyage en Arabie et en d'autres pays de l'Orient.* Amsterdam, 1780

OLEARIUS, ADAM, *Voyages très curieux et très renommés faits en Muscovie, Tartarie et Perse par le Sr . . . .* (1636). Amsterdam, 1727

OLMSTEAD, A. T. *History of the Persian Empire.* Phoenix Books, The University of Chicago Press, Chicago and London, 1966

OUSELEY, SIR WILLIAM, *Travels in various countries of the East, more particularly Persia.* London, Rodwell and Martin, 1819

PAHLAVI, MOHAMMAD REZA SHAH, SHAHANSHAH OF IRAN, *Mission for my Country.* Hutchinson, 1961
The White Revolution. Kayhan Press, Tehran, 1967

PAKRAVAN, EMINEH, *Kazvine, capitale oubliée.* Ed. Institut Franco-Iranien, Tehranien, Tehran
Abbas Mirza. Editions de l'Institut Franco-Iranien, Tehran, 195

Vieux Teheran. Editions de l'Institut Franco-Iranien, Tehran, 1961

Agha Mohammad Ghadjar. Nouvelles Editions Debresse (re-edition 1962)

POPE, ARTHUR UPHAM, *A Survey of Persian Art.* 6 vols. Oxford University Press, 1938–39

Persian Architecture (1 vol.) Thames & Hudson, 1965

PORADA, EDITH, *Ancient Iran* (Art of the World series) Methuen, 1965

PORTER, SIR ROBERT KER, *Travels in Georgia, Persia and Armenia.* London, 1821

POWELL, E. ALEXANDER, *By Camel and Car to the Peacock Throne.* The Century Co., N.Y. and London, 1923

ROSE, ED., *The Dervishes.* Oxford University Press, 1927

ROSS, SIR E. DENISON, *The Persians.* Oxford University Press, 1931

SACKVILLE-WEST, V., *Passenger to Tehran.* Hogarth Press, 1926

SAMI, ALI, *Pasargadae.* Shiraz, March 1956

Persepolis. Shiraz, Spring 1958

Shiraz. Shiraz, Spring 1958

SCHMIDT, E. F., *Persepolis I.* Chicago, 1953

SITWELL, SACHEVERELL, *Arabesque and Honeycomb.* Robert Hale, 1957

SKRINE, SIR CLARMONT, *World War in Iran.* Constable, 1962

SMITH, ANTHONY, *Blind White Fish in Persia.* George Allen & Unwin, 1953

STARK, FREYA, *The Valleys of the Assassins.* J. Murray, 1934

STEIN, AUREL, *Archaeological Reconnaissances in N.W. India and S.E. Iran.* Macmillan, 1937

Old Routes of West Iran. Macmillan, 1940

SURATGAR, OLIVE, *I sing in the Wilderness.* Edward Stanford, London, 1951

SYKES, CHRISTOPHER, *Wassmuss.* Longmans, Green, 1936

Four Studies in Loyalty. Collins, 1946

SYKES, ELLA C., *Through Persia on a Side Saddle.* John Macqueen, London, 1901

SYKES, SIR PERCY, *A History of Persia.* 2 vols. Macmillan, 1915

SYKES, MAJOR PERCY MOLESWORTH, *Ten Thousand Miles in Persia or Eight Years in Iran.* J. Murray, 1902

TANCOIGNE (attaché to the Embassy of General Gardane), *Journey into Persia and Residence at Teheran.* William Wright, London, 1820

TAVERNIER, J. B., *Six Voyages through Turkey and Persia to the Indies.* London, 1678

ULLENS DE SCHOOTEN, MARIE-THERESE, *Lords of the Mountains* (Qashgais). Chatto & Windus, 1956

UPTON, JOSEPH M., *The History of Modern Iran.* Harvard University Press, 1965

VANDEN BERGHE, PROFESSOR L., *Archéologie de l'Iran Ancien.* E. J. Brill, Leiden, 1959
'On the Track of the Civilizations of Ancient Iran'. *Memo from Belgium, September–October 1968,* Belgian MFA, Brussels

WHEELER, SIR MORTIMER, *Flames over Persepolis.* Weidenfeld & Nicolson, 1968

WILBER, DONALD N., *Architecture of Islamic Iran.* Princeton University Press, 1955
Persian Gardens and Pavilions. Chas. E. Tuttle Co., Rutland, Vermont and Tokyo, 1962
Persepolis. Cassell, 1969

WILKINSON, CHARLES K., *Iranian Ceramics.* Asia House N.Y., 1963

WILLEY, PETER, *The Castles of the Assassins.* Geo. G. Harrap & Co., 1963

WILLS, C. J., M.D., *In the Land of the Lion and Sun, or Modern Persia.* Ward, Lock & Co., 1891

WILSON, SIR ARNOLD T., *Persian Gulf.* Oxford University Press, 1928
Persia. The Modern World Series, Benn, 1932
South-West Persia. Oxford University Press, 1941

XENOPHON, *The Persian Expedition.* Penguin Books, 1949

THIRD EDITION
Addendum to Bibliography

BENY, ROLOFF, *Persia, Bridge of Turquoise.* Toronto, 1975

CAMERON, GEORGE G., *History of Early Iran*. University of Chicago Press, 1936

GHIRSHMAN, MINORSKY and SANGVI, *Persia, the Immortal Kingdom*. London, 1971

HINZ, WALTHER, *The Lost World of Elam*. Sidgwick and Jackson, 1972

KRUZINSKI, J. T., *Histoire de la Derniere Revolution en Perse*. The Hague, 1728

LANE FOX, ROBIN, *Alexander the Great*. Allen Lane, 1973

LOCKHART, LAURENCE, *The Fall of the Safavi Dynasty*. Cambridge University Press, 1958

MATHESON, SYLVIA, *Persia: an Archaeological Guide*. Faber and Faber, 1972

SEHERR-THOSS, SONIA, P. and HANS C., *Design and Color in Islamic Architecture*. Smithsonian Institution Press, 1968

STRONACH, DAVID, *Pasargadae*. Oxford University Press, 1978

VALLE, PIETRO della, *Viaggi*. Brighton, 1843

VARIOUS AUTHORS, *Persia: History and Heritage*. Henry Melland, 1978

WRIGHT, SIR DENIS, *The English amongst the Persians*. Heinemann, 1977

Index

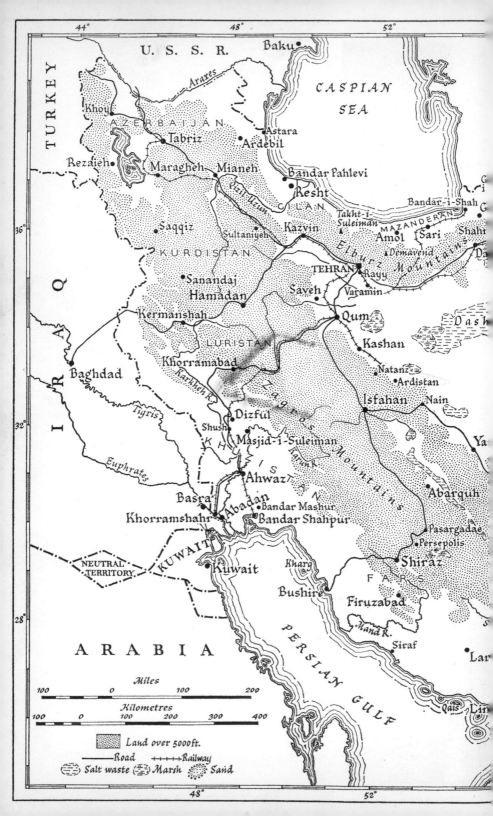